Advance Praise for
Imaginative Writing: The Elements of Craft

"*Imaginative Writing* is an excellent introductory text, providing far clearer and more substantial insight into the complex issues of craft than any other text that I have encountered."

Michael Ritterbrown
Glendale College

"Burroway's book provides the work in both technique and genres, as well as much-needed exposure to drafts, workshops, and revisions, that inexperienced writers need to hone their skills and recognize their strengths."

Debra Peterson
Wayne State University

"The rhythm and pace of this text demonstrates a great empathy for the creative writing classroom, one that pauses and reflects, and then with great creative force launches forward into refreshing new territory. Each section is written and shaped according to its own special niche in the world of imaginative writing."

Almeda Glenn Miller
Koolenay School of the Arts and *Selkirk College*

"Professor Burroway's writing style is engaging, witty, specific, absolutely clear and propelled by the kind of energetic prose that inspires students to write and write well."

Porter Shreve
University of North Carolina, Greensboro

"Today's students require real world attachments to new concepts that their instructors ask them to absorb and practice. Burroway's book provides these; reinforcing new skills with examples and exercises that encourage the student to interact with the textbook rather than remain a passive reader."

Sarah L. Stecher
Tulsa Community College

Photo: Peter Ruppert

Janet Burroway is the author of plays, poetry, children's books, and seven novels including *The Buzzards*, *Raw Silk* (runner up for the National Book award), *Opening Nights*, and *Cutting Stone*. A collection of personal essays, *Embalming Mom*, has been recently published, in addition to a volume of poetry, *Material Goods*, and two children's books in verse, *The Truck on the Track* and *The Giant Jam Sandwich*. Her most recent plays, *Medea With Child* (The Reva Shiner Award), *Sweepstakes*, and *Division of Property* (2001 *Arts & Letters* Award), have received readings and productions in New York, London, San Francisco, Hollywood, and various regional theatres. Her textbook *Writing Fiction*, now in its sixth edition, is used in more than three hundred colleges and universities in the United States. She is Robert O. Lawton Distinguished Professor Emeritus at the Florida State University in Tallahassee.

Imaginative Writing

The Elements of Craft

Janet Burroway

Florida State University

PENGUIN ACADEMICS

New York   San Francisco   Boston
London   Toronto   Sydney   Tokyo   Singapore   Madrid
Mexico City   Munich   Paris   Cape Town   Hong Kong   Montreal

For Neal, Eleanor, Holly, and Thyra
who inherit the language

Vice President and Editor-in-Chief: Joseph Terry
Acquisitions Editor: Erika Berg
Development Manager: Janet Lanphier
Development Editor: Adam Beroud
Senior Marketing Manager: Melanie Craig
Production Manager: Mark Naccarelli
Project Coordination, Text Design, and Electronic Page Makeup: Elm Street
    Publishing Services, Inc.
Cover Designer/Manager: Nancy Danahy
Cover Photo: Paul Klee (1879–1949) "Hoffmaneske Geschichte", 1921, 18
    (DETAIL), "Tale a la Hoffman", 31.1 × 24.1 cm; oil transfer drawing and water-
    colour on paper. The Metropolitan Museum of Art, New York, The Berggruen Klee
    Collection, 1984. (1984.315.26) Photograph Copyright 1992 The Metropolitan
    Museum of Art, Copyright 2003 Artist Rights Society (ARS), New York/
    VG Bild-Kunst, Bonn.
Photo Researcher: Photosearch, Inc. Kunst, Bonn.
Manufacturing Buyer: Roy Pickering
Printer and Binder: The Maple-Vail Book Manufacturing Group
Cover Printer: Phoenix Color Corps

For permission to use copyrighted material, grateful acknowledgment is made to the
copyright holders on pp. 407–410, which are hereby made part of this copyright page.

Burroway, Janet.
    Imaginative writing: the element of craft / Janet Burroway.
        p. cm.
    Includes bibliographical references and index.
    ISBN 0-321-08191-9
    1. English language–Rhetoric. 2. Creative writing (Higher education) 3. College
readers. I. Title.

PE1408 .B8843 2003
808'.042–dc21   2001050823

Please visit our website at http://www.ablongman.com

ISBN 0-321-08191-9

3 4 5 6 7 8 9 10—MA—05 04 03

Contents

Preface to the Instructor xv

INVITATION TO THE WRITER xx

You . . .   xx
. . . and writing . . .   xxi
. . . and reading . . .   xxii
. . . and this book . . .   xxii
. . . and your journal . . .   xxiii
. . . and your workshop xxvi

PART I THE ELEMENTS OF CRAFT

CHAPTER 1 IMAGE 2

Image and Imagination   3
Concrete, Significant Details   7
Metaphor and Simile   11

Essays   14

ANNIE DILLARD
   "The Giant Water Bug"   14

DAVE EGGERS
   from *A Heartbreaking Work of Staggering Genius*   15

Fiction   19

LOUISE ERDRICH
   "Sister Godzilla"   19

DENIS JOHNSON
   "Car Crash While Hitchhiking"   26

Poems

TED HUGHES
   "The Hawk in the Rain"   31

ROBERT PINSKY
  "The Haunted Ruin" 32

YUSEF KOMUNYAKAA
  "Facing It" 33

MAY SWENSON
  "The Surface" 34

DAVID KIRBY
  "How to Use This Body" 35

GALWAY KINNELL
  "Why Regret?" 36

Drama 37

SAMUEL BECKETT
  Act Without Words 37

ATHOL FUGARD
  The Drummer 40

CHAPTER 2 VOICE 42

Your Voice 44
Persona 45
Character Voice 47
Point of View 49

Essays 55

FRANK MCCOURT
  from *Angela's Ashes* 55

VLADIMIR NABOKOV
  "Invitation to a Transformation" 63

Fiction 64

HA JIN
  "In the Kindergarten" 64

DONALD BARTHELME
  "The School" 72

Poems 74

DONALD JUSTICE
  "Order in the Streets" 74

GARY SOTO
  "Black Hair" 75

TED HUGHES
  "Hawk Roosting" 76
WILLIAM TROWBRIDGE
  "Kong Looks Back on His Tryout with the Bears" 77
HILDA RAZ
  "Father" 78
LYDIA DAVIS
  "A Mown Lawn" 79
BARBARA HAMBY
  "The Language of Bees" 80
Drama 82
JANE MARTIN
  from *Talking With . . . Handler and French Fries* 82

CHAPTER 3 CHARACTER 86

As Desire 87
As Image 89
As Voice 91
As Action 94
As Thought 96
As Presented by the Author 97
As Conflict 98

Essay 99
SCOTT RUSSELL SANDERS
  "The Inheritance of Tools" 99

Fiction 106
JUNOT DÍAZ
  "Ysrael"

Poems 115
THEODORE ROETHKE
  "I Knew a Woman" 115
CAROLE SIMMONS OLES
  "Stonecarver" 116
STEPHEN DUNN
  "My Brother's Work" 116
FRED WAH
  "Old man Hansen comes in at ten to" 117

ELIZABETH JENNINGS
  "One Flesh"   118

B.H. FAIRCHILD
  "Old Men Playing Basketball"   118

EDWARD HIRSCH
  "Portrait of a Writer"   119

Drama   121

MARY GALLAGHER
  Brother   121

CHAPTER 4   SETTING   128

As the World   130
As a Camera   133
As Mood and Symbol   136
As Action   137

Essays   139

JOAN DIDION
  "At the Dam"   139

BARRY LOPEZ
  "Landscape and Narrative"   141

Fiction   147

CHARLES BAXTER
  "Snow"   147

Poems   156

JOY HARJO
  "Deer Ghost"   156

HEATHER McHUGH
  "Earthmoving Malediction"   157

RITA DOVE
  "Vacation"   158

YUSEF KOMUNYAKAA
  "Nude Interrogation"   158

GEORGE MACBETH
  "Advice From the Extractor"   159

Drama   161

IMAMU AMIRI BARAKA
  Dutchman   161

CHAPTER 5 **STORY 178**

As a Journey 179
As a Power Struggle 181
As Connection/Disconnection 183

Essay 190

PATRICIA HAMPL
"Red Sky in the Morning" 190

Fiction 194

ROBERT OLEN BUTLER
"Missing" 194

RON WALLACE
"Worry" 201

Poems 202

ROBERT HASS
"A Story About the Body" 202

RICHARD WILBUR
"Digging for China" 202

ELLEN BRYANT VOIGT
"Short Story" 203

MAXINE KUMIN
"Woodchucks" 204

LI-YOUNG LEE
"The Hammock" 205

LOUISE GLÜCK
"Vita Nova" 206

Drama 208

CAROLE REAL
The Battle of Bull Run Always Makes Me Cry 208

CHAPTER 6 **DEVELOPMENT AND REVISION 216**

Developing a Draft 218
Revision and Editing 222
The Workshop 226

Examples 229

ELIZABETH BISHOP
First and final drafts of "One Art" 229

JANET BURROWAY
  "The Opening of *Time Lapse:* a revision narrative"   231
Developing Scene   237
Undrafting   238
Line Editing   239

PART II THE GENRES

CHAPTER 7   ESSAY   242

Kinds of Essay   244
Essay Techniques   247
Fact and Truth   251

Readings   254

MARGARET ATWOOD
  "The Female Body"   254

JAMAICA KINCAID
  "Those Words That Echo . . . Echo . . . Echo Through Life"   257

RICHARD SELZER
  "The Knife"   261

SUSAN LESTER
  "Belongings"   268

CHAPTER 8   FICTION   272

Story and Plot   273
Scene and Summary   276
Backstory and Flashback   278
Text and Subtext   281

Readings   283

NADINE GORDIMER
  "The Diamond Mine"   283

RICK DE MARINIS
  "Your Fears Are Justified"   289

LAURIE BERRY
  "Mockingbird"   290

HEATHER SELLERS
  "It's Water, It's Not Going to Kill You"   291

IAN FRAZIER
"Tomorrow's Bird"   302

CHAPTER 9   POETRY   306

Free Verse and Formal Verse   308
Imagery, Connotation, and Metaphor   310
Density and Intensity   312
Prosody, Rhythm, and Rhyme   316
Readings   322

SYLVIA PLATH
"Stillborn"   322

STEVE KOWIT
"The Grammar Lesson"   323

PETER MEINKE
"The Poet, Trying to Surprise God"   323

ADRIENNE RICH
"Like This Together"   324

ENID SHOMER
"Romantic, at Horseshoe Key"   326

RAYMOND CARVER
"Locking Yourself Out, Then Trying to Get Back In"   327

JAMES TATE
"Prose Poem"   328

DAVE SMITH
"Black Silhouettes of Shrimpers"   329

RUTH STONE
"Repetition"   330

AGHA SHAHID ALI
"Ghazal"   331

SHARON OLDS
"The Language of the Brag"   332

JOHN BERRYMAN
"Dream Song 14"   333

YVONNE SAPIA
"My Uncle Guillermo Speaks at His Own Funeral"   334

CHAPTER 10 DRAMA 336

The Difference Between Drama and Fiction 337
Sight: Sets, Action, Costumes, Props 339
Sound: Nonverbal and Verbal 342
Some Notes on Screenwriting 347

Readings 349

RICHARD DRESSER
  The Road to Ruin 349

SYBIL ROSEN
  Duet for Bear and Dog 357

JOSÉ RIVERA
  Gas 362

LANFORD WILSON
  Eukiah 367

DAVID IVES
  The Philadelphia 371

APPENDIX A Collaborative Exercises 379

APPENDIX B Formats 387

1. Prose fiction and nonfiction 387
2. Poetry 387
3. Drama 387

APPENDIX C A Basic Prosody 393

Glossary 401

Index 407

Preface to the Instructor

Imaginative Writing addresses one feature of the widespread growth of creative writing as a college subject: the multigenre course. Many liberal arts and community colleges that do not have the funds or faculty for full-scale writing programs nevertheless offer courses at the basic level. Increasing numbers of universities, too, offer introductory classes in creative writing, often as a premajor tryout for the writing programs.

These courses typically cover more than one genre, and *Imaginative Writing* is organized on the principle that students in them can benefit from playing with various writing techniques before they settle into a particular form. Much if not most of the advice given to students is relevant to any sort of writing and to most of the genres: the need for significant detail, for example, applies equally to narrative scene, poetic line, and theatrical dialogue; voice is a concept that applies to a character, a narrator, a memoir, or a lyric persona, and so forth. My expectation is that by discussing techniques and offering exercises that allow students to experiment with them *before* they lock themselves into a formal project, such instruction will prove less threatening and encourage a sense of adventure. Beginning this way will also make it possible to illustrate the extent to which *all* writing is imaginative (as well as autobiographical), and the fact that different genres share similar sources and build on similar skills.

I have taken fiction and poetry as givens in a multigenre course. I have personally been convinced of drama's usefulness in developing a writer's facility (with characterization, dialogue, plot, pace, symbol). I have also wanted to acknowledge the growing popularity of the personal essay, the continuity of imaginative writing with the essay form students have inevitably studied, and the fact that emerging writers may find it easiest to begin with the material of their own lives.

The book is organized on the assumption that a college semester is about fifteen or sixteen weeks long and that one or two weeks are always lost to administration, holidays, exams, and illness, so that material for fourteen weeks is about right. Roughly, the first five weeks are intended to cover five areas of imaginative technique (Image, Voice, Character, Setting, and Story), the sixth the processes of Development and Revision, and two weeks each can then be devoted to Personal Essay, Fiction, Poetry, and Drama.

Each chapter begins with a graphic or photographic image accompanied by a "Warm-up" prompt, which may be assigned in class or as a journal entry or replaced by one of the instructor's invention.

Each of the technique chapters proceeds with a discussion of that technique, including illustrations from more than one genre (some invented and some taken from established writers); contains exercises (*"Try This"*) throughout, linked to particular aspects of the topic; and is followed by complete selections in the various genres. Again, the "Try This" exercises could be used as in-class practice, assigned for journal entries, or left for the students to choose from. I think it's important, at least sometimes, to discuss resulting pieces in class, in order to get students used to a nonjudgmental discussion of roughs and written play. (This neutral way of workshopping is described at the end of the next section, "Invitation to the Writer.") Further comments and exercises among the selections at the end of each chapter link the readings to the techniques discussed and suggest *briefly*—there are no questions aimed at literary interpretation—how to read the selections for what can be taken away from them and made part of a repertoire of skills. But of course all the selections illustrate many things, and they can be assigned in any order or quantity that suits the individual instructor.

Chapter Six, Development and Revision, suggests ways to use the material generated in the first five weeks toward the writing of finished pieces, and here too the workshop may prove a positive help to the writer through exploration rather than praise and critique. The "Try This" exercises in this chapter can again be used in class or out, and if it feels right, students can be encouraged to exchange journal pieces and try developing and revising passages not their own. This chapter is followed by some examples, with discussion, of aspects of the rewriting process.

I've envisioned that for each of the final four chapters, dealing with the essay, fiction, poetry, and drama, one week will be spent discussing the genre and roughing out a draft, a second workshopping and working at revision. (Instructors will know what is comfortable and doable for their classes; my inclination would be to assign a short story and an essay of about 1500 words each, three poems, and one ten-minute play.) Each of these chapters attempts to outline what is unique and defining about each of the genres, to suggest ways of exploiting the particular nature of that genre, and to help the students use what they have learned in the first six weeks. The exercises in these chapters are designed to promote development of some aspect of the genre under discussion or to aid revision in terms of focus, cutting, attention to language, originality, and so forth. At this point the critical component of the workshop becomes relevant; students will no doubt be ready to talk about not only what sort of thing this piece of work is but whether and where it "works."

The order of presentation is always problematic in a writing text—everything really needs to be said at once—and many instructors will find that they would have chosen a different sequence for the techniques or the genres or both, so I'll say a little about my rationale. When I laid out the plan for the text *Writing Fiction* many years ago, I had, out of my classroom experience, a strong sense that students focusing on that form needed a sense of its structure and to face the question: what is a story? But for the more playful and process-oriented course for which *Imaginative Writing* is intended, it seems to me that the core need and the first skill is the one represented by the irreplaceable maxim *show–don't–tell*. Again and again I have seen the moment of revelation in the classroom as a grasp of how to address the senses—so simple once it is achieved, so elusive until it is. After that, it is valuable, and also often a revelation, to gain an awareness of how diction and point of view direct meaning. From image and voice to character is a logical progression; then to the outside world of setting, and only then to a consideration of what it means to tell a story, whether in memoir, poetic, fictional, or dramatic form.

I put Development and Revision together, in the middle of the book, in the hope of suggesting that these are ongoing parts of the same process, rather than representing a beginning and an end.

When I came to ordering the genres I reasoned that the essay offers beginning writers the easiest segue from the material of their own lives and also from the kind of writing they find most familiar. From there to fiction may prove a short step. Poetry leads them then to focus on density and the effects of language. Finally, drama in many ways asks that they distance themselves farthest from autobiography, that they externalize everything verbally or visually.

There is nothing sacred about this order, and I have tried to balance the chapters between self-containment and linkage, so that an instructor who prefers another sequence may shop around in the text and shape his or her course to fit. In practice I think it may be most difficult to alter the sequence of the five techniques chapters, and no problem at all to switch—or omit—any of the genres.

In addition to the "Try This" in each chapter, Appendix A contains a *bricolage* of collaborative in-class exercises, which are like the "Try This" exercises addressed to the student, though teachers may want to alter the wording to fit their own style. Some of these activities involve writing but many are taken from theater, art, dance, meditation, or physical therapy. Some instructors will be eager to try these; others may recoil from them as disruptively boisterous or dreamily new-age. Students are often resistant to getting out of their chairs, embarrassed to pick up a felt-tip, reluctant to make a nonverbal sound. But if I have any proselytizing to do, it is at this pulpit. I say to my students, and also to teachers reading this preface: *don't worry about it, go with it, give it a shot.* Simple stretching and breathing can break down the rigidity of the classroom. Repeated improvisations such as the "word-at-a-time story" sometimes become the cohesive social force in a writing class. Mask-making sometimes begins with the groans of the artistically challenged and leads to breakthrough on character. "Mirroring" can teach more about narrative than a lecture on conflict or connection. I have over several years become convinced of the useful energy generated by each one of these exercises, and I've tried to indicate the purpose of each one. In the meantime, however, I've relegated them to an appendix for those determined to avoid them.

Further appendices give the basic formats for each of the genres, a basic prosody for those who want further information about and practice in poetic form, and a glossary of the terms covered in the text.

It often seems pretty well impossible to teach a course across the genres—a semester to do everything, as if you were asked to teach an Intro to Human Nature or The History of Work in sixteen weeks. My hope is that this book will make it feel a little more possible. What *Imaginative Writing* is *not*, is comprehensive. It tries to cover the basics in a way that is sound but brief, overwhelming to neither the student nor the personality and methods of the instructor. I will be interested to hear from anyone who teaches from the book how well I have succeeded in this, and how I might improve the book in future editions. (jburroway@english.fsu.edu)

Meanwhile I am grateful to numbers of people, especially my beloved coven of colleagues Pam Ball, Claudia Johnson, and Elizabeth Stucky-French; and always to my students and former students, of whom I would like to name especially Heather Sellers, Ann Turkle, Michael McClelland, Beth Watzke, Carissa Neff, Debbie Olander, Thom Mannarino, Pat Murphy, and William Nesbitt. Many of the ideas and exercises in this book are here thanks to their invention and their spirited help. Creative writing exercises tend to be, like scientific information in a more generous time, freely offered, freely shared, and passed from hand to hand. I know that I have cadged, cobbled, and adapted my "Try This" exercises from Marta Mihalyi, Maria Irene Fornes, Aimee Beal, Margaret Rozga, Cheril Dumesnil, Laura-Gray Street, Mary Ann Lando, Gerald Shapiro, Matt Zambito, and Michael Kardos, many of them from the Pedagogy Panels of the Associated Writing Programs. Other ideas will have come to me third-hand, or I will have forgotten where I read or heard them; to those unacknowledged, equal thanks and apologies.

I have relied on the incisiveness and generosity of my reviewers: Lawrence Coates, Southern Utah University; Almeda Glenn Miller, Koolenay School of the Arts and Selkirk College; Debra Peterson, Wayne State University; Michael Ritterbrown, Glendale College; Porter Shreve, University of North Carolina–Greensboro; Sarah L. Stecher, Tulsa Community College; and Susan Swartout, Southeast Missouri State University; and on the insight and cheer of my editors Adam Beroud and Erika Berg, to all of whom great thanks. My husband, Peter Ruppert, brings light to life and lit.

Janet Burroway

Invitation to the Writer

I just realize that we start out in these very awkward
ways, and we do look a little stupid as we draft, and that's
all right . . . You have to be willing to go into the chaos
and bring back the beauties.

Tess Gallagher

You . . .

You started learning to write—at the latest—as soon as you were born. You
learned within hours to recognize an "audience," and within a few days that
expressing yourself would elicit a response. Your basic desires created the fundamental form of story—I want, *I want*, I WANT!—with its end in gratifica-
tion (comedy) or denial (tragedy). Within a year you had begun to understand
the structure of sentences and to learn rules of immense subtlety and complexity, so that for no precisely understood reason you would always say "little red
wagon" rather than "red little wagon." You responded to rhythm and rhyme
(*One, two. Buckle my shoe*). You matched images and explained their meanings (*This is a giraffe. Dog is hungry*). You invented metaphors (*My toes are sol-
diers*). By the time you could speak you were putting together personal essays
about what you had done and what had happened to you and forecasting fantasies of your future exploits. By the time you started school you had (mostly
thanks to television) watched more drama than the nobility of the Renaissance,
and you understood a good deal about how a character is developed, how a
joke is structured, how a narrative expectation is met, how dramatic exposition, recognition, and reversal are achieved. You understood the unspoken rules
of specific traditions—that Bugs Bunny may change costume but the Road Runner may not, that the lovers will marry, that the villain must die.

You are, in fact, a literary sophisticate. You have every right to write.

This needs saying emphatically and often, because writing is one of those things—like public speaking, flying, and garden snakes—that often calls up unnecessary panic. Such fear is both normal (a high percentage of people feel it) and based in reason (some speakers do humiliate themselves, some planes do crash, some snakes are poisonous) and irrational (statistically, the chances of disaster are pretty low). Nevertheless, people do learn to speak, fly, and garden. And people learn to shrug at their dread and write.

. . . and writing . . .

All writing is imaginative. The translation of experience or thought into words is of itself an imaginative process. Although there is certainly such a thing as truth in writing, and we can spot falsity when we encounter it in print, these qualities are hard to define, hard to describe, and do not always depend on factual accuracy or inaccuracy. Often what is *most* original, that is, imaginative, is precisely what "rings true."

Aristotle said that when you change the form of a thing you change its purpose. For example, the purpose of an algebra class is to teach algebra. But if you take a photo of the class, the purpose of the photo *cannot* be to teach algebra. The picture would probably serve the purpose of commemorating the class and the people in it. On the other hand, if you wrote a short story about that class, its purpose might be (not to teach algebra or to commemorate the class, but) to reveal something about the emotional undertow, the conflict in or between students, the hidden relationships in that apparently staid atmosphere.

It's impossible to tell *the truth, the whole truth, and nothing but the truth* in words, because words are of a different form than experience, and their choice is determined by the vast array of cultural and personal influences. Writers learn very quickly that a thing is not necessarily credible because it "really happened" and that saying so is no defense of the unconvincing. When you write about an experience, you cast it in a new form and therefore furnish it with a new purpose. Part of the hard work and the pleasure of writing is discovering what that purpose is. You will never exactly "catch" an experience you have lived, but you may both discover and reveal new insights in the recasting of that experience.

All writing is autobiographical as well as invented. Just as it's impossible to write the whole and literal truth about any experience, so it's also impossible to invent without drawing on your own experience, which has furnished your brain. Your view of yourself, the place you live, the people you know, the institutions you live with, your view of nature and God or the gods will inform not only your dreams and daydreams, what you say, wear, think, and do, but also everything you write. What you write will ineluctably reveal to a certain extent both what you think the world is like and what you think it *should* be like.

The two impossibilities—of perfectly capturing your experience and of avoiding it altogether—offer great freedom if you accept them in that light. Begin by writing whatever comes to you, recording your observations, trying out your ideas, indulging your fantasies. *Then* figure out what you want to make of it, what its purpose is, and what it means. Then work toward making it "work"— that is, toward making it meaningful for the reader who is your partner in the imaginative act.

. . . and reading . . .

At the same time, you yourself need to become a reader of a writerly sort, reading greedily, not just for entertainment but also focusing on the craft, the choices, and techniques of the author; "reading the greats," in novelist Alan Cheuse's words, "in that peculiar way that writers read, attentive to the peculiarities of the language . . . soaking up numerous narrative strategies and studying various approaches to that cave in the deep woods where the human heart hibernates."

Reading as a writer involves not asking *What does this mean?* so much as *How does it work? Why has the author made this choice of imagery, voice, atmosphere? What techniques of language, pacing, character contribute to this effect?*

Reader/writers sometimes become impatient with this process. "How do you know the author didn't just want to do it that way?" The answer is: you don't. But everything on the page is there because the writer chose that it should be there, and the effectiveness of the piece depends on those choices. The British critic F. R. Leavis used to observe that a poem is not a frog. In order to understand the way a frog works you must kill it, then splay out the various respiratory, digestive, muscular systems, and so forth. But when you "take apart" a piece of literature to discover how it is made, it is more alive than before, it will resonate with all you have learned, and you as a writer know a little better how to reproduce such vitality.

. . . and this book . . .

My creative writing workshop exchanged a few classes with a group of student choreographers. The first time we came into the dance theater, we writers sat politely down in our seats with our notebooks on our laps. The choreographer-dancers did stretches on the carpet, headstands on the steps; some sat backward on the chairs; one folded herself down into a seat like a teabag in a teacup. When they started to dance they were given a set of instructions: *Group A is rolling through, up and under; Group B is blue Tuesday; Group C is weather comes from the west.* The choreographers began to invent movement; each made up a "line" of dance. They repeated and altered it. They bumped into each other, laughed, repeated, rearranged, and danced it through. They did it again. They adjusted. They repeated. They danced it through. Nobody was embarrassed and nobody gave up. They tried it again. One of the young writers turned to me with a face of luminous discovery. "We don't *play* enough," she said.

That's the truth. Writing is such a solitary occupation, and we are so used to moiling at it until it's either perfect or *due*, that our first communal experience of our writing also tends to be awful judgment. Even alone, we internalize the criticism we anticipate and become harsh critics of ourselves. "The progress of any writer," said the great poet Ted Hughes, "is marked by those moments when he manages to outwit his own police system."

Imaginative Writing assumes that you will play before you work—dance before performing, doodle before fiddling with, fantasize before forming, *anything goes* before *finish something*. This is not an unusual idea among writers and teachers of writing. ("Indulge yourself in your first drafts," says novelist Jonathan Lethem, "and write against yourself in revisions.") But it is easier to preach than to practice.

Nevertheless, most of the techniques that writers use are relevant to most forms of imaginative writing and can be learned by playing around in any form. So the first five sections of this book talk about some techniques that are useful in any sort of writing, or relevant to more than one genre, and suggest ways to play with those techniques. The purpose of these chapters is to free the imagination. The sixth chapter talks about ways to develop and revise your experiments into a finished piece. The last four sections discuss what is particular to each of four forms: Personal Essay, Fiction, Poetry, and Drama; and how you can mold some of what you have written toward each of them.

There is a lot of "do this" in the following pages, but a good deal more of "try this." The overriding idea of the book is *play*—serious, strenuous, dedicated, demanding, exhilarating, enthusiastic, repeated, perfected play. It is the kind of play that makes you a superior swimmer or singer, a first-rank guitar, pool, polo, piano, or chess player. As with any sport or musical skill, a writer's power grows by the practice of the moves and the mastering of the instrument.

Insofar as writing is a skill, it can only be learned by doing. Insofar as writing is "inspired," it may pour out of you obsessively, feverishly, without your seeming to have to make any effort or even without your seeming to have any responsibility for it. When that happens, it feels wonderful, as any writer will tell you. Yet over and over again, writers attest to the fact that the inspiration only comes with, and as a result of, the doing.

. . . and your journal . . .

While you use this book you will be writing one—a journal that should be, first of all, a physical object with which you feel comfortable. Some writers keep notes in a shoebox or under the bed, but your journal probably needs to be light enough to carry around easily, sturdy enough to stand up to serious play, large enough to operate as a capacious hold-all for your thoughts. Think of it as a handbag, a backpack, a trunk, a cupboard, an attic, a warehouse of your mind. Everything can go into it: stuff you like and what you paid too much for, what Aunt Lou gave you and the thing you found in the road, this out-of-date what-sit and that high-tech ware. You never know what you're going to need; absolutely anything may prove useful later on.

Try This

In other words, write any sort of thing in your journal, and write various kinds of things:

- An observation
- An overheard conversation
- Lists
- Longings
- Your response to a piece of music
- A rough draft of a letter
- Names for characters
- Quotations from what you are reading
- The piece of your mind you'd like to give so-and-so
- An idea for a story
- A memory
- A dream
- A few lines of a poem
- A fantasy conversation
- Titles of things you are never going to write
- Something else

Your journal is totally forgiving; it is one hundred percent rough draft; it passes no judgments.

Throughout *Imaginative Writing* there will be prompts, trigger lines, and ideas for playing in your journal. Here are a few general suggestions:

- **Freewrite.** Gertrude Stein called this "automatic writing." Either on a regular schedule or at frequent intervals, sit down and write without any plan whatsoever of what you are going to write. Write anything that comes into your head. It doesn't matter what it is *at all*. This is the equivalent of volleying at tennis or improvisation at the piano; it puts you in touch with the instrument and limbers the verbal muscles.

- **Focused freewrite.** Pick a topic and then do the same thing: focusing on this topic, write for five or ten minutes saying anything at all about it—*anything at all*—in any order.

- **Cluster.** This is a technique you may have learned in composition class, and it helps focus and shape a freewrite. Write the word that represents your subject in the middle of a blank page. Circle it. Free-associate on the page around that word, absolutely anything that pops into your head. When you see a connection between two words, circle them and draw a line connecting them. When your associations come at longer intervals than it takes to write them down (the kernels slowing down in the popcorn bag), stop. Look over what you have. Freewrite.

- **Brainstorm.** A problem-solving technique that can also generate ideas for an imagined situation. Whatever problem the characters might face, whatever idea might be struggling to surface in this poem or essay, brainstorm it—free associate a list of ideas, connections, solutions, no matter how bizarre. Then use these as prompts for your writing. Brainstorming is also useful for coming up with fresh ideas. Start with the question *"What if . . . ?"* and let your mind loose on the rest of the question.

Make a habit, rather than a chore, of writing in your journal. If you skip a day, it's not the end of the world, but it may well be that, as with a physical workout, you have to coax or cajole yourself into writing regularly before you get to the point when you look forward to that part of your life, can't wait for it, can't do without it. You will know some of the patterns that help you create a habit. Write first thing in the morning? At the same hour every day? After a shower? With a cup of coffee? Before you fall asleep? Use your self-discipline to make yourself sit down and write, but once you get there, tell your inner critic to hush, give yourself permission to write whatever you please, and *play*.

Try This

Here is a list of lists. Pick any one of them to generate a list in your journal. Write a single line about each item on the list; is this the start of a poem? Then pick a word from your list and write a paragraph on the subject; is this a memoir or a story?
- Things on which I am an expert
- Things I have lost
- Signs of winter
- What is inside my body
- Things people have said to me
- What to take on the journey
- Things I have forgotten
- Things to make lists of

Only part of the journal habit is the writing of it. Perhaps more important, knowing that you are going to write every day will give you a habit of listening and seeing with writing in mind. A writer is a kind of benevolent cannibal who eats the world. Or at least, you'll begin to observe and hear the world with an eye and ear toward what use you can make of it.

. . . and your workshop.

Many of us think of the primary function of a writing workshop as being to criticize, in order to improve, whatever piece of writing is before us. This is, again, absolutely natural, not only because of the way the writing workshop has evolved over the years but because nothing is more natural than to judge art. We do it all the time and we do it out of a valid impulse. If you tell me you've just seen a movie, I don't ask the plot, I ask: *how was it?* Art *sets out to* affect us emotionally and intellectually, and whether it has achieved this is of the first interest. The poet and critic John Ciardi said of literature that "it is never only about ideas, but about the experience of ideas," and the first thing we want to know is, naturally, "how was the experience?"

But if the first thing you expect of yourself as a writer is *play*, and if in order to play you banish your inner critic and give yourself permission to experiment, doodle, and dance, it doesn't make a lot of sense to subject that play to immediate assessment. I'm going to suggest that for most of the time this book is being used, you avoid the phrases, *I like, I don't like, this works, this doesn't work*—and all their equivalents. It may be harder to forgo praise than blame, but praise should be a controlled substance too. Instead, discipline yourself to explore whatever is in front of you. Not *what I like*, but *what this piece is like*. Interrogate it, suggest its context, explore its nature and its possibilities:

- *Is there a drama in this situation?*
- *I'm wondering what this word suggests.*
- *This reminds me of . . .*
- *It's like . . .*
- *I think this character wants . . .*
- *What if . . . ?*
- *The rhythm is . . .*
- *Could this be expanded to . . . ?*
- *Is the conflict between . . . ?*
- *Does this connect with . . . ?*
- *The atmosphere seems . . .* and so forth.

This kind of descriptive, inquisitive, and neutral discussion of writing is *hard*. It will pay off in the freedom that each writer feels to write and in the flexibility of critical response you're developing in the workshop. In the later part of the course, when everyone is writing in a particular form and revision is the legitimate focus of the work, there will be a time to discuss not only *what this piece is trying to do* but also whether it succeeds. At that point, critique will help.

Try This

Make use of these prompts or trigger lines for easy freewrites. Pick one of them— quickly; don't think about it too much—write it down and keep writing. Anything at all. Whatever the prompt suggests. Keep going. A little bit more.

- This journal is
- My mother used to have
- There was something about the way he
- The house we lived in
- In this dream I was
- She got out of the car
- The first thing I want in the morning

More to Read

Brande, Dorothea. *Becoming a Writer.* Los Angeles: Jeremy P. Tarcher, 1981.

Friedman, Bonnie. *Writing Past Dark.* New York: HarperCollins, 1993.

Imaginative Writing

Warm-up

Write a paragraph about a single small part of this picture (not the whole beast, but its leash or feet, for example). Include the color, the smell, sound, texture of the thing described. What is the emotional effect of what you have written? How does it differ from the impact of the picture as a whole?

CHAPTER ONE

IMAGE

Image and Imagination
Concrete, Significant Details
Metaphor and Simile

> When I talk about pictures in my mind I am talking, quite
> specifically, about images that shimmer round the edges . . .
> You just lie low and let them develop.
>
> *Joan Didion*

Image and Imagination

It's no accident that the words *image* and *imagination* have the same root (Latin *imago*, a picture or portrayal), because what all imaginative writing has in common is that it calls up pictures in the mind. Reports may be accurate, explanations may be clear, philosophical treatises may be profound, theories may be brilliant—and any of these may be enlivened by images. But the kinds of writing we group under the heading *imaginative*—poetry, song lyrics, playscripts, filmscripts, personal essays, memoirs, stories, novels—exist fundamentally as re-presentations. They bring people, places, objects, and actions to the mind as if physically present. Any particular piece of imaginative writing may or may not be "imaginary" in the sense of made-up; it may or may not have its origins in "real" people or what "really" happened. What all such pieces invariably have in common is that the writing calls up sense impressions in the mind.

Novelist Robert Olen Butler points out that *all* art objects are sensuous and are produced by a process that is sensuous rather than logical. Artists in other media than literature are clear about the nature of their process, because they work with material that is fundamentally of the senses. The musician deals in sound, the painter in color and composition, the sculptor in texture, the dancer in bodily movement. But because as writers we deal in a medium of abstract symbols, we may find it harder to set logic and argument aside. Writing as an art begins when we surrender ourselves to the world of images.

An image is a word or series of words that appeals to one or more of the five senses. *An image appeals to the senses.* This is the foundation of imaginative writing. If you can "grok" that fact (a useful word that means to understand in the gut as well as the head), you are on your way to being a writer.

Here is a thought that does not contain an image:

Not everything that appears to be valuable is actually valuable.

Here is an image that contains the same thought:

All that glistens is not gold.

A thought without an image:

It is best to consider consequences before proceeding.

An image that contains the thought:

Look before you leap.

A thought without an image:

I will do everything in my power to overturn this unjust verdict.

An image that contains the thought:

I will fall like an ocean on that court! (Arthur Miller, *The Crucible*)

A thought without an image:

The verses I am writing have no vitality; they are unattractive and stale.

An image that contains the thought:

They are not pigs, they are not even fish, /Though they have a piggy and a fishy air— (Sylvia Plath, "Stillborn")

Notice that every case of flat writing above is full of abstractions (*actually, power, vitality, before*), generalizations (*everything, all, consequences, verses*), and judgments (*valuable, best, unjust, have no vitality, unattractive, stale*). When these are replaced with nouns that call up a sense image (*gold, ocean, court, pigs, fish*) and with verbs that represent actions we can visualize (*glisten, look, leap, fall*), the writing comes alive. At the same time, the ideas, generalizations, and judgments are *also* present in the images.

Notice too that Plath's image of poems that have a "fishy air" suggests not just the sight of a fish but its smell; Miller's image "fall like an ocean" has weight and texture. All of the five senses go into the making of imagery, and a writer working at full stretch will make use of them all.

It's not that abstractions, generalizations, and judgments are useless: on the contrary, they are important to all human communication.

- *Abstractions* are the names of ideas or concepts, which cannot in themselves be visualized, such as *intelligence, criticism, love, anger.*

- *Generalizations* can only be vaguely visualized because they include too many of a given group: *something, creatures, kitchen equipment.*

- *Judgments* tell us what to think about something instead of showing it: *beautiful, insidious, suspiciously.*

Human beings are able to communicate largely because they are capable of these kinds of conceptual thinking.

But it is sense impressions that make writing vivid, and there is a physiological reason for this. Information taken in through the five senses is processed in the *limbic system* of the brain, which generates sensuous responses in the body: heart rate, blood/oxygen flow, muscle reaction, and so forth. Emotional response consists of these physiological reactions, and so in order to have an effect on your reader's emotions, you must literally get into the limbic system, which you can only do through the senses. Now, the images of a film strike the eye directly, *as images*, just as the sounds of music strike the ear directly as sound, the smells of perfume or food strike the nose directly, and so forth. But the images of written literature (including sound, smell, taste, feel) strike the eye as little symbols on the page, which must be translated by the brain into the sound that these symbols represent, which must then be translated into the sense that our language signifies by that particular sound. It's a complicated process that demands a lot of a reader, who will thank you for making it worthwhile.

And it is a dynamic process. Words not only *denote*, or literally refer to their meaning, but *connote*, suggest or imply through layers of connection in our experience and culture. Often using the imagery of one sense will suggest the other senses as well, and will resonate with ideas, qualities, and emotions that are not stated. Strong images tend to demand active verbs that make for energy in the prose or the poetic line.

Here is a single sentence from Margaret Atwood's *Cat's Eye*, in which the heroine describes the zoology building where her father worked when she was a child.

> The cellar smells strongly of mouse droppings, a smell which wafts upward through the whole building, getting fainter as you go up, mingling with the smell of green Dustbane used to clean the floors, and with the other smells, the floor polish and furniture wax and formaldehyde and snakes.

We are ostensibly given only a series of smells from a child's point of view, but as those smells rise we experience traveling upward through the building, also seeing the floors, the furniture, the snakes. The "rising" smells also help build the suggestion of the sinister, from *mouse* to *Dustbane* to *formaldehyde* to *snakes*. There is an echo of fear implied in "getting fainter as you go up," which seems to apply to courage as well as smells.

Notice also how this passage bristles with active verbs. These smells don't just lie there, they *waft, get fainter, mingle;* you *go;* the Dustbane is *used to clean.* This is important. Active verbs are images too. "Look before you leap" contains no visible objects, but we can see the actions. Passive verbs, linking verbs, all forms of the verb *to be*, invite flat, generalized writing, whereas active verbs jump-start the mind.

Try This

Open a textbook, a how-to book, a form letter, something not intended to be a work of the imagination. Identify words that represent abstractions, generalizations, and/or judgments. Make a list of at least ten of these. Pick two or three of them and invent an image that suggests each word. Let your imagination loose—this is a sense impression, not a definition! Examples:

Capitalism
Dotted line across Nevada
Rollerblade straight:
Sign here.

Shame
Okra in the gumbo.
One cross-section surfaces:
Perfect flower,
Pool of slime.

Or this succinct example from Barbara Drake:

Hunger
How terrible—this little blob of jelly
has a mouth.

> The greatest writers are effective largely because they deal
> in particulars and report the details that matter.
>
> *William H. Strunk*

Concrete, Significant Details

Writers are frequently advised: *show, don't tell.* What this means is that it is crucial to address the senses. Vivid writing contains **concrete, significant details.**

- *Concrete* means that there is an image, something that can be seen, heard, smelled, tasted, or touched.

- *Detail* means that there is a degree of focus and specificity.

- *Significant* means that the specific image also suggests an abstraction, generalization, or judgment.

The notion of *detail* is important to the image because it moves away from the generalized and toward the particular. For example, *creature* is a generalized notion, hard to see except in the vaguest way. *Animal* is still vague; *four-legged animal* is a little more specific; *domestic animal* a little more; *dog* narrows the field; *mix-breed Shepherd* we can see; *old Sammy asleep on the red rug, his haunches twitching in his dream* brings the dog into sharp focus in our minds. At the same time this last sentence resonates with the ideas of age and uneasy sleep. If it said *his teeth bared and gnashing in his dream,* we'd also guess that old Sam has a capacity for meanness. Notice how the narrowing specificity of the noun invites active verbs.

Try This
Begin with the largest general category you can think of—minerals, food, structures—think big. Then narrow the category step by step, becoming more specific until you have a single detailed image. Try it again with the same large category but narrow in another direction. Can you, *without naming a quality*, make your image suggest an idea or direct our attitude toward the thing you describe?

If specificity as well as concreteness is crucial to vivid writing, so too is the significance carried in those concrete details, the ideas or qualities that they suggest, the way they reveal character, attract or warn us; the way they lead us to think and feel. A list of physical details without such hints will not move us: *The lawn is green; there are four trees; there is a white picket fence about three feet high and a flagstone walk leading up to the white door.* We want to have our intellects and emotions also directed toward the *meaning* of the details.

A survey of any bookshelf will turn up dozens of examples of this principle. Here, for instance, in a scene from Anne Tyler's *Accidental Tourist*, the protagonist's wife has left him and he is having trouble sleeping.

> The dog, sighing, roused himself and dropped off the bed to pad downstairs behind him. The floorboards were cool underfoot, the kitchen linoleum cooler still; there was a glow from the refrigerator as Macon poured himself a glass of milk. He went to the living room and turned on the TV. Generally some black-and-white movie was running—men in suits and felt hats, women with padded shoulders. He didn't try to follow the plot. He took small, steady sips of milk, feeling the calcium traveling to his bones. Hadn't he read that calcium cures insomnia? He absently stroked the cat, who had somehow crept into his lap. It was much too hot to have a cat in his lap, especially this one—a loose-strung, gray tweed female who seemed made of some unusually dense substance. And the dog, most often, would be lying on top of his feet. "It's just you and me, old buddies," Macon would tell them. The cat made a comma of sweat across his bare thighs.

In this passage, Tyler makes continual reference to the senses, letting us feel the floor, the cat, and the heat; see the glow of the refrigerator and the TV; taste the milk and the "calcium traveling to his bones"; hear the dog sigh and the man talking to the animals. The writing is alive because we do in fact live through our sense perceptions, and Tyler takes us past words and through thought to let us perceive the scene in this way.

At the same time, a number of ideas not stated reverberate off the images. We are aware of generalizations the author does not need to make because we will make them ourselves. Tyler could have had her character "tell" us: *The house felt eerie. I was desperately lonely and neither the television nor the animals were really company. I thought if I did something sensible and steady it would help, but I just felt trapped. When I tried to be cheerful it got worse.*

This version would be very flat, and none of it is necessary. The eeriness is inherent in the light of the refrigerator and TV; the loneliness in the sigh, the sips, and the absent stroking of the cat. The sense of entrapment is in the cat on his thighs and the dog on his feet. The emotion of the paragraph begins with a sigh and ends in sweat. Notice how deftly Tyler tells us—"men in suits and felt hats, women with padded shoulders"—that at this late hour, all there is on TV is *film noir*, which adds a connotation of further eeriness, seediness, and despair.

John Gardner in *The Art of Fiction* speaks of concrete details as "proofs," which establish in the reader such firm confidence that the author is an authority, that we will believe whatever she or he tells us. An author who is vague and opinionated, on the other hand, makes us uneasy and suspicious. And this applies to characters as well—a fact you can exploit. Any character—whether in a memoir, a fiction, poetry, or drama—who speaks in generalizations and judgments will undermine our trust.

It is odd but I must tell you that I have never felt so self-assured, so splendid, so brilliant…Apparently, it is necessary to find someone completely inferior to appreciate one's own excellence. To be a prince in name is nothing. To be a prince in essence—it's heaven, it's pure joy.

"*Ivona, Princess of Burgundia,*" *Witold Gombrowicz*

We don't have to know anything about this character or the play he comes from to know that we mistrust his judgment.

This book has begun by insisting on imagery because it is so central to literature and also because many beginning writers try to make their, or their characters', emotions felt by merely naming them, and so fail to let us experience those emotions. Here is a passage from a young writer, which fails through lack of appeal to the senses.

> Debbie was a very stubborn and completely independent person and was always doing things her way despite her parents' efforts to get her to conform. Her father was an executive in a dress manufacturing company and was able to afford his family all the luxuries and comforts of life. But Debbie was completely indifferent to her family's affluence.

This passage contains a number of judgments we might or might not share with the author, and she has not convinced us that we do. What constitutes stubbornness? Independence? Indifference? Affluence? Further, since the judgments are supported by generalizations, we have no sense of the individuality of the characters, which alone would bring them to life on the page. What things was she always doing? What efforts did her parents make to get her to conform? What sort of executive is the father? What dress manufacturing company? What luxuries and comforts?

> Debbie would wear a tank top to a tea party if she pleased, with fluorescent earrings and ankle-strap sandals.
> "Oh, sweetheart," Mrs. Chiddister would stand in the doorway wringing her hands. "It's not *nice.*"
> "Not who?" Debbie would say, and add a fringed belt.
> Mr. Chiddister was Artistic Director of the Boston branch of Cardin, and had a high respect for what he called "elegant textures," which ranged from handwoven tweed to gold filigree, and which he willingly offered his daughter. Debbie preferred her laminated wrist bangles.

We have not passed a final judgment on the merits of these characters, but we know a good deal more about them, and we have drawn certain interim conclusions that are our own and have not been not forced on us by the author. Debbie is independent of her parents' values, rather careless of their feelings, energetic, a little trashy. Mrs. Chiddister is quite ineffectual. Mr. Chiddister is a snob, though maybe Debbie's taste is so bad we'll end up on his side.

But maybe that isn't at all what the author had in mind. The point is that we weren't allowed to know what the author did have in mind. Perhaps it was more like this version.

> One day Debbie brought home a copy of *Ulysses*. Mrs. Strum called it "filth" and threw it across the sunporch. Debbie knelt on the parquet and retrieved her bookmark, which she replaced. "No, it's not," she said.
> "You're not so old I can't take a strap to you!" Mr. Strum reminded her.
> Mr. Strum was controlling stockholder of Readywear Conglomerates, and was proud of treating his family, not only on his salary, but also on his expense account. The summer before he had taken them to Belgium, where they toured the American Cemetery and the torture chambers of Ghent Castle. Entirely ungrateful, Debbie had spent the rest of the trip curled up in the hotel with a shabby copy of some poems.

Now we have a much clearer understanding of *stubbornness, independence, indifference,* and *affluence,* both their natures and the value we are to place on them. This time our judgment is heavily weighted in Debbie's favor—partly because people who read books have a sentimental sympathy with people who read books—but also because we hear hysteria in "filth" and "take a strap to you," whereas Debbie's resistance is quiet and strong. Mr. Strum's attitude toward his expense account suggests that he's corrupt, and his choice of "luxuries" is morbid. The passage does contain two overt judgments, the first being that Debbie was "entirely ungrateful." Notice that by the time we get to this, we're aware that the judgment is Mr. Strum's and that Debbie has little enough to be grateful for. We understand not only what the author says but also that she means the opposite of what she says, and we feel doubly clever to get it; that is the pleasure of irony. Likewise, the judgment that the book of poems is "shabby" shows Mr. Strum's crass materialism toward what we know to be the finer things.

Try This
Rewrite the passage about Debbie twice more, changing her character by changing the details. Or, if you like, change the gender and write about Darren or David as the independent offspring.

> A metaphor goes out and comes back; it is a fetching
> motion of the imagination.
>
> *Tony Hoagland*

Metaphor and Simile

Metaphor, including its subset **simile**, brings special intensity to imagery by asking the mind to compare and find similar two unlike things.

A *metaphor* assumes or states the comparison, without acknowledging that it is a comparison: *my electric muscles shock the crowd; her hair is seaweed and she is the sea.* The metaphor may come in the form of an adjective: *they have a piggy and a fishy air.* Or it may come as a verb: *the bees shouldering the grass.*

A simile makes a comparison between two things using the words *like* or *as: his teeth rattled like dice in a box; my head is light as a balloon; I will fall like an ocean on that court!*

Both metaphor and simile compare things that are both alike and different, and it is in the tension between this likeness and difference that their literary power lies.

From earliest infancy, our brains are busy registering likeness and difference. This is a major way we learn, about both behavior and what things mean. A smile on mother's face expresses and promises pleasure, so a smile on a different face also reassures us. If we fall and are told to "be careful," then "be careful" will suggest alarm when we reach for the glass of milk. We compare an experience in the past to a current problem in order to predict the future. The habit of comparison is so natural that our language is full of metaphor and simile we use without knowing we are doing so—and English is especially rich in this respect. *That's old hat. He's crazy as a loon. The sky's the limit. Don't hand me that. It won't compute.* Many of the most popular metaphors, like these, are reused until they become *clichés*, comparisons that have lost their freshness.

Metaphor is central to imaginative writing because it offers a particularly exact and resonant kind of concrete detail. When we speak of "the eyes of a potato," or "the eye of the needle," we mean simply that the leaf bud and the thread hole *look like* eyes. We don't mean to suggest that the potato or the needle can see. The comparisons do not suggest any essential or abstract quality to do with sight. But in literature both metaphor and simile have developed so that the resonance of comparison is precisely in the essential or abstract quality that the two objects share. When a writer speaks of "the eyes of the houses" or "the windows of the soul," the comparison of eyes to windows does contain the idea of transmitting vision between the inner and the outer. When Shakespeare's Jacques claims that "All the world's a stage," the significance lies not in the physical similarity of the world to a stage (he isn't backtracking in history to claim the world is flat), but in the essential qualities that such similarity implies: the pretense of the actors, the briefness of the play, the parts that men and women must inevitably play from babyhood to old age.

The *resonance of a comparison depends on the abstractions conveyed in the likeness of the things compared*. A good metaphor reverberates with the essential; this is the writer's principle of choice. So Peter Hoeg, in *Smilla's Sense of Snow*, speaks of rain showers that "slap me in the face with a wet towel." Well, rain showers can patter gently on your face, or dribble down your neck, or bring May flowers. But the rain showers that Hoeg is talking about have a vicious nature that lies in the metaphor: they hit hard, they sting, and they seem to hurt on purpose.

Hoeg's metaphor contains a complex of meanings; yet it is *brief*. Because a metaphor condenses so many connotations into the tension between the images, it tends to be not only concrete but concise. So although you might in one context choose to say, "He was so angry that I thought he was going to hit me," if you sense that the moment wants the special intensity of metaphor, you could also pack that meaning into: "His face was a fist."

A metaphor is a particular and particularly imaginative kind of significant detail, comparing two sensible images and letting the abstraction remain unvoiced between them. But even if part of the comparison is an abstraction, that part will be made vivid by the "thingness" of the comparison. Robert Frost's famous "Fire and Ice" develops a simple but striking metaphor in which the objects are compared to the qualities themselves:

> Some say the world will end in fire,
> Some say in ice.
> From what I've tasted of desire
> I hold with those who favor fire.
> But if it had to perish twice,
> I think I know enough of hate
> To say that for destruction ice
> Is also great
> And would suffice.

Try This

Write this poem: The first line consists of an abstraction, plus a verb, plus a place. The second line describes attire. The third line summarizes an action. Let it flow; don't worry too much about making sense.

Examples (by Carissa Neff):

Beauty creeps out the window
Wearing nothing but taut bare skin.
Leaving a trail of wrinkles behind her.

continued

Hunger yells in the hallway,
Draped in cymbals;
He stomps and shouts, "Hear me now!"

The major danger of metaphor is cliché. Those "windows of the soul," those "eyes like pools" are so familiar that they no longer hold any interest, whereas a fresh metaphor surprises us with the unlikeness of the two things compared while at the same time convincing us of the aptness or truth of the likeness. A cliché metaphor fails to surprise us and so fails to illuminate. Sometimes as a writer you will find yourself with a gift of fresh comparison, and sometimes the first image that comes to mind will be tired and stale. All writers experience this, and the goods ones learn to overcome it. The first thing to do is to make yourself alert to clichés in your own writing and the world around you, and then to labor (which may mean dream) your way toward those images that illuminate the everyday and make the familiar strange.

Try This
Quickly list as many cliché metaphors as you can think of: *the path of life, eyes like pools, crazy as a bedbug, nose to the grindstone,* and so forth. Then switch half a dozen of the comparisons: *eyes like bedbugs, nose to the path, the grindstone of life.* Some of these might be fresh and apt! In any case, the exercise will help you become aware of clichés and so help you avoid them.

My own long relationship with cliché is a paradox, for I find that my language is least fresh when I am most determined to write well. If I sit rigid with good intentions, my inner critic takes up residence on my shoulder, sneering *that's silly, that's far-fetched, what a crock, nobody'll believe that!*—with the result that I fall back on usual phrases. But if I knock her off her perch and let myself try anything that comes to mind, *some* of it will be silly, some far-fetched, and among the verbal rubble there is almost bound to be a salvageable building block, a serviceable cooking pot, a precious stone.

More to Read

Burke, Carol, and Molly Best Tinsley. *The Creative Process.* New York: St. Martin's Press, 1993.

Rico, Gabriele Lusser. *Writing the Natural Way.* Los Angeles: J.P. Tarcher, Inc., 1983.

Essays

The readings that follow this chapter employ imagery and metaphor in a wide variety of ways. For example, Annie Dillard's "The Giant Water Bug," a short essay from her book *Pilgrim at Tinker Creek*, represents a single sharp observation of nature, dense with metaphor. In the scene excerpted from Dave Eggers memoir, *A Heartbreaking Work of Staggering Genius*, sights, sounds, smells and tastes propel us, fast, through a series of actions. In Louise Erdrich's short story "Godzilla," reptiles real and imaginary form a metaphoric frame—and so forth through the prose pieces, poems, and plays.

Read each selection once, fast, for content and pleasure; a second time consciously aware of images and metaphors. What affect do they have on you? How? What technique might you imitate, absorb, try, steal?

Among the readings you'll find some triggers for play in your journal. These are not connected to the readings in any direct or literal way, but may suggest peripheral ways to practice some shape, subject, or skill the writers display.

Annie Dillard

The Giant Water Bug

A couple of summers ago I was walking along the edge of the island to see what I could see in the water, and mainly to scare frogs. Frogs have an inelegant way of taking off from invisible positions on the bank just ahead of your feet, in dire panic, emitting a froggy "Yike!" and splashing into the water. Incredibly, this amused me, and, incredibly, it amuses me still. As I walked along the grassy edge of the island, I got better and better at seeing frogs both in and out of the water. I learned to recognize, slowing down, the difference in texture of the light reflected from mudbank, water, grass, or frog. Frogs were flying all around me. At the end of the island I noticed a small green frog. He was exactly half in and half out of the water, looking like a schematic diagram of an amphibian, and he didn't jump.

He didn't jump; I crept closer. At last I knelt on the island's winter-killed grass, lost, dumb-struck, staring at the frog in the creek just four feet away. He was a very small frog with wide, dull eyes. And just as I looked at him, he slowly crumpled and began to sag. The spirit vanished from his eyes as if snuffed. His skin emptied and drooped; his very skull seemed to collapse and settle like a kicked tent. He was shrinking before my eyes like a deflating football. I watched the taut, glistening skin on his shoulders ruck and rumple and fall. Soon, part of his skin, formless as a pricked balloon, lay in floating folds like bright scum on top of the water: it was a monstrous and terrifying thing. I gaped bewildered, appalled. An oval shadow hung in the water behind the drained frog; then the shadow glided away. The frog skin bag started to sink.

I had read about the giant water bug, but never seen one. "Giant water bug" is really the name of the creature, which is an enormous, heavy-bodied brown beetle. It eats insects, tadpoles, fish, and frogs. Its grasping forelegs are mighty and hooked inward. It seizes a victim with these legs, hugs it tight, and paralyzes it with enzymes injected during a vicious bite. That one bite is the only bite it ever takes. Through the puncture shoot the poisons that dissolve the victim's muscles and bones and organs—all but the skin—and through it the giant water bug sucks out the victim's body, reduced to a juice. This event is quite common in warm fresh water. The frog I saw was being sucked by a giant water bug. I had been kneeling on the island grass; when the unrecognizable flap of frog skin settled on the creek bottom, swaying, I stood up and brushed the knees of my pants. I couldn't catch my breath.

Dave Eggers
from *A Heartbreaking Work of Staggering Genius*

At home it's returning library books late, and getting posterboard for Toph's map of Africa, and grocery shopping at the place where they know us and know that we don't need a cart to carry the bags to the car, not us, because two men can carry six bags four for me and two for Toph, we love carrying the stuff, side by side, and thus insist upon it. And one night after the grocery store and immediately after a bookstore visit, from the north of Shattuck Avenue, right in the left-middle of Berkeley's downtown there comes a moving, gurgling volcano of lights. White lights popping from motorcycles, police cars yelling in red and blue, and then a slow river of shiny black. A procession. Too late for a funeral—it's already dark—but then, what—

They drive past, and about when we think they'll be out of sight, they stop.

A man walks toward us, from the direction of the caravan.

"It's Clinton," he says. "He's eating at Chez Panisse."

We run.

Toph and I are among the first there. I am wild with excitement. (This was, remember, around '93–'94.) I explain to Toph how thrilling this is, that inside this building is the president, and not just any president—though admittedly that probably would not have mattered—but this is a president that, fuck, we have some sort of crush on this man. He speaks like a president, not always authoritative or anything but he can form sentences, complex sentences with beginnings and ends, subordinate clauses—you can *hear* his semicolons! He knows the answers to questions. He knows acronyms and the names of foreign leaders, their deputies. It is heartening, it makes our country look smart, and this is an important thing, something we have too long been without. Oh many were the times when Toph and I lay on my bed, my legs on his back, watching Clinton talk, points a and b and c, *Jesus, how does he do it?* Toph, I would say, Toph, this man is actually bright, could be brilliant. This man still reads books; encyclopedic and charming and so seemingly real—he is real, yes, certainly more real than the last few, who were too old to know—never did we know people that old so they were something else, unintelligible—and though we hope that he is real even if he is not entirely real he is more real, and smart enough to seem real, and wins both ways—And now he is here, mere feet away, eating the fresh and adventurous food stylings of California Cuisine!

We decide that we're staying until he comes out. I run to a phone to call Kirsten. She's in bed but says she'll be there. Toph runs to the convenience store to get provisions—Fig Newtons and root beer and caramel.

"No comic books," I say.

"Okay," he says.

"Really. I'm timing you. This is the president, little man."

"Okay, okay," he says.

While he's gone more people arrive. There is a commotion, a civic bustle just as Frank Capra would have imagined it:

"Charlie, what's all the hullabaloo about?"

"Word is the president's inside!"

"The president? Well, I'll be . . . "

When Toph gets back there are about twenty people, gathered on either side of the restaurant's door. Across the street the cars and vans of the slow caravan stand still, doors open. Agents walk and squint and whisper, doing their agent things, wishing their friends could see them now.

Kirsten arrives, in her pajamas. It's been about twenty minutes, and there are now about fifty people around the door, some across the street, camped near the limos.

We are standing at the very front, to the right side of the door, no more than twenty feet away. We eat the snacks and Toph drinks his root beer, which he's set on the ground, holding it steady with his feet. He is careful about the things he loves.

Another half hour passes and a hundred more gather. There are people ten deep behind us, a throng across Shattuck Avenue. We cannot fathom why people would stand across the street, easily a hundred feet away, when they could be so close, near us.

"Suckers." I tell Toph, thumbing toward those watching from so far away. It is important, I feel, that the boy knows what suckers look like.

To pass the time, we bounce on our toes. We trip each other. We play the game where you're not supposed to look at the (show), and when you do, you are punched on the arm. We stop when given a sidelong look from one of the Secret Service people. *Do we look menacing, or just pathetic?*

Any minute now.

Something occurs to me, though. How much time will Clinton have to mingle? Surely not much at all. So then, how will he decide where in the crowd to plunge? No way will he have time to shake the hands of us all, or even a portion of us, however doting. He will have to choose an area, a slice of us most deserving and representative.

I try to get Toph to take his hat off. He's always wearing the goddamn Cal hat with the smell of urine. He wears it to school, between classes, every moment until bedtime. He is trying to resist the onset of the curly hair— already his hair is thickening—and the hat straightens it out but now the hat is ruining our chances. The hat makes us look disrespectful. We're a young hoodlum and his . . . drug dealer.

"Off with the hat."

"No."

"Off with the hat."

"No."

Good God, the door opens. A few randoms pour out and then this huge grey-haired man. Jesus Christ, he's a big man. His face is so pink. What happened to his face that it's so pink? I ask Toph why his face is so pink. Toph thinks for a second but does not know.

Flashbulbs of course, and the screaming of things, mostly things like We Love You Bill, because everyone does love him now, because he is in the Bay Area, and he is our man, he says things we believe and is so thrillingly articulate, and he knows we love him and has come here to bask, in Berkeley even, at Chez Panisse, our town, our restaurant, and here he is, to be adored and received and thanked and urged on. Because we are in Berkeley and the president is here we are, Toph and Kirsten and I—at the white-hot center of the entire world and history to date.

But Toph can't see, because suddenly some ugly rat bastard has shoved himself in front of us. It's unbelievable. I want to push this guy over, want to throw him to one side. How could we wait for so long and be so devoted and ready, only to have this round-backed asshole devour our chance for an audience with Bill?

This will not stand. I will toss him aside if need be. *But will the president come our way? Will he know that we have been chosen?* Surely he will know. If anyone will know, he will.

After waving to the throng for a minute, Bill heads . . . toward us. Of course! Of course! Here he comes! Here he comes! Good lord his face is huge! Why so pink? Why so weirdly pink? Toph is being crushed, his face pressed against the back of this round-backed bastard-man, and so I grab Toph and lift him, and his hat falls off, and Clinton is making his way from our left, where our side began, to us, in the middle. Hands reach toward him, grasping for his flesh, and he reaches into the anemone of fingers and as he reaches toward us I lunge and take Toph's hand and thrust it toward the president's, because close will not do here, chance is not good enough, and just as I throw Toph's little soft hand forward, Bill's fat pink hand is there—perfect timing— and the president grabs and squeezes the little hand of my brother, and I feel the jolt through me because we have completed the moment, have destroyed and begun a new world at this moment when we did all that was necessary.

Toph touched his hand! Oh if only there were a picture. Then, decades from now, when Toph was running for president himself, there would be the shot of he and Clinton touching, like God's finger lazily extended toward Adam's, like the photograph of Clinton shaking the hand of Kennedy.

And who will Toph thank, during his own inauguration? Oh yes, we know who he will thank. He will thank me. He will be there, in his blue suit, so tall and filled out and finally not wearing his urine-smelling hat, and he will say:

"I'll never forget when my brother, who tried so hard and suffered so long, lifted me over the heads of the throng to meet my destiny." Destiny spoken in a whisper, accent on first syllable.

Try this

Make a quick list of objects you can see around you from where you sit now. Take the number that represents the month of your birth and count down your list that many places. Take the word there and begin writing about it. Write anything the word suggests to you—memory, metaphor, ideas, other objects, colors, places—anything. Don't worry about the order of your ideas or the form of what you write. Sentences are

continued

good—but not necessary. Keep writing for ten minutes; it will seem a long time. You will probably have a page or two. Do the ideas connect in any way? Are some metaphors? Do some suggest a larger idea or a reaching out from the object you started with? Are there any words, ideas, images that you'd like to expand on?

FICTION

Louise Erdrich

Sister Godzilla

The door banged shut, and then the children were alone with their sixth-grade teacher. It was the first day of school, in the fall of 1963. The habits of Franciscan nuns still shrouded all but their faces, so each of the new nun's features was emphasized, read forty times over in astonishment. Outlined in a stiff white frame of starched linen, Sister's eyes, nose, and mouth leaped out, a mask from a dream, a great rawboned jackal's muzzle.

"Oh, Christ," Toddy Crieder said, just loud enough for Dot to hear.

Dot Adare, a troublemaker, knew Toddy was in love with her and usually ignored him, but the nun's extreme ugliness was irresistible.

"Godzilla," she whispered.

The teacher's name was Sister Mary Anita Groff. She was young, in her twenties or thirties, and so swift of movement, for all her hulking size, that walking from the back of the room to the front, she surprised her students, made them picture an athlete's legs and muscles concealed in the flow of black wool. When she swept the air in a gesture meant to include them all in her opening remarks, her hands fixed their gazes. They were the opposite of her face. Her hands were beautiful, as white as milk glass, the fingers straight and tapered. They were the hands in the hallway print of Mary underneath the cross. They were the hands of the Apostles, cast in plastic and lit at night on the tops of television sets. Praying hands.

Ballplayer's hands. She surprised them further by walking onto the graveled yard at recess, her neckpiece cutting hard into the flesh beneath her heavy jaw. When, with a matter-of-fact grace, she pulled from the sleeve of her gown a mitt of dark mustard-colored leather and raised it, a thrown softball dropped in. Her skill was obvious. Good players rarely stretch or change their expressions. They simply tip their hands toward the ball like magnets, and there it is. As a pitcher, Mary Anita was a swirl of wool, as graceful as the windblown cape of Zorro, an emotional figure that stirred Dot so thoroughly that as she pounded home plate—a rubber dish mat—and beat the air twice in practice swings, choked up on the handle, tried to concentrate, Dot knew she would have no choice but to slam a home run.

She did not. In fact, she whiffed, in three strikes, never ticking the ball or fouling. Purely disgusted with herself, she sat on the edge of the bike rack and watched as Sister gave a few balls away and pitched easy hits to the rest of the team. It was as if the two had sensed from the beginning what was to come. Or, then again, perhaps Mary Anita's information came from Dot's former teachers, living in the red-brick convent across the road. Hard to handle. A smart-off. Watch out when you turn your back. They were right. After recess, her pride burned, Dot sat at her desk and drew a dinosaur draped in a nun's robe, its mouth open in a roar. The teeth, long and jagged, grayish-white, held her attention. She worked so hard on the picture that she barely noticed as the room hushed around her. She felt the presence, though, the shadow of attention that dropped over her as Mary Anita stood watching. As a mark of her arrogance, Dot kept drawing.

She shaded in the last tooth and leaned back to frown at her work. The page was plucked into the air before she could pretend to cover it. No one made a sound. Dot's heart beat with excitement.

"You will remain after school," the nun pronounced.

The last half hour passed. The others filed out the door. And then the desk in front of Dot filled suddenly. There was the paper, the carefully rendered dinosaur caught in mid-roar. Dot stared at it furiously, her mind a blur of anticipation. She was not afraid.

"Look at me," Mary Anita said.

Dot found that she didn't want to, that she couldn't. Then her throat filled. Her face was on fire. Her lids hung across her eyeballs like lead shades. She traced the initials carved into her desktop.

"Look at me," Mary Anita said to her again, and Dot's gaze was drawn upward, upward on a string, until she met the eyes of her teacher, deep brown, electrically sad. Their very stillness shook Dot.

"I'm sorry," she said.

When those two unprecedented words dropped from her lips, Dot knew, beyond reason and past bearing, that something terrible had occurred. She felt dizzy. The blood rushed to her head so fast that her ears ached, yet the tips of her fingers fell asleep. Her eyelids prickled and her nose wept, but at the same time her mouth went dry. Her body was a thing of extremes, contradicting itself.

"When I was young," Sister Mary Anita said, "as young as you are, I felt a great deal of pain when I was teased about my looks. I've long since accepted my . . . deformity. A prognathic jaw runs in our family, and I share it with an uncle. But I must admit, the occasional insult, or drawing such as yours, still hurts."

Dot began to mumble and then stopped, desperate. Sister Mary Anita waited, and then handed her her own handkerchief.

"I'm sorry," Dot said again. She wiped her nose. The square of white material was cool and fresh. "Can I go now?"

"Of course not," Mary Anita said.

Dot was confounded. The magical two words, an apology, had dropped from her lips. Yet more was expected. What?

"I want you to understand something," the nun said. "I've told you how I feel. And I expect that you will never hurt me again."

The nun waited, and waited, until their eyes met. Then Dot's mouth fell wide. Her eyes spilled over. She knew that the strange feelings that had come upon her were the same feelings that Mary Anita had felt. Dot had never felt another person's feelings, never in her life.

"I won't do anything to hurt you," she blubbered passionately. "I'll kill myself first."

"I'm sure that will not be necessary," Sister Mary Anita said.

Dot tried to rescue her pride then, by turning away very quickly. Without permission, she ran out the schoolroom door, down the steps, and on into the street, where at last the magnetic force of the encounter weakened, and suddenly she could breathe. Even that was different, though. As she walked, she began to realize that her body was still fighting itself. Her lungs filled with air like two bags, but every time they did so, a place underneath them squeezed so painfully that the truth suddenly came dear.

"I love her now," she blurted out. She stopped on a crack, stepping on it, sickened. "Oh, god, I am *in love.*"

Toddy Crieder was a hollow-chested, envious boy whose reputation had never recovered from the time he was sent home for eating tree bark. In the third grade he had put two crayons up his nose, pretend tusks. The pink one got stuck, and Toddy had to visit the clinic. This year, already, his stomach had been pumped in the emergency room. Dot despised him, but that only seemed to fuel his adoration of her.

Coming into the schoolyard the second day, a bright, cool morning, Toddy ran up to Dot, his thin legs knocking.

"Yeah," he cried. "Godzilla! Not bad, Adare."

He wheeled off, the laces of his tennis shoes dragging. Dot looked after him and felt the buzz inside her head begin. How she wanted to stuff that name back into her mouth, or at least Toddy's mouth.

"I hope you trip and murder yourself!" Dot screamed.

But Toddy did not trip. For all of his clumsiness, he managed to stay upright, and as Dot stood rooted in the center of the walk, she saw him whiz from clump to clump of children, laughing and gesturing, filling the air with small and derisive sounds. Sister Mary Anita swept out the door, a wooden-handled brass bell in her hand, and when she shook it up and down, the children, who played together in twos and threes, swung toward her and narrowed or widened their eyes and turned eagerly to one another. Some began to laugh. It seemed to Dot that all of them did, in fact, and that the sound, jerked from their lips was large, uncanny, totally and horribly delicious.

"Godzilla, Godzilla," they called under their breath. "Sister Godzilla."

Before them on the steps, the nun continued to smile into their faces. She did not hear them—yet. But Dot knew she would. Over the bell her eyes were brilliantly dark and alive. Her horrid jagged teeth showed in a smile when she saw Dot, and Dot ran to her, thrusting a hand into her lunch bag and grabbing the cookies that her mother had made from whatever she could find around the house—raisins, congealed Malt-O-Meal, the whites of eggs.

"Here!" Dot shoved a sweet, lumpy cookie into the nun's hand. It fell apart, distracting Sister as the children pushed past.

The students seemed to forget the name off and on all week. Some days they would move on to new triumphs or disasters—other teachers occupied them, or some small event occurred in the classroom. But then Toddy Crieder would lope and careen among them at recess, would pump his arms and pretend to roar behind Sister Mary Anita's back as she stepped up to the plate. As she swung and connected with the ball and gathered herself to run, her veil lifting, the muscles in her shoulders like the curved hump of a raptor's wings, Toddy would move along behind her, rolling his legs the way Godzilla did in the movie. In her excitement, dashing base to base, her feet long and limber in black laced shoes, Mary Anita did not notice. But Dot looked on, the taste of a penny caught in her throat.

"Snakes live in holes. Snakes are reptiles. These are Science Facts." Dot read aloud to the class from her Discovery science book. "Snakes are not wet. Some snakes lay eggs. Some have live young."

"Very good," Sister said. "Can you name other reptiles?"

Dot's tongue fused to the back of her throat.

"No," she croaked.

"Anyone else?" Sister asked.

Toddy Crieder raised his had. Sister recognized him.

"How about Godzilla?"

Gasps. Small noises of excitement. Mouths agape. Admiration for Toddy's nerve rippled through the rows of children like a wind across a field. Sister Mary Anita's great jaw opened, opened, and then snapped shut. Her shoulders shook. No one knew what to do at first. Then she laughed. It was a high-pitched, almost birdlike sound, a thin laugh like the highest notes on the piano. The children all hesitated, and then they laughed with her, even Toddy Crieder. Eyes darting from on child to the next, to Dot, Toddy laughed.

Dot's eyes crossed with urgency. When Sister Mary Anita turned to new work, Dot crooked her arm beside her like a piston and leaned across Toddy's desk.

"I'm going to give you one right in the breadbasket," she said.

With a precise boxer's jab she knocked the wind out of Toddy, left him gasping, and turned to the front, face clear, as Sister began to speak.

Furious sunlight. Black cloth. Dot sat on the iron trapeze, the bar pushing a sore line into the backs of her legs. As she swung, she watched Sister Mary Anita. The wind was harsh, and the nun wore a pair of wonderful gloves, black, the fingers cut off of them so that her hands could better grip the bat. The ball arced toward her sinuously and dropped. Her bat caught it with a thick, clean sound, and off it soared. Mary Anita's habit swirled open behind her. The cold bit her cheeks red. She swung to third, glanced, panting, over her shoulder, and then sped home. She touched down lightly and bounded off.

Dot's arms felt heavy, weak, and she dropped from the trapeze and went to lean against the brick wall of the school building. Her heart thumped in her ears. She saw what she would do when she grew up: declare her vocation, enter the convent. She and Sister Mary Anita would live in the nuns' house together, side by side. They would eat, work, eat, cook. To relax, Sister Mary Anita would hit pop flies and Dot would catch them.

Someday, one day, Dot and Mary Anita would be walking, their hands in their sleeves, long habits flowing behind.

"Dear Sister," Dot would say, "remember that old nickname you had the year you taught the sixth grade?"

"Why, no," Sister Mary Anita would say, smiling at her. "Why, no."

And Dot would know that she had protected her, kept her from harm.

It got worse. Dot wrote some letters, tore them up. Her hand shook when Sister passed her in the aisle, and her eyes closed, automatically, as she breathed in the air that closed behind the nun. Soap–a harsh soap. Faint carbolic mothballs. That's what she smelled like. Dizzying. Dot's fists clenched. She pressed her knuckles to her eyes and very loudly excused herself. She went to the girls' bathroom and stood in a stall. Her life was terrible. The thing was, she didn't want to be a nun.

"I don't want to!" she whispered, desperate, to the whitewashed tin walls that shuddered if a girl bumped them. "There must be another way."

She would have to persuade Mary Anita to forsake her vows, to come and live with Dot and her mother in the house just past the edge of town. How would she start, how would she persuade her teacher?

Someone was standing outside the stall. Dot opened the door a bit and stared into the great craggy face.

"Are you feeling all right? Do you need to go home?" Sister Mary Anita was concerned.

Fire shot through Dot's limbs. The girls' bathroom. A place of secrets, of frosted glass, its light mute and yet brilliant, paralyzed her. But she gathered herself. Here was her chance, as if God had given it to her.

"Please," Dot said, "let's run away together!"

Sister paused. "Are you having troubles at home?"

"No," Dot said.

Sister's milk-white hand came through the doorway and covered Dot's forehead. Dot's anxious thoughts throbbed against the lean palm. Staring into the eyes of the nun, Dot gripped the small metal knob on the inside of the door and pushed. Then she felt herself falling forward, slowly turning like a leaf in the wind, upheld and buoyant in the peaceful roar. It was as though she would never reach Sister's arms, but when she did, she came back with a jolt.

"You *are* ill," Sister said. "Come to the office, and we'll call your mother."

As Dot had known it would, perhaps from that moment in the girls' bathroom, the day came. The day of her reckoning.

Outside, in the morning schoolyard, after mass and before first bell, everyone crowded around Toddy Crieder. In his arms he held a wind-up tin Godzilla, a big toy, almost knee-high, a green-and-gold replica painted with a fierce eye for detail. The scales were perfect overlapping crescents, and the eyes were large and manic, pitch-black, oddly human. Toddy had pinned a sort of cloak on the thing, a black scarf. Dot's arms thrust through the packed shoulders, but the bell rang, and Toddy stowed the toy under his coat. His eyes picked Dot from the rest.

"I had to send for this!" he cried. The punch hadn't turned him against Dot, only hardened his resolve to please her. He vanished through the heavy wine-red doors of the school. Dot stared at the ground. The world went stark, the colors harsh in her eyes. The small brown pebbles of the playground leaped off the tarred and sealed earth. She took a step. The stones seemed to crack and whistle under her feet.

"Last bell!" Sister Mary Anita called. "You'll be late!"

Morning prayer. The pledge. Toddy drew out the suspense of his audience, enjoying the glances and whispers. The toy was in his desk. Every so often he lifted the lid and then looked around to see how many children were watching him duck inside to make adjustments. By the time Sister started the daily reading lesson, the tension in the room was so acute that not even Toddy could bear it any longer.

The room was large, high-ceilinged, floored with slats of polished wood. Round lights hung on thick chains, and the great rectangular windows let through enormous sheaves of radiance. This large class had been in the room for more than two years. Dot had spent most of every day in this room. She knew its creaks, the muted clunk of desks rocking out of floor bolts, the mad thrumping in the radiators like the sound of a thousand imprisoned elves, and so she heard and immediately registered the click and grind of Toddy's wind-up key. Sister Mary Anita did not. The teacher turned to the chalkboard, her book open on the desk, and began to write instructions for the children to copy.

She was absorbed, calling out the instructions as she wrote. Her arm swept up and down, it seemed to Dot, in a frighteningly innocent joy. She was inventing a lesson, some way of doing things, not a word of which was being taken in. All eyes were on the third row, where Toddy Crieder sat. All eyes were on his hand as he wound the toy up to its limit and bent over and set it on the floor. Then the eyes were on the toy itself, as Toddy lifted his hand away and the thing moved forward on its own.

The scarf it wore did not hamper the beast's progress, the regular thrash of its legs. The tiny claw hands beat forward like pistons and the thick metal tail whipped from side to side as the toy moved down the center of the aisle toward the front of the room, toward Sister Mary Anita, who stood, back turned, immersed in her work at the board.

Dot had gotten herself placed in the first row, to be closer to her teacher, and so she saw the creature up close just before it headed into the polished open space of floor at the front of the room. Its powerful jaws thrust from the black scarf; its great teeth were frozen, exhibited in a terrible smile. Its painted eyes had an eager and purposeful look.

Its movement faltered as it neared Mary Anita. The children caught their breath, but the thing inched forward, made slow and fascinating progress, directly toward the hem of her garment. She did not seem to notice. She continued to talk, to write, circling numbers and emphasizing certain words with careful underlines. And as she did so, as the moment neared, Dot's brain finally rang. She jumped as though it were the last bell of the day. She vaulted from her desk. Two steps took her across that gleaming space of wood at the front of the room. But just as she bent down to scoop the toy to her chest, a neat black boot slashed, inches from her nose. Sister Mary Anita had whirled, the chalk fixed in her hand. Daintily, casually, she had lifted her habit and kicked the toy dinosaur into the air. The thing ascended, pedaling its clawed feet, the scarf blown back like a sprung umbrella. The trajectory was straight and true. The toy knocked headfirst into the ceiling and came back down in pieces. The children ducked beneath the rain of scattered tin. Only Dot and Mary Anita stood poised, unmoving, focused on the moment between them.

Dot could look nowhere but at her teacher. But when she lifted her eyes this time, Sister Mary Anita was not looking at her. She had turned her face away, the rough cheek blotched as if it had borne a slap, the gaze hooded and set low. Sister walked to the window, her back again to Dot, to the class, and as the laughter started, uncomfortable and groaning at first, then shriller, fuller, becoming its own animal, Dot felt an unrecoverable tenderness boil up in her. Inwardly she begged the nun to turn and stop the noise. But Sister did not. She let it wash across them both without mercy. Dot lost sight of her unspeakable profile as Mary Anita looked out into the yard. Bathed in a brilliant light, the nun's face went as blank as a sheet of paper, as the sky, as featureless as all things that enter heaven.

Try This

Pain is notoriously difficult to describe. Describe a pain you remember, in images of all five senses—its size, shape, location, color, smell, sound, taste. Then find a few quick metaphors for it—perhaps suggested by these concrete details.

Denis Johnson
Car Crash While Hitchhiking

A salesman who shared his liquor and steered while sleeping . . . A Cherokee filled with bourbon . . . A VW no more than a bubble of hashish fumes, captained by a college student . . .

And a family from Marshalltown who head-onned and killed forever a man driving west out of Bethany, Missouri . . .

. . . I rose up sopping wet from sleeping under the pouring rain, and something less than conscious, thanks to the first three of the people I've already named—the salesman and the Indian and the student—all of whom had given me drugs. At the head of the entrance ramp I waited without hope of a ride. What was the point, even, of rolling up my sleeping bag when I was too wet to be let into anybody's car? I draped it around me like a cape. The downpour raked the asphalt and gurgled in the ruts. My thoughts zoomed pitifully. The traveling salesman had fed me pills that made the linings of my veins feel scraped out. My jaw ached. I knew every raindrop by its name. I sensed everything before it happened. I knew a certain Oldsmobile would stop for me even before it slowed, and by the sweet voices of the family inside it I knew we'd have an accident in the storm.

I didn't care. They said they'd take me all the way.

The man and the wife put the little girl up front with them and left the baby in back with me and my dripping bedroll. "I'm not taking you anywhere very fast," the man said. "I've got my wife and babies here, that's why."

You are the ones, I thought. And I piled my sleeping bag against the left-hand door and slept across it, not caring whether I lived or died. The baby slept free on the seat beside me. He was about nine months old.

. . . But before any of this, that afternoon, the salesman and I had swept down into Kansas City in his luxury car. We'd developed a dangerous cynical camaraderie beginning in Texas, where he'd taken me on. We ate up his bottle of amphetamines, and every so often we pulled off the Interstate and bought another pint of Canadian Club and a sack of ice. His car had cylindrical glass holders attached to either door and a white, leathery interior. He said he'd take me home to stay overnight with his family, but first he wanted to stop and see a woman he knew.

Under Midwestern clouds like great grey brains we left the superhighway with a drifting sensation and entered Kansas City's rush hour with a sensation of running aground. As soon as we slowed down, all the magic of traveling together burned away. He went on and on about his girlfriend. "I like this girl, I think I love this girl—but I've got two kids and a wife, and there's certain obligations there. And on top of everything else, I love my wife. I'm gifted with love. I love my kids. I love all my relatives." As he kept on, I felt jilted and sad: "I have a boat, a little sixteen-footer. I have two cars. There's room in the back yard for a swimming pool." He found his girlfriend at work. She ran a furniture store, and I lost him there.

The clouds stayed the same until night. Then, in the dark, I didn't see the storm gathering. The driver of the Volkswagen, a college man, the one who stoked my head with all the hashish, let me out beyond the city limits just as it began to rain. Never mind the speed I'd been taking, I was too overcome to stand up. I lay out in the grass off the exit ramp and woke in the middle of a puddle that had filled up around me.

And later, as I've said, I slept in the back seat while the Oldsmobile—
the family from Marshalltown—splashed along through the rain. And yet I
dreamed I was looking right through my eyelids, and my pulse marked off
the seconds of time. The Interstate through western Missouri was, in that era,
nothing more than a two-way road, most of it. When a semi truck came
toward us and passed going the other way, we were lost in a blinding spray
and a warfare of noises such as you get being towed through an automatic
car wash. The wipers stood up and lay down across the windshield without
much effect. I was exhausted, and after an hour I slept more deeply.

I'd known all along exactly what was going to happen. But the man
and his wife woke me up later, denying it viciously.

"Oh—*no!*"

"NO!"

I was thrown against the back of their seat so hard that it broke. I commenced bouncing back and forth. A liquid which I knew right away was
human blood flew around the car and rained down on my head. When it
was over I was in the back seat again, just as I had been. I rose up and looked
around. Our headlights had gone out. The radiator was hissing steadily.
Beyond that, I didn't hear a thing. As far as I could tell, I was the only one
conscious. As my eyes adjusted I saw that the baby was lying on its back
beside me as if nothing had happened. Its eyes were open and it was feeling its cheeks with its little hands.

In a minute the driver, who'd been slumped over the wheel, sat up
and peered at us. His face was smashed and dark with blood. It made my
teeth hurt to look at him—but when he spoke, it didn't sound as if any of
his teeth were broken.

"What happened?"

"We had a wreck," he said.

"The baby's okay," I said, although I had no idea how the baby was.
He turned to his wife.

"Janice," he said. "Janice, Janice!"

"Is she okay?"

"She's dead!" he said, shaking her angrily.

"No, she's not." I was ready to deny everything myself now.

The little girl was alive, but knocked out. She whimpered in her sleep.
But the man went on shaking his wife.

"Janice!" he hollered.

His wife moaned.

"She's not dead," I said, clambering from the car and running away.

"She won't wake up," I heard him say.

I was standing out here in the night, with the baby, for some reason, in my arms. It must have still been raining, but I remember nothing about the weather. We'd collided with another car on what I now perceived was a two-lane bridge. The water beneath us was invisible in the dark.

Moving toward the other car I began to hear rasping, metallic snores. Somebody was flung halfway out the passenger door, which was open, in the posture of one hanging from a trapeze by his ankles. The car had been broadsided, smashed so flat that no room was left inside it even for this person's legs, to say nothing of a driver or any other passengers. I just walked right on past.

Headlights were coming from far off. I made for the head of the bridge, waving them to a stop with one arm and clutching the baby to my shoulder with the other.

It was a big semi, grinding its gears as it decelerated. The driver rolled down his window and I shouted up to him, "There's a wreck. Go for help."

"I can't turn around here," he said.

He let me and the baby up on the passenger side, and we just sat there in the cab, looking at the wreckage in his headlights.

"Is everybody dead?" he asked.

"I can't tell who is and who isn't," I admitted.

He poured himself a cup of coffee from a thermos and switched off all but his parking lights.

"What time is it?"

"Oh, it's around quarter after three," he said.

By his manner he seemed to endorse the idea of not doing anything about this. I was relieved and tearful. I'd thought something was required of me, but I hadn't wanted to find out what it was.

When another car showed coming in the opposite direction, I thought I should talk to them. "Can you keep the baby?" I asked the truck driver.

"You'd better hang on to him," the driver said. "It's a boy, isn't it?"

"Well, I think so," I said.

The man hanging out of the wrecked car was still alive as I passed, and I stopped, grown a little more used to the idea of how really badly broken he was, and made sure there was nothing I could do. He was snoring so loudly and rudely. His blood bubbled out of his mouth with every breath. He wouldn't be taking many more. I knew that, but he didn't, and therefore I looked down into the great pity of a person's life on this earth. I don't mean that we all end up dead, that's not the great pity. I mean that he couldn't tell me what he was dreaming, and I couldn't tell him what was real.

Before too long there were cars backed up for a ways at either end of the bridge, and headlights giving a night-game atmosphere to the steaming rubble, and ambulances and cop cars nudging through so that the air pulsed with color. I didn't talk to anyone. My secret was that in this short while I had gone from being the president of this tragedy to being a faceless onlooker at a gory wreck. At some point an officer learned that I was one of the passengers, and took my statement. I don't remember any of this, except that he told me, "Put out your cigarette." We paused in our conversation to watch the dying man being loaded into the ambulance. He was still alive, still dreaming obscenely. The blood ran off him in strings. His knees jerked and his head rattled.

There was nothing wrong with me, and I hadn't seen anything, but the policeman had to question me and take me to the hospital anyway. The word came over his car radio that the man was now dead, just as we came under the awning of the emergency-room entrance.

I stood in a tiled corridor with my wet sleeping bag bunched against the wall beside me, talking to a man from the local funeral home.

The doctor stopped to tell me I'd better have an X-ray.

"No."

"Now would be the time. If something turns up later . . . "

"There's nothing wrong with me."

Down the hall came the wife. She was glorious, burning. She didn't know yet that her husband was dead. We knew. That's what gave her such power over us. The doctor took her into a room with a desk at the end of the hall, and from under the closed door a slab of brilliance radiated as if, by some stupendous process, diamonds were being incinerated in there. What a pair of lungs! She shrieked as I imagined an eagle would shriek. It felt wonderful to be alive to hear it! I've gone looking for that feeling everywhere.

"There's nothing wrong with me"—I'm surprised I let those words out. But it's always been my tendency to lie to doctors, as if good health consisted only of the ability to fool them.

Some years later, one time when I was admitted to the Detox at Seattle General Hospital, I took the same tack.

"Are you hearing unusual sounds or voices?" the doctor asked.

"Help us, oh God, it hurts," the boxes of cotton screamed.

"Not exactly," I said.

"Not exactly," he said. "Now, what does that mean."

"I'm not ready to go into all that," I said. A yellow bird fluttered close to my face, and my muscles grabbed. Now I was flopping like a fish. When I squeezed shut my eyes, hot tears exploded from the sockets. When I opened them, I was on my stomach.

"How did the room get so white?" I asked.

A beautiful nurse was touching my skin. "These are vitamins," she said, and drove the needle in.

It was raining. Gigantic ferns leaned over us. The forest drifted down a hill. I could hear a creek rushing down among rocks. And you, you ridiculous people, you expect me to help you.

Try This

Write down a bumper sticker you like. (It's a good idea to bring them to class and exchange them so you are working with one you don't actually remember.) Describe the car (van, truck) this bumper sticker is stuck on—make, model, year, color, and condition. Anything else on the body? As an observer of this vehicle, give a justification for looking inside. Open the door. Name three smells you encounter. Describe two textures. Name three objects you see on the seats, the floor. Name a fourth object that is surprising to find there. You look up. Here comes the owner of the vehicle. Who, wearing what, moving how? The owner says something to you. What?

POEMS

Ted Hughes
The Hawk in the Rain

I drown in the drumming ploughland, I drag up
Heel after heel from the swallowing of the earth's mouth,
From clay that clutches my each step to the ankle
With the habit of the dogged grave, but the hawk

Effortlessly at height hangs his still eye.
His wings hold all creation in a weightless quiet,
Steady as a hallucination in the streaming air.
While banging wind kills these stubborn hedges,

Thumbs my eyes, throws my breath, tackles my heart,
And rain hacks my head to the bone, the hawk hangs
The diamond point of will that polestars
The sea drowner's endurance: and I,

Bloodily grabbed dazed last-moment-counting
Morsel in the earth's mouth, strain towards the master-
Fulcrum of violence where the hawk hangs still.
That maybe in his own time meets the weather

Coming from the wrong way, suffers the air, hurled upside down,
Fall from his eye, the ponderous shires crash on him,
The horizon trap him; the round angelic eye
Smashed, mix his heart's blood with the mire of the land.

Robert Pinsky

The Haunted Ruin

Even your computer is a haunted ruin, as your
Blood leaves something of itself, warming
The tool in your hand.

From far off, down the billion corridors
Of the semiconductor, military
Pipes grieve at the junctures.

This too smells of the body, its heated
Polymers smell of breast milk
And worry-sweat.

Hum of so many cycles in current, voltage
Of the past. Sing, wires. Feel, hand. Eyes,
Watch and form

Legs and bellies of characters:
Beak and eye of A. Serpentine hiss
S of the foregoers, claw-tines

Of E and the claw hammer
You bought yesterday, its head
Tasting of light oil, the juice

Of dead striving—the haft
Of ash, for all its urethane varnish, is
Polished by body salts.

Pull, clawhead. Hold, shaft. Steel face,
Strike and relieve me. Voice
Of the maker locked in the baritone

Whine of the handsaw working.
Lost, lingerer like the dead souls of
Wilno, revenant. Machine-soul.

Yusef Komunyakaa
Facing It

My black face fades,
hiding inside the black granite.
I said I wouldn't,
dammit: No tears.
I'm stone. I'm flesh.
My clouded reflection eyes me
like a bird of prey, the profile of night
slanted against morning. I turn
this way—the stone lets me go.
I turn that way—I'm inside
the Vietnam Veterans Memorial
again, depending on the light
to make a difference.
I go down the 58,022 names,
half-expecting to find
my own in letters like smoke.
I touch the name Andrew Johnson;
I see the booby trap's white flash.
Names shimmer on a woman's blouse
but when she walks away
the names stay on the wall.
Brushstrokes flash, a red bird's
wings cutting across my stare.
The sky. A plane in the sky.
A white vet's image floats
closer to me, then his pale eyes
look through mine. I'm a widow.
He's lost his right arm
inside the stone. In the black mirror
a woman's trying to erase names:
No, she's brushing a boy's hair.

May Swenson

The Surface

First I saw the surface,
then I saw it flow,
then I saw the underneath.

In gradual light below
I saw a kind of room,
the ceiling was a veil,

a shape swam there
slow, opaque and pale.
I saw enter by a shifting corridor

other blunt bodies
that sank toward the floor.
I tried to follow deeper

with my avid eye.
Something changed the focus:
I saw the sky,

a glass between inverted trees.
Then I saw my face.
I looked until a cloud

flowed over that place.
Now I saw the surface
broad to its rim,

here gleaming, there opaque,
far out, flat and dim.
Then I saw it was an Eye:

I saw the Wink that slid
from underneath the rushes
before it closed its lid.

Try This

Write a paragraph or a poem exploring your relationship with an animal or a machine.
Describe the animal or machine using at least three of the senses.

continued

or:

Write a poem or paragraph about a relationship between surface and depth—in an eye, a mirror, water, metal . . .

David Kirby

How to Use This Body

Remove clothes and put to one side.
Body will look awkward, which is normal.
Arrange body on sheets, adjust temperature,
and turn out lights.

At this point,
any number of things can go wrong:
phone can ring, vase or book can fall
from shelf, memory can quicken, love can beat
its wings against the window, and so on.
In that case read to body, give body

hot drink or bath, return body to bed,
and repeat steps two through four (above).
After several hours, remove body from bed
and wash.

Put body into clothes again.
Feed and love body. Do not cut, shoot,
hang, poison, or throw body from window.
Keep body from drafts and solitude.
Write us if you are happy with body, and
could we use your name in our next poem?

Try This
Pick an ordinary activity that you do every, or nearly every, day. Write instructions for how to do it. The instructions may be in the form of a list, a poem, a paragraph, a speech, or whatever you like, but make them so detailed and specific that someone who had never done this particular thing could see how it is done. How to make a peanut butter sandwich. How to back out of the driveway. How to feed the cat.

Galway Kinnell
Why Regret?

Didn't you like the way the ants help
the peony globes open by eating the glue off?
Weren't you cheered to see the ironworkers
sitting on an I-beam dangling from a cable,
in a row, like starlings, eating lunch, maybe
baloney on white with fluorescent mustard?
Wasn't it a revelation to waggle
from the estuary all the way up the river,
the kill, the pirle, the run, the rent, the beck,
the sike nearly dry, to the shock of a spring?
Didn't you almost shiver, hearing the book lice
clicking their sexual dissonance inside the old
Webster's *New International*, perhaps having just
eaten out of it *izle*, *xyster* and *thalassacon*?
What did you imagine lay in store anyway
at the end of a world whose sub-substance is
gleyme, gleet, birdlime, slime, mucus, muck?
Don't worry about becoming emaciated—think of the wren
and how little flesh is needed to make a song.
Didn't it seem somehow familiar when the nymph
split open and the mayfly struggled free
and flew and perched and then its own back
split open and the imago, the true adult,
somersaulted out backwards and took flight
toward the swarm, mouth-parts vestigial,
alimentary canal unfit to digest food,
a day or hour left to find the desired one?
Or when Casanova took up the platter of linguine
in squid's ink and slid the stuff off it
out the window, telling his startled companion,
"The perfected lover does not eat."
As a child didn't you find it calming to think
of the pinworms as some kind of tiny batons
giving cadence to the squeezes and releases
around the downward march of debris?
Didn't you once glimpse what seemed your own
inner blazonry in the monarchs flapping
and gliding, in desire, in the middle air?
Weren't you reassured at the thought that these flimsy,
hinged beings might navigate their way to Mexico
by the flair of the dead bodies of ancestors
who fell in the same migration a year ago?

Isn't it worth missing whatever joy
you might have dreamed, to wake in the night and find
you and your beloved are holding hands in your sleep?

Try This

The Jungian psychologist James Hillman proposes an exercise that he calls "befriending the dream." Quickly write down a dream you have had. Then begin "It's like . . . " and write whatever comes into your head. Every time you come to the end of that thought, write "It's like . . . " and keep going. "It's like . . . it's like . . . it's like . . ." Some of your phrases may be metaphors, some may be colors, some memories, some nonsense, some deep emotions. Whenever you feel yourself "stuck" on a piece of writing, or just want to explore what more may be in it, or what it might be about, you can also befriend the piece.

DRAMA

Samuel Beckett

Act Without Words

A Mime for One Player

Desert. Dazzling light.

The man is flung backwards on stage from right wing. He falls, gets up immediately, dusts himself, turns aside, reflects.

Whistle from right wing.

He reflects, goes out right.

Immediately flung back on stage he falls, gets up immediately, dusts himself, turns aside, reflects.

Whistle from left wing.

He reflects, goes out left.

Immediately flung back on stage he falls, gets up immediately, dusts himself, turns aside, reflects.

Whistle from left wing.

He reflects, goes towards left wing, hesitates, thinks better of it, halts, turns aside, reflects.

A little tree descends from flies, lands. It has a single bough some three yards from ground and at its summit a meager tuft of palms casting at its foot a circle of shadow.

He continues to reflect.

Whistle from above.

He turns, sees tree, reflects, goes to it, sits down in its shadow, looks at his hands.

A pair of tailor's scissors descends from flies, comes to rest before tree, a yard from ground.

He continues to look at his hands.

Whistle from above.

He looks up, sees scissors, takes them and starts to trim his nails.

The palms close like a parasol, the shadow disappears.

He drops scissors, reflects.

A tiny carafe, to which is attached a huge label inscribed WATER, descends from flies, comes to rest some three yards from ground.

He continues to reflect.

Whistle from above.

He looks up, sees carafe, reflects, gets up, goes and stands under it, tries in vain to reach it, renounces, turns aside, reflects.

A big cube descends from flies, lands.

He continues to reflect.

Whistle from above.

He turns, sees cube, looks at it, at carafe, reflects, goes to cube, takes it up, carries it over and sets it down under carafe, tests its stability, gets up on it, tries in vain to reach carafe, renounces, gets down, carries cube back to its place, turns aside, reflects.

A second smaller cube descends from flies, lands.

He continues to reflect.

Whistle from above.

He turns, sees second cube, looks at it, at carafe, goes to second cube, takes it up, carries it over and sets it down under carafe, tests it stability, gets up on it, tries in vain to reach carafe, renounces, gets down, takes up second cube to carry it back to its place, hesitates, thinks better of it, sets it down, goes to big cube, takes it up, carries it over and puts it on small one, tests their stability, gets up on them, the cubes collapse, he falls, gets up immediately, brushes himself, reflects.

He take up small cube, puts it on big one, tests their stability, gets up on them and is about to reach carafe when it is pulled up a little way and comes to rest beyond his reach.

He gets down, reflects, carries cubes back to their place, one by one, turns aside, reflects.

A third still smaller cube descends from flies, lands.

He continues to reflect.

Whistle from above.

He turns, sees third cube, looks at it, reflects, turns aside, reflects.

The third cube is pulled up and disappears in flies.

Beside carafe a rope descends from flies, with knots to facilitate ascent.

He continues to reflect.

Whistle from above.

He turns, sees rope, reflects, goes to it, climbs up it and is about to reach the carafe when rope is let out and deposits him back on ground.

He reflects, looks around for scissors, sees them, goes and picks them up, returns to rope and starts to cut it with scissors.

The rope is pulled up, lifts him off ground, he hangs on, succeeds in cutting rope, falls back on ground, drops scissors, falls, gets up again immediately, brushes himself, reflects.

The rope is pulled up quickly and disappears in flies.

With length of rope in his possession he makes a lasso with which he tries to lasso carafe.

The carafe is pulled up quickly and disappears in flies.

He turns aside, reflects.

He goes with lasso in his hand to tree, looks at bough, turns and looks at cubes, looks again at bough, drops lasso, goes to cubes, takes up small one, carries it over and sets it down under bough, goes back for big one, takes it up and carries it over under bough, makes to put it on small one, hesitates, thinks better of it, sets it down, takes up small one and puts it on big one, tests their stability, turns aside and stoops to pick up lasso.

The bough folds against trunk.

He straightens up with lasso in his hand, turns and sees what has happened.

He drops lasso, turns aside, reflects.

He carries back cubes to their place, one by one, goes back for lasso, carries it over to cubes and lays it in a neat coil on small one.

He turns aside, reflects.

Whistle from right wing.

He reflects, goes out right.

Immediately flung back on stage he falls, gets up immediately, brushes himself, turns aside, reflects.

Whistle from left wing.

He does not move.

He looks at his hands, looks around for scissors, sees them, goes and picks them up, starts to trim his nails, stops, reflects, runs his finger along blade of scissors, goes and lays them on small cube, turns aside, opens his collar, frees his neck and fingers it.

The small cube is pulled up and disappears in flies, carrying away rope and scissors.

He turns to take scissors, sees what has happened.

He turns aside, reflects.

He goes and sits down on big cube.

The big cube is pulled from under him. He falls. The big cube is pulled up and disappears in flies.

He remains lying on his side, his face towards auditorium, staring before him.

The carafe descends from flies and comes to rest a few feet from his body.
He does not move.
Whistle from above.
He does not move.
The carafe descends further, dangles and plays about his face.
He does not move.
The carafe is pulled up and disappears in flies.
The bough returns to horizontal, the palms open, the shadow returns.
Whistle from above.
He does not move.
The tree is pulled up and disappears in flies.
He looks at his hands.

Curtain

Athol Fugard

The Drummer

Commissioned and First Produced by Actors Theatre of Louisville

CHARACTERS
The Man

A city pavement.

Scene: *A pile of rubbish on a pavement, waiting to be cleared away. This consists of an overfilled trash-can and a battered old chair with torn upholstery on which is piled an assortment of cardboard boxes and plastic bags full of discarded junk. Distant and intermittent city noises. These will increase in volume and frequency as the action demands.*

At Rise: *A bum enters. He walks over to the pile of rubbish and starts to work his way through it . . . looking for something useful in terms of that day's survival. He has obviously just woken up and yawns from time to time. After a few seconds he clears the chair, sits down, makes himself comfortable and continues his search. One of the boxes produces a drumstick. He examines it and then abandons it. A little later he finds a second drumstick. He examines it. Remembers! He scratches around in the pile of rubbish at his feet and retrieves the first. Two drumsticks! His find intrigues him. Another dip into the rubbish but it produces nothing further of interest. Two drumsticks! He settles back in his chair and surveys the world.*

An ambulance siren approaches and recedes stage right. He observes indif-ferently. A fire engine approaches and recedes stage left. He observes. While this is going on he taps idly on the lid of the trash-can with one of the drumsticks. He becomes aware of this little action. Two drumsticks and a trash-can! It takes him a few seconds to realize the potential. He straightens up in his chair and with a measure of caution, attempts a little tattoo on the lid of the can. The result is not very impressive. He makes a second attempt, with the same result. Prob-lem. Solution! He gets up and empties the trash-can of its contents, replaces the lid and makes a third attempt. The combination of a serious intention and the now resonant bin produces a decided effect. He develops it and in doing so starts to enjoy himself. His excitement gets him onto his feet. He has one last flash of inspiration. He removes the lid from the can, up-ends it, and with great bravuro drums out a final tattoo . . . virtually an accompaniment to the now very loud and urgent city noises all around him. Embellishing his appearance with some item from the rubbish . . . a cape? . . . and holding his drumsticks ready he chooses a direction and sets off to take on the city. He has discovered it is full of drums . . . and he has got drumsticks.

The Beginning

Try This

The preceding two pieces are mimes, or plays in which no word is spoken. Beckett and Fugard create very different characters, moods, and stories through action and objects alone. Write a very short mime involving one character and two or three objects. How do these visual equivalents of verbs and images convey an idea?

Warm-up
Write a few sentences that might be coming out of the mouth of each of these three
characters.

CHAPTER TWO

VOICE

Your Voice
Persona
Character Voice
Point of View

We can only talk about ourselves in the language we have available. If that language is rich, it illuminates us. But if it is narrow or restricted, it represses and conceals us.

Jaan Whitehead

Literature is made of words. Neither the meaning nor the emotional impact of a given piece can be separated from the language in which it is expressed, nor does "creativity" amount to making "something out of nothing." Perhaps such making belongs to God or to the Big Bang; but creation as we know it, whether of a vegetable, a human being, a symphony, or a poem, consists in the selection and arrangement of elements already there.

In this sense, words are the cells of written meaning. **Diction** (which is a combination of **vocabulary**, the words chosen, and **syntax**, the order in which they are used) will impart particularity to a poem or prose just as the nature and arrangement of cells make up a particular self. Diction will convey not only the facts but what we are to make of them, not only the situation but its emotional coloration, not only the identity but also the tone and attitude of the person whose voice speaks to us from the page.

"All I know about grammar," says Joan Didion in the essay "Why I Write,"

... is its infinite power. To shift the structure of a sentence alters the meaning of that sentence, as definitely and inflexibly as the position of a camera alters the meaning of the object photographed. Many people know about camera angles now, but not so many people know about sentences. The arrangement of the words matters, and the arrangement you want can be found in the picture in your mind.

Your Voice

An "author's **voice**" is a particular recognizable style and tone that lets us know, as if we'd picked up the phone, that this is so-and-so talking. This voice has a quality developed over time, involving recurrent word choice, syntax, imagery, idiom, rhythm, and range. It comes about by a mostly automatic process, the result of practice and the growing confidence that practice brings. Don't worry about finding your voice. Worry about saying things as clearly, precisely, and vividly as you can. Make your language as rich, flexible, and varied as you can make it. In other words: seek *to voice*, and *your voice* will follow.

The language that comes naturally to you is the fine and proper foundation of your voice. Nothing rings more false than a writer who puts on the airs of critical jargon, or medieval fantasy, or high culture, without having a convincing command of that language. On the other hand, training your awareness of language, stretching both the quantity and the flexibility of your vocabulary, playing at different human voices, can all expand your range.

It can't hurt to go about adding to your vocabulary in even a self-improvement sort of way—buy a word-a-day calendar, subscribe to "Wordsmith" or "Merriam Webster's Word of the Day" on e-mail, read "On Language" in the Sunday magazine of the *New York Times*. Buy a really good dictionary. Dissect the diction of the authors you read, and if you don't know a word, look it up. Every writer I know owns a *Roget's Thesaurus*, a blessed aid to locating—not a fancier word to say what you mean! (that *chicken* is not, really, a *chanticleer*)—but the word with that exact shade of meaning you almost have in mind (it might well be a *broiler* or a *bantam* or a *Rhode Island Red*).

Try This

Play at making your vocabulary flexible by picking a word of two or more syllables and recombining its parts, adding rhymes or sounds close in other ways. Example: *wardrobe, wordrobe, rosewood, woodbine, wood bin, rose vine, vineyard, yard rows, wood yard, woodshed, Shadrack, shad roe, word rows*. Make nonsense sentences using your words: *The rose vine grows its rows on the wood shed like these word rows make my wordrobe.*

Alert yourself to language as it is used around you. Listen to people talking, note the flavor of different idioms, record bits of conversation, wander around in the dictionary, push the words around on the page. When you get to the point of revising your manuscript, pay attention to the small unease this or that word occasions in you and focus on how it might please you better.

Begin by knowing, and exploring, the fact that you already have a number of different voices. You speak differently in class from the way you speak (even to the same people) at a party or a bar. You have one diction for your diary and another for your history paper. You use one style of vocabulary and syntax to console a friend and another to ditch a date.

You also have a different vocabulary for shades of meaning, so that according to the circumstances you might describe someone as *stuck-up, snobbish, arrogant, haughty,* or *imperious.* There is no such thing as an exact synonym. Each word would be appropriate to a description of a different person, a different mood or tone, a different medium, even a different speaker.

Try This
Stuck-up, snobbish, arrogant, haughty, imperious. Pick three of these words and produce an image in words of a person who fits each of them. To what extent does "the picture dictate the arrangement" of the words?

Persona

A **persona** is a mask adopted by the author, which may be a public manifestation of the author's self; or a distorted or partial version of that self; or a fictional, historical, or mythological character. The concept of a persona allows us to acknowledge that, just as no written account can tell the whole truth about an event, so no "I" of a poem, essay, or story is exactly the same as the person who writes. When you write "as yourself" in your own voice—in a personal essay or a lyric poem, for example—there is nevertheless a certain distance between the person you are as you go about living your daily life and the *persona* in which you write. The version of yourself that you choose to reveal is part of your meaning. No matter how earnest your attempt to tell "exactly what happened," "the author" is always a partial or slightly idealized you, writing from a frame of mind more focused and consistent—and probably more virtuous—than any person ever possessed. Even if you are confessing terrible sins, you write as one-who-confesses, which is a particular, and admirable, version of your composite total self.

When you speak in your "own" voice, that voice may be relatively intimate and confiding, one that, though artful, we trust to be as honest with us as possible, as in this memoir-poem of Anne Sexton's, "Young."

A thousand doors ago
when I was a lonely kid
in a big house with four
garages and it was summer

as long as I could remember
I lay on the lawn at night,
clover wrinkling under me,
the wise stars bedding over me,
my mother's window a funnel
of yellow heat running out,
my father's window, half shut,
an eye where sleepers pass
and the boards of the house
were smooth and white as wax
and probably a million leaves
sailed on their strange stalks
as the crickets ticked together
and I, in my brand new body,
which was not a woman's yet,
told the stars my questions
and thought God could really see
the heat and the painted light,
elbows, knees, dreams, goodnight.

Here one may feel how the words are "found in the picture" in the poet's mind, how for example the "thousand doors ago" or the "window a funnel of yellow heat running out" reach for an exactness of image, mood, and memory. But the diction might instead signal a more fanciful mask, like this one in which Anne Sexton plays on a conventional image of power and malevolence for her persona.

Her Kind
I have gone out, a possessed witch,
haunting the black air, braver at night;
dreaming evil, I have done my hitch
over the plain houses, light by light:
lonely thing, twelve-fingered, out of mind.
A woman like that is not a woman, quite.
I have been her kind. . .

Prose writers can exercise a similar range of personae. One way of looking at the author of a memoir or personal essay is that that writer is the main character or protagonist of a true story. Again, the persona may be confessional and direct:

When my family packed up and moved from the backwoods of Tennessee to the backwoods of Ohio I was not quite six years old. Like most children at that age I was still a two-legged smudge. Hardly a thing about me was definite except my way of talking, and that soon landed me in trouble. The kids in Ohio took one listen to my Tennessee accent and decided I was a hick. They let me know their opinion by calling me not only hick but hillbilly, ridge runner, clodhopper, and hayseed.

"Coming from the Country," Scott Russell Sanders

But this is far from the only way you might choose to present your "self" as author. Any number of masks may be donned. Here is Dave Barry writing from the persona of Ignorant Literal-Minded Guy, a mask that has been enormously popular among American essayists since Mark Twain:

> . . . obviously the real cause of the California electricity shortage is: college students. I base this statement on widespread observation of my son, who is a college student, and who personally consumes more electricity than Belgium. If my son is in a room, then every electrical device within 200 yards of that room—every light, computer, television, stereo, video game, microwave oven, etc.—will be running. My son doesn't even have to turn the devices on; they activate themselves spontaneously in response to his presence.

This comic persona depends partly on exaggeration and an inflated vocabulary, out of tone in relation to the content: *widespread observation, personally consumes, electrical device, spontaneously in response*. It also mocks scientific logic, "basing the statement" on a single case.

Try This

Imagine (remember?) that you have borrowed ("borrowed"?) a car and been involved in a fender bender. Write an explanation for the police report. Write a **monologue** (a speech for one voice) explaining the accident to the friend whose car you borrowed. Write a letter telling about it to a friend who thinks you are truly cool.

"I'll tell my state as though 'twere none of mine."

Robert Browning

Character Voice

You may also choose to speak in the persona of a character who is largely or totally unlike you. This **character**'s voice is a chosen mimicry and is one of the most rewarding devices of imaginative writing, a skill to pursue in order to develop rich characters both in their narratives and in their dialogue. Your voice will never be entirely absent from the voice of the characters you create, but the characters too can be distinct and recognizable.

The voice of a character requires, beyond invention, an imaginative leap into the mind and diction of another person. The best way to develop this capability is first, to listen to other people speaking and to become aware of their speech patterns, vocabulary choice, habits of diction; and then to practice launching yourself into the voices you have heard. You already have a foundation for this skill through your knowledge of other writers' efforts. Here, for example, are some very brief examples, most of them familiar to you, of characters announcing their own identities. Notice how much they tell you about themselves, the worlds they inhabit, and their attitudes, in a very few words:

Call me Ishmael.

My name is Bond—James Bond.

My name is Ozymandias, King of Kings.
Look on my works, ye mighty, and despair.

Out of the ash
I rise with my red hair.
And I eat men like air.

I am but mad north-northwest: when the wind is southerly, I know a hawk from a handsaw.

I am the Way and the Light. Whosoever believeth in Me shall not perish, but have everlasting life.

I am a man more sinn'd against than sinning.

If you really want to hear about it, the first thing you'll probably want to know is where I was born, and what my lousy childhood was like, and how my parents were occupied and all before they had me, and all that David Copperfield kind of crap. . . (*The Catcher in the Rye*, J.D. Salinger)

When I look back on my childhood, I wonder how I survived at all. It was, of course, a miserable childhood: the happy childhood is hardly worth your while. Worse than the ordinary miserable childhood is the miserable Irish childhood, and worse yet is the miserable Irish Catholic childhood. (*Angela's Ashes*, Frank McCourt)

Try This

Write a short character sketch of someone in your family. Write a monologue in which that person tells you an anecdote from his or her childhood.

You could say, and be roughly accurate, that there is a hierarchy of distance between the author and the voice. The memoirist or personal essayist is most likely to be closest to the person writing; the lyric poet is somewhat more distanced by the artifice of the language; the fiction writer has a range of masks from "author" to characters; and the dramatist speaks only through the characters, theoretically never speaking in his/her own voice except in stage directions.

Great potential for contrast, irony, and conflict enters the writing when one voice is set off against another. Characters reveal themselves in conversation and confrontation not only in the ideas they consciously express but in the diction they use, the things that "just slip out," and the things they refuse or fail to say. The next chapter will look at dialogue, which can lead not only to character revelation but to the heart of story, which is discovery and decision. In the meanwhile:

Try This
Go back to the character in your "bumper sticker" exercise on p. 31. Find a few more details to describe that character. Then pick a trigger line from those below and use it to start a monologue in that character's voice. If you feel you are not catching the voice, never mind; keep going.
- I don't normally dress this way, but
- I had a dream last night
- I'll tell you what doesn't make any sense
- I'm sorry, I didn't see you
- What I need is some kind of work that
- I remember when you could

> I am the narrator. I am just up in the sky telling the story.
> I just know everything. So pay no attention to me.
>
> *Josiah Sable, ten years old*

Point of View

Closely allied to the concept of voice is **point of view**. We're used to using the phrase "point of view" as a synonym for "opinion," as in, "It's my point of view that young people watch too much television." But point of view as a literary technique is a complex and specific concept, dealing with vantage point and addressing the question: *Who* is standing *where* to watch the scene? The answer will involve the voice of the teller, the intended listener, and the distance or closeness of both the action and the diction. An author's view of the world, as it is and as it ought to be, will ultimately be revealed by manipulation of the point of view, but not vice versa—identifying the author's beliefs will not describe the point of view of the work.

The first point of view decision that you as a writer must make is the **person** in which you speak: *first person* (I walked out into the rain), *second person* (You walked out into the rain), or *third person* (She walked out into the rain).

All of the examples of persona in this chapter so far are in the **first person**: *I was a lonely kid. . . I have gone out, a possessed witch. . . I was not quite six years old. . . I base this statement. . . Call me Ishmael,* and so forth. The first person is the point of view most frequent in memoir, personal essay, and lyric poetry. Characters in a play speak, of course, in the first person. It is also the voice of much fiction, in which case it will be the voice of the **central narrator**, the *I* writing *my* story as if it were memoir; or else of a **peripheral narrator**, someone on the edge of the action, but nevertheless our eyes and ears in the story and therefore the person with whom we identify, and with whom we must be moved or changed if the story is to succeed.

Notice that when you are writing in the first person voice of a fictional or dramatic character, the whole range of intimacy and distance is also possible in the diction. Bohumil Hrabel's young railway employee in the novel *Closely Observed Trains* tells his own story and takes us into his confidence as if he were writing a confessional memoir, in spite of the fact that he never existed:

> I always had the impression—and I still have and always shall have—that behind every window there was at the very least one pair of eyes watching me. If anyone spoke to me I blushed, because I felt uncomfortably aware that there was something about me that disturbed and upset everybody. Three months ago I slashed my wrists, and on the face of it I had no reason to do such a thing, but I did have a reason, and I knew what it was, and I was only afraid that everyone who looked at me was guessing at what that reason could be.

By contrast, in the play *Our Country's Good*, Timberlake Wertenberger's Judge Collins of eighteenth-century Australia uses the distanced diction of profound and self-satisfied authority:

> This land is under English law. The court found them guilty and sentenced them accordingly. . . I commend your endeavor to oppose the baneful influence of vice with the harmonizing acts of civilization, Governor, but I suspect your edifice will collapse without the mortar of fear.

The **second person** is the basic point of view of a piece only when the "you" is a character—usually in fact the reader, whom the author turns into a character by assuming she knows just how "you" behave in the situation she invents. Here is an example from Lorrie Moore's story "How to Be a Writer:"

> First, try to be something, anything, else. A movie star/astronaut. A movie star/missionary. The movie star/kindergarten teacher. President of the World. Fail miserably. It is best if you fail at an early age—say, fourteen. Early, critical disillusionment is necessary so that at fifteen you can write long haiku sequences

about thwarted desire. It is a pond, a cherry blossom, a wind brushing against sparrow wing leaving for mountain. Count the syllables. Show it to your mom.

More frequently, when there is a "you" addressed, it represents the person who is assumed to read or receive the piece—look again at the powerful last sentence of Denis Johnson's "Car Crash While Hitchhiking" on p. 31. The basic point of view in that story is still first person, as it is in Sharon Olds's poem "Feared Drowned," of which these are the first two stanzas:

Suddenly nobody knows where you are,
your suit black as seaweed, your bearded
head slick as a seal's.

Somebody watches the kids. I walk down the
edge of the water, clutching the towel
like a widow's shawl around me. . .

This use of the second person as someone to whom a poem or story (or in the case of drama, a speech) is addressed can enhance a sense of intimacy, even make us feel as readers/viewers that we are overhearing something private. The second person as a basic point of view, in which "you" become the character, tends to be experimental and self-conscious, and may be set aside or saved for special effects.

Try This
Write about something that happened to you. But write about it in the first person *from the point of view of someone else* who was present.
Or write about it in the second person, keeping in mind that you're trying to make your reader identify and "become you."

The **third person** is frequently used in poetry and fiction, as well as being the voice of the "objective" journalist or essayist. This voice in imaginative writing can be roughly divided into three techniques: that of the **omniscient** or god-like narrator, who may know anything past, present, or future and is free to tell us what to think; the **limited omniscient**, who may go into the mind of one or perhaps two characters and also observe from the outside; and the **objective**, who may know no more than a person observing the scene—the facts and whatever is present to the senses.

The omniscient author was a frequent stance of nineteenth-century fiction, where the persona of "author" took on an all-knowing quality:

Caroline Helstone was just eighteen years old; and at eighteen the true narrative of life has yet to be commenced. Before that time, we sit listening to a tale, a marvelous fiction; delightful sometimes, and sad sometimes; almost always unreal. . . Hope, when she smiles on us, and promises happiness tomorrow, is implicitly believed;— Love, when he comes wandering like a lost angel to our door, is at once admitted, welcomed, embraced. . . Alas, Experience! No other mentor has so wasted and frozen a face. . .

Shirley, Charlotte Brontë

In the twentieth century it became usual for "the author" to assume the more modest capability of the limited omniscient, able to go into one character's mind and to tell us objectively what, if we were present, we would be able to perceive for ourselves, but not to leap from the mind of one character to another.

Years later, Orno Tarcher would think of his days in New York as a seduction. A seduction and a near miss, a time when his memory of the world around him— the shining stone stairwells, the taxicabs, the sea of nighttime lights—was glinting and of heroic proportion. Like a dream. He had almost been taken away from himself. That was the feeling he had looking back. Smells and sounds: the roll and thunder of the number 1 train; the wind like a flute through the deck rafters of the Empire State Building; the waft of dope in the halls.

For Kings and Planets, Ethan Canin

The perception in these two passages is very much alike, of the vulnerability and ignorance of youth, but in the first the convention of "the author" holds all the answers, whereas in the second "the author" is an unvoiced presence, seeing and remembering through the character's eyes. It is the character himself looking back who "realizes," "feels," and "smells."

In the objective viewpoint, the author may choose a strictly journalistic stance, reporting only what may be seen, heard, smelled, tasted, touched, and objectively known. This is a favorite stance of Ernest Hemingway. In the story "Hills Like White Elephants," Hemingway reports what is said and done by a quarreling couple, both without any direct revelation of the characters' thoughts and without comment.

The American and the girl with him sat at a table in the shade, outside the building. It was very hot and the express from Barcelona would come in forty minutes. It stopped at this junction for two minutes and went on to Madrid.

"What should we drink?" the girl asked. She had taken off her hat and put it on the table.

"It's pretty hot," the man said.

"Let's drink beer."

"Dos cervezas," the man said into the curtain.

"Big ones?" a woman asked from the doorway.

"Yes. Two big ones."

The woman brought two glasses of beer and two felt pads. She put the felt pads and the beer glasses on the table and looked at the man and the girl. The girl was looking off at the line of hills. They were white in the sun and the country was brown and dry.

The narrative remains clipped, austere, and external. What Hemingway gains by this pretense of objective reporting is that the reader is allowed to discover what is really happening through gestures, repetitions, and slips of the tongue, as in life.

Try This

Take any passage you have written in the first person and recast it in the objective voice. Try to reveal the thoughts and feelings of the original through speech, gesture, action, and image.

Beyond the choice of person, point of view importantly involves the question of the **distance** between the author/reader and the characters. John Gardner in *The Art of Fiction* succinctly illustrates some of the possibilities of distance in the third person:

1. It was winter of the year 1853. A large man stepped out of a doorway.
2. Henry J. Warburton had never cared much for snowstorms.
3. Henry hated snowstorms.
4. God how he hated these damn snowstorms.
5. Snow. Under your collar, down inside our shoes, freezing and plugging up your miserable soul.

From the impersonality of *large man* through increasingly familiar designations (full name, first name, pronoun), to the identification implied in the second person (*your collar, your shoes, your soul*), these examples reduce the formality of the diction and therefore the psychic and psychological distance between the author-and-reader and the character.

The degree of distance will involve a series of questions, of which "who speaks?" is only the first. It will also involve *to whom?* (the reader? another character? the self?), *in what form?* (a story? a journal? a report? a daydream?), *at what distance?* (an old man telling the story of his youth? a prisoner recounting his crime?), and *with what limitations?* (is the narrator a liar, a child, crazy?). The voice of the speaker, whether autobiographical, poetic persona, narrator, or character, always involves these issues. Because the author *inevitably wants to convince us to share the same perspective*, the answers will also help reveal her or his final opinion, judgment, attitude, or message.

Point of view is a slippery concept, but one over which you gradually gain control as you write. Apart from significant detail, there is no more important skill for a writer to grasp, for, as Carol Bly says in *The Passionate, Accurate Story*, these are the two skills that "divide master from apprentice." Once you have chosen a point of view, you have in effect made a "contract" with the reader, and it will be difficult to break the contract gracefully. If you have restricted yourself to the mind of Sally Anne for five pages, as she longingly watches Chuck and his R&B band, you will violate the contract by suddenly dipping into Chuck's mind to let us know what he thinks of groupies. We are likely to feel misused—and likely to cancel the contract altogether, if you suddenly give us an omniscient lecture on the failings of the young.

In many ways, our language has been impoverished—by politics, ads, ignorance, and suspicion of eloquence. In the Renaissance it was socially valuable to be able to speak well; you could talk yourself into court or into bed. Whereas in America, and especially in the latter half of the twentieth century, we have tended to equate eloquence with arrogance at best and dishonesty at worst, preferring people who, like, you know, well, kinda couldn't exactly, like, say what they mean. Sort of. Whole concepts have disappeared via advertising from our fund of expression. We no longer have meaningful ways to say: *the real thing*, or: *the right choice*, or: *new and improved*, or: *makes you feel young again*, or: *just do it*. The words *wonderful, great, grand, distinctive, elegant, exclusive, purity, pleasure, passion, mastery, mystery*, and *natural*, have been co-opted and corrupted. If I say: *I love what you do to me*, it is clear that I've got something to sell.

Paradoxically, this impoverishment allows the writer myriad ways to characterize. Though it may be difficult to write convincingly from the lofty perspective of all-knowing author-ity, a rich awareness of voice and voices, their particular idioms and diction, can give you a range of perspectives from which to write. You can make legitimate and revealing use of jargon, cliché, malapropisms (misused words), overstatement, and so forth, in the mouth of a character. Such language is a way of signaling distance between author and character, a distance that the reader understands and shares. A famous example is Amanda Wingfield of Tennessee Williams' "Glass Menagerie," who here berates her son:

> Oh, I can see the handwriting on the wall as plain as I see the nose in front of my face! It's terrifying! More and more you remind me of your father! He was out all hours without explanation—then *left*! And me with the bag to hold.

Try This

Write a speech in which a character strings together a bunch of clichés or jargon phrases. Let the clichés characterize. However, be sure you have some sympathy for the character.

If you persevere in writing, "your voice" will inevitably take on a coloration that is entirely your own. At the same time, voice is a powerful force for exploring the inner lives of others. Story writer Grace Paley describes the process: ". . . what we write about is *what we don't know about what we know*. . . when you take this other voice—you're making a 'pull.' You're pulling towards another head. And that pull toward what you *don't* know. . . well, that's the story itself. The story is that stretching. . . that *act* of stretching."

More to Read

Oliver, Mary. *A Poetry Handbook.* New York: Harcourt Brace, 1994.

Sloane, William. *The Craft of Writing.* New York: W.W. Norton, 1979.

ESSAYS

Of the four prose pieces that begin these readings, three are written in the first person, and one in the third person, limited omniscient, through the eyes of the central character; but they present four very different voices. Explore what choices of diction and imagery create the comic intimacy of McCourt, the genial erudition of Nabokov, the childlike curiosity of Jin, the sharp satire of Barthelme. Contrast them with the authorial third-person voice of "Sister Godzilla" at the end of the preceding chapter on "Image."

Frank McCourt

from *Angela's Ashes*

Eugene is sleeping under a coat on the bed. Dad sits by the fireplace with Oliver on his lap. I wonder why Dad is telling Oliver a Cuchulain story. He knows the Cuchulain stories are mine, but when I look at Oliver I don't mind. His cheeks are bright red, he's staring into the dead fire, and you can see he has no interest in Cuchulain. Mam puts her hand on his forehead. I think he has a fever, she says. I wish I had an onion and I'd boil it in milk and pepper. That's good for the fever. But even if I had what would I boil the milk on? We need coal for that fire.

She gives Dad the docket for the coal down the Dock Road. He takes me with him but it's dark and all the coal yards are closed.

What are we going to do now, Dad?

I don't know, son.

Ahead of us women in shawls and small children are picking up coal along the road.

There, Dad, there's coal.

Ooh, no, son. We won't pick coal off the road. We're not beggars.

He tells Mam the coal yards are closed and we'll have to drink milk and eat bread tonight, but when I tell her about the women on the road she passes Eugene to him.

If you're too grand to pick coal off the road I'll put on my coat and go down the Dock Road.

She gets a bag and takes Malachy and me with her. Beyond the Dock Road there is something wide and dark with lights glinting in it. Mam says that's the River Shannon. She says that's what she missed most of all in America, the River Shannon. The Hudson was lovely but the Shannon sings. I can't hear the song but my mother does and that makes her happy. The other women are gone from the Dock Road and we search for the bits of coal that drop from lorries. Mam tells us gather anything that burns, coal, wood, cardboard, paper. She says, There are them that burn the horse droppings but we're not gone that low yet. When her bag is nearly full she says, Now we have to find an onion for Oliver. Malachy says he'll find one but she tells him, No, you don't find onions on the road, you get them in shops.

The minute he sees a shop he cries out, There's a shop, and runs in.

Oonyen, he says. Oonyen for Oliver.

Mam runs into the shop and tells the woman behind the counter, I'm sorry. The woman says, Lord, he's a dote. Is he an American or what?

Mam says he is. The woman smiles and shows two teeth, one on each side of her upper gum. A dote, she says, and look at them gorgeous goldy curls. And what is it he wants now? A sweet?

Ah, no, says Mam. An onion.

The woman laughs, An onion? I never heard a child wanting an onion before. Is that what they like in America?

Mam says, I just mentioned I wanted to get an onion for my other child that's sick. Boil the onion in milk, you know.

True for you, missus. You can't beat the onion boiled in milk. And look, little boy, here's a sweet for yourself and one for the other little boy, the brother, I suppose.

Mam says, Ah, sure, you shouldn't. Say thank you, boys.

The woman says, Here's a nice onion for the sick child, missus.

Mam says, Oh, I can't buy the onion now, missus. I don't have a penny on me.

I'm giving you the onion, missus. Let it never be said a child went sick in Limerick for want of an onion. And don't forget to sprinkle in a little pepper. Do you have pepper, missus?

Ah, no, I don't but I should be getting it any day now.

Well, here, missus. Pepper and a little salt. Do the child all the good in the world.

Mam says, God bless you, ma'am, and her eyes are watery.

Dad is walking back and forth with Oliver in his arms and Eugene is playing on the floor with a pot and a spoon. Dad says, Did you get the onion?

I did, says Mam, and more. I got coal and the way of lighting it.

I knew you would. I said a prayer to St. Jude. He's my favorite saint, patron of desperate cases.

I got the coal. I got the onion, no help from St. Jude.

Dad says, you shouldn't be picking up coal off the road like a common beggar. It isn't right. Bad example for the boys.

Then you should have sent St. Jude down the Dock Road.

Malachy says, I'm hungry, and I'm hungry, too, but Mam says, Ye'll wait till Oliver has his onion boiled in milk.

She gets the fire going, cuts the onion in half, drops it in the boiling milk with a little butter and sprinkles the milk with pepper. She takes Oliver on her lap and tries to feed him but he turns away and looks into the fire.

Ah, come on, love, she says. Good for you. Make you big and strong.

He tightens his mouth against the spoon. She puts the pot down, rocks him till he's asleep, lays him on the bed and tells the rest of us be quiet or she'll demolish us. She slices the other half of the onion and fries it in butter with slices of bread. She lets us sit on the floor around the fire where we eat the fried bread and sip at the scalding sweet tea in jam jars. She says, That fire is good and bright so we can turn off that gaslight till we get money for the meter.

The fire makes the room warm and with the flames dancing in the coal you can see faces and mountains and valleys and animals leaping. Eugene falls asleep on the floor and Dad lifts him to the bed beside Oliver. Mam puts the boiled onion pot up on the mantelpiece for fear a mouse or rat might be at it. She says she's tired out from the day, the Vincent de Paul Society, Mrs. McGrath's shop, the search for coal down the Dock Road, the worry over

Oliver not wanting the boiled onion, and if he's like this tomorrow she's taking him to the doctor, and now she's going to bed.

Soon we're all in bed and if there's the odd flea I don't mind because it's warm in the bed with the six of us and I love the glow of the fire the way it dances on the walls and ceiling and makes the room go red and black, red and black, till it dims to white and black and all you can hear is a little cry from Oliver turning in my mother's arms.

In the morning Dad is lighting the fire, making tea, cutting the bread. He's already dressed and he's telling Mam hurry up and get dressed. He says to me, Francis, your little brother Oliver is sick and we're taking him to the hospital. You are to be a good boy and take care of your two brothers. We'll be back soon.

Mam says, When we're out go easy with that sugar. We're not millionaires.

When Mam picks up Oliver and wraps him in a coat Eugene stands on the bed. I want Ollie, he says. Ollie play.

Ollie will be back soon, she says, and you can play with him. Now you can play with Malachy and Frank.

Ollie, Ollie, I want Ollie.

He follows Oliver with his eyes and when they're gone he sits on the bed looking out the window. Malachy says, Genie, Genie, we have bread, we have tea. Sugar on your bread, Genie. He shakes his head and pushes away the bread Malachy is offering. He crawls to the place where Oliver slept with Mam, puts his head down and stares out the window.

Grandma is at the door. I heard your father and mother were running down Henry Street with the child in their arms. Now where are they gone to?

Oliver is sick, I said. He wouldn't eat the boiled onion in milk.

What are you blatherin' about?

Wouldn't eat the boiled onion and got sick.

And who's minding ye?

I am.

And what's up with the child in the bed? What's his name?

That's Eugene. He misses Oliver. They're twins.

I know they're twins. That child looks starved. Have ye any porridge here?

What's porridge? Says Malachy.

Jesus, Mary and Holy St. Joseph! What's porridge! Porridge is porridge. That's what porridge is. Ye are the most ignorant bunch o' Yanks I ever seen. Come on, put on yeer clothes and we'll go across the street to your aunt Aggie. She's there with the husband, Pa Keating, and she'll give ye some porridge.

She picks up Eugene, wraps him in her shawl and we cross the street to Aunt Aggie's. She's living with Uncle Pa again because he said she wasn't a fat cow after all.

Do you have any porridge? Grandma says to Aunt Aggie.

Porridge? Am I supposed to be feeding porridge to a crowd of Yanks?

Pity about you, says Grandma. It won't kill you to give them a little porridge.

And I suppose they'll be wanting sugar and milk on top of everything or they might be banging on my door looking for an egg if you don't mind. I don't know why we have to pay for Angela's mistakes.

Jesus, says Grandma, 'tis a good thing you didn't own that stable in Bethlehem or the Holy Family would still be wanderin' the world crumblin' with the hunger.

Grandma pushes her way past Aunt Aggie, puts Eugene on a chair near the fire and makes the porridge. A man comes in from another room. He has black curly hair and his skin is black and I like his eyes because they're very blue and ready to smile. He's Aunt Aggie's husband, the man who stopped the night we were attacking the fleas and told us all about fleas and snakes, the man with the cough he got from swallowing gas in the war.

Malachy says, Why are you all black? And Uncle Pa Keating laughs and coughs so hard he has to ease himself with a cigarette. Oh, the little Yanks, he says. They're not a bit shy. I'm black because I work at the Limerick Gas Works shoveling coal and coke into the furnaces. Gassed in France and back to Limerick to work in the gas works. When you grow up you'll laugh.

Malachy and I have to leave the table so the big people can sit and have tea. They have their tea but Uncle Pa Keating, who is my uncle because he's married to my Aunt Aggie, picks up Eugene and takes him on his lap. He says, This is a sad little fella, and makes funny faces and silly sounds. Malachy and I laugh but Eugene only reaches up to touch the blackness of Pa Keating's skin, and then when Pa pretends to bite his little hand, Eugene laughs and everyone in the room laughs. Malachy goes to Eugene and tries to make him laugh even more but Eugene turns away and hides his face in Pa Keating's shirt.

I think he likes me, says Pa, and that's when Aunt Aggie puts down her teacup and starts to bawl, Waah, waah, waah, big teardrops tumbling down her fat red face.

Aw, Jesus, says Grandma, there she is again. What's up with you this time?

And Aunt Aggie blubbers, To see Pa there with a child on his lap an' me with no hope of having my own.

Grandma barks at her, Stop talkin' like that in front of the children.

Have you no shame? When God is good and ready He'll send you your family.

Aunt Aggie sobs, Angela with five born an' one just gone an' her so useless she couldn't scrub a floor an' me with none an' I can scrub an' clean with the best and make any class of a stew or a fry.

Pa Keating laughs, I think I'll keep this little fella.

Malachy runs to him. No, no, no. That's my brother, that's Eugene. And I say, No, no, no, that's our brother.

Aunt Aggie pats the tears on her cheeks. She says, I don't want nothing of Angela's. I don't want nothing that's half Limerick and half North of Ireland, so I don't, so ye can take him home. I'll have me own someday if I have to do a hundred novenas to the Virgin Mary and her mother, St. Ann, or if I have to crawl from here to Lourdes on me two bended knees.

Grandma says, That's enough. Ye have had yeer porridge and 'tis time to go home and see if yeer father and mother are back from the hospital.

She puts on her shawl and goes to pick up Eugene but he clutches so hard at Pa Keating's shirt she has to pull him away though he keeps looking back at Pa till we're out the door.

We followed Grandma back to our room. She put Eugene in the bed and gave him a drink of water. She told him to be a good boy and go to sleep for his little brother, Oliver, would be home soon and they'd be playing again there on the floor.

But he kept looking out the window.

She told Malachy and me we could sit on the floor and play but to be quiet because she was going to say her prayers. Malachy went to the bed and sat by Eugene and I sat on a chair at the table making out words on the newspaper that was our tablecloth. All you could hear in the room was Malachy whispering to make Eugene happy and Grandma mumbling to the click of her rosary beads. It was so quiet I put my head on the table and fell asleep.

Dad is touching my shoulder. Come on, Francis, you have to take care of your little brothers.

Mam is slumped on the edge of the bed, making small crying sounds like a bird. Grandma is pulling on her shawl. She says, I'll go down to Thompson the undertaker about the coffin and the carriage. The St. Vincent de Paul Society will surely pay for that, God knows.

She goes out the door. Dad stands facing the wall over the fire, beating on his thighs with his fists, sighing, Och, och, och.

Dad frightens me with his och, och, och, and Mam frightens me with her small bird sounds and I don't know what to do though I wonder if anyone will light the fire in the grate so that we can have tea and bread because it's a long time since we had the porridge. If Dad would move away from the fireplace I could light the fire myself. All you need is paper, a few bits of coal or turf, and a match. He won't move so I try to go around his legs while he's beating on his thighs but he notices me and wants to know why I'm trying to light the fire. I tell him we're all hungry and he lets out a crazy laugh. Hungry? He says. Och, Francis, your wee brother Oliver is dead. Your wee sister is dead and your wee brother is dead.

He picks me up and hugs me so hard I cry out. Then Malachy cries, my mother cries, Dad cries, I cry, but Eugene stays quiet. Then Dad sniffles, We'll have a feast. Come on, Francis.

He tells my mother we'll be back in awhile but she has Malachy and Eugene on her lap in the bed and she doesn't look up. He carries me through the streets of Limerick and we go from shop to shop with him asking for food or anything they can give a family that has two children dead in a year, one in America, one in Limerick and danger of losing three more for the want of food and drink. Most shopkeepers shake their heads. Sorry for your troubles but you could go to the St. Vincent de Paul Society or get the public assistance.

Dad says he's glad to see the spirit of Christ alive in Limerick and they tell him they don't need the likes of him with his northern accent to be telling them about Christ and he should be ashamed of himself dragging a child around like that like a common beggar, a tinker, a knacker.

A few shopkeepers give bread, potatoes, tins of beans and Dad says, We'll go home now and you boys can eat something, but we meet Uncle Pa Keating and he tells Dad he's sorry for his troubles and would Dad like to have a pint in this pub here?

There are men sitting in this pub with great glasses of black stuff before them. Uncle Pa Keating and Dad have the black stuff, too. They lift their glasses carefully and slowly drink. There is creamy white stuff on their lips, which they lick with little sighs. Uncle Pa gets me a bottle of lemonade and Dad gives me a piece of bread and I don't feel hungry anymore. Still, I wonder how long we'll sit here with Malachy and Eugene hungry at home, hours from the porridge, which Eugene didn't eat anyway.

Dad and Uncle Pa drink their glass of black stuff and have another. Uncle Pa says, Frankie, this is the pint. This is the staff of life. This is the best thing for nursing mothers and for those who are long weaned.

He laughs and Dad smiles and I laugh because I think that's what you're supposed to do when Uncle Pa says something. He doesn't laugh when he tells the other men about Oliver dying. The other men tip their hats to Dad. Sorry for your troubles, mister, and surely you'll have a pint.

Dad says yes to the pints and soon he's singing Roddy McCorley and Kevin Barry and song after song I never heard before and crying over his lovely little girl, Margaret, that died in America and his little boy, Oliver, dead beyond in the City Home Hospital. It frightens me the way he yells and cries and sings and I wish I could be at home with my three brothers, no, my two brothers, and my mother.

The man behind the bar says to Dad, I think now, mister, you've had enough. We're sorry for your troubles but you have to take that child home to his mother that must be heartbroken by the fire.

Dad says, One, one more pint, just one, eh? and the man says no. Dad shakes his fist. I did me bit for Ireland, and when the man comes out and takes Dad's arm, Dad tries to push him away.

Uncle Pa says, Come on now, Malachy, stop the blaguarding. You have to go home to Angela. You have a funeral tomorrow and the lovely children waiting for you.

But Dad struggles till a few men push him out into the darkness. Uncle Pa stumbles out with the bag of food. Come on, he says. We'll go back to your room.

Dad wants to go to another place for a pint but Uncle Pa says he has no more money. Dad says he'll tell everyone his sorrows and they'll give him pints. Uncle Pa says that's a disgraceful thing to do and Dad cries on his shoulder. You're a good friend, he tells Uncle Pa. He cries again till Uncle Pa pats him on the back. It's terrible, terrible, says Uncle Pa, but you'll get over this in time.

Dad straightens up and looks at him. Never, he says. Never.

Next day we rode to the hospital in a carriage with a horse. They put Oliver in a white box that came with us in the carriage and we took him to the graveyard. They put the white box into a hole in the ground and covered it with earth. My mother and Aunt Aggie cried, Grandma looked angry, Dad, Uncle Pa Keating, and Uncle Pat Sheehan looked sad but did not cry and I thought that if you're a man you can cry only when you have the black stuff that is called the pint.

I did not like the jackdaws that perched on trees and gravestones and I did not want to leave Oliver with them. I threw a rock at a jackdaw that waddled over toward Oliver's grave. Dad said I shouldn't throw rocks at jackdaws, they might be somebody's soul. I didn't know what a soul was but I didn't ask him because I didn't care. Oliver was dead and I hated jackdaws. I'd be a man someday and I'd come back with a bag of rocks and I'd leave the graveyard littered with dead jackdaws.

Vladimir Nabokov

Invitation to a Transformation

There was a Chinese philosopher who all his life pondered the problem whether he was a Chinese philosopher dreaming that he was a butterfly or a butterfly dreaming that she was a philosopher. . .

Transformation. Transformation is a marvelous thing. I am thinking especially of the transformation of butterflies. Though wonderful to watch, transformation from larva to pupa or from pupa to butterfly is not a particularly pleasant process for the subject involved. There comes for every caterpillar a difficult moment when he begins to feel pervaded by an odd sense of discomfort. It is a tight feeling—here about the neck and elsewhere, and then an unbearable itch. Of course he has molted a few times before but *that* is nothing in comparison to the tickle and urge that he feels now. He must shed that tight dry skin, or die. As you have guessed, under that skin, the armor of a pupa—and how uncomfortable to wear one's skin over one's armor—is already forming: I am especially concerned at the moment with those butterflies that have carved golden pupa, called also chrysalis, which hang from some surface in the open air.

Well, the caterpillar must do something about that horrible feeling. He walks about looking for a suitable place. He finds it. He crawls up a wall or a tree trunk. He makes for himself a little pad of silk on the underside of that perch. He hangs himself by the tip of his tail or last legs, from the silk patch, so as to dangle head downwards in the position of an inverted question mark, and there is a *question*—how to get rid now of his skin. One wriggle, another wriggle—and zip the skin bursts down the back, and he gradually gets out of it working with shoulders and hips like a person getting out of a sausage dress. Then comes the most critical moment. You understand that we are hanging head down by our last pair of legs, and the problem now is to shed the whole skin—even the skin of those last legs by which we hang—but how to accomplish this without falling?

So what does he do, this courageous and stubborn little animal who is already partly disrobed? Very carefully he starts working out his hind legs, dislodging them from the patch of silk from which he is dangling, head down—and then with an admirable twist and jerk he sort of jumps *off* the silk pad, sheds his last shred of hose, and immediately, in the process of the same jerk-and-twist-jump he attaches himself anew by means of a hook that was under the shed skin on the tip of his body. Now all the skin has come off, thank God, and the bared surface, now hard and glistening, is the pupa, a swathed-baby-like thing hanging from that twig—a very beautiful chrysalis with golden knobs and plate-armor wing cases. This pupal stage lasts from a few days to a few years. I remember as a boy keeping a hawk moth's pupa in a box for something like seven years, so that I actually finished high school while the thing was asleep—and then finally it hatched—unfortunately, it happened during a journey on the train—a nice case of misjudgment after all those years. But to come back to our butterfly pupa.

After, say, two or three weeks something begins to happen. The pupa hangs quite motionless, but you notice one day that through the wing cases, which are many times smaller than the wings of the future perfect insect— you notice that through the hornlike texture of each wing case you can see in miniature the pattern of the future wing, the lovely flush of the ground color, a dark margin, a rudimentary eyespot. Another day or two—and the final transformation occurs. The pupa splits as the caterpillar had split—it is really a last glorified molt, and the butterfly creeps out—and in its turn hangs down from the twig to dry. She is not handsome at first. She is very damp and bedraggled. But those limp implements of hers that she has disengaged gradually dry, distend, the veins branch and harden—and in 20 minutes or so she is ready to fly. You have noticed that the caterpillar is a *he*, the pupa an *it*, and the butterfly a *she*. You will ask—what is the feeling of hatching? Oh, no doubt, there is a rush of panic to the head, a thrill of breathless and strange sensation, but then the eyes see, in a flow of sunshine, the butterfly sees the world, the large and awful face of the gasping entomologist.

Let us now turn to the transformation of Jekyll into Hyde.

FICTION

Ha Jin
In the Kindergarten

Shaona kept her eyes shut, trying to sleep. Outside, the noonday sun was blazing, and bumblebees were droning in the shade of an elm. Time and again one of them would bump into the window's wire screen with a thud and then a louder buzz. Soon Teacher Shen's voice in the next room grew clearer.

"Oh please!" the teacher blubbered on the phone. "I'll pay the money back in three months. You've already helped me so much, why can't you help me out?"

Those words made Shaona fully awake. She moved her head closer to the wall and strained her ears to listen. The teacher begged, "Have mercy on me, Doctor Niu. I've an old mother at home. My mother and I have to live…You know, I lost so much blood, because of the baby, that I have to eat some eggs to recuperate. I'm really broke now. Can you just give me another month?"

Shaona was puzzled, thinking how a baby could injure her teacher's health. Her grandmother used to say that babies were dug out from pumpkin fields in the countryside. Why did her teacher sound as though the baby had come off from her body? Why did she bleed for the baby?

Teacher Shen's voice turned desperate. "Please, don't tell anyone about the abortion! I'll try my best to pay you back…very soon. I'll see if I can borrow some money from a friend."

What's an abortion? Shaona asked herself. Is it something that holds a baby? What does it look like? Must be very expensive.

Her teacher slammed the phone down, then cried, "Heaven help me!"

Shaona couldn't sleep anymore. She missed her parents so much that she began sobbing again. This was her second week in the kindergarten, and she was not used to sleeping alone yet. Her small iron bed was uncomfortable, in every way different from the large soft bed at home, which could hold her entire family. She couldn't help wondering if her parents would love her the same as before, because three weeks ago her mother had given her a baby brother. These days her father was so happy that he often chanted opera snatches.

In the room seven other children were napping, one of them wheezing with a stuffy nose. Two large bronze moths, exhausted by the heat, were resting on the ceiling, their powdery wings flickering now and again. Shaona yawned sleepily but still couldn't go to sleep.

At two-thirty the bell rang, and all the nappers got out of their beds. Teacher Shen gathered the whole class of five- and six-year-olds in the corridor. Then in two lines they set out for the turnip field behind the kindergarten. It was still hot. A steamer went on blowing her horn in the north, and a pair of jet fighters were flying in the distant sky, drawing a long double curve. Shaona wondered how a pilot could stay inside those planes that looked as small as pigeons. In the air lingered a sweetish odor of dichlorvos, which had been sprayed around in the city to get rid of flies, fleas, mosquitoes. The children were excited, because seldom could they go beyond the stone wall topped with shards of dark brown glass. Today, instead of playing games within the yard as the children of the other classes were doing, Teacher Shen was going to teach them how to gather purslane. Few of them knew what a purslane looked like, but they were all eager to search for the herb.

On the way their teacher turned around to face them, flourishing her narrow hand and saying, "Boys and girls, you'll eat sautéed purslanes this evening. It tastes great, different from anything you've ever had. Tell me, do you all want to have purslanes for dinner or not?"

"Yes, we want," a few voices cried.

The teacher smacked her lips. Her sunburned nose crinkled, a faint smile playing on her face. As she continued walking, the ends of her two braids, tied with green woolen strings, were stroking the baggy seat of her pants. She was a young woman, tall and angular, with crescent eyebrows. She used to sing a lot; her voice was fruity and clear. But recently she was quiet, her face rather pallid. It was said that she had divorced her husband the previous summer because he had been sentenced to thirteen years in prison for embezzlement.

When they arrived at the field, Teacher Shen plucked a purslane from between two turnip seedlings. She said to the children standing in a horseshoe, "Look, its leaves are tiny, fleshy, and egg-shaped. It has reddish stems, different from regular veggies and grass. Sometimes it has small yellow flowers." She dropped the purslane into her duffel bag on the ground and went on, "Now, you each take charge of one row."

Following her orders, the children spread out along the edge of the field and then walked into the turnip seedlings.

Shaona lifted up the bottom of her checked skirt to form a hollow before her stomach and set out to search. Purslanes weren't difficult to find among the turnips, whose greens were not yet larger than a palm. Pretty soon every one of the children had gathered some purslanes.

"Don't stamp on the turnips!" Uncle Chang shouted at them from time to time. Sitting under an acacia, he was puffing away at a long pipe that had a brass bowl, his bald crown coated with beads of sweat. He was in charge of a few vegetable fields and the dilapidated pump house.

Shaona noticed Dabin, a rambunctious boy, sidling up to her, but she pretended she hadn't seen him. He nudged her and asked, "How many did you get?" He sniffed—two lines of dark mucus disappeared from his nostrils, then poked out again.

She lowered the hollow of her skirt, showing him about a dozen purslanes.

He said with one eye shut, "You're no good. Look at mine." He held out his peaked cap, which was full.

She felt a little hurt, but kept quiet. He turned away to talk to other children, telling them that purslane tasted awful. He claimed he had once eaten a bowl of purslane stew when he had had diarrhea. He would never have touched that stuff if his parents hadn't forced him. "It tastes like crap, more bitter than sweet potato vines," he assured them.

"Not true," said Weilan, a scrawny girl. "Teacher Shen told us it tastes great."

"How can you know?"

"I just know it."

"You know your granny's fart!"

"Big asshole," Weilan said, and made a face at him, sticking out her tongue.

"Say that again, bitch!" He went up to her, grabbed her shoulder, pushed her to the ground, and kicked her butt. She burst out crying.

Their teacher came over and asked who had started the fight. Shaona pointed at Dabin. To her surprise, the teacher walked up to the boy and seized him by the ear, saying through her teeth, "You can't live for a day without making trouble. Come now, I'm going to give you a trouble-free place to stay." She was dragging him away.

"Ouch!" he cried with a rattling noise in his throat. "You're pulling off my ear."

"You'll have the other one left."

Passing Uncle Chang, Teacher Shen stopped to ask him to keep an eye on the children for a short while. Then she pulled Dabin back to the kindergarten.

Shaona's mouth fell open. That boy would be "jailed" and he might get even with her after he was released. On the second floor of their building there was a room, an unused kitchen, in which three bedside cupboards sat on the cooking range. Sometimes a troublesome boy would be locked in one of them for hours. Once in a while his teacher might forget to let him out in time, so that he had to go without lunch or dinner.

About ten minutes later Teacher Shen returned, panting hard, as though she had just finished a sprint. She counted the children to make sure nobody was missing.

Shaona, immersed in looking for more purslanes, soon forgot Dabin. For most of the children this was real work. Few of them had ever tasted anything gathered by themselves, so they were searching diligently. Whenever their little skirts or caps were full, they went over to unload the purslanes into the duffel bag, from which their teacher was busy picking out grass and other kinds of herbs mixed into the purslanes. The children were amazed that in just one and a half hours the bag was filled up and that they had almost combed the entire field. Their teacher kept reminding them of the proverb they had learned lately—"Many hands provide great strength."

When they had searched the field, they were lined up hand in hand behind the pump house, ready to return to the kindergarten. But before leaving, for some reason their teacher gave several handfuls of purslanes to Uncle Chang. With grudging eyes they watched her drop almost a third of their harvest into the old man's wicker basket, but none of them made a peep. The old man went on smiling at the young woman, saying, "All right, enough, enough. Keep the rest for yourself." As he was speaking, spittle was emitted through his gapped teeth.

Shaona's mind was full, and she couldn't wait for dinner. She thought, If purslanes taste real good, I'll pick some for Mom and Dad. She knew a place in the kindergarten—inside the deserted pigsty—where she had seen a few purslanes.

To her dismay, dinner was similar to other days': corn glue, steamed sweet potatoes, and sautéed radishes. There wasn't even a purslane leaf on the table. Every one of her classmates looked upset. Not knowing what to say, some children were noisily stirring the corn glue with spoons. Shaona wanted to cry, but she controlled herself. She remembered seeing her teacher leave for home with the bulging duffel clasped on the carrier of her bicycle. At that moment Shaona had thought the green bag must contain laundry or something, because it was so full. Now she understood—their teacher took their harvest home.

Shaona liked sweet potato, but she didn't eat much. Anger and gas filled her stomach. Despite their sullen faces and disappointed hearts, none of the children mentioned purslanes. Everyone looked rather dejected except for Dabin. He had kept glaring at Shaona ever since he was let out of the cupboard for dinner. She knew he was going to take his revenge. What should she do?

In the dusk, when the children were playing in the yard, Shaona caught sight of Dabin. She called and beckoned to him. He came over and grunted, "What's up, little telltale?"

"Dabin, would you like to have these?" In her palm were two long peanuts. Her father had given her six of them when she was coming back to the kindergarten two days ago.

"Huh!" he exclaimed with pursed lips. "I never saw a peanut with four seeds in it." He snatched them from her hand and without another word cracked one. His eyes glittered and his mouth twitched like a rabbit's while he was chewing the roasted kernels.

Within a few seconds he finished the peanuts off. Then he asked, "Do you have more?"

"Uh-uh." She shook her head, her slant eyes fixed on the ground.

He touched her sweater pocket, which was empty. She had hidden the other four peanuts in her socks. He said, "You must be nice to me from now on. Remember to save lots of goodies for me, got it?"

She nodded without looking at him.

Standing below a slide, she watched him running away with his bowlegs to join the boys who were hurling paper bombers and imitating explosions. Behind the cypress hedge, near the closed front gate, a couple of children were playing hide-and-go-seek, their white clothes flickering and their ecstatic cries ringing in the twilight.

That night Shaona didn't sleep well. She was still scared of the dark room. One of her roommates, Aili, snored without stopping. An owl or a hawk went on hooting like an old man's coughing. A steam hammer in the shipyard on the riverbank pounded metal now and then. Unable to sleep, Shaona ate a peanut, though the rule didn't allow her to eat anything after she had brushed her teeth for bed. She took care to hide the shells under her pillow. How she missed her mother's warm, soft belly; again she cried quietly.

It rained the next morning, but the clouds began lifting after nine o'clock, so the children were allowed to go out and play. In the middle of the yard stood a miniature merry-go-round, sky blue and nine feet across. A ring of boys were sitting on it, revolving and yelling happily. Dabin and Shuwen, who was squint-eyed, were among them, firing wooden carbines at treetops, people, birds, smokestacks, and anything that came into sight. They were shouting out "rat-a-tat" as if the spinning platform were a tank turret. Shaona dared not go take a spin. The previous week she had ridden on that thing and had been spun giddy, sick for two days.

So instead she played court with a bunch of girls. They elected her the queen, saying she looked the most handsome among them. With four maids waiting on her, she had to sit on the wet ground all the time. Weilan and Aili were her amazons, each holding a whittled branch as a lance. The girls wished they could have made a strong boy the king, but only Dun was willing to stay with them. He was a mousy boy, and most of the girls could beat him easily. He should have been a courtier rather than the ruler. Soon Shaona couldn't stand remaining the queen anymore, because she felt silly calling him "Your Majesty" and hated obeying his orders. She begged other girls to replace her, but none of them would. She got up from the ground, shouting, "I quit!" To keep the court from disintegrating, Aili agreed to be vice-queen.

Because of the soggy ground, many of the children had their clothes soiled by lunchtime. Teacher Shen was angry, especially with those who had played mud pies. She said that if they were not careful about their clothes, she wouldn't let them go out in the afternoon. "None of you is a good child," she declared. "You all want to create more work for me."

After lunch, while the children were napping, Teacher Shen collected their clothes to scrub off the mudstains. She was unhappy because she couldn't take a nap.

Too exhausted to miss her parents, Shaona fell asleep the moment her head touched her pillow. She slept an hour and a half. When she woke up, she was pleased to find her sweater and skirt clean, without a speck of mud. But as her hand slotted into the sweater pocket she was surprised—the three peanuts were gone. She removed the toweling coverlet and rummaged through her bedding but couldn't find any trace of them; even the shells under her pillow had disappeared. Heartbroken, she couldn't stop her tears, knowing that her teacher must have confiscated the peanuts.

The sun came out in the afternoon, and the ground in the yard turned whitish. Again Teacher Shen led the twenty-four children out to the turnip field. On their way they sang the song "Red Flowers," which they had learned the week before:

> Red flowers are blooming everywhere.
> Clapping our hands, we sing
> And play a game in the square,
> All happy like blossoms of spring.

When they arrived at the field, Uncle Chang was not in view, but the water pump was snarling, tiny streams glinting here and there among the turnip rows.

The sight of the irrigation made their teacher hesitate for a moment. Then she said loudly to the children, "We're going to gather more purslanes this afternoon. Aunt Chef couldn't cook those we got yesterday because we turned them in too late, but she'll cook them for us today. So everybody must be a good child and work hard. Understood?"

"Understood," they said, almost in unison. Then they began to search among the turnips.

Although most of the children were as high-spirited as the day before, there weren't many purslanes left in the field, which was muddy and slippery. A number of them fell on their buttocks and had their clothes soiled. Their shoes were ringed with dark mud.

Yet the hollow of Shaona's skirt was soon filled with several puny purslanes, and some children had even dropped a load into the duffel, which began to swell little by little. Unlike the silly boys and girls who were still talking about what purslanes tasted like, Shaona was sulky the whole time, though she never stopped searching.

In front of her appeared a few tufts of wormwood, among which were some brownish rocks partly covered by dried grass. A swarm of small butterflies rested on the wormwood, flapping their white wings marked with black spots. Now and then one of them took off, flying sideways to land on a rock. Shaona went over to search through the grass; her motion set the butterflies in flight all at once, like a flurry of snowflakes. Suddenly a wild rabbit jumped out, racing away toward a group of girls, who all saw it and broke out hollering. The animal, frightened by their voices, swerved and bolted away toward the back wall of the kindergarten. At the sight of the fleeing creature, Teacher Shen yelled, "Catch him! Don't let him run away!"

All at once several boys started chasing the rabbit, which turned out to have a crippled hind leg. Now their teacher was running after it too, motioning to the children ahead to intercept the animal. Her long braids swayed from side to side as she was dashing away. Within seconds all the children except Shaona joined the chase. The turnip field was being ruined, with a lot of seedlings trampled and muddy water splashing from the running feet. Shrieks and laughter were rising from the west side of the field.

Shaona was not with them because she wanted to pee. Looking around, she saw nobody near, so she squatted down over the duffel, made sure to conceal her little behind with her skirt, and peed on the purslanes inside the bag. But she dared not empty her bladder altogether; she stopped halfway, got up, and covered the wet purslanes with the dry ones she had gathered. Then with a kicking heart she ran away to join the chasers.

The rabbit had fled out of sight, but the children were still excited, boys huffing and puffing and bragging about how close they had got to the animal. Dabin swore that his toes, caged in a pair of open-headed sandals, had touched that fluffy tail. Shuwen said that the wild rabbit tasted much better than the domestic rabbit; a few children were listening to him describe how his uncle had shot a pair of wild rabbits in the mountain and how his aunt had cut them to pieces and stewed them with potato and carrot cubes. Their teacher stopped him from finishing his story. Without delay she assembled the children and led them out of the field, fearful that Uncle Chang would call her names for the trampled turnips.

Before dinner Shaona was worried for fear the chef might cook the soiled purslanes for them. To her relief, dinner turned out to be similar. She was thrilled. For the first time in the kindergarten she ate a hearty meal— three sweet potatoes, two bowls of corn glue, and many spoonfuls of fried eggplant. The whole evening she was so excited that she joined the boys in playing soldier, carrying a toy pistol, as though all of a sudden she had become a big girl. She felt that from now on she would no longer cry like a baby at night.

Donald Barthelme

The School

Well, we had all these children out planting trees, see, because we figured that
. . . that was part of their education, to see how, you know, the root systems
. . . and also the sense of responsibility, taking care of things, being individually responsible. You know what I mean. And the trees all died. They were
orange trees. I don't know why they died, they just died. Something wrong
with the soil possibly or maybe the stuff we got from the nursery wasn't the
best. We complained about it. So we've got thirty kids there, each kid had his
or her own little tree to plant, and we've got these thirty dead trees. All these
kids looking at these little brown sticks, it was depressing.

It wouldn't have been so bad except that just a couple of weeks before
the thing with the trees, the snakes all died. But I think that the snakes—well,
the reason that the snakes kicked off was that. . . you remember, the boiler
was shut off for four days because of the strike, and that was explicable. It
was something you could explain to the kids because of the strike. I mean,
none of their parents would let them cross the picket line and they knew there
was a strike going on and what it meant. So when things got started up
again and we found the snakes they weren't too disturbed.

With the herb gardens it was probably a case of overwatering, and at
least now they know not to overwater. The children were very conscientious
with the herb gardens and some of them probably. . . you know, slipped them
a little extra water when we weren't looking. Or maybe. . . well, I don't like
to think about sabotage, although it did occur to us. I mean, it was something that crossed our minds. We were thinking that way probably because
before that the gerbils had died, and the white mice had died, and the salamander. . . well, now they know not to carry them around in plastic bags.

Of course we *expected* the tropical fish to die, that was no surprise.
Those numbers, you look at them crooked and they're belly-up on the surface.
But the lesson plan called for tropical-fish input at that point, there was noth-
ing we could do, it happens every year, you just have to hurry past it.

We weren't even supposed to have a puppy.

We weren't even supposed to have one, it was just a puppy the Mur-
doch girl found under a Gristede's truck one day and she was afraid the truck
would run over it when the driver had finished making his delivery, so she
stuck it in her knapsack and brought it to school with her. So we had this
puppy. As soon as I saw the puppy I thought, Oh Christ, I bet it will live for
about two weeks and then. . . And that's what it did. It wasn't supposed to
be in the classroom at all, there's some kind of regulation about it, but you

can't tell them they can't have a puppy when the puppy is already there, right in front of them, running around on the floor and yap yap yapping. They named it Edgar—that is, they named it after me. The had a lot of fun running after it and yelling, "Here, Edgar! Nice Edgar!" Then they'd laugh like hell. They enjoyed the ambiguity. I enjoyed it myself. I don't mind being kidded. They made a little house for it in the supply closet and all that. I don't know what it died of. Distemper, I guess. It probably hadn't had any shots. I got it out of there before the kids got to school. I checked the supply closet each morning, routinely, because I knew what was going to happen. I gave it to the custodian.

And then there was this Korean orphan that the class adopted through the Help the Children program, all the kids brought in a quarter a month, that was the idea. It was an unfortunate thing, the kid's name was Kim and maybe we adopted him too late or something. The cause of death was not stated in the letter we got, they suggested we adopt another child instead and sent us some interesting case histories, but we didn't have the heart. The class took it pretty hard, they began (I think, nobody ever said anything to me directly) to feel that maybe there was something wrong with the school. But I don't think there's anything wrong with the school, particularly, I've seen better and I've seen worse. It was just a run of bad luck. We had an extraordinary number of parents passing away, for instance. There were I think two heart attacks and two suicides, one drowning, and four killed together in a car accident. One stroke. And we had the usual heavy mortality rate among the grandparents, or maybe it was heavier this year, it seemed so. And finally the tragedy.

The tragedy occurred when Matthew Wein and Tony Mavrogordo were playing over where they're excavating for the new federal office building. There were all these big wooden beams stacked, you know, at the edge of the excavation. There's a court case coming out of that, the parents are claiming that the beams were poorly stacked. I don't know what's true and what's not. It's been a strange year.

I forgot to mention Billy Brandt's father, who was knifed fatally when he grappled with a masked intruder in his home.

One day, we had a discussion in class. They asked me, where did they go? The trees, the salamander, the tropical fish, Edgar, the poppas and mommas, Matthew and Tony, where did they go? And I said, I don't know, I don't know. And they said, who knows? and I said, nobody knows. And they said, is death that which gives meaning to life? And I said, no, life is that which gives meaning to life. Then they said, but isn't death, considered as a fundamental datum, the means by which the taken-for-granted mundanity of the everyday may be transcended in the direction of—

I said, yes, maybe.

They said, we don't like it.

I said, that's sound.

They said, it's a bloody shame!

I said, it is.

They said, will you make love now with Helen (our teaching assistant) so that we can see how it is done? We know you like Helen.

I do like Helen but I said that I would not.

We've heard so much about it, they said, but we've never seen it.

I said I would be fired and that it was never, or almost never, done as a demonstration. Helen looked out of the window.

They said, please, please make love with Helen, we require an assertion of value, we are frightened.

I said that they shouldn't be frightened (although I am often frightened) and that there was value everywhere. Helen came and embraced me. I kissed her a few times on the brow. We held each other. The children were excited. Then there was a knock on the door, I opened the door, and the new gerbil walked in. The children cheered wildly.

Try This

Pick a paragraph from *Angela's Ashes* and rewrite it in the third-person objective point of view. Pick another from "Invitation to a Transformation" and recast it in a tone of intimate confessional. Pick a third from "In the Kindergarten" and put it in the second person in the voice of the teacher speaking to Shaona. Take another from "The School" and turn it into a first-person poem from the viewpoint of a grieving pupil.

POEMS

Donald Justice

Order in the Streets

(From instructions printed on a child's toy, Christmas 1968, as reported in the New York Times.)

1. 2. 3.
Switch on.

Jeep rushes
to the scene
of riot

Jeep goes
in all directions
by mystery action.

Jeep stops periodically
to turn hood over

machine gun appears
with realistic
shooting noise.

After putting down riot,
jeep goes
back to the headquarters.

> **Try This**
> Justice's "Order in the Streets" is a "found poem," which is a good device for making
> yourself aware of the possibilities of language. Take any single source of words: the
> signs along a particular street, a menu, a food packet, a map, a clothing catalogue, a
> circular from a job or government office, and so forth. You will find a source that calls
> to you. Rearrange the words and phrases into a new meaning.

The three first-person poems that follow are written in the personae of the
poet, a hawk, and King Kong, respectively. What differences of diction distinguish these voices? How intimate or distanced is each? To whom is each poem
addressed? Can you copy any of these tricks for your own purposes?

Gary Soto
Black Hair

At eight I was brilliant with my body.
In July, that ring of heat
We all jump through, I sat in the bleachers
Of Romain Playground, in the lengthening
Shade that rose from our dirty feet.
The game before us was more than baseball.
It was a figure—Hector Moreno

Quick and hard with turned muscles,
His crouch the one I assumed before an altar
Of worn baseball cards, in my room.

I came here because I was Mexican, a stick
Of brown light in love with those
Who could do it—the triple and hard slide,
The gloves eating balls into double plays.
What could I do with 50 pounds, my shyness,
My black torch of hair, about to go out?
Father was dead, his face no longer
Hanging over the table or our sleep,
And mother was the terror of mouths
Twisting hurt by butter knives.

In the bleachers I was brilliant with my body,
Waving players in and stomping my feet,
Growing sweaty in the presence of white shirts.
I chewed sunflower seeds. I drank water
And bit my arm through the late innings.
When Hector lined balls into deep
Center, in my mind I rounded the bases
With him, my face flared, my hair lifting
Beautifully, because we were coming home
To the arms of brown people.

Ted Hughes
Hawk Roosting

I sit in the top of the wood, my eyes closed.
Inaction, no falsifying dream
Between my hooked head and hooked feet:
Or in sleep rehearse perfect kills and eat.

The convenience of the high trees!
The air's buoyancy and the sun's ray
Are of advantage to me;
And the earth's face upward for my inspection.

My feet are locked upon the rough bark.
It took the whole of Creation
To produce my foot, my each feather:
Now I hold Creation in my foot

Or fly up, and revolve it all slowly—
I kill where I please because it is all mine.
There is no sophistry in my body:
My manners are tearing off heads—

The allotment of death.
For the one path of my flight is direct
Through the bones of the living.
No arguments assert my right:

The sun is behind me.
Nothing has changed since I began.
My eye has permitted no change.
I am going to keep things like this.

William Trowbridge

Kong Looks Back On His Tryout With the Bears

If it had worked out, I'd be on a train to Green Bay,
not crawling up this building with the air corps
on my ass. And if it weren't for love, I'd drop
this shrieking little bimbo sixty stories
and let them take me back to the exhibit,
let them teach me to rumba and do imitations.
They tried me on the offensive line, told me
to take out the right cornerback for Nagurski.
Eager to please, I wadded up the whole secondary,
then stomped the line, then the bench and locker room,
then the east end of town, to the river.
But they were not pleased: they said
I had to learn my position, become a team player.
The great father Bear himself said that,

so I tried hard to know the right numbers
and how the arrows slanted toward the little o's.
But the o's and the wet grass and the grunts
drowned out the count, and the tight little cheers
drew my arrow straight into the stands,
and the wives tasted like flowers and raw fish.
So I was put on waivers right after camp,
and here I am, panty sniffer, about to die a clown,
who once opened a hole you could drive Nebraska through.

Try This

Write from the point of view of anything not human—an insect, an android, a potato, a belly button. Try to invent and develop a diction that represents the frame of reference of this thing. For instance, if you are writing from the point of view of a shoe, it is likely to have extensive knowledge of and opinions about flooring, but a limited concept of the sky or human heads.

Hilda Raz

Father

is never home but she loves him—
adores him, really, and so does Mom:
his big, burly body, his flannel shirts,
woolens over interesting scars
with stories to tell. Oh, he is a raconteur
with racks of bottles in the fragrant breakfront.

He tells her not to talk so much.
His talk holds the world intact;
when it stops, the key piece
drops out the bottom and the whole
plastic globe fragments. Nothing's
the same ever again.

The size of him! The size of them all,
uncles, cousins, the brothers:
wide shoulders jutting through cigar smoke
in the breakfast nook. The deep black marks
of their synthetic heels never quite scrub out.

Under the huge dining table,
under the carpet where his big feet wait,
is the bell. When he pushes it with his shoe
an aunt, or mother, or a maid
brings out another dish
from the steaming kitchen.

But he paid for it, paid for it all,
sweaters, teak tables with brass inlay,
steaks, furs, wicks for the memorial
candles, silk stockings, full tin box
the color of sky, plants
and their white rings on the mahogany,
and the cars, deep greens, metallic,
and the cashmere lap-robes,
and the aunts and out-of-work uncles.

He was best loved, best beloved in the family,
    whose very shadow, even absent,
absorbed all color, sucked short
the seasons, colored grey
even the lavish lilacs of that northern city

she never visits. She sends money
to an old woman who tends the graves,
sends money when the pencilled bills come in.

Try This

"Father" is written in the third person, as if from the point of view of an outsider, aimed at no one in particular but the convention of "the reader" or "the listener." Why did the poet make this decision? Try recasting a few lines into first person. What happens?

Lydia Davis
A Mown Lawn

She hated a *mown lawn*. Maybe that was because *mow* was the reverse of *wom*, the beginning of the name of what she was—a *woman*. A *mown lawn* had a sad sound to it, like a *long moan*. From her, a *mown lawn* made a *long moan*. *Lawn* had some of the letters of *man*, though the reverse of man would be *Nam*, a bad war. A *raw war*. *Lawn* also contained the letters of *law*. In fact, *lawn* was a contraction of *lawman*. Certainly a *lawman* could and did *mow a lawn*. *Law and order* could be seen as starting from *lawn order*, valued by so many Americans. *More lawn* could be made using a *lawn mower*. A *lawn mower* did make *more lawn*. *More lawn* was a contraction of *more lawmen*. Did *more lawn* in America make *more lawmen* in America? Did *more lawn* make *more Nam*? *More mown lawn* made *more long moan*, from her. Or a *lawn mourn*. So often, she said, Americans wanted *more mown lawn*. All of America might be one *long mown lawn*. A *lawn* not *mown* grows *long*, she said: better a *long lawn*. Better a *long lawn* and a *mole*. Let the *lawman* have the *mown lawn*, she said. Or the *moron*, the *lawn moron*.

Try This

Pick any three-syllable word and fool around with its syllables. Write it in the middle of a page and then fill the page at random with words that it reminds you of *not necessarily in meaning but in sound*. Example: *handkerchief: handy, hanky, hunky, hankering, hungering, kerchief, curtain, kerchoo, choo-choo, chieftain, chief, chef, handle, haggle, handoff, handout, hanging, chipper, cheaper. . .*

Pick any three words from your list and combine them in a poem or a scene of fiction.

Barbara Hamby
The Language of Bees

The language of bees contains 76 distinct words for stinging,
    distinguishes between a prick, puncture, and mortal wound,
    elaborates on cause and effect as in a sting made to retaliate,
    irritate, insinuate, infuriate, incite, rebuke, annoy,
    nudge, anger, poison, harangue.
The language of the bees has 39 words for queen—regina apiana,
    empress of the hive, czarina of nectar, maharani of the ovum,
    sultana of stupor, *principessa* of dark desire.
The language of bees contains 22 words for sunshine,
Two for rain—big water and small water, so that a man urinating
    on an azalea bush in the full fuchsia of April
    has the linguistic effect of a light shower in September.
For man, two words—roughly translated—"hands" and "feet,"
    the first with the imperialistic connotation of beekeeper,
    the second with the delicious resonance of bareness.
All colors are variations on yellow, from the exquisite

sixteen-syllable word meaning "diaphanous golden fall,"
to the dirty ochre of the bitter pollen
stored in the honeycomb and used by bees for food.

The language of bees is the language of war. For what is peace
without strife but the boredom of enervating day-after-day,
obese with sweetness, truculent with ennui?
Attack is delightful to bees, who have hundreds of verbs
embracing strategy, aim, location, velocity:
swift, downward swoop to stun an antagonist,
brazen, kamikaze strike for no gain but momentum.
Yet stealth is essential to bees, for they live to consternate
their enemies, flying up pantslegs, hovering in grass.
No insect is more secretive than the bee, for they have two
thousand words describing the penetralia of the hive
—octagonal golden chamber of unbearable moistness,
opaque tabernacle of nectar,
sugarplum of polygonal waxy walls.

The language of bees is the language of aeronautics,
for they have wings—transparent, insubstantial,
black-veined like the fall of an exotic iris.
For they are tiny dirigibles, aviators of orchard and field.
For they have ambition, cunning, and are able to take direct aim.
For they know how to leave the ground, to drift, hover, swarm,
sail over the tops of trees.
The language of bees is a musical dialect, a full, humming
congregation of hallelujahs and amens,
at night blue and disconsolate,
in the morning bright and bedewed.
The language of bees contains lavish adjectives
praising the lilting fertility of their queen
—fat, red-bottomed progenitor of millions,
luscious organizer of coitus,
gelatinous distributor of love.
The language of bees is in the jumble of leaves before rain,
in the quiet night rustle of small animals,
for it is eloquent and vulgar in the same mouth,
and though its wound is sweet it can be distressing,
as if words could not hurt or be meant to sting.

Try This
Invent a language for something nonhuman. Describe it in poetry or prose.

DRAMA

Jane Martin

Talking With. . .

HANDLER

A young woman in a simple, country-print dress. On the floor before her is a handmade wooden box about two feet long and eighteen inches high with a sliding wire screen top.

CARO: My Dada* was gonna do this tonight but the Lord froze his face so he sent me. I learned this from my Dada and he learned it up from great Gran, who took it on from the Reverend Soloman Bracewood, who had him a mule ministry 'round these parts way back when. Dada taught Miss Ellie, my ma, and my brother Jamie. . . he was in it too, 'fore he went for Detroit.

See, what I got in here is snakes. Lotta people don't like snakes. Gives it its nature, I guess. This here is water mocs. Jamie, he said they got the dirtiest, nastiest bite of all. . . well, rattlers is yer biggest. Lotta venom. You milk you a rattler, you can half fill up a juice glass. Dada said Jamie should do rattlers, but he never. Did 'heads, copperheads. Now they're slower and safer but it ain't such a good show. You know those dang snakes smell like cucumbers? Well, they do. Miss Ellie, she favored mocassins. Dada too. . . well, Dada he did all kinds, all ways. Your mocassin now, he's your good ol' boy snake. Flat out mean an' lots of get up n' go. Heck, they'll chase ya. They will. Ol' Dada he didn't like Miss Ellie doin' 'em. 'You lay off them mocs 'fore they lay you down.' Made Miss Ellie laugh. Lotta handlers think mocassins are slimy. Couldn't get me to touch one. They'll do rattlers. . . got him a nice dry feel. Little bit sandpapery. Rattler can find ya in the pitch dark though. They git on to yer body heat. Snake handlin'. *All* my blood does it. Only Dada an' me now though. Snake handlin', with the Holiness Church. Down where I come from we take God pretty serious. If you got the spirit, snake don't bite. If he bites you, you know you ain't got the spirit. Makes the difference real clear, don't it?

It's right there in the scripture. . . Mark, Chapter 16, verses 17 and 18, 'And these signs shall follow them that believe. In my name they shall cast out devils; they shall speak in new tongues; they shall take up serpents; and if they shall drink any deadly thing, it shall not hurt them; they shall lay hands on the sick and they shall recover.' Don't figure it could be much clearer than that. There's some churches don't use snakes, use strychnine, powdered poison, same idea though. They mix it with Cherry kool-ade, sing 'em a hymn, drink it off, and then just stand around waitin' to see if they fall over. Ain't much of a show. Not like snakes. Dada does fire but I can't do it. Pours some kerosene in a coke

---

* Pronounced "Dád-aw".

bottle, sticks a rag in the top and lights it up. Holds that fire under his chin, passes it down the arm, puts his hand in it, you know, that kind of stuff. He says there's people do blow torches down to Tennessee. I don't know. Jamie give it a try 'fore he went to Detroit. Just about burned his ass off. Sorry.

When I handle, I keep 'em in this box. Dada gimme this and some Heidi doll on my ninth birthday. Sometimes I'll just open up the lid and put my foot in or, uh, maybe stick it open side to my chest. There's some lay it to their face. I don't. Scares my eyes. Durin' service we take 'em right out, pass 'em around. It's more dangerous than a single handler. Snake gets to comparin' who got the spirit a whole lot an' who jes got it some. Somebody's jes about bound to come in second. Don't get me wrong now. Y' don't die everytime yer bit. I been bit seven times. Four times by the same serpent. Dada says he got the sweet tooth for me. Dada been bit thirty-two times an' never saw him a doctor. Used to let me kiss him on the marks. Last one got him here. (*Points to eye.*) Froze him right up. Dada says he'll thaw but I don't know.

Day after Jamie took off Miss Ellie did mocassins standin' in the back of the pickup over to Hard Burley. Shouldn't ought to 'cause her mind weren't there. Coal truck backfired and she got bit. Snake bit her three more times 'fore she hit the ground. Dada layed hands on her but she died anyway. There was ten of us handled right there at the funeral. Snake handlin'.

Snake knows what you feel. You can fool a person but you can't fool a snake. You got the spirit, God locks their jaws. Keeps you safe. Tell you what though. . . I don't believe in a God. Left me. Gone with Miss Ellie. I was handlin' when I knew it sure. Snake was jes comin' on down the line. Marita she yells out, 'The Lord. Lord's in me and with me. In me and with me.' Noah he was ululatin', talkin' in tongues. Couple of folks was rollin' and singing. Dada was doin' switch grips. Had Miss Ellie's weddin' ring on his little finger. And it came on me, heck, there ain't no God in here. There's just a bunch of shouters gettin' tranced. There ain't no God in here at all. 'Bout that time they layed that serpent to me. Felt fussy. Nasty. Just lookin' for an excuse y'know? An' I was an empty vessel, worse nor a pharasee, grist for the mill. My blood went so cold I coulda crapped ice-cubes. Snake knew. Started to get leverage. So I said, 'Snake. You Satan' hand-maiden. You're right, there ain't no God in me. I'm just a woman, but I'm the only woman in my Dada's house and he needs me home. Outta his faith and his need, you lock yer jaws.' I let that snake feel a child's pure love and it sponged it up offa my hands and then ol' wiggley went limp. I tranced it. It was a real good service. Didn't nobody handlin' get bit. (*Takes the snake out of the box.*) Yes, you got to believe. Holiness Church is dead right about that. Makes me wonder, you know? I git to lookin' at people and wonderin' if they got anything in 'em could lock a serpent's jaws. Any power or spirit or love or whatever. I look at 'em and I wonder, could they handle? Tell you what though, you can see it in a face. You can read it. You look me full in the face it don't take me 30 seconds. It's like I was the snake, some ol' pit viper, an' I can read yer heart. Maybe you could handle and maybe you can't, but there's but one sure thing in this world. . . yer empty, yer gonna get bit.

FADE OUT

FRENCH FRIES

An old woman in a straight-back chair holding a McDonald's cup. She is sur-
rounded by several bundles of newspapers. She wears thick glasses that distort
her eyes to the viewer.

ANNA MAE: If I had one wish in my life, why I'd like to live in McDonald's.
Right there in the restaurant. 'Stead of in this old place. I'll come up to the brow
of the hill, bowed down with my troubles, hurtin' under my load and I'll see
that yellow horseshoe, sort of like part of a rainbow, and it gives my old spirit
a lift. Lord, I can sit in a McDonald's all day. I've done it too. Walked the seven
miles with the sun just on its way, and then sat on the curb till five minutes of
seven. First one there and the last one to leave. Just like some ol' french fry they
forgot.

I like the young people workin' there. Like a team of fine young horses when
I was growin' up. All smilin'. Tell you what I really like though is the plastic. God
gave us plastic so there wouldn't be no stains on his world. See, in the human
world of the earth it all gets scratched, stained, tore up, faded down. Loses its
shine. All of it does. In time. Well, God he gave us the idea of plastic so we'd know
what the everlasting really was. See if there's plastic then there's surely eternity. It's God's hint.

You ever watch folks when they come on in the McDonald's? They always
speed up, almost run the last few steps. You see if they don't. Old Dobbin with
the barn in sight. They know it's safe in there and it ain't safe outside. Now it
ain't safe outside and you know it.

I've see a man healed by a Big Mac. I have. I was just sittin' there. Last
summer it was. Oh, they don't never move you on. It's a sacred law in McDonald's, you can sit for a hundred years. Only place in this world. Anyway, a fella,
maybe thirty-five, maybe forty, come on in there dressed real nice, real bright tie,
bran' new baseball cap, nice white socks and he had him that disease. You know
the one I mean, Cerebral Walrus they call it. Anyway, he had him a cock leg.
His poor old body had it two speeds at the same time. Now he got him some
coffee, with a lid on, and sat him down and Jimmy the tow-head cook knew him,
see, and he brought over a Big Mac. Well, the sick fella ate maybe half of it and
then he was just sittin', you know, suffering those tremors, when a couple of *ants*
come right out of the burger. Now there ain't no ants in McDonald's no way. Lord
sent those ants, and the sick fella he looked real sharp at the burger and a bunch
more ants marched on out nice as you please and his head lolled right over and
he pitched himself out of that chair and banged his head on the floor, loud.
Thwack! Like a bowling ball dropping. Made you half sick to hear it. We jump
up and run over but he was cold out. Well those servin' kids, so cute, they watered
him, stuck a touch pepper up his nostril, slapped him right smart, and bang,
up he got. Standin' an' blinkin'. 'Well, how are you?,' we say. An he looks us over,
looks right in our eyes, and he say, 'I'm fine.' And he was. He was fine! Tipped
his Cincinnati Reds baseball cap, big 'jus'-swallowed-the-canary' grin, paraded
out of there clean, straight like a pole-bean poplar, walked him a plumb line without no trace of the 'walrus.' Got outside, jumped up, whooped, hollered, sang

him the National Anthem, flagged down a Circle Line bus, an' rode off up Muhammad Ali Boulevard wavin' an' smilin' like the King of the Pharoahs. Healed by a Big Mac. I saw it.

McDonald's. You ever seen anybody die in a McDonald's? No sir. No way. Nobody ever has died in one. Shoot, they die in Burger Kings all the time. Kentucky Fried Chicken's got their own damn ambulances. Noooooooooo, you can't die in a McDonald's no matter how hard you try. It's the spices. Seals you safe in this life like it seals in the flavor. Yesssssss, yes!

I asked Jarrell could I live there. See they close up around ten, and there ain't a thing goin' on in 'em till seven a.m. I'd just sit in those nice swingy chairs and lean forward. Rest my head on those cool, cool, smooth tables, sing me a hymn and sleep like a baby. Jarrell, he said he'd write him a letter up the chain of command and see would they let me. Oh, I got my bid in. Peaceful and clean.

Sometimes I see it like the last of a movie. You know how they start the picture up real close and then back it off steady and far? Well, that's how I dream it. I'm living in McDonald's and it's real late at night and you see me up close, smiling, and then you see the whole McDonald's from the outside, lit up and friendly. And I get smaller and smaller, like they do, and then it's just a light in the darkness, like a star, and I'm in it. I'm part of that light, part of the whole sky, and it's all McDonald's, but part of something even bigger, something fixed and shiny. . . like plastic.

I know. I know. It's just a dream. Just a beacon in the storm. But you got to have a dream. It's our dreams make us what we are.

BLACKOUT

Try This

Unlike the mimes that follow chapter one, the props in Jane Martin's monologues are subordinated to the voices of the characters. Write a short monologue in which a character reveals him- or herself through speech, and also through relation to an object onstage.

Warm-up

What does this woman want? Write about what she misses, covets, regrets, dreams of, longs for, deeply desires. What does she want for her daughter? How much of this will she be willing to tell the daughter? What will she admit to no one? Will the daughter share her desires?

CHAPTER THREE

CHARACTER

As Desire
As Image, Voice, Action, Thought
As Presented by the Author
As Conflict

I write because I want to have more than one life.

Anne Tyler

Character as Desire

A character is somebody who wants, and that's what a character is.

The importance of desire in creating character can scarcely be overstated. Whether persona or entirely fictional, a person-on-the-page who engages the attention and emotions of your reader will be a person who reveals desire—novelist Robert Olen Butler calls it *yearning*, to indicate its poignant and obsessive nature. Nor is such desire a small thing. Aristotle declared that the nature of a man's desire determined the nature of his morality: he who wants good is good; he who wants evil is evil. (And it follows pretty well that he who wants the trivial is trivial, she who wants peace is peaceful, and so forth.)

I think the importance of desire is the first principle to grasp in the creation of character, because those of us who write are often excellent observers, and we can fall into the trap of creating fictional people who passively observe. Such passive characters lie flat on the page. The characters who stand up and make us care are so in love that they are willing to risk their reputations and their souls (Anna Karenina, for example); or so committed to a cause that they will devote their lives to it (Robin Hood, among many); driven by a passion to know (like Faust); or to revenge (as in *Hamlet*); to solve the mystery, climb the mountain, uncover the past, find out who they really are. Of course, the desire need not be as grand as these examples, and in modern literature the questing, conflicted nature of the desire is often and profoundly the point. But it is nevertheless so, that this quality of yearning or determination is what makes us catch our breath, hope for the best, fear the worst, and in short identify with what is, after all, a series of little squiggly lines on a page. "We know rationally," says William Logan, "that Prospero and Miranda never existed, much less Ariel or Caliban; that the real Caesar was not Shakespeare's Caesar; but we can be moved to tears by Ophelia's death, or Cordelia's. The bundles of words behave as if they had private psychologies."

You will have the makings of a character when you can fill out this sentence: _____(name)_____ is a _____(adj.)_____ _____-year-old _____(noun)_____ who wants _____.

It isn't so important to trace the motive back to some childhood experience or trauma as it is to explore the nature and reality of the character's desire. What is her deepest need, longing, hope; apart from food and air? What can't he live without?

In thinking about your character's desire, it's a good idea to think both generally and specifically, or about the deep desire and the immediate desire. In filling in the sentence above, you might think: *Jeremy Glazer is a belligerent 17-year-old basketball player who wants respect.* "Respect" in this case, an abstraction, represents what Jeremy deeply desires. As a writer you need to ask what, in the particular situation he finds himself in, would represent respect for Jeremy? Being placed on the starting team? Being included in the locker room banter? Or is it his father's acknowledgement that basketball matters as much as his grades? What a character wants, deeply (and which can be expressed in an abstraction), will always have a particular manifestation in a particular situation and can be expressed in a way that leads to image and action.

Try This

Choose a character you have thought and written about before. Fill out the sentence above. Then quickly jot down what makes your character:

- laugh
- afraid
- angry
- awed
- tender
- ashamed
- obsessed
- other . . . ?

Imagine your character in a situation that produces one of these emotions. What does he or she *want* in that situation? What is the deep, abstract desire? What, in this

continued

specific situation, does he or she want that would at least for the moment fulfill that desire?

Once you've decided on a character, there are essentially five methods of presenting him or her to the reader:

Directly, through:

1. image (or "appearance")

2. voice (or "speech")

3. action

4. thought

Or **indirectly**, through:

5. "telling" or interpreting as an author

> The first thing is to see the people every minute . . . You have got to learn to paint with words.
>
> *Flannery O'Connor*

Character as Image

Everything we know about other people we know through our five senses. The outer expresses the inner. Words, actions, and things, which can be seen and heard, express and reveal character and feeling that can be neither seen nor heard.

Nadia sits across from me at dinner; she is petite, dark-haired. She gestures delicately with her fork. She makes a political point to the famous, bald man beside me, who is sweating and drinking his fourth glass of wine. Nadia's voice is light, her phrases follow each other steadily. The famous man takes another piece of pie. He wipes his forehead with a knuckle, wipes the knuckle on his napkin, flaps the napkin toward Nadia as he replies to her question with a little explosion of sound. I miss some of what he says because his mouth is full of pie. I think: *she's smarter than he is, but he doesn't realize it because he's so impressed with his own fame; actually, underneath, he is terrified of being found out, and he's going to eat and drink himself to death trying to fill the void of his own ego.*

I hardly know these people! How did I come to such conclusions?!

Literature allows us a freedom that life does not, to be both inside and outside a character, to know thoughts as we can only know them in ourselves, and to see the externals as we can for everyone *except* ourselves. Sometimes a beginning writer skips the externals in order to try to take us directly to the abstract essence of a character. But if you let your reader get to know your characters through the sense details, as in life, these images will convey the essence in the way discussed in Chapter 1, through concrete significant detail: how does this character laugh, what is he wearing, how does she move, what gesture does he make, what objects does he carry, what does she eat and drink, what is the tone of her voice, his laugh, the texture of his skin, the smell of her hair?

> Swollen feet
> tripping on vines in the heat,
> palms thick and green-knuckled,
> sweat drying on top of old sweat.
> She flicks her tongue over upper lip
> where the salt stings her cracked mouth.
>
> *"sus plumas el viento," Gloria Anzaldua*

The first half dozen lines of this sharply realized miniature portrait convey much more than the images themselves. We already know the basic elements of this woman's life, her gender and status, her suffering. We know how poverty feels and tastes, the toll on the body of long overwork.

Traditionally, the characters in a play may be minimally described (*Lisa, in her teens, scruffy; Ludovico, blind, a former spy*), for the very good reason that the people in the audience will have the live actor in front of them to offer a sense impression, heightened by costume, makeup, and lighting. But playwrights can and often do vividly signal in their stage directions the physical attributes, gestures, and clothes of their characters; and actors can and often do gratefully make use of this information to explore the character's inner life.

> Leaning on the solitary table, his head cupped in one hand as he pages through one of his comic books, is Sam. A black man in his mid-forties. He wears the white coat of a waiter.
>
> *"Master Harold" . . . and the Boys, Athol Fugard*

Or:

> . . . Lou, the magician, enters. He is dressed in the traditional costume of Mr. Interlocutor: tuxedo, bow tie, top hat festooned with all kinds of whatnots that are obviously meant for good luck, he does a few catchy "soft shoe" steps & begins singing a traditional version of a black play song.
>
> *spell # 7, Ntozake Shange*

Try This

If people are characterized by the objects they choose, own, wear, and carry with them, they are also revealed in what they throw away. *Garbology* is the study of society or

continued

culture by examining and analyzing its refuse. Write a character sketch by describing the contents of your character's waste basket.

Character as Voice

In order to move beyond remembering or inventing a character to the mental state where you are living inside that character, you need to hear his/her voice in your head, and it's always good practice to write a monologue in that voice. Sometimes using the clustering technique described on page xxv, thinking *from the point of view of that character*, will help you to find the voice. It's always useful to keep going even if you feel you haven't "caught" the diction, because sometimes the very fact of continuing will allow you to slip or sidle into the voice you seek.

Try This
Write a quick sketch of a character you have already worked with, no more than two or three focused details. Then pick one of the trigger lines below and write a monologue in that character's voice. Keep going a little bit past the place you want to stop.
- It doesn't take much, does it, for
- And what I said was true
- I know right away I'm going to
- I've become a different person since
- I don't like anyone to watch me
- You call that music?

Now look over the monologue and highlight a few phrases that seem to you to catch that character's voice. Pick one of these and use it to begin another short monologue.

One of the ways we understand what is going on among people is by assessing, partly instinctively and partly by learning through experience, what is expressed voluntarily and what is involuntary. When someone chooses to wear baggy jeans as opposed to slim-fits, or a shaved head, a tuxedo, body piercing, a string of pearls—these are choices, largely conscious, that signal: *I am a member of this group*. Other "body language" will strike the viewer as involuntary (dishevelment, poor taste, blushing, slurring, staring, sweating, clumsiness) and so as a betrayal of feelings that have not been chosen. On the whole, it is human nature to give the involuntary more credibility than the chosen. We say that *what he said was very generous, but he kept checking to see how it was going over*. His glances *belied* his words. In this case, we say that the words represent the *text*, and that what we read by other means is the *subtext*.

Speech belongs largely in the voluntary category, though like appearance it can (and does) betray us. Talking is an intentional attempt to express the inner as the outer. But when people talk in literature they convey much more than the information in their speech. They are also working for the author—to reveal themselves, advance the plot, fill in the past, control the pace, establish the tone, foreshadow the future, establish the mood. What busy talk!

NELL: So just fill me in a bit more could you about what you've been doing.

SHONA: What I've been doing. It's all down there.

NELL: The bare facts are down here but I've got to present you to an employer.

SHONA: I'm twenty-nine years old.

NELL: So it says here.

SHONA: We look young. Youngness runs in our family.

NELL: So just describe your present job for me.

SHONA: My present job at present. I have a car. I have a Porsche. I go up the M1 a lot. Burn up the M1 a lot. Straight up the M1 in the fast lane to where the clients are, Staffordshire, Yorkshire, I do a lot in Yorkshire. I'm selling electric things. Like dishwashers, washing machines, stainless steel tubs are a feature and the reliability of the program . . .

"Top Girls," Caryl Churchill

Notice how the characters produce tension by contradicting each other (*Fill me in; it's all down there; but I've got to present you; I'm twenty-nine; so it says*). This is known as "no dialogue," in which characters are in many and various ways saying "no" to each other. They may be angry or polite, disagreeing, contradicting, qualifying, or frankly quarreling, but whatever the tone, they spark our interest because we want to find out what will happen in this overt or implied conflict.

Notice also how Shona's description of her job reveals the subtext. She falters between concrete imagery and flimsy generalization, contradicting in generalization what she tries to prove by making up convincing details. She is spinning lies without sufficient information or imagination, so it's no great surprise when Nell ends the exchange with, "Christ, what a waste of time . . . Not a word of this is true, is it?"

Dramatic dialogue is always **direct** as in this example, all the words spoken. In fiction, essays, or poems, direct dialogue of this sort is lively and vivid, but sometimes the narrative needs to cover ground faster, and then dialogue may be **indirect** or **summarized**. Summarized dialogue, efficient but textureless, gives us a brief report:

Shona claimed she had sales experience, but Nell questioned both her age and her expertise.

Indirect dialogue gives the flavor of the dialogue without quoting directly:

Nell wanted her to fill in the facts, so Shona repeated that she was twenty-nine, claimed that looking young ran in the family, and that she drove a Porsche up to Staffordshire to sell dishwashers and washing machines. But she couldn't seem to come up with the word "appliances."

There's a strong temptation to make dialogue eloquent (you are a writer, after all), and the result is usually that it becomes stilted. People are often *not* eloquent, precisely about what moves them most. Half the time we aren't really sure what we mean, and if we are, we don't want to say it, and if we do, we can't find the words, and if we do, the others aren't listening, and if they are, they don't understand . . . In fact, the various failures to communicate can make the richest sort of dialogue, just as the most stunted language is sometimes the most revealing of character.

In this example from Mark Winegardner's *Crooked River Burning*, David, who has just begun dating a rich society girl, is fishing with his Uncle Stan.

David had no idea exactly where Uncle Stan came down on yesterday. Finally, he just broke down and asked. "Uncle Stan? What . . . ?"

But he could not find the words. His uncle just watched him stammer.

"The thing I was wondering, is . . . " Couldn't do it.

"This isn't my strong suit," said Stan. "As you know." He licked his lips. "Cigar?"

"Um, OK," David said. This was a new one.

Stan killed the engine. They lit up. "Fella at work," he said. "Twins."

"Great." They drifted.

"I know you don't feel like this," said Stan.

"Like what?"

"Like what I'm about to say," said his uncle. "Don't take this wrong. But you have no idea how young you are . . . "

Debate and argument can make interesting dialogue if the matter itself is interesting, but in imaginative writing debate and argument are usually too static to be of interest, too simple and too single. Eudora Welty explained in an interview with the *Paris Review*, "Sometimes I needed to make a speech do four or five things at once—reveal what the character said but also what he thought he said, what he hid, what others were going to think he meant, and what they misunderstood—and so forth—all in this single speech...I used to laugh out loud sometimes when I wrote it."

If a character expresses in dialogue what he/she means, that character has done only one thing, whereas as a writer you are constantly trying to mean more than you say, to give several clues at once to the inner lives of your characters. If Jeannine says:

I feel that civilization is encroaching on nature, and that the greed of the developers will diminish the value of all our lives—

—she has expressed an opinion, but little of her inner life is revealed, her emotions, her history, her particularities. This is the dialogue equivalent of the vague category images described in Chapter 1. But if she says:

They should lock up that builder. He's massacred the neighborhood. I remember how the lilac and wisteria used to bloom, and then the peonies, and the daffodils. What fragrance in this room! But now. Smell the stink of that site next door. It just makes me sick.

—the same opinion is expressed, but her emotions—anger, nostalgia, and defeat—also are vividly revealed—and through particular detail.

Try This

Write a "dialogue" between two characters, only one of whom can speak. The other is physically, emotionally, or otherwise prevented from saying what he/she wants to say. Write only the words of the one, only the appearance and actions of the other.

By our actions we discover what we really believe and, simultaneously, reveal ourselves to others.

John Gardner

Character as Action

One reason that debate and argument seem static is that characters holding forth with well-thought-out positions seem unlikely to change. A character is somebody who wants; a *dynamic* character is somebody who is capable of change. The dialogue that is dramatic, that moves us, is the dialogue that displays this potential for change.

Human beings achieve or suffer change though the agents of *discovery* and *decision*. Playwright Sam Smiley observes that "Any significant discovery forces change in conditions, relationships, activity or all three." And, he says, "The quickest and best way to know someone is to see that person make a significant decision...At the instant a character makes a choice, he changes from one state to another; his significant relationships alter; and usually he must follow a new line of action as a consequence."

In dramatic dialogue, in ways large and small, characters are constantly making discoveries and decisions. Look again at the exchange above between Nell and Shona. What does Nell discover about Shona? What does Shona decide to say to prove herself? Look at the exchange between David and his Uncle Stan.

What change occurs between them when Stan decides to offer his nephew a cigar? How is the relationship further changed, when he decides (with difficulty: "Don't take this wrong.") to speak his mind?

Such change may seem most obvious in literature with a strong story line, such as fiction or drama, but in even the gentlest piece of memoir or the slightest nature lyric, the persona is made aware of something that seems important, something that has not before been present to the mind, and now is, and so changes the entire mental landscape. Frequently (by no means always; still, frequently) in the tradition of memoir this mental change has to do with a new perspective of the complexity of life and human beings; frequently in lyric poetry it has to do with the ephemeral quality of beauty, and therefore an awareness of death.

Since discovery and decision are the two agents of human change, characters will be *in action* when these are possible. Action as in *action-packed* is a crude but effective way of getting discovery and decision into a work (*There's the bad guy!* [discovery] *Quick, I will load my revolver, hide behind this pillar, turn and shoot.* [decision] *But wait! There's his accomplice on the catwalk above me!* [discovery] *I will roll under this forklift to avoid his bullet!* [decision]).

The change from alive-to-dead is a major one, as is the change from in-danger-to-triumphant-hero. But discovery and decision are no less present in the subtle and profound exchanges of ordinary life.

Loveliest of trees, the cherry now
Is hung with snow along the bough
And stands about the woodland ride
Wearing white for Easter tide.

Now of my threescore years and ten
Twenty will not come again,
And take from seventy springs a score,
That only leaves me fifty more.

And since, to look at things in bloom,
Fifty years is little room,
About the woodland I will go
To see the cherry hung with snow.

"II" from A Shropshire Lad, A.E. Housman

In this very low-key poem (you can hear the stillness, the deliberate pace, in the rhythm), the poet makes two discoveries and a decision. The first discovery is of the snow on the trees; the second is of the brevity of life. The decision is simply to walk in the woods, but in following this "new line of action" he also "changes from one state to another," and acknowledges his mortality.

> **Try This**
> Take a monologue you have already written and add actions, in the form of either narration or stage directions. Make the action contradict or qualify the speech. ("I'm not worried about it at all. These things don't throw me." [*She twists her hands.*]) and so forth. Remember that a good way to reveal characters' feelings is through their relationships to objects.

Character as Thought

Although decision and discovery necessarily imply thought; image, speech, and action are all external manifestations, things that we could observe. Imaginative writing has the power also to take us inside the minds of characters to show us directly what they are thinking. Again, the various forms of literature suggest a certain hierarchy of possibility here. In a memoir or personal essay we can't credibly see into the minds of other characters. (Though even this quasi-rule is sometimes broken; Tom Wolfe in his techniques of "new journalism" frequently turns what his interviewees say into a kind of mental patter or stream-of consciousness, as if these quotations were in fact their thoughts.) A character in a drama is necessarily speaking and therefore making his thoughts external, but there are a number of theatrical traditions to let us know that we are overhearing his/her thoughts—as in soliloquy, aside, voice-over. Many characters in modern drama speak directly to the audience, and usually do so with an assumed honesty toward what is going on in their minds, whereas in dialogue with other characters they may lie, conceal, stumble, or become confused. A persona in poetry is usually sharing thoughts. Poetry also has the same freedom as fiction, to be presented from the point of view of a character—and this character may reveal what's on her mind. Fiction usually gives us the thoughts of at least the central character.

Aristotle suggested a useful way of looking at thought in relation to desire. A persona or character begins with a certain desire, and therefore a certain specific goal in mind. Thought is the process by which she works backward to decide what to do in the immediate situation that presents itself. "Loveliest of Trees" is a condensed poetic demonstration of this process. *The chances are I will die at about seventy. I'm twenty now. That means I have fifty years left. That's not many years to look at these trees. I will look at them now.* My apologies to Housman for this rude paraphrase—but it does show, not only Aristotle's understanding of the thought process, but also how crucial to the beauty of the poem is Housman's diction.

Thought, like dialogue, is also action when it presents us with the process of change. Since both discovery and decision take place in the mind, thought is material to every character and is in fact the locus of action and the dwelling place of desire. In the first lines of any poem, the first page of every story, the curtain rise of every drama, is a human consciousness with a yearning for whatever might occur in the last line, on the last page, in the last scene. The action proceeds because that consciousness makes a lightning-fast leap backward to the present moment, to decide what action can be taken now, at this moment, in this situation, to achieve that goal. At every new discovery, the mind repeats the process, ever changing in the service of a fixed desire.

Character as Presented by the Author

Appearance, speech, action, and thought are the direct methods of presenting character. The *indirect method* is **authorial interpretation**—"telling" us the character's background, motives, values, virtues, and the like. The advantages of the indirect method are enormous, for its use leaves you free to move in time and space; to know anything you choose to know whether the character knows it or not; and godlike, to tell us what we are to feel. The indirect method allows you to convey a great deal of information in a short time.

> The port town of Veracruz is a little purgatory between land and sea for the traveler, but the people who live there are very fond of themselves and the town they have helped to make . . . and they carry on their lives of alternate violence and lethargy with a pleasurable contempt for outside opinion . . .
> *Katherine Anne Porter, Ship of Fools*

The disadvantage of this indirect method is that it bars us readers from sharing the immediacy and vividness of detail and the pleasure of judging for ourselves. In the summarized judgments of the passage above, for example, we learn more about the attitude of the narrator than about the town. Nevertheless, the indirect method is very efficient when you want to cover the exposition quickly, as A.S. Byatt does in this passage from "Crocodile Tears."

> The Nimmos spent their Sundays in those art galleries that had the common sense to open on that dead day . . . They liked buying things, they liked simply looking, they were happily married and harmonious in their stares, on the whole. They engaged a patch of paint and abandoned it, usually simultaneously, they lingered in the same places, considering the same things. Some they remembered, some they forgot, some they carried away.

Thus in a few sentences of the first paragraph, Byatt tells us everything we need to know about the Nimmos' marriage—especially since Mr. Nimmo is going to die on the next page, and the story will concern itself with Mrs. Nimmo's flight from the scene. In such an instance, authorial interpretation functions for pace and structure. But it is not a very useful mode to describe human change, which calls for the immediacy of scene, and of the direct presentation of character.

Try This

Take a monologue you have written and copy it, adding both the thoughts of the character and your own authorial comments. Let it flow; feel free to alter the character's feelings or the meaning of the speech, to allow new discoveries, to let the character change.

> The meaning of life must be conceived in terms of the specific meaning of a personal life in a given situation.
>
> *Victor Frankl*

Character as Conflict

Rich characterization can be effectively (and quite consciously) achieved by producing a conflict between methods of presentation. A character can be directly revealed to us through *appearance, speech, action,* and *thought*. If you set one of these methods at odds with the others, then dramatic tension will be produced. Imagine, for example, a character who is impeccable and expensively dressed, who speaks eloquently, who acts decisively, and whose mind is revealed to us as full of order and determination. He is inevitably a flat character. But suppose that he is impeccable, eloquent, decisive, and that his mind is a mess of wounds and panic. He is at once interesting.

Here is the opening passage of Saul Bellow's *Seize the Day*, in which appearance and action are blatantly at odds with thought. Notice that it is the tension between suppressed thought and what is expressed through appearance and action that produces the rich character conflict.

> When it came to concealing his troubles, Tommy Wilhelm was not less capable than the next fellow. So at least he thought, and there was a certain amount of evidence to back him up. He had once been an actor—no, not quite, an extra—and he knew what acting should be. Also, he was smoking a cigar, and when a man is smoking a cigar, wearing a hat, he has an advantage: it is harder to find out how he feels. He came from the twenty-third floor down to the lobby on the mezzanine to collect his mail before breakfast, and he believed—he hoped—he looked passably well: doing all right.

Thought is most frequently at odds with one or more of the other three methods of direct presentation—reflecting the difficulty we have expressing ourselves openly or accurately—but this is by no means always the case. The author may be directly telling us what to think and contradicting herself by showing the character to be someone else entirely. A character may be successfully, calmly, even eloquently expressing fine opinions while betraying himself by pulling at his ear, or herself by crushing her skirt. Captain Queeg of Herman Wouk's *The Caine*

Mutiny is a memorable example of this, maniacally clicking the steel balls in his hand as he defends his disciplinary code. Often we are not privy to the thoughts of a character at all, so that the conflicts must be expressed in a contradiction between the external methods of direct presentation, appearance, speech, and action. Notice that the notion of "betraying oneself" is again important here. We're more likely to believe the evidence unintentionally given than deliberate expression.

Try This

Write a short character sketch (it may be from life), focusing on how your character makes a living. Put your character in a working situation and let us know by a combination of direct and indirect methods what that work is, how well he/she does it, what it looks, sounds, smells like, and how the character feels about it. Contrast the methods.

More to Read

Chiarella, Tom. *Writing Dialogue*. Cincinnati: Story Press, 1998.

Minot, Stephen. *Three Genres*. Upper Saddle River, N.J.: Prentice Hall, 1998.

ESSAYS

Scott Russell Sanders

The Inheritance of Tools

At just about the hour when my father died, soon after dawn one February morning when ice coated the windows like cataracts, I banged my thumb with a hammer. Naturally I swore at the hammer, the reckless thing, and in the moment of swearing I thought of what my father would say: "If you'd try hitting the nail it would go in a whole lot faster. Don't you know your thumb's not as hard as that hammer?" We both were doing carpentry that day, but far apart. He was building cupboards at my brother's place in Oklahoma; I was at home in Indiana putting up a wall in the basement to make a bedroom for my daughter. By the time my mother called with news of his death—the long distance wires whittling her voice until it seemed too thin to bear the weight of what she had to say—my thumb was swollen. A week or so later a white scar in the shape of a crescent moon began to show above the cuticle, and month by month it rose across the pink sky of my thumbnail. It took the better part of a year for the scar to disappear, and every time I noticed it I thought of my father.

The hammer had belonged to him, and to his father before him. The three of us have used it to build houses and barns and chicken coops, to upholster chairs and crack walnuts, to make doll furniture and bookshelves and jewelry boxes. The head is scratched and pockmarked, like an old plowshare that has been working rocky fields, and it gives off the sort of dull sheen you see on fast creek water in the shade. It is a finishing hammer, about the weight of a bread loaf, too light really for framing walls, too heavy for cabinetwork, with a curved claw for pulling nails, a rounded head for pounding, a fluted neck for looks, and a hickory handle for strength.

The present handle is my third one, bought from a lumberyard in Tennessee down the road from where my brother and I were helping my father build his retirement house. I broke the previous one by trying to pull sixteen-penny nails out of floor joists—a foolish thing to do with a finishing hammer, as my father pointed out. "You ever head of a crowbar?" he said. No telling how many handles he and my grandfather had gone through before me. My grandfather used to cut down hickory trees on his farm, saw them into slabs, cure the planks in his hayloft, and carve handles with a drawknife. The grain in hickory is crooked and knotty, and therefore tough, hard to split, like the grain in the two men who owned this hammer before me.

After proposing marriage to a neighbor girl, my grandfather used this hammer to build a house for his bride on a stretch of river bottom in northern Mississippi. The lumber for the place, like the hickory for the handle, was cut on his own land. By the day of the wedding he had not quite finished the house, and so right after the ceremony he took his wife home and put her to work. My grandmother had worn her Sunday dress for the wedding, with a fringe of lace tacked on around the hem in honor of the occasion. She removed this lace and folded it away before going out to help my grandfather nail siding on the house. "There she was in her good dress," he told me some fifty-odd years after that wedding day, "holding up them long pieces of clapboard while I hammered, and together we got the place covered up before dark." As the family grew to four, six, eight, and eventually thirteen, my grandfather used this hammer to enlarge his house room by room, like a chambered nautilus expanding his shell.

By and by the hammer was passed along to my father. One day he was up on the roof of our pony barn nailing shingles with it, when I stepped out the kitchen door to call him for supper. Before I could yell, something about the sight of him straddling the spine of the roof and swinging the hammer caught my eye and made me hold my tongue. I was five or six years old, and the world's commonplaces were still news to me. He would pull a nail from the pouch at his waist, bring the hammer down, and a moment later the *thunk* of the blow would reach my ears. And that is what had stopped me in my tracks and stilled my tongue, that momentary gap between seeing and hearing the blow. Instead of yelling from the kitchen door, I ran to the barn and climbed two rungs up the ladder—as far as I was allowed to go—and spoke quietly to my father. On our walk to the house he explained that sound takes time to make its way through air. Suddenly the world seemed larger, the air more dense, if sound could be held back like any ordinary traveler.

By the time I started using this hammer, at about the age when I discovered the speed of sound, it already contained houses and mysteries for me. The smooth handle was one my grandfather had made. In those days I needed both hands to swing it. My father would start a nail in a scrap of wood, and I would pound away until I bent it over.

"Looks like you got ahold of some of those rubber nails," he would tell me. "Here, let me see if I can find you some stiff ones." And he would rummage in a drawer until he came up with a fistful of more cooperative nails. "Look at the head," he would tell me. "Don't look at your hands, don't look at the hammer. Just look at the head of that nail and pretty soon you'll learn to hit it square."

Pretty soon I did learn. While he worked in the garage cutting dovetail joints for a drawer or skinning a deer or tuning an engine, I would hammer nails. I made innocent blocks of wood look like porcupines. He did not talk much in the midst of his tools, but he kept up a nearly ceaseless humming, slipping in and out of a dozen tunes in an afternoon, often running back over the same stretch of melody again and again, as if searching for a way out. When the humming did cease, I knew he was faced with a task requiring great delicacy or concentration, and I took care not to distract him.

He kept scraps of wood in a cardboard box—the ends of two-by-fours, slabs of shelving and plywood, odd pieces of molding—and everything in it was fair game. I nailed scraps together to fashion what I called boats or houses, but the results usually bore only faint resemblance to the visions I carried in my head. I would hold up these constructions to show my father, and he would turn them over in his hands admiringly, speculating about what they might be. My cobbled-together guitars might have been alien spaceships, my barns might have been models of Aztec temples, each wooden contraption might have been anything but what I had set out to make.

Now and again I would feel the need to have a chunk of wood shaped or shortened before I riddled it with nails, and I would clamp it in a vice and scrape at it with a handsaw. My father would let me lacerate the board until my arm gave out, and then he would wrap his hand around mine and help me finish the cut, showing me how to use my thumb to guide the blade, how to pull back on the saw to keep it from binding, how to let my shoulder do the work.

"Don't force it," he would say, "just drag it easy and give the teeth a chance to bite."

As the saw teeth bit down the wood released its smell, each kind with its own fragrance, oak or walnut or cherry or pine—usually pine, because it was the softest and easiest for a child to work. No matter how weathered and gray the board, no matter how warped and cracked, inside there was this smell waiting, as of something freshly baked. I gathered every smidgen of sawdust and stored it away in coffee cans, which I kept in a drawer of the workbench. When I did not feel like hammering nails I would dump my sawdust on the concrete floor of the garage and landscape it into highways and farms and towns, running miniature cars and trucks along miniature roads. Looming as huge as a colossus, my father worked over and around me, now and again bending down to inspect my work, careful not to trample my creations. It was a landscape that smelled dizzyingly of wood. Even after a bath my skin would carry the smell, and so would my father's hair, when he lifted me for a bedtime hug.

I tell these things not only from memory but also from recent observation, because my own son now turns blocks of wood into nailed porcupines, dumps cans full of sawdust at my feet and sculpts highways on the floor. He learns how to swing a hammer from the elbow instead of the wrist, how to lay his thumb beside the blade to guide a saw, how to tap a chisel with a wooden mallet, how to mark a hole with an awl before starting a drill bit. My daughter did the same before him, and even now, on the brink of teenage aloofness, she will occasionally drag out my box of wood scraps and carpenter something. So I have seen my apprenticeship to wood and tools reenacted in each of my children, as my father saw his own apprenticeship renewed in me.

The saw I use belonged to him, as did my level and both of my squares, and all four tools had belonged to his father. The blade of the saw is the bluish color of gun barrels, and the maple handle, dark from the sweat of hands, is inscribed with curving leaf designs. The level is a shaft of walnut two feet long, edged with brass and pierced by three round windows in which air bubbles float in oil-filled tubes of glass. The middle window serves for testing whether a surface is horizontal, the others for testing whether it is plumb or vertical. My grandfather used to carry this level on the gun rack behind the seat in his pickup, and when I rode with him I would turn around to watch the bubbles dance. The larger of the two squares is called a framing square, a flat steel elbow so beat up and tarnished you can barely make out the rows of numbers that show how to figure the cuts on rafters. The smaller one is called a try square, for marking right angles, with a blued steel blade for the shank and a brass-faced block of cherry for the head.

I was taught early on that a saw is not to be used apart from a square: "If you're going to cut a piece of wood," my father insisted, "you owe it to the tree to cut it straight."

Long before studying geometry, I learned there is a mystical virtue in right angles. There is an unspoken morality in seeking the level and the plumb. A house will stand, a table will bear weight, the sides of a box will hold together only if the joints are square and the members upright. When the bubble is lined up between two marks etched in the glass tube of a level, you have aligned yourself with the forces that hold the universe together. When you miter the corners of a picture frame, each angle must be exactly forty-five degrees, as they are in the perfect triangles of Pythagoras, not a degree more or less. Otherwise the frame will hang crookedly, as if ashamed of itself and of its maker. No matter if the joints you are cutting do not show. Even if you are butting two pieces of wood together inside a cabinet, where no one except a wrecking crew will ever see them, you must take pains to insure that the ends are square and the studs are plumb.

I took pains over the wall I was building on the day my father died. Not long after that wall was finished—paneled with tongue-and-groove boards of yellow pine, the nail holes filled with putty and the wood all stained and sealed—I came close to wrecking it one afternoon when my daughter ran howling up the stairs to announce that her gerbils had escaped from their cage and were hiding in my brand-new wall. She could hear them scratching and squeaking behind her bed. Impossible! I said. How on earth could they get inside my drum-tight wall? Through the heating vent, she answered. I went downstairs, pressed my ear to the honey-colored wood, and heard the scritch scritch of tiny feet.

"What can we do?" my daughter wailed. "They'll starve to death, they'll die of thirst, they'll suffocate."

"Hold on," I soothed. "I'll think of something."

While I thought and she fretted, the radio on her bedside table delivered us the headlines. Several thousand people had died in a city in India from a poisonous cloud that had leaked overnight from a chemical plant. A nuclear-powered submarine had been launched. Rioting continued in South Africa. An airplane had been hijacked in the Mediterranean. Authorities calculated that several thousand homeless people slept on the streets within sight of the Washington Monument. I felt my usual helplessness in face of all these calamities. But here was my daughter weeping because her gerbils were holed up in a wall. This calamity I could handle.

"Don't worry," I told her. "We'll set food and water by the heating vent and lure them out. And if that doesn't do the trick, I'll tear the wall apart until we find them."

She stopped crying and gazed at me. "You'd really tear it apart? Just for my gerbils? The *wall?*" Astonishment slowed her down only for a second, however, before she ran to the workbench and began tugging at drawers, saying, "Let's see, what'll we need? Crowbar. Hammer. Chisels. I hope we don't have to use them—but just in case."

We didn't need the wrecking tools. I never had to assault my handsome wall, because the gerbils eventually came out to nibble at a dish of popcorn. But for several hours I studied the tongue-and-groove skin I had nailed up on the day of my father's death, considering where to begin prying. There were no gaps in that wall, no crooked joints.

I had botched a great many pieces of wood before I mastered the right angle with a saw, botched even more before I learned to miter a joint. The knowledge of these things resides in my hands and eyes and the webwork of muscles, not in the tools. There are machines for sale—powered miter boxes and radial arm saws, for instance—that will enable any casual soul to cut proper angles in boards. The skill is invested in the gadget instead of the person who uses it, and this is what distinguishes a machine from a tool. If I had to earn my keep by making furniture or building houses, I suppose I would buy powered saws and pneumatic nailers; the need for speed would drive me to it. But since I carpenter only for my own pleasure or to help neighbors or to remake the house around the ears of my family, I stick with hand tools. Most of the ones I own were given to me by my father, who also taught me how to wield them. The tools in my workbench are a double inheritance, for each hammer and level and saw is wrapped in a cloud of knowing.

All of these tools are a pleasure to look at and to hold. Merchants would never paste NEW NEW NEW! signs on them in stores. Their designs are old because they work, because they serve their purpose well. Like folk-songs and aphorisms and the grainy bits of language, these tools have been pared down to essentials. I look at my claw hammer, the distillation of a hundred generations of carpenters, and consider that it holds up well beside those other classics—Greek vases, Gregorian chants, *Don Quixote*, barbed fish-hooks, candles, spoons. Knowledge of hammering stretches back to the earliest humans who squatted beside fires chipping flints. Anthropologists have a lovely name for those unworked rocks that served as the earliest hammers. "Dawn stones" they are called. Their only qualification for the work, aside from hardness, is that they fit the hand. Our ancestors used them for grinding corn, tapping awls, smashing bones. From dawn stones to this claw hammer is a great leap in time, but no great distance in design or imagination.

On that iced-over February morning when I smashed my thumb with the hammer, I was down in the basement framing the wall that my daughter's gerbils would later hide in. I was thinking of my father, as I always did whenever I built anything, thinking how he would have gone about the work, hearing in memory what he would have said about the wisdom of hitting the nail instead of my thumb. I had the studs and plates nailed together all square and trim, and was lifting the wall into place when the phone rang upstairs. My wife answered, and in a moment she came to the basement door and called down softly to me. The stillness in her voice made me drop the framed wall and hurry upstairs. She told me my father was dead. Then I heard the details over the phone from my mother. Building a set of cupboards for my brother in Oklahoma, he had knocked off work early the previous afternoon because of cramps in his stomach. Early this morning, on his way into the kitchen of my brother's trailer, maybe going for a glass of water, so early that no one else was awake, he slumped down on the linoleum and his heart quit.

For several hours I paced around inside my house, upstairs and down, in and out of every room, looking for the right door to open and knowing there was no such door. My wife and children followed me and wrapped me in arms and backed away again, circling and staring as if I were on fire. Where was the door, the door, the door? I kept wondering. My smashed thumb turned purple and throbbed, making me furious. I wanted to cut it off and rush outside and scrape away the snow and hack a hole in the frozen earth and bury the shameful thing.

I went down into the basement, opened a drawer in my workbench, and stared at the ranks of chisels and knives. Oiled and sharp, as my father would have kept them, they gleamed at me like teeth. I took up a clasp knife, pried out the longest blade, and tested the edge on the hair of my forearm. A tuft came away cleanly, and I saw my father testing the sharpness of tools on his own skin, the blades of axes and knives and gouges and hoes, saw the red hair shaved off in patches from his arms and the backs of his hands. "That will cut bear," he would say. He never cut a bear with his blades, now my blades, but he cut deer, dirt, wood. I closed the knife and put it away. Then I took up the hamper and went back to work on my daughter's wall, snugging the bottom plate against a chalkline on the floor, shimming the top plate against the joists overhead, plumbing the studs with my level, making sure before I drove the first nail that every line was square and true.

Try This

Write a few paragraphs about a family member you associate with particular equipment, tools, paraphernalia, or gear. How do those objects reveal that person? Scott Russell Sanders' portrait of his father is entirely loving, and yours may be so as well. Or not.

FICTION

"Ysreal" is a story told in the limited omniscient through the eyes of the youngest of three characters. Examine the ways that all three are characterized through image, voice, action, and thought. What is the relative power of each, and how do you know?

Junot Díaz

Ysrael

1.

We were on our way to the colmado for an errand, a beer for my tío, when Rafa stood still and tilted his head, as if listening to a message I couldn't hear, something beamed in from afar. We were close to the colmado; you could hear the music and the gentle clop of drunken voices. I was nine that summer, but my brother was twelve, and he was the one who wanted to see Ysrael, who looked out towards Barbacoa and said, We should pay that kid a visit.

2.

Mami shipped me and Rafa out to the campo every summer. She worked long hours at the chocolate factory and didn't have the time or the energy to look after us during the months school was out. Rafa and I stayed with our tíos, in a small wooden house just outside Ocoa; rose bushes blazed around the yard like compass points and the mango trees spread out deep blankets of shade where we could rest and play dominos, but the campo was nothing like our barrio in Santo Domingo. In the campo there was nothing to do, no one to see. You didn't get television or electricity and Rafa, who was older and expected more, woke up every morning pissy and dissatisfied. He stood out on the patio in his shorts and looked out over the mountains, at the mists that gathered like water, at the brucal trees that blazed like fires on the mountain. This, he said, is shit.

Worse than shit, I said.

Yeah, he said, and when I get home, I'm going to go crazy—chinga all my girls and then chinga everyone else's. I won't stop dancing either. I'm going to be liked those guys in the record books who dance four or five days straight.

Tío Miguel had chores for us (mostly we chopped wood for the smokehouse and brought water up from the river) but we finished these as easy as we threw off our shirts, the rest of the day punching us in the face. We caught jaivas in the streams and spent hours walking across the valley to see girls who were never there; we set traps for jurones we never caught and toughened up our roosters with pails of cold water. We worked hard at keeping busy.

I didn't mind these summers, wouldn't forget them the way Rafa would. Back home in the Capital, Rafa had his own friends, a bunch of tígueres who liked to knock down our neighbors and who scrawled chocha and toto on walls and curbs. Back in the Capital he rarely said anything to me except Shut up, pendejo. Unless, of course, he was mad and then he had about five hundred routines he liked to lay on me. Most of them had to do with my complexion, my hair, the size of my lips. It's the Haitian, he'd say to his buddies. Hey Señor Haitian, Mami found you on the border and only took you in because she felt sorry for you.

If I was stupid enough to mouth off to him—about the hair that was growing on his back or the time the tip of his pinga had swollen to the size of a lemon—he pounded the hell out of me and the I would run as far as I could. In the Capital Rafa and I fought so much that our neighbors took to smashing broomsticks over us to break it up, but in the campo it wasn't like that. In the campo we were friends.

The summer I was nine, Rafa shot whole afternoons talking about whatever chica he was getting with—not that the campo girls gave up ass like the girls back in the Capital but kissing them, he told me, was pretty much the same. He'd take the campo girls down to the dams to swim and if he was lucky they let him put it in their mouth or in their asses. He'd done La Muda that way for almost a month before her parents heard about it and barred her from leaving the house forever.

He wore the same outfit when he went to see these girls, a shirt and pants that my father had sent him from the States last Christmas. I always followed Rafa, trying to convince him to let me tag along.

Go home, he'd say. I'll be back in a few hours.

I'll walk you.

I don't need you to walk me anywhere. Just wait for me.

If I kept on he'd punch me in the shoulder and walk on until what was left of him was the color of his shirt filling in the spaces between the leaves. Something inside of me would sag like a sail. I would yell his name and he'd hurry on, the ferns and branches and flower pods trembling in his wake.

Later, while we were in bed listening to the rats on the zinc roof he might tell me what he'd done. I'd hear about the tetas and chochas and leche and he'd talk without looking over at me. There was a girl he'd gone to see, half-Haitian but he ended up with her sister. Another who believed she wouldn't get pregnant if she drank a Coca-Cola afterwards. And one who was pregnant and didn't give a damn about anything. His hands were behind his head and his feet were crossed at the ankles. He was handsome and spoke out of the corner of his mouth. I was too young to understand most of what he said, but I listened to him anyway, in case these things might be useful in the future.

3.

Ysrael was a different story. Even on this side of Ocoa people had heard of him, how when he was a baby a pig had eaten his face off, skinned it like an orange. He was something to talk about, a name that set the kids to screaming, worse than el Cuco or la Vieja Calusa.

I'd seen Ysrael my first time the year before, right after the dams were finished. I was in town, farting around, when a single-prop plane swept in across the sky. A door opened on the fuselage and a man began to kick out tall bundles that exploded into thousands of leaflets as soon as the wind got to them. They came down as slow as butterfly blossoms and were posters of wrestlers, not politicians, and that's when us kids started shouting at each other. Usually the planes only covered Ocoa, but if extras had been printed the nearby towns would also get leaflets, especially if the match or the election was a big one. The paper would cling to the trees for weeks.

I spotted Ysrael in an alley, stooping over a stack of leaflets that had not come undone from its thin cord. He was wearing his mask.

What are you doing? I said.

What do you think I'm doing?

He picked up the bundle and ran down the alley, away from me. Some other boys saw him and wheeled around, howling but, coño, could he run.

That's Ysrael! I was told. He's ugly and he's got a cousin around here but we don't like him either. And that face of his would make you sick!

I told my brother later when I got home and he sat up in his bed. Could you see under the mask?

Not really.

That's something we got to check out. I hear it's bad.

The night before we went to look for him my brother couldn't sleep. He kicked at the mosquito netting and I could hear the mesh tearing just a little. My tío was yukking it up with his buddies in the yard. One of tío's roosters had won big the day before and he was thinking of taking it to the Capital.

People around here don't bet worth a damn, he was saying. Your average campesino only bets big when he feels lucky and how many of them feel lucky?

You're feeling lucky right now.

You're damn right about that. That's why I have to find myself some big spenders.

I wonder how much of Ysrael's face is gone, Rafa said.

He has his eyes.

That's a lot, he assured me. You'd think eyes would be the first thing a pig would go for. Eyes are soft. And salty.

How do you know that?

I licked one, he said.

Maybe his ears.

And his nose. Anything that sticks out.

Everyone had a different opinion on the damage. Tío said it wasn't bad but the father was very sensitive about anyone taunting his oldest son, which explained the mask. Tía said that if we were to look on his face we would be sad for the rest of our lives. That's why the poor boy's mother spends her day in church. I had never been sad more than a few hours and the thought of that sensation lasting a lifetime scared the hell out of me. My brother kept pinching my face during the night, like I was a mango. The cheeks, he said. And the chin. But the forehead would be a lot harder. The skin's tight.

All right, I said. Ya.

The next morning the roosters were screaming. Rafa dumped the ponchera in the weeds and then collected our shoes from the patio, careful not to stop on the pile of cacao beans Tía had set out to dry. Rafa went into the smokehouse and emerged with his knife and two oranges. He peeled them and handed me mine. When we heard Tía coughing in the house, we started on our way. I kept expecting Rafa to send me home and the longer he went without speaking, the more excited I became. Twice I put my hands over my mouth to stop from laughing. We went slow, grabbing saplings and fenceposts to keep from tumbling down the rough brambled slope. Smoke was rising from the fields that had been burned the night before, and the trees that had not exploded or collapsed stood in the black ash like spears. At the bottom of the hill we followed the road that would take us to Ocoa. I was carrying the two Coca-Cola empties Tío had hidden in the chicken coop.

We joined two women, our neighbors, who were waiting by the colmado on their way to mass.

I put the bottles on the counter. Chicho folded up yesterday's *El Nacional*. When he put fresh Cokes next to the empties, I said, We want the refund.

Chicho put his elbows on the counter and looked me over. Are you supposed to be doing that?

Yes, I said.

You better be giving this money back to your tío, he said. I stared at the pastelitos and chicharrón he kept under a fly-specked glass. He slapped the coins onto the counter. I'm going to stay out of this, he said. What you do with this money is your own concern. I'm just a businessman.

How much of this do we need? I asked Rafa.

All of it.

Can't we buy something to eat?

Save it for a drink. You'll be real thirsty later.

Maybe we should eat.

Don't be stupid.

How about if I just bought us some gum?

Give me that money, he said.

OK, I said. I was just asking.

Then stop. Rafa was looking up the road, distracted; I knew that expression better than anyone. He was scheming. Every now and then he glanced over at the two women, who were conversing loudly, their arms crossed over their big chests. When the first autobus trundled to a stop and the women got on, Rafa watched their asses bucking under their dresses. The cobrado leaned out from the passenger door and said, Well? And Rafa said, Beat it, baldie.

What are we waiting for? I said. That one had air conditioning.

I want a younger cobrador, Rafa said, still looking down the road. I went to the counter and tapped my finger on the glass case. Chico handed me a pastelito and after putting it in my pocket, I slid him a coin. Business is business, Chicho announced but my brother didn't bother to look. He was flagging down the next autobus.

Get to the back, Rafa said. He framed himself in the main door, his toes out in the air, his hands curled up on the top lip of the door. He stood next to the cobrador, who was a year or two younger than he was. This boy tried to get Rafa to sit down but Rafa shook his head with that not-a-chance grin of his and before there could be an argument the driver shifted into gear, blasting the radio. *La chica de la novela* was still on the charts. Can you believe that? The man next to me said. They play that vaina a hundred times a day.

I lowered myself stiffly into my seat but the pastelito had already put a grease stain on my pants. Coño, I said and took out the pastelito and finished it in four bites. Rafa wasn't watching. Each time the autobus stopped he was hopping down and helping people bring on their packages. When a row filled he lowered the swing-down center seat for whoever was next. The cobrador, a thin boy with an Afro, was trying to keep up with him and the driver was too busy with his radio to notice what was happening. Two people paid Rafa—all of which Rafa gave to the cobrador, who was himself busy making change.

You have to watch out for stains like that, the man next to me said. He had big teeth and wore a clean fedora. His arms were ropy with muscles.

These things are too greasy, I said.

Let me help. He spit in his fingers and started to rub at the stain but then he was pinching at the tip of my pinga through the fabric of my shorts.

He was smiling. I shoved him against his seat. He looked to see if anybody had noticed.

You pato, I said.

The man kept smiling.

You low-down pinga-sucking pato, I said. The man squeezed my bicep, quietly, hard, the way my friends would sneak me in church. I whimpered.

You should watch your mouth, he said.

I got up and went over to the door. Rafa slapped the roof and as the driver slowed the cobrador said, You two haven't paid.

Sure we did, Rafa said, pushing me down into the dusty street. I gave the money for those two people there and I gave you our fare too. His voice was tired, as if he got into these discussions all the time.

No you didn't.

Fuck you I did. You got the fares. Why don't you count and see?

Don't even try it. The cobrador put his hands on Rafa but Rafa wasn't having it. He yelled up to the driver, Tell your boy to learn how to count.

We crossed the road and went down into a field of guineo; the cobrado was shouting after us and we stayed in the field until we heard the driver say, Forget them.

Rafa took off his shirt and fanned himself and that's when I started to cry.

He watched for a moment. You, he said, are a pussy.

I'm sorry.

What the hell's the matter with you? We didn't do anything wrong.

I'll be OK in a second. I sawed my forearm across my nose.

He took a look around, drawing in the lay of the land. If you can't stop crying, I'll leave you. He headed towards a shack that was rusting in the sun.

I watched him disappear. From the shack you could hear voices, as bright as chrome. Columns of ants had found a pile of meatless chicken bones at my feet and were industriously carting away the crumbling marrow. I could have gone home, which was what I usually did when Rafa acted up, but we were far—eight, nine miles away.

I caught up with him beyond the shack. We walked about a mile; my head felt cold and hollow.

Are you done?

Yes, I said.

Are you always going to be a pussy?

I wouldn't have raised my head if God himself had appeared in the sky and pissed down on us.

Rafa spit. You have to get tougher. Crying all the time. Do you think our papi's crying? Do you think that's what he's been doing the last six years? He turned from me. His feet were crackling through the weeds, breaking stems.

Rafa stopped a schoolboy in a blue and tan uniform, who pointed us down a road. Rafa spoke to a young mother, whose baby was hacking like a miner. A little further, she said and when he smiled she looked the other way. We went too far and a farmer with a machete showed us the easiest loop back. Rafa stopped when he saw Ysrael standing in the center of a field; he was flying a kite and despite the string he seemed almost unconnected to the distant wedge of black that finned back and forth in the sky. Here we go, Rafa said. I was embarrassed. What the hell were we supposed to do?

Stay close, he said. And get ready to run. He passed me his knife, then trotted down towards the field.

4.

The summer before I pegged Ysrael with a rock and the way it bounced off his back I knew I'd clocked a shoulder blade.

You did it! You fucking did it! The other boys yelled.

He'd been running from us and he arched in pain and one of the other boys nearly caught him but he recovered and took off. He's faster than a mongoose, someone said, but in truth he was faster than that. We laughed and went back to our baseball games and forgot him until he came to town again and then we dropped what we were doing and chased him. Show us your face, we cried. Let's see it just once.

5.

He was about a foot bigger than either of us and looked like he'd been fattened on that supergrain the farmers around Ocoa were giving their stock, a new product which kept my tío up at night, muttering jealously, Proxyl Feed 9, Proxyl Feed 9. Ysrael's sandals were of stiff leather and his clothes were North American. I looked over at Rafa but my brother seemed unperturbed.

Listen up, Rafa said. My hermanito's not feeling too well. Can you show us where a colmado is? I want to get him a drink.

There's a faucet up the road, Ysrael said. His voice was odd and full of spit. His mask was handsewn from thin blue cotton fabric and you couldn't help but see the scar tissue that circled his left eye, a red waxy crescent, and the saliva that trickled down his neck.

We're not from around here. We can't drink the water.

Ysrael spooled in his string. The kite wheeled but he righted it with a yank.

Not bad, I said.

We can't drink the water around here. It would kill us. And he's already sick.

I smiled and tried to act sick, which wasn't too difficult. I was covered with dust and I saw Ysrael looking us over.

The water here is probably better than up in the mountains, he said.

Help us out, Rafa said in a low voice.

Ysrael pointed down a path. Just go that way, you'll find it.

Are you sure?

I've lived here all my life.

I could hear the plastic kite flapping in the wind; the string was coming in fast. Rafa huffed and started on his way. We made a long circle and by then Ysrael had his kite in hand—the kite was no handmade local job. It had been manufactured abroad.

We couldn't find it, Rafa said.

How stupid are you?

Where did you get that? I asked.

Nueva York, he said. From my father.

No shit! Our father's there too! I shouted.

I looked at Rafa, who, for an instant, frowned. Our father only sent us letters and an occasional shirt or pair of jeans at Christmas.

What the hell are you wearing that mask for anyway? Rafa asked.

I'm sick, Ysrael said.

It must be real hot.

Not for me.

Don't you take it off?

Not until I get better. I'm going to have an operation soon.

You better watch out for that, Rafa said. Those doctors will kill you faster than the guardia.

These are American doctors.

Rafa sniggered. You're lying.

I saw them last spring. They want me to go next year.

They're lying to you. They probably just felt sorry.

Do you want me to show you where the colmado is or not?

Sure.

Follow me, he said, wiping the spit on his neck. At the colmado he stood off while Rafa bought me the Cola. The owner was playing dominos with the beer delivery man and didn't bother to look up, though he put a hand in the air for Ysrael. He had that lean look of every colmado owner I'd ever met. On the way back to the road I left the bottle with Rafa to finish and caught up with Ysrael, who was ahead of us. Are you still into wrestling? I asked.

He turned to me and something rippled under the mask. How did you know that?

I heard, I said. Do they have wrestling in the States?

I hope so.

Are you a wrestler?

I'm a great wrestler. I almost went to fight in the Capital.

My brother laughed, swinging on the bottle.

You want to try it, pendejo?

Not right now.

I didn't think so.

I tapped his arm. The planes haven't dropped anything this year.

It's still too early. The first Sunday of August is when it starts.

How do you know?

I'm from around here, he said. The mask twitched. I realized he was smiling and then my brother brought his arm around and smashed the bottle on top of his head. It exploded, the thick bottom spinning away like a crazed eyeglass and I said, Holy fucking shit. Ysrael stumbled once and slammed into a fencepost that had been sunk into the side of the road. Glass crumbled off his mask. He spun towards me, then fell down on his stomach. Rafa kicked him in the side. Ysrael seemed not to notice. He had his hands flat in the dirt and was concentrating on pushing himself up. Roll him on his back, my brother said and we did, pushing like crazy. Rafa took off his mask and threw it spinning into the grass.

His left ear was a nub and you could see the thick veined slab of his tongue through a hole in his cheek. He had no lips. His head was tipped back and his eyes had gone white and the cords were out on his neck. He'd been an infant when the pig had come into the house. The damage looked old but I still jumped back and said, Rafa, let's go! Rafa crouched and using only two of his fingers, turned Ysrael's head from side to side.

6.

We went back to the colmado where the owner and the delivery man were now arguing, the dominos chattering under their hands. We kept walking and after one hour, maybe two, we saw an autobus. We boarded and went right to the back. Rafa crossed his arms and watched the fields and roadside shacks scroll past, the dust and smoke and people almost frozen by our speed.

Ysrael will be OK, I said.

Don't bet on it.

They're going to fix him.

A muscle fluttered between his jaw bone and his ear. Yunior, he said tiredly. They aren't going to do shit to him.

How do you know?

I know, he said.

I put my feet on the back of the chair in front of me, pushing on an old lady, who looked back at me. She was wearing a baseball cap and one of her eyes was milky. The autobus was heading for Ocoa, not for home.

Rafa signaled for a stop. Get ready to run, he whispered.

I said, OK.

Try This

Write about an incident involving three characters from the viewpoint of the weakest of them; characterize all three.

POEMS

Theodore Roethke

I Knew a Woman

I knew a woman, lovely in her bones,
When small birds sighed, she would sigh back at them;
Ah, when she moved, she moved more ways than one:
The shapes a bright container can contain!
Of her choice virtues only gods should speak,
Or English poets who grew up on Greek
(I'd have them sing in chorus, cheek to cheek).

How well her wishes went! She stroked my chin,
She taught me Turn, and Counter-turn, and Stand;
She taught me Touch, that undulant white skin;
I nibbled meekly from her proffered hand;
She was the sickle; I, poor I, the rake,
Coming behind her for her pretty sake
(But what prodigious mowing we did make).

Love likes a gander, and adores a goose:
Her full lips pursed, the errant note to seize;
She played it quick, she played it light and loose;
My eyes, they dazzled at her flowing knees;
Her several parts could keep a pure repose,
Or one hip quiver with a mobile nose
(She moved in circles, and those circles moved).

Let seed be grass, and grass turn into hay:
I'm martyr to a motion not my own;
What's freedom for? To know eternity.
I swear she cast a shadow white as stone.
But who would count eternity in days?
These old bones live to learn her wanton ways:
(I measure time by how a body sways).

Carole Simmons Oles
Stonecarver

for Father

Don't look at his hands now.
Stiff and swollen, small finger
curled in like a hermit:
needing someone to open the ketchup,
an hour to shave.
That hand held the mallet,
made the marble say
Cicero, Juno, and *laurel.*

Don't think of his eyes
behind thick lenses squinting
at headlines, his breath
drowning in stonedust and Camels,
his sparrow legs.

Think of the one who slid
3 floors down scaffolding ropes
every lunchtime,
who stood up to Donnelly the foreman
for more time to take care.

Keep him the man in the photo,
straight-backed on the park bench
in Washington, holding hands
with your mother.
Keep his hands holding
calipers, patterns, and pointer,
bringing the mallet down
fair on the chisel,
your father's hands sweeping off dust.

Stephen Dunn
My Brother's Work

My brother who knows
the indignity of work
rides home with the taste of it
turning peptic, that odor

of swallowed pride rising
into his breath, his wife waiting
for the kiss that's so full
of the day she can't bear it.
My brother who hears the shout
of bosses, who is no boss himself,
only shouts at home,
thinks shouting is what permits
the bosses to move
with the easy self-
fulfilled gait of leopards
who've eaten all they've killed.
My brother who will not leave
his job wonders how Gauguin left
the world and found himself
on the other side of it.
"What *balls*," he says, "braver
than a suicide." My brother
who is no less than anyone
circumstance has made
to do its bidding, who wants
to rise one morning against
all odds and slip
into his leopard body,
my brother is
coming home now and his wife
is waiting for the kiss.

Fred Wah

Old man Hansen comes
in at ten to

six, when things aren't even ready yet. He's always the first.
He takes a paper and puts a dime on the stack, and then shuffles down
to booth number three, hangs up his hat and overcoat, and sits facing the front, silent and stonefaced. Hansen is in his eighties,
always wears a dark suit, rooms alone down in the Arlington,
depends on the Diamond for breakfast and some suppers. The cafe
even opens by six on Christmas and New Years mornings so
Hansen will be able to get breakfast. Wordlessly, Fred brings

Hansen his coffee and a jug of syrup on the way to the kitchen to order. Stack a hot! Side a sausage!

Shu, the cook, doesn't even look up. He's ready. He echoes stack a hot! and his hands sweep up the bowl of batter and ladle three perfect pancakes already on the grill. He's been waiting for that first order shouted into the kitchen air. That's the switch, the buzz. Now the day has measure.

Elizabeth Jennings

One Flesh

Lying apart now, each in a separate bed,
He with a book, keeping the light on late,
She like a girl dreaming of childhood,
All men elsewhere—it is as if they wait
Some new event: the book he holds unread,
Her eyes fixed on the shadows overhead.

Tossed up like flotsam from a former passion,
How cool they lie. They hardly ever touch,
Or if they do it is like a confession
Of having little feeling—or too much.
Chastity faces them, a destination
For which their whole lives were a preparation.

Strangely apart, yet strangely close together,
Silence between them like a thread to hold
And not wind in. And time itself's a feather
Touching them gently. Do they know they're old,
These two who are my father and my mother
Whose fire from which I came, has now grown cold?

B.H. Fairchild

Old Men Playing Basketball

The heavy bodies lunge, the broken language
of fake and drive, glamorous jump shot
slowed to a stutter. Their gestures, in love
again with the pure geometry of curves,

rise toward the ball, falter, and fall away.
On the boards their hands and fingertips
tremble in tense little prayers of reach
and balance. Then, the grind of bone

and socket, the caught breath, the sigh,
the grunt of the body laboring to give
birth to itself. In their toiling and grand
sweeps, I wonder, do they still make love

to their wives, kissing the undersides
of their wrists, dancing the old soft-shoe
of desire? And on the long walk home
from the VFW, do they still sing

to the drunken moon? Stands full, clock
moving, the one in army fatigues
and houseshoes says to himself, *pick and roll*,
and the phrase sounds musical as ever,

radio crooning songs of love after the game,
the girl leaning back in the Chevy's front seat
as her raven hair flames in the shuddering
light of the outdoor movie, and now he drives,

gliding toward the net. A glass wand
of autumn light breaks over the backboard.
Boys rise up in old men, wings begin to sprout
at their backs. The ball turns in the darkening air.

Edward Hirsch

Portrait of a Writer

Keys on a battered typewriter,
　　　letters waiting absentmindedly
　　　　　to come together in words that will
　　　　　　　save the night from a grave stillness.

Pages and pages of low-grade
　　　white paper, some of it blank,
　　　　　some festooned with mistakes and
　　　　　　　sentenced to death in a wicker basket.

How many books has he pro-
posed to this room? How many
selves has he discarded while
the dog slept restlessly at his feet

and the moon burrowed a hole
in the clouds? He has stared
at scars rivered into the desk
and wondered about the stranger

he has become to himself and
others. What exile is this?
And who are these solitaries glow-
ering from photographs in the hallway,

always dropping their suitcases
and wandering off into the un-
suspecting fate that awaits them?
They are a tribe of failures on the move . . .

He is tired of this broken-
hearted tradition of losses,
Lord, tired of these breaches
and ruptures, these promissory notes

to the dead hand of the past.
He is tired of memories advancing
into the future, fanatical dust,
and a dispossession without grace.

This sleeplessness has lasted
forty years in the desert.
He knows its delirious exile
and in the midst of night

he wrestles with absence
like a mysterious stranger,
he strives against darkness
until daybreak when he can sleep.

Try This

Take any monologue or character sketch you have written and read it over. Highlight any phrase that strikes you as particularly interesting, image that seems vivid, metaphor you'll stand by, forceful verb. Then take a fresh sheet of paper and put down as a title the name or other identification of the character. Write down only those words and phrases you have highlighted. Arrange them in lines. Fool around with their order.

continued

Cluster an image for fresh associations, brainstorm a word to find similar sounds. Incorporate whatever of this seems good to you. Restore any syntax necessary to make grammatical sense. Try repeating a phrase or word in several lines throughout. Is that interesting? Does the word or phrase change meaning in its different contexts? Have you written a poem?

DRAMA

Mary Gallagher

Brother

CHARACTERS
Kitty
Charlie

It's five o'clock in the morning. Kitty's entering in her bathrobe and heading for the refrigerator as Charlie enters from outside, wearing a worn-looking winter jacket.

CHARLIE: Oh great—   **KITTY**: Oh God,
     I was afraid Mom was   you scared me—
     up—How the hell are ya?   Hi! How *are* you . . . ?

(They kiss and hug awkwardly, he whirls her around as:)

CHARLIE: Jeez, whenja get so skinny?

KITTY: God, I don't know . . . has it been that long since we—?

CHARLIE: Yeah, gotta be   **KITTY**: Well, yeah, I guess we
     a couple years   didn't make it last
     or something . . .   Christmas, so—

KITTY: You look big! I always forget, I expect you to look weedy, like when you were sixteen or something . . .

CHARLIE: That was many moons ago.

KITTY: I know, but I forget. Listen, I still picture you in that dalmatian outfit you had to wear in the kindergarten play.

CHARLIE: Oh, yeah? You wanta wrestle? Now that you're a fly-weight. Give you two falls out of three. How was the trip down?

KITTY: Average. There was a wreck on 90 so everything was backed up—and poor Matt got carsick, twice—your average turnpike nightmare . . . Are you just getting home?

CHARLIE: Yup. Had too good a time tonight, couldn't tear myself away. What is it, five o'clock or something? What're you doing up?

KITTY: I just *got* up, I've gotta make this damn potato salad for the reception and I want to get it done before the kids get up. I must've been crazy to say I'd do this . . .

(She takes a bowl of hard-boiled eggs from the fridge and starts peeling them.)

KITTY: So what's the story, you seeing somebody?

CHARLIE: Nah. I was just up at Dink's.

KITTY: That biker bar? I mean, it *was* . . . now is it . . . like, fun, or—?

CHARLIE: That's my club. There're some good guys hang out there. They call me the King. I walk in, they say, "The King is here." Plus they got a pool table—

KITTY: You didn't walk home, did you? God. I mean, it's none of my business, but you don't want to get mugged again—

CHARLIE: I was a kid when I got mugged, I don't even remember it. *You* remember—

KITTY: Well, but it's cold out, too—

CHARLIE: Haddaya *think* I get around? It's not like I can use Mom's car. Hey, I'm the champeen walker.

KITTY: Right . . . don't you have gloves, at least?

CHARLIE: I had some great gloves. Did you give me those? Blue wool with leather pads?

KITTY: Yeah, probably . . .

CHARLIE: They were great. But I lost 'em. That red shirt you gave me was great too, I lost that too. They're great while they last, though. Man, I am starving. Mom made that chicken stuff for dinner, right?

KITTY: We killed it.

CHARLIE: Thanks, guys.

KITTY: There's salad left, though.

CHARLIE: Salad! Hey, this is me you're talking to—Oh shit, I better close this door or Mom'll be out here bitching, make me do the Breathalyzer . . .

(He closes the door to the hall, goes to cupboards, takes out a can of Chef Boy-ar-Dee Ravioli and a loaf of Wonder Bread, opens the can and makes cold ravioli sandwiches.)

CHARLIE: Couple months ago I was a bad boy, really let myself go . . . she tell you about this?

KITTY: *(nods yes, but blankly)* What.

CHARLIE: It was pretty funny, or it woulda been if somebody'd been there to see it besides us . . . I came in real late, and I mean I was loaded, and coming through the living room, I tripped over her fucking sewing box and I fell flat, like, with this huge crash! And I couldn't get back up. It was wild, the whole room was going nuts around me . . . and then, Jesus, here comes Mom, with the electric carving knife!—she thought someone was breaking in—

KITTY: (*appalled but has to laugh*) What was she gonna do with the electric knife, she would've had to go get the extension cord so she could plug it in—

CHARLIE: (*laughs*) Yeah, right . . . yeah . . . but she doesn't sleep through stuff like she used to. That was great, how when she was sleeping, we'd go in and ask her stuff, like if we could do stuff or buy stuff, like donuts or something, and she'd always say—

BOTH: "Sure, honey . . . "

KITTY: She'd still be asleep . . .

CHARLIE: We got away with fucking everything. Forget it, *now*. The slightest thing, she wakes up screaming . . .

KITTY: Listen though, Mom says you're doing great at your new job, she says they really like you.

CHARLIE: Well, my boss keeps telling me I'm the best worker they got . . .

KITTY: Well, good for you . . . just keep it up. I mean I always knew if you got on a good roll . . .

CHARLIE: I figure she'd be telling you to shape me up—

KITTY: No, listen . . . I mean sure, she . . . she *cares*, that's all . . . but I don't want to . . . be telling you . . . we oughta be past that . . .

CHARLIE: Jesus, *I* think so, but Mom . . . she's really getting crotchety. Like ever since that night, she won't give me a ride anywhere except to work, and that's just if I oversleep. It's like, in her mind, the only life I should have is work. You know? I go, "Hey, Ma, I'm not gonna just work and come straight home and sit around watching the boob tube all night long, like the living dead . . . "

(*starts eating ravioli sandwiches, sees her watching*)

What.

KITTY: You really do still eat like that.

CHARLIE: Hey, the Chef's my man. Mom, once in a while she'll try to palm off some gourmet brand, what they call "pasta" now. I tell her, "Ma, I got my loyalties."

KITTY: So you psyched for the wedding?

CHARLIE: . . . Oh, right! Right . . . great!

KITTY: All the cousins are coming in—

CHARLIE: Oh yeah? Old Eddie's coming, too?

KITTY: Yeah, didn't Mom tell you?

CHARLIE: Hey. You're the one she talks to.

KITTY: Well . . . that's because I'm gone. But listen, Jen has hot plans to dance with you. Uncle Charlie. Like, rad.

CHARLIE: Oh, yeah?

KITTY: Oh, please. Don't tell her I said so, but she never stops playing that Jackson Browne tape you gave her.

CHARLIE: She's a babe, that kid, she's gonna break some hearts. Yeah, I wanted to make it home to see her tonight, but . . .

KITTY: And Matt's dying to see you too. You'll have to show him your MAD collection one more time.

CHARLIE: He remembers that?

KITTY: Are you serious? That's on the list now, that's required.

CHARLIE: Oh, shit.

KITTY: What.

CHARLIE: I think I have to work today.

KITTY: Oh, no, Charlie, you can't miss this—

CHARLIE: Shit. Get me up at eight, I'll call in sick.

KITTY: Well . . . wait . . .

CHARLIE: Nah, fuck it. If he doesn't like it, he can fire me.

KITTY: No, wait, Charlie, I shouldn't've . . . that wouldn't be too cool with Mom, or . . . you know, just . . . for *you*, I mean . . . this is a decent job . . .

CHARLIE: Pearl-diving, it's a privilege—

KITTY: Well, but if you stick it out there, maybe you can move up—

CHARLIE: Move up, how? To waiter? I'd rather wash dishes my whole life than be a fucking waiter. You know how much shit they have to take from these assholes? Come in ordering "Chivas and Coke," like that's a sign of class!

KITTY: Well, but you'd make a lot more money—

CHARLIE: Hey, I go in, I do my job, and I don't have to take any shit from anybody—including my "superior." The crew chief? What a dick-head! Keeps telling me about "technique"—which he doesn't know zilch what he's talking about—and when I tell him "Back off," he goes, "I am your superior!" Dickhead's never read a book, can't even speak English hardly, here he is telling me . . .

KITTY: Well, sure, but on any job—

CHARLIE: Then yesterday, I had a couple beers in the bar on my lunch hour—then my boss comes in and tells me the staff isn't *allowed* to drink on the "premises"—how's that for life in a democracy?

KITTY: That stinks. But, you know, why give them your money anyway—

CHARLIE: Man, I was seeing red, I went back in the kitchen, my "superior" starts in on me about "technique," I told him, "Yeah, you spent your whole life washing other people's dirty dishes, and you think that make you my *superior*? I find that sad."

KITTY: Well, but Charlie, don't . . . this looks like a job you can keep for a while, right?

CHARLIE: Listen, there are a million—a zillion jobs like this. Pearl-diving, busing tables, washing floors—nobody wants these fucking jobs. Every kitchen is a zoo, they got no-shows, they got walkouts, guys right off the boat who can't even speak English, you gotta do a pantomime to show 'em what they're sposeta do . . . . This is one thing I know more about than you, okay? With my experience, I can walk into any restaurant and any bar in this city, and I can get hired, and I am not exaggerating, any day I ask—

KITTY: Okay, but asking is the hard part, and—Jesus, I swore I wasn't getting into this—Mom wants you to be working—

CHARLIE: No matter what scutwork it is—

KITTY: Now that's not fair—or true—God, Charlie—you're so bright—

CHARLIE: Oh shit, what, did you guys spend the whole night talking about getting me motivated—?

KITTY: (*overlapping*) No, I told her, I told everyone, I don't want to get into this! But when I hear you talking about—

CHARLIE: (*overlapping*) You come home every two years—

KITTY: (*overlapping*)It's not just me who's saying it—

CHARLIE: You wouldn't last one day washing dishes in a restaurant.

KITTY: Okay, fine . . . let's not do this, huh? I'm really . . . want to see you, I want to spend some time with you—

CHARLIE: You know, she keeps ragging me about "if you'd just get your equivalency"—like a high school diploma's gonna open the golden doors—McDonald's, that's the golden doors it'll open—and I'd rather haul shit! Listen, I couldn't make Mom happy unless I wore a suit to work—Shit.

KITTY: What.

CHARLIE: I forgot to get my good pants cleaned.

KITTY: I'll just iron 'em, they'll be fine—

CHARLIE: No, they're gross, got puke on 'em or something . . .

KITTY: Well, maybe Joe brought extra pants—

CHARLIE: Well, I was gonna ask him if he brought extra shoes. All I've got is tennis shoes.

KITTY: God, I sort of doubt it. Joe's not exactly Mr. Style, you know. I mean you don't have to worry about the family standards here. Last week his boss took us out to dinner, and they wouldn't even let Joe in the restaurant because no tie, right?

CHARLIE: (*half-listening*) Assholes . . .

KITTY: So Joey takes off down the street and zips into some discount store and zips out with this plastic tie—God, did it feel sleazy, like it was made out of a shower curtain, or—well, most likely he'll wear it tomorrow at the wedding—

CHARLIE: I've got ties to lend him, God, they're still in the boxes—but I better find that white shirt, throw it in the washer. Can you wake me? Like at nine. And I'll call in. What time's the wedding?

KITTY: Noon. I'll prob'ly still be making this goddamn potato salad as they're marching down the aisle . . .

CHARLIE: Joe's gonna wear a suit, right?

KITTY: No, just a sportscoat, you don't have to—

CHARLIE: Would he have an extra one?

KITTY: . . . I don't think . . . but you don't have to . . . or we can go buy one, in a couple hours here. We can put it on the card and you can pay us back.

CHARLIE: Yeah? When?

KITTY: Oh, who cares? Shoes, too. Charlie. You should have a decent pair of shoes, you know? A decent jacket . . . for your life. Okay?

CHARLIE: (*beat; then:*) I can get away with a shirt and tie, huh?

KITTY: . . . Sure, this is very casual . . . home-catering, the whole trip . . .

CHARLIE: Okay, I'm gonna hit the rack. Wake me up, okay? Wake me at ten, ten's good enough.

KITTY: I'll send the kids in—

CHARLIE: Better not, you ain't seen my room.

(as he exits)

> And listen, at the wedding? Just keep Uncle Bill away from me. I can get through anything if he just doesn't ask me what I'm "up to these days."

(He exits, with remains of sandwiches. She keeps peeling eggs.)

Blackout

Try this

Write a short dialogue in which one person explains or defends him- or herself to another. The listener is sympathetic, and believes the explanation. We aren't and don't. How can you make the talker unreliable in both image/action and speech? Why does the listener believe what we do not?

Warm-up

Let your mind float among images of place; pick a couple of geographical or physical features that don't naturally occur together, like the sandcastle in the dining room above. Then combine them and describe the "surreal" landscape that results. Make your description as detailed, realistic, and convincing as you can.

CHAPTER FOUR

SETTING

As the World
As a Camera
As Mood and Symbol
As Action

"... place is a definer and a confiner of what I'm doing
... It saves me. Why, you couldn't write a story that happened nowhere.

Eudora Welty

A love of home. A passion for travel. The grief of exile. The fragility of nature.
The excitement of the metropolis. A fascination with the past. An obsession
with the future. The search to belong. The need to flee. A sense of alienation. The
thrill of outer space. The romance of real estate. Fear of the dark. The arctic
waste. The swamp. The summit. The sea. The slums. The catacombs. The palace.
The rocking chair. The road.

Writer after writer will tell you that **setting** fuels the drive to write. Virtually any writer you ask will profess a profound relation to place and time, whether
as patriot, refugee, homebody, adventurer, flaneur, or time traveler; and each will
tell you that creating the sensuous particularity of a place and period is crucial
to writing. Setting is not merely scenery against which the significant takes place;
it is part and parcel of the significant; it is heritage and culture; it is identity or
exile.

Like so many Americans raised in suburbia [Deborah Tall writes], I have never
really belonged to an American landscape . . . The land's dull tidiness was hard
to escape, except in the brief adventures of childhood when I could crawl beneath
a bush or clothe myself in a willow tree. Before long, tall enough to look out the
kitchen window, I saw the tree tamed by perspective, the bush that could be

hurdled, my yard effectively mimicked all up and down the block: one house, two trees, one house, two trees, all the way to the vanishing point.

"Here"

In rejecting the suburban landscape as her rightful home, Tall creates its oppressive tidiness for us, its suggestive or even symbolic importance to her sense of the "vanishing point." Though the description is of a deliberately static scene, the forceful verbs—*escape, crawl, clothe, tame, hurdle, mimick*—carry the energy of her desire to be gone from it. And readers can connect with the pictures and emotions she evokes in many ways: the image of suburbia itself, the childhood desire to hide, the changing perspective as she grows, the need for independence. For myself, though I grew up in the desert and would have been grateful for two trees, I powerfully identify with the sense of knowing even as a child that the place I lived was not the place I belonged, and the implication that this sense of exile is common among writers.

If a piece of literature does not create the setting for us, if it seems to occur in no-place no-time, or in vague-place fuzzy-time, we cannot experience it, or else we must experience that vagueness itself as crucial to the action. Samuel Butler's Utopia is set in *Erewhon* (*nowhere* spelled backwards) because the point of such a place, where philosophers reign and children select their parents, is that it cannot exist. Tom Stoppard's heroes in *Rosencrantz and Guildenstern Are Dead* do not know where they are, or where they came from, or where the sun comes up, or what time it is, and therefore *do not know who they are.*

Yet there's a resistance and even a measure of boredom that greets the subject of setting, and I can think of at least two reasons for this. The first is that tedious and sentimental descriptions of nature tend to be part of our early schooling, operating as a sort of admonishment that we should pay less attention to Mickey Mouse and Eminem, and more to the (ho-hum) wonders of nature. The other is that in daily life we take our surroundings ninety percent for granted. The world you know is what you're told to write about. What's the big deal? Isn't it everybody's world? Well, no.

> Don't think that any place is "typical."
>
> *Steven Schoen*

Setting as the World

Your routine, your neighborhood, your take on home, history, climate, and the cosmos is unique, like your voice, and inseparable from your voice. As a writer you need to be alert to your own vision and to create for us, even make strange to us, the world you think most familiar. If the world you are writing about is itself in some way exotic, you will need to work in the opposite direction, to make it seem as familiar to us as the nearest mall.

Try This
Draw the floor plan of the first house you remember living in. Take a mental tour through this house, pausing (and marking on the floor plan) where significant events occurred. Walk through again, remembering, marking. Make a list of the events. Pick one of them and write about it. Pay attention to the setting and the atmosphere of the event. How does your relation to the space, light, weather, walls, furniture, objects affect what you are doing and feeling? Does the place represent safety or confinement?

Description has earned a bad rap with overlong, self-indulgent eulogies to wildflowers, furniture, or alien planets. But setting involves everything that supports and impinges on your characters. The props of the world—artifacts and architecture, infrastructure, books, food, fabrics, tools and technology—create and sustain identity. People behaving in relation to their surroundings define both space and time, and reveal much more.

Take the example of a simple stage setting. The stage is bare; it could be anywhere at any time. Now place on it an ordinary straight-backed chair. What portion of history is now eliminated? How much of the contemporary world can the setting now *not* represent—in what portion of the planet do people not sit on chairs? You don't know the answer. Neither do I. That neither of us knows the answer proves how particular and limited is our vision of the world.

A male actor enters the space. He sits in the chair. He holds his arms and head rigid, as if strapped. Where is he now? What will happen? Or he sweeps in and sits, miming the flinging aside of his robe. Where is he now? To what tradition does the scene belong? He drops a briefcase, slumps in the chair, and slips off his shoes with a toe on the heel of each. Where? What is he feeling? Or he sets the briefcase down, opens it, removes something, clears a space before him and begins to study, frowning. Where? Who is he? He tips back, one fist over the other in front of him, fighting the pull of the thing in his hands. Where? How much do you know about him? He kneels in front of the chair, one hand on his heart. What is he up to? He stands on the chair, fingering his neck, eyeing the ceiling. What is he thinking?

The male actor exits. A female actor enters. What does *she* do in relation to the chair? Which of the above actions would she not be likely to perform? What would she do that he would not?

Each of these actions, in relation to the absolute rock-bottom-simplest setting, represents a narrowing of possibility, an intensifying of situation, a range of emotions, and a shape of story. Each depends on the historical, geographical, psychological, and narrative potential that we have learned throughout a lifetime. Dancers have been so enamored of these possibilities that the use of chairs in dance has become a cliché. When a playwright wishes to indicate the most minimal set imaginable, she will usually indicate something like: *bare stage, three chairs.*

Try This
Write a short mime for one actor (male or female) and chair. Describe the actions in such a way as to let us know where and when the action takes place, and the emotions and the intentions of the character. The more unexpected the setting, the more specific the actions will have to be, and the more original the result.

In this simplest of examples, the playwright is relying on the body and mobility of the actor to create the world around the chair, and those represent a powerful collaborative presence. If your medium is poetry, essay, or fiction, you need to supply the whole of that vitality in words. Think of your characters as the point and center of what you write. Setting is everything else. It is the world. You need to make that world for us even as you present your characters, in order to let us care about them. Novelist and short-story writer Ron Carlson nicely catches the necessity and the priority:

> . . . if the story is about a man and a woman changing a tire on a remote highway . . . you've nonetheless got to convince me of the highway, the tire, the night, the margin, the shoulder, the gravel under their knees, the lug nuts, the difficulty getting the whole thing apart and back together, and the smells. You must do that. But that's not what you're there to deliver. That's the way you're going to seduce me . . . after you've got my shirt caught in the machine of the story and you've drawn me in, what you're really going to crush me with are these hearts and these people. Who are they?
>
> *interview with Ron Carlson by Susan McInnis*

The techniques of setting—"the machine of the story"—are those you have already encountered as image and voice. Create a place by the selection of concrete detail in your particular diction or that of your narrating character. When you focus on offering us the particularity of place, time, and weather, you will also be able to manipulate the mood, reveal the character, and advance the action.

The details you choose to evoke place will also, if you choose them well, signal the period. Albert Einstein invented the word *chronotope* to indicate the "space-time-continuum," or the fact that space and time are different manifestations of the same thing. Metaphorically this is true of imagery, and of the imagery of space and time. You will indicate something about period as well as architecture if your characters live in a *hogan, bungalow, cottage, sod house, split-level* or *high-rise.* Likewise you will tell us something about where and when we are likely to be if your heroine is carrying a *reticule, porte monnaie, poke, duffle,* or *fanny pack.*

> My father walked beside me to give me courage, his palm touching gently the back laces of my bodice. In the low-angled glare already baking the paving stones of the piazza and the top of my head, the still shadow of the Inquisitor's noose hanging above the Tor di Nona, the papal court, stretched grotesquely down the wall, its shape the outline of a tear.
> "A brief unpleasantness, Artemesia," my father said, looking straight ahead. "Just a little squeezing."
>
> *The Passion of Artemesia, Susan Vreeland*

This is a voice of relative calm in a situation of high drama. What objects, images, architecture, diction create at once the place and time in which that drama will unfold?

Try This

A memory, a poem, or a short-short story: Two characters sit down to eat. Don't tell us where or when, but let us know through the architecture, décor, implements, and food when and where the scene takes place.

Setting as a Camera

Setting often begins a piece, for the very good reason that this is the first thing we register in life. Entering a place, we take it in as a panorama (sit in a restaurant and watch people enter; their eyes go left and right, even up and down before they fix on the approaching hostess). Waking with the sense "where am I?" is notoriously disconcerting. It is no less so in literature. This does not mean setting has to be the very first thing, but it does mean that we can't go far without some sort of orientation.

As a model, consider the western, which typically begins with a *long shot* (the camera at distance) of the horsemen coming over the rise. We get a sense of the landscape, then we see the far-off arrival of the riders. Then there might be a *middle shot*, say four riders in the frame, to give us a sense of the group. Then a *close-up*: this is our hero, his head and shoulders. Screenwriters and directors are taught that they need such an "establishing shot" at the beginning of *each* scene. This parallels the action that often takes place on stage: the curtain opens on an empty room; we register it, read its clues. Someone enters. What is the relationship of this person to this space? Someone else comes in; they begin to talk and the situation is revealed.

Carl Sandburg, in *Good Morning, America*, demonstrates the long shot opening:

> In the evening there is a sunset sonata to the cities.
> There is a march of little armies to the dwindling of drums.
> The skyscrapers throw their tall lengths of walls into black bastions on the red west.

Only once this cityscape, its sound, sight, and time of day, is established, does he introduce the puny maker of these great structures, man.

The process of orientation somehow takes place in every piece that tells a story. Consider again the beginning of the Housman poem in the last chapter:

> Loveliest of trees, the cherry now
> Is hung with snow along the bough
> And stands about the woodland ride
> Wearing white for Easter tide
>
> Now of my threescore years and ten
> Twenty will not come again . . .

Notice how this poem follows both the pattern of a film opening (and also, incidentally, the "seduction" process that Ron Carlson describes). Actually, we begin with a middle shot (cherry tree, bough with the snow that tells us the season), pull back to a long shot (woodland ride), and then zoom in on the persona in relation to the scene (my whole life, and where I am in it now).

The practice of beginning with a wide angle and moving to closer focus is important for introducing us to an exotic locale:

> The thin light of the approaching daybreak always seemed to emphasize the strangeness and foreignness of our battalion's bivouac area on a country road outside Casablanca. Every morning a heavy mist covered the land just before the sun rose. Then, as the light grew, odd-looking shapes and things came slowly into view . . . .Dim, moving figures behind the mist, dressed in ghostly white, materialized as Arabs perched on the hindquarters of spindly donkeys or walking along the road.
>
> *"On the Fedala Road," John McNeel*

But this technique is no less useful to present a domestic scene:

> Throughout my childhood our family's evening meals were expeditious and purposeful, more reliable than imaginative. We were French Canadians, which meant we knew pork and maple syrup. My grandfather liked to eat salt pork,

sautéed in a frying pan, or cold, right out of the fridge, with a schmear of horse-radish, a side of string beans, and a bottle of Tadcaster ale.

"Nothing to Eat but Food: Menu as Memoir," John Dufresne

Part of the long shot is temporal here, involving the whole sweep of *throughout my childhood*. Then it places us at table (*evening meals*). The diction also begins on a wide scale, with the generalizations (*expeditious, purpose-ful*) narrowing to an ethnicity and a region (*French Canadians*) and then comically to an image (*pork and maple syrup*). The character of grandfather is introduced and the closeup begins, narrowing toward his plate while the details and diction also give us the ethnic oddities of voice and flavor: *sautéed* and *schmear* and *Tadcaster ale*.

Of course, it is equally possible, and potentially interesting, to begin with the close-up and then move to middle and long shots—an opening image, say, of a fly crawling up three-day's worth of stubble to disappear in a nostril—only then you had better pull back to show us the bad guy's whole face, and the way he is wedged in the rock, and the wide-sky emptiness of the desert he has to cross. Sandra Cisneros demonstrates the technique in the short story "Salvador Late or Early":

Salvador with eyes the color of a caterpillar, Salvador of the crooked hair and crooked teeth, Salvador whose name the teacher cannot remember, is a boy who is no one's friend, runs along somewhere in that direction where homes are the color of bad weather, lives behind a raw wood doorway, shakes the sleepy brothers awake, ties their shoes, combs their hair with water, feeds them milk and corn flakes from a tin cup in the dim dark of morning.

In this dense miniature portrait, notice how the focus begins on Salvador, then places him in a classroom, then chases him *somewhere in that direction*, so that we know the very vivid images of his poverty are the narrator's invention, impressions of the *dim dark* setting in which he lives.

Try This

Pick a scene you consider typical of your own childhood. Describe it in the pattern *long shot, middle shot, close-up*. Make sure that you begin with a wide sweep and end with a tight focus.

Pick another scene. Begin with a very small, close image. Widen the lens until you have placed that scene in the context of the entire continent.

> If the atmosphere is to be foreboding, you must forebode
> on every page. If it is to be cold, you must chill, not once
> or twice, but until your readers are shivering.
>
> *Jerome Stern*

Setting as Mood and Symbol

Each of the scenes above creates a **mood** or **atmosphere** for the events that
will unfold there—fearful in the Vreeland, majestic in the Sandburg, elegiac in
the Housman, mysterious in the McNeel, comic in the Dufresne, poignant in
the Cisneros. (Do you agree with these characterizations? Which words and
images are responsible for the mood created?)

Setting in the sense of atmosphere is one of the writer's most adaptable tools.
Mood will inevitably contain some element of time and weather—wet or dry, dark
or light, winter or summer, calm or storm, and so forth. These, together with the
textures and colors of objects, the smells of vegetation, the shapes of buildings,
are all rich with the mood from which the unique action and its meaning emerge.

> When we came back to Paris it was clear and cold and lovely. The city had accom-
> modated itself to winter, there was good wood for sale at the wood and coal place
> across our street, and there were braziers outside of many of the good cafés so that
> you could keep warm on the terraces.
>
> *A Moveable Feast, Ernest Hemingway*

Mood is a state of mind or emotion, and when we speak of setting as mood,
we are speaking of an external manifestation of the inner, the concrete expressing the abstract, the contingent standing for the essential. In this sense, setting is often to some degree **symbolic**. It may be deliberately and specifically
so, like the deranged planets that stand for the disordered society in *King Lear*,
or the subway that is "the flying underbelly of the city . . . heaped in modern
myth" in Imamu Amiri Baraka's "Dutchman," which appears at the end of
this chapter.

More often, the setting is suggestive of a larger meaning, reaching out from
a particular place and time toward a cosmic or universal reading. In this opening passage from Don DeLillo's *Underworld*, a boy is playing hookey to be at a
New York baseball stadium that becomes the symbolic locus of American longing. (Notice the close-up/long-shot/close-up/long-shot structure.)

> It's a school day, sure, but he's nowhere near the classroom. He wants to be here
> instead, standing in the shadow of this old rust-hulk of a structure, and it's hard
> to blame him . . .
>
> Longing on a large scale is what makes history. This is just a kid with a local
> yearning but he is part of an assembling crowd, anonymous thousands off the
> buses and trains, people in narrow columns tramping over the swing bridge above
> the river, and even if they are not a migration or a revolution, some vast shaking

of the soul, they bring with them the body heat of a great city and their own small reveries and desperations, the unseen something that haunts the day . . .

Our relation to place, time, and weather, like our relation to clothes and other objects, is charged with emotion more or less subtle, more or less profound. It is filled with judgment mellow or harsh. And it alters according to what happens to us. In some rooms you are always trapped; you enter them with grim purpose and escape them as soon as you can. Others invite you to settle in, to nestle or carouse. Some landscapes lift your spirits; others depress you. Cold weather gives you energy and bounce, or else it clogs your head and makes you huddle, struggling. You describe yourself as a night person or a morning person. The house you loved as a child now makes you, precisely because you were once happy there, think of loss and death.

All such emotion can be used or heightened (or invented) to dramatic effect in your writing. Nothing happens nowhere. Just as significant detail calls up a sense impression and also an abstraction, so setting and atmosphere impart both information and emotion. Just as dialogue must do more than one thing at a time, so can setting characterize, reveal mood, and signal change.

Try This

Choose one of the clichés below. Without using the words of the cliché, create a setting that expresses the scene more vividly. In memoir, poem, or fiction, make it fresh and specific again. You might begin with a single sharply focused image, then pull back to reveal the larger landscape. Use a persona or introduce a character if you choose.

- a dark and stormy night
- not a fit night out for man or beast
- raining cats and dogs
- freeze you to death
- scorching hot
- foggy as pea soup
- balmy weather
- fragrant as new-mown hay

Setting as Action

If character is the foreground, and setting the background, then there may be harmony or conflict between character and background. The persons of your poems, play, memoir, or fiction may be comfortably at ease in the world around them, or they may be uneasy, uncomfortable, full of foreboding.

I will wait for her in the yard that Maggie and I made so clean and wavy yesterday afternoon. A yard like this is more comfortable than most people know. It is not just a yard. It is like an extended living room. When the hard clay is swept clean as a floor and the fine sand around the edges lined with tiny, irregular grooves, anyone can come and sit and look up into the elm tree and wait for the breezes that never come inside the house.

"Everyday Use," Alice Walker

Here the setting is a place full of comfort and community, and any conflict comes from an outside threat to that balance—perhaps, we suspect, the "her" being waited for. But where there is menace in the setting, or conflict between the character and the setting, there is already an element of "story."

There is a city surrounded by water with watery alleys that do for streets and roads and silted up back ways that only the rats can cross. Miss your way, which is easy to do, and you may find yourself staring at a hundred eyes guarding a filthy palace of sacks and bones. Find your way, which is easy to do, and you may meet an old woman in a doorway. She will tell your fortune, depending on your face.

The Passion, Jeanette Winterson

When a character is in harmony with his surroundings, the atmosphere suggested is static, and it will take a disruption of some kind to introduce the possibility of change. But when setting and character, background and foreground, are set in opposition to each other, the process of discovery and decision is already in motion, and we know we are in for a seismic or a psychic shift.

Try This

On the left is a list of times, places, and/or weather. On the right are words that represent a mood or quality of atmosphere. Pick one item from the left and one from the right. Write a poem or paragraph in which you make the setting suggest the atmosphere. If the connection is not obvious, your piece will be more interesting. Introduce a character if you please.

- the city in the rain   sinister
- midnight on the farm   sick with love
- 1890, in the parlor   full of promise
- high noon on the river   suicidal
- a spring morning   dangerous
- in the bar, after hours   suspense
- the dusty road   happy-go-lucky
- dawn in a foreign place   lonely

One great advantage of being a writer is that you may create the world. Places and the elements have the significance and the emotional effect you give them in language. As a person you may be depressed by rain, but as an author you are free to make rain mean freshness, growth, bounty, and God. You may love winter, but you are free to make the blank white field symbolize oblivion.

As with character, the first requisite of effective setting is to know it fully, to experience it mentally, and the second is to create it through significant detail. What sort of place is this, and what are its peculiarities? What is the weather like, the light, the season, the time of day? What are the contours of the land and architecture? What are the social assumptions of the inhabitants, and how familiar and comfortable are the characters with this place and its lifestyle? These things are not less important in literature than in life, but more, since their selection inevitably takes on significance.

Try This

Take a road map, close your eyes, and point to it at random. Have a character drive or walk through the nearest town and stop in at a bank, shop, or restaurant. Study the surrounding area on the map if you like. Invent the details.

or:

Write about a place you can't return to.

More to Read

Baxter, Charles. *Burning down the House: Essays on Fiction.* Graywolf Press, 1997.

Bickham, Jack M. *Setting.* Cincinnati: Writer's Digest Books, 1994.

ESSAYS

Joan Didion
At the Dam

Since the afternoon in 1967 when I first saw Hoover Dam, its image has never been entirely absent from my inner eye. I will be talking to someone in Los Angeles, say, or New York, and suddenly the dam will materialize, its pristine concave face gleaming white against the harsh rusts and taupes and mauves of that rock canyon hundreds or thousands of miles from where I am. I will be driving down Sunset Boulevard, or about to enter a freeway, and abruptly those power transmission towers will appear before me, canted vertiginously over the tailrace. Sometimes I am confronted by the intakes and sometimes by the shadow of the heavy cable that spans the canyon and sometimes by the ominous outlets to unused spillways, black in the lunar clarity of the desert light. Quite often I hear the turbines. Frequently I wonder what is happening at the dam this instant, at this precise intersection of time and space, how much water is being released to fill downstream orders and what lights are flashing and which generators are in full use and which just spinning free.

I used to wonder what it was about the dam that made me think of it at times and in places where I once thought of the Mindanao Trench, or of the stars wheeling in their courses, or of the words *As it was in the beginning, is now and ever shall be, world without end, amen.* Dams, after all, are commonplace: we have all seen one. This particular dam had existed as an idea in the world's mind for almost forty years before I saw it. Hoover Dam, showpiece of the Boulder Canyon project, the several million tons of concrete that made the Southwest plausible, the *fait accompli* that was to convey, in the innocent time of its construction, the notion that mankind's brightest promise lay in American engineering.

Of course the dam derives some of its emotional effect from precisely that aspect, that sense of being a monument to a faith since misplaced. "They died to make the desert bloom," reads a plaque dedicated to the 96 men who died building this first of the great high dams, and in context the worn phrase touches, suggests all of that trust in harnessing resources, in the meliorative power of the dynamo, so central to the early Thirties. Boulder City, built in 1931 as the construction town for the dam, retains the ambience of a model city, a new town, a toy triangular grid of green lawns and trim bungalows, all fanning out from the Reclamation building. The bronze sculptures at the dam itself evoke muscular citizens of a tomorrow that never came, sheaves of wheat clutched heavenward, thunderbolts defied. Winged Victories guard the flagpole. The flag whips in the canyon wind. An empty Pepsi-Cola can clatters across the terrazzo. The place is perfectly frozen in time.

But history does not explain it all, does not entirely suggest what makes the dam so affecting. Nor, even, does energy, the massive involvement with power and pressure and the transparent sexual overtones to that involvement. Once when I revisited the dam I walked through it with a man from the Bureau of Reclamation. For a while we trailed behind a guided tour, and then we went on, went into parts of the dam where visitors do not generally go. Once in a while he would explain something, usually in that recondite language having to do with "peaking power," with "outages" and "dewatering," but on the whole we spent the afternoon in a world so alien, so complete and so beautiful unto itself that it was scarcely necessary to speak at all. We saw almost no one. Cranes moved above us as if under their own volition. Generators roared. Transformers hummed. The gratings on which we stood vibrated. We watched a hundred-ton steel shaft plunging down to that place where the water was. And finally we got down to that place where the water was, where the water sucked out of Lake Mead roared through thirty-foot penstocks and then into thirteen-foot penstocks and finally into the turbines themselves. "Touch it," the Reclamation man said, and I did, and for a long time I just stood there with my hands on the turbine. It was a peculiar moment, but so explicit as to suggest nothing beyond itself.

There was something beyond all that, something beyond energy, beyond history, something I could not fix in my mind. When I came up from the dam that day the wind was blowing harder, through the canyon and all across the Mojave. Later, toward Henderson and Las Vegas, there would be dust blowing, blowing past the Country-Western Casino FRI & SAT NITES and blowing past the Shrine of Our Lady of Safe Journey STOP & PRAY, but out at the dam there was no dust, only the rock and the dam and a little greasewood and a few garbage cans, their tops chained, banging against a fence. I walked across the marble star map that traces a sidereal revolution of the equinox and fixes forever, the Reclamation man had told me, for all time and for all people who can read the stars, the date the dam was dedicated. The star map was, he had said, for when we were all gone and the dam was left. I had not thought much of it when he said it, but I thought of it then, with the wind whining and the sun dropping behind a mesa with the finality of a sunset in space. Of course that was the image I had seen always, seen it without quite realizing what I saw, a dynamo finally free of man, splendid at last in its absolute isolation, transmitting power and releasing water to a world where no one is.

1970

Barry Lopez
Landscape and Narrative

One summer evening in a remote village in the Brooks Range of Alaska, I sat among a group of men listening to hunting stories about the trapping and pursuit of animals. I was particularly interested in several incidents involving wolverine, in part because a friend of mine was studying wolverine in Canada, among the Cree, but, too, because I find this animal such an intense creature. To hear about its life is to learn more about fierceness.

Wolverines are not intentionally secretive, hiding their lives from view, but they are seldom observed. The range of their known behavior is less than that of, say, bears or wolves. Still, that evening no gratuitous details were set out. This was somewhat odd, for wolverine easily excite the imagination; they can loom suddenly in the landscape with authority, with an aura larger than their compact physical dimensions, drawing one's immediate and complete attention. Wolverine also have a deserved reputation for resoluteness in the worst winters, for ferocious strength. But neither did these attributes induce the men to embellish.

I listened carefully to these stories, taking pleasure in the sharply observed detail surrounding the dramatic thread of events. The story I remember most vividly was about a man hunting a wolverine from a snow machine in the spring. He followed the animal's tracks for several miles over rolling tundra in a certain valley. Soon he caught sight ahead of a dark spot on the crest of a hill—the wolverine pausing to look back. The hunter was catching up, but each time he came over a rise the wolverine was looking back from the next rise, just out of range. The hunter topped one more rise and met the wolverine bounding toward him. Before he could pull his rifle from its scabbard the wolverine flew across the engine cowl and the windshield, hitting him square in the chest. The hunter scrambled his arms wildly, trying to get the wolverine out of his lap, and fell over as he did so. The wolverine jumped clear as the snow machine rolled over, and fixed the man with a stare. He had not bitten, not even scratched the man. Then the wolverine walked away. The man thought of reaching for the gun, but no, he did not.

The other stories were like this, not so much making a point as evoking something about contact with wild animals that would never be completely understood.

When the stories were over, four or five of us walked out of the home of our host. The surrounding land, in the persistent light of a far northern summer, was still visible for miles—the striated, pitched massifs of the Brooks Range; the shy, willow-lined banks of the John River flowing south from Anaktuvuk Pass; and the flat tundra plain, opening with great affirmation to the north. The landscape seemed alive because of the stories. It was precisely these ocherous tones, this kind of willow, exactly this austerity that had informed the wolverine narratives. I felt exhilaration, and a deeper confirmation of the stories. The mundane tasks which awaited me I anticipated now with pleasure. The stories had renewed in me a sense of the purpose of my life.

This feeling, an inexplicable renewal of enthusiasm after storytelling, is familiar to many people. It does not seem to matter greatly what the subject is, as long as the context is intimate and the story is told for its own sake, not forced to serve merely as the vehicle for an idea. The tone of the story need not be solemn. The darker aspects of life need not be ignored. But I think intimacy is indispensable—a feeling that derives from the listener's trust and a storyteller's certain knowledge of his subject and regard for his audience. This intimacy deepens if the storyteller tempers his authority with humility, or when terms of idiomatic expression, or at least the physical setting for the story, are shared.

I think of two landscapes—one outside the self, the other within. The external landscape is the one we see—not only the line and color of the land and its shading at different times of the day, but also its plants and animals in season, its weather, its geology, the record of its climate and evolution. If you walk up, say, a dry arroyo in the Sonoran Desert you will feel a mounding and rolling of sand and silt beneath your foot that is distinctive. You will anticipate the crumbling of the sedimentary earth in the arroyo bank as your hand reaches out, and in that tangible evidence you will sense a history of water in the region. Perhaps a black-throated sparrow lands in a paloverde bush—the resiliency of the twig under the bird, that precise shade of yellowish-green against the milk-blue sky, the fluttering whir of the arriving sparrow, are what I mean by "the landscape." Draw on the smell of creosote bush, or clack stones together in the dry air. Feel how light is the desiccated dropping of the kangaroo rat. Study an animal track obscured by the wind. These are all elements of the land, and what makes the landscape comprehensible are the relationships between them. One learns a landscape finally not by knowing the name or identity of everything in it, but by perceiving the relationships in it—like that between the sparrow and the twig. The difference between the relationships and the elements is the same as that between written history and a catalog of events.

The second landscape I think of is an interior one, a kind of projection within a person of a part of the exterior landscape. Relationships in the exterior landscape include those that are named and discernible, such as the nitrogen cycle, or a vertical sequence of Ordovician limestone, and others that are uncodified or ineffable, such as winter light falling on a particular kind of granite, or the effect of humidity on the frequency of a black-poll warbler's burst of song. That these relationships have purpose and order, however inscrutable they may seem to us, is a tenet of evolution. Similarly, the speculations, intuitions, and formal ideas we refer to as "mind" are a set of relationships in the interior landscape with purpose and order; some of these are obvious, many impenetrably subtle. The shape and character of these relationships in a person's thinking, I believe, are deeply influenced by where on this earth one goes, what one touches, the patterns one observes in nature—the intricate history of one's life in the land, even a life in the city, where wind, the chirp of birds, the line of a falling leaf, are known. These thoughts are arranged, further, according to the thread of one's moral, intellectual, and spiritual development. The interior landscape responds to the character and subtlety of an exterior landscape; the shape of the individual mind is affected by land as it is by genes.

In stories like those I heard at Anaktuvuk Pass about wolverine, the relationship between separate elements in the land is set forth clearly. It is put in a simple framework of sequential incidents and apposite detail. If the exterior landscape is limned well, the listener often feels that he has heard something pleasing and authentic—trustworthy. We derive this sense of confidence I think not so much from verifiable truth as from an understanding that lying has played no role in the narrative. The storyteller is obligated to engage the reader with a precise vocabulary, to set forth a coherent and dramatic rendering of incidents—and to be ingenuous.

When one hears a story one takes pleasure in it for different reasons—for the euphony of its phrases, an aspect of the plot, or because one identifies with one of the characters. With certain stories certain individuals may experience a deeper, more profound sense of well-being. This latter phenomenon, in my understanding, rests at the heart of storytelling as an elevated experience among aboriginal peoples. It results from bringing two landscapes together. The exterior landscape is organized according to principles or laws or tendencies beyond human control. It is understood to contain an integrity that is beyond human analysis and unimpeachable. Insofar as the storyteller depicts various subtle and obvious relationships in the exterior landscape accurately in his story, and insofar as he orders them along traditional lines of meaning to create the narrative, the narrative will "ring true." The listener who "takes the story to heart" will feel a pervasive sense of congruence within himself and also with the world.

Among the Navajo and, as far as I know, many other native peoples, the land is thought to exhibit a sacred order. That order is the basis of ritual. The rituals themselves reveal the power in that order. Art, architecture, vocabulary, and costume, as well as ritual, are derived from the perceived natural order of the universe—from observations and meditations on the exterior landscape. An indigenous philosophy—metaphysics, ethics, epistemology, aesthetics, and logic—may also be derived from a people's continuous attentiveness to both the obvious (scientific) and ineffable (artistic) orders of the local landscape. Each individual, further, undertakes to order his interior landscape according to the exterior landscape. To succeed in this means to achieve a balanced state of mental health.

I think of the Navajo for a specific reason. Among the various sung ceremonies of this people—Enemyway, Coyoteway, Red Antway, Uglyway—is one called Beautyway. In the Navajo view, the elements of one's interior life—one's psychological makeup and moral bearing—are subject to a persistent principle of disarray. Beautyway is, in part, a spiritual invocation of the order of the exterior universe, that irreducible, holy complexity that manifests itself as all things changing through time (a Navajo definition of beauty, hózhǫ́ǫ́). The purpose of this invocation is to recreate in the individual who is the subject of the Beautyway ceremony that same order, to make the individual again a reflection of the myriad enduring relationships of the landscape.

I believe story functions in a similar way. A story draws on relationships in the exterior landscape and projects them onto the interior landscape. The purpose of storytelling is to achieve harmony between the two landscapes, to use all the elements of story—syntax, mood, figures of speech—in a harmonious way to reproduce the harmony of the land in the individual's interior. Inherent in story is the power to reorder a state of psychological confusion through contact with the pervasive truth of those relationships we call "the land."

These thoughts, of course, are susceptible to interpretation. I am convinced, however, that these observations can be applied to the kind of prose we call nonfiction as well as to traditional narrative forms such as the novel and the short story, and to some poems. Distinctions between fiction and nonfiction are sometimes obscured by arguments over what constitutes "the truth." In the aboriginal literature I am familiar with, the first distinction made among narratives is to separate the authentic from the inauthentic. Myth, which we tend to regard as fictitious or "merely metaphorical," is as authentic, as real, as the story of the wolverine in a man's lap. (A distinction is made, of course, about the elevated nature of myth—and frequently the circumstances of myth-telling are more rigorously prescribed than those for the telling of legends or vernacular stories—but all of these narratives are rooted in the local landscape. To violate *that* connection is to call the narrative itself into question.)

The power of narrative to nurture and heal, to repair a spirit in disarray, rests on two things: the skillful invocation of unimpeachable sources and a listener's knowledge that no hypocrisy or subterfuge is involved. This last simple fact is to me one of the most imposing aspects of the Holocene history of man.

We are more accustomed now to thinking of "the truth" as something that can be explicitly stated, rather than as something that can be evoked in a metaphorical way outside science and Occidental culture. Neither can truth be reduced to aphorism or formulas. It is something alive and unpronounceable. Story creates an atmosphere in which it becomes discernable as a pattern. For a storyteller to insist on relationships that do not exist is to lie. Lying is the opposite of story. (I do not mean to confuse ignorance with deception, or to imply that a storyteller can perceive all that is inherent in the land. Every storyteller falls short of a perfect limning of the landscape—perception and language both fail. But to make up something that is not there, something which can never be corroborated in the land, to knowingly set forth a false relationship, is to be lying, no longer telling a story.)

Because of the intricate, complex nature of the land, it is not always possible for a storyteller to grasp what is contained in a story. The intent of the storyteller, then, must be to evoke, honestly, some single aspect of all that the land contains. The storyteller knows that because different individuals grasp the story at different levels, the focus of his regard for truth must be at the primary one—with who was there, what happened, when, where, and why things occurred. The story will then possess similar truth at other levels—the integrity inherent at the primary level of meaning will be conveyed everywhere else. As long as the storyteller carefully describes the order before him, and uses his storytelling skill to heighten and emphasize certain relationships, it is even possible for the story to be more successful than the storyteller himself is able to imagine.

I would like to make a final point about the wolverine stories I heard at Anaktuvuk Pass. I wrote down the details afterward, concentrating especially on aspects of the biology and ecology of the animals. I sent the information on to my friend living with the Cree. When, many months later, I saw him, I asked whether the Cree had enjoyed these insights of the Nunamiut into the nature of the wolverine. What had they said?

"You know," he told me, "how they are. They said, 'That could happen.'"

In those uncomplicated words the Cree declared their own knowledge of the wolverine. They acknowledged that although they themselves had never seen the things the Nunamiut spoke of, they accepted them as accurate observations, because they did not consider story a context for misrepresentation. They also preserved their own dignity by not overstating their confidence in the Nunamiut, a distant and unknown people.

Whenever I think of this courtesy on the part of the Cree I think of the dignity that is ours when we cease to demand the truth and realize that the best we can have of those substantial truths that guide our lives is metaphorical—a story. And the most of it we are likely to discern comes only when we accord one another the respect the Cree showed the Nunamiut. Beyond this—that the interior landscape is a metaphorical representation of the exterior landscape, that the truth reveals itself most fully not in dogma but in the paradox, irony, and contradictions that distinguish compelling narratives—beyond this there are only failures of imagination: reductionism in science; fundamentalism in religion; fascism in politics.

Our national literatures should be important to us insofar as they sustain us with illumination and heal us. They can always do that so long as they are written with respect for both the source and the reader, and with an understanding of why the human heart and the land have been brought together so regularly in human history.

FICTION

Charles Baxter

Snow

Twelve years old, and I was so bored I was combing my hair just for the hell
of it. This particular Saturday afternoon, time was stretching out unpleas-
antly in front of me. I held the comb under the tap and then stared into the
bathroom mirror as I raked the wave at the front of my scalp upward so
that it would look casual and sharp and perfect. For inspiration I had my
transistor radio, balanced on the doorknob, tuned to an AM Top Forty station. But the music was making me jumpy, and instead of looking casual
my hair, soaking wet, had the metallic curve of the rear fins of a De Soto. I
looked aerodynamic but not handsome. I dropped the comb into the sink and
went down the hallway to my brother's room.

　　Ben was sitting at his desk, crumpling up papers and tossing them into
a wastebasket near the window. He was a great shot, particularly when he
was throwing away his homework. His stainless-steel sword, a souvenir of
military school, was leaning against the bookcase, and I could see my pen-
cil-thin reflection in it as I stood in his doorway. "Did you hear about the
car?" Ben asked, not bothering to look at me. He was gazing through his window at Five Oaks Lake.

　　"What car?"

　　"The car that went through the ice two nights ago. Thursday. Look.
You can see the pressure ridge near Eagle Island."

　　I couldn't see any pressure ridge; it was too far away. Cars belonging
to ice fishermen were always breaking through the ice, but swallowing up a
car was a slow process in January, though not in March or April, and the
drivers usually got out safely. The clear lake ice reflected perfectly the flat
gray sky this drought winter, and we could still see the spiky brown grass
on our back lawn. It crackled and crunched whenever I walked on it.

"I don't see it," I said. "I can't see the hole. Where did you hear about this car? Did Pop tell you?"

"No," Ben said. "Other sources." Ben's sources, his network of friends and enemies, were always calling him on the telephone to tell him things. He basked in information. Now he gave me a quick glance. "Holy smoke," he said. "What did you do to your hair?"

"Nothing," I said. "I was just combing it."

"You look like that guy," he said. "The one in the movies."

"Which guy?"

"That Harvey guy."

"Jimmy Stewart?"

"Of course not," he said. "You know the one I mean. Everybody knows that guy. The Harvey guy." When I looked blank, he said, "Never mind. Let's go down to the lake and look at the car. You'd better tell them we're going." He gestured toward the other end of the house.

In the kitchen I informed my parents that I was headed somewhere with my brother, and my mother, chopping carrots for one of her stews, looked up at me and my hair. "Be back by five," she said. "Where did you say you were off to?"

"We're driving to Navarre," I said. "Ben has to get his skates sharpened."

My stepfather's eyebrows started to go up; he exchanged a glance with my mother—the usual pantomime of skepticism. I turned around and ran out of the kitchen before they could stop me. I put on my boots, overcoat, and gloves, and hurried outside to my brother's car, a 1952 Rocket 88. He was already inside. The motor roared.

The interior of the car smelled of gum, cigarettes, wet wool, analgesic balm, and after-shave. "What'd you tell them?" my brother asked.

"I said you were going to Navarre to get your skates sharpened."

He put the car into first gear, then sighed. "Why'd you do that? I have to explain everything to you. Number one: my skates aren't in the car. What if they ask to see them when we get home? I don't have them. That's a problem, isn't it? Number two: when you lie about being somewhere, you make sure you have a friend who's there who can say you *were* there, even if you weren't. Unfortunately, we don't have any friends in Navarre."

"Then we're safe," I said. "No one will say we *weren't* there."

He shook his head. Then he took off his glasses and examined them as if my odd ideas were visible right there on the frames. I was just doing my job, being his private fool, but I knew he liked me and liked to have me around. My unworldliness amused him; it gave him a chance to lecture me. But now, tired of wasting words on me, he turned on the radio. Pulling out onto the highway, he steered the car in his customary way. He had explained to me that only very old or very sick people actually grip steering wheels. You didn't have to hold the wheel to drive a car. Resting your arm over the top of the wheel gave a better appearance. You dangled your hand down, preferably with a cigarette in it, so that the car, the entire car, responded to the mere pressure of your wrist.

"Hey," I said. "Where are we going? This isn't the way to the lake."

"We're not going there first. We're going there second."

"Where are we going first?"

"We're going to Five Oaks. We're going to get Stephanie. Then we'll see the car."

"How come we're getting her?"

"Because she wants to see it. She's never seen a car underneath the ice before. She'll be impressed."

"Does she know we're coming?"

He gave me that look again. "What do they teach you at that school you go to? Of course she knows. We have a date."

"A date? It's three o'clock in the afternoon," I said. "You can't have a date at three in the afternoon. Besides, I'm along."

"Don't argue," Ben said. "Pay attention."

By the time we reached Five Oaks, the heater in my brother's car was blowing out warm air in tentative gusts. If we were going to get Stephanie, his current girlfriend, it was fine with me. I liked her smile—she had an overbite, the same as I did, but she didn't seem self-conscious about it—and I liked the way she shut her eyes when she laughed. She had listened to my crystal radio set and admired my collection of igneous rocks on one of her two visits to our house. My brother liked to bring his girlfriends over to our house because the house was old and large and, my brother said, they would be impressed by the empty rooms and the long hallways and the laundry chutes that dropped down into nowhere. They'd be snowed. Snowing girls was something I knew better than to ask my brother about. You had to learn about it by watching and listening. That's why he had brought me along.

Ben parked outside Stephanie's house and told me to wait in the car. I had nothing to do but look at houses and telephone poles. Stephanie's front-porch swing had rusted chains, and the paint around her house seemed to have blistered in cobweb patterns. One drab lamp with a low-wattage bulb was on near an upstairs window. I could see the lampshade: birds—I couldn't tell what kind—had been painted on it. I adjusted the dashboard clock. It didn't run, but I liked to have it seem accurate. My brother had said that anyone who invented a clock that would really work in a car would become a multimillionaire. Clocks in cars never work, he said, because the main-springs can't stand the shock of potholes. I checked my wristwatch and yawned. The inside of the front window began to frost over with my breath. I decided that when I grew up I would invent a new kind of timepiece for cars, without springs or gears. At three-twenty I adjusted the clock again. One minute later, my brother came out of the house with Stephanie. She saw me in the car, and she smiled.

I opened the door and got out. "Hi, Steph," I said. "I'll get in the back-seat."

"That's okay, Russell," she said, smiling, showing her overbite. "Sit up in front with us."

"Really?"

She nodded. "Yeah. Keep us warm."

She scuttled in next to my brother, and I squeezed in on her right side, with my shoulder against the door. A soon as the car started, she and my brother began to hold hands: he steered with his left wrist over the steering wheel, and she held his right hand. I watched all this, and Stephanie noticed me watching. "Do you want one?" she asked me.

"What?"

"A hand." She gazed at me, perfectly serious. "My other hand."

"Sure." I said.

"Well, take my glove off," she said. "I can't do it by myself." My brother started chuckling, but she stopped him with a look. I took Stephanie's wrist in my left hand and removed her glove, finger by finger. I hadn't held hands with anyone since second grade. Her hand was not much larger than mine, but holding it gave me an odd sensation, because it was a woman's hand, and where my fingers were bony, hers were soft. She was wearing a bright-green cap, and when I glanced up at it she said, "I like your hair, Russell. It's kind of slummy. You're getting to look dangerous. Is there any gum?"

I figured she meant in the car. "There's some up there on the dash-board." Ben said. His car always had gum in it. It was a museum of gum. The ashtrays were full of cigarette butts and gum, mixed together, and the floor was flecked silver from the foil wrappers.

"I can't reach it," Stephanie said. "You two have both my hands tied down."

"Okay," I said. I reached up with my free hand and took a piece of gum and unwrapped it. The gum was light pink, a sunburn color.

"Now what?" I asked.

"What do you think?" She looked down at me, smiled again, then opened her mouth. I suddenly felt shy. "Come on, Russell," she said. "Haven't you ever given gum to a girl before?" I raised my hand with the gum in it. She kept her eyes open and on me. I reached forward, and just as I got the gum close to her mouth she opened wider, and I slid the gum in over her tongue without even brushing against her lipstick. She closed and began chewing.

"Thank you," she said. Stephanie and my brother nudged each other. Then they broke out in short quick laughs—vacation laughter. I knew that what had happened hinged on my ignorance, but that I wasn't exactly the butt of the joke and could laugh, too, if I wanted. The sky had turned darker, and I wondered whether, if I was still alive fifty years from now, I would remember any of this. I saw an old house on the side of the highway with a cracked upstairs window, and I thought, that's what I'll remember from this whole day when I'm old—that one cracked window.

Stephanie was looking out at the dry winter fields and suddenly said, "The state of Michigan. You know who this state is for? You know who's really happy in this state?"

"No," I said. "Who?"

"Chickens and squirrels," she said. "They love it here."

My brother parked the car on the driveway down by our dock, and we walked out onto the ice on the bay. Stephanie was stepping awkwardly, a high-center-of-gravity shuffle. "Is it safe?" she asked.

"Sure, it's safe," my brother said. "Look." He began to jump up and down. Ben was heavy enough to be a tackle on his high-school football team, and sounds of ice cracking reverberated all through the bay and beyond into the center of the lake, a deep echo. Already, four ice fishermen's houses had been set up on the ice two hundred feet out—four brightly painted shacks, male hideaways—and I could see tire tracks over the thin layer of sprinkled snow. "Clear the snow and look down into it," he said.

After lowering herself to her knees, Stephanie dusted the snow away. She held her hands to the side of her head and looked. "It's real thick," she said. "Looks a foot thick. How come a car went through?"

"It went down in a channel." Ben said, walking ahead of us and calling backward so that his voice seemed to drift in and out of the wind. "It went over a pressure ridge, and that's all she wrote."

"Did anyone drown?"

He didn't answer. She ran ahead to catch up to him, slipping, losing her balance, then recovering it. In fact I knew that no one had drowned. My stepfather had told me that the man driving the car had somehow—I wasn't sure how a person did this—pulled himself out through the window. Apparently the front end dropped through the ice first, but the car had stayed up for a few minutes before it gradually eased itself into the lake. The last two nights had been very cold, with lows around fifteen below zero, and by now the hole the car had gone through had iced over.

Both my brother and Stephanie were quite far ahead of me, and I could see them clutching at each other, Stephanie leaning against him, and my brother trying out his military-school peacock walk. I attempted this walk for a moment, then thought better of it. The late-afternoon January light was getting very raw: the sun came out for a few seconds, lighting and coloring what there was, then disappeared again, closing up and leaving us in a kind of sour grayness. I wondered if my brother and Stephanie actually liked each other or whether they were friends because they had to be.

I ran to catch up to them. "We should have brought our skates," I said, but they weren't listening to me. Ben was pointing at some clear ice, and Stephanie was nodding.

"Quiet down," my brother said. "Quiet down and listen."

All three of us stood still. Some cloud or other was beginning to drop snow on us, and from the ice underneath our feet we heard a continual chinging and barking as the ice slowly shifted.

"This is exciting," Stephanie said.

My brother nodded, but instead of looking at her he turned slightly to glance at me. Our eyes met, and he smiled.

"It's over there," he said, after a moment. The index finger of his black leather glove pointed toward a spot in the channel between Eagle Island and Crane Island where the ice was ridged and unnaturally clear. "Come on," he said.

We walked. I was ready at any moment to throw myself flat if the ice broke beneath me. I was a good swimmer—Ben had taught me—but I wasn't sure how well I would swim wearing all my clothes. I was absorbent and would probably sink headfirst, like that car.

"Get down," my brother said.

We watched him lowering himself to his hands and knees, and we followed. This was probably something he had learned in military school, this crawling. "We're ambushing this car," Stephanie said, creeping in front of me.

"There it is," he said. He pointed down.

This new ice was so smooth that it reminded me of the thick glass in the Shedd Aquarium, in Chicago. But instead of seeing a loggerhead turtle or a barracuda I looked through the ice and saw this abandoned car, this two-door Impala. It was wonderful to see—white-painted steel filtered by ice and lake water—and I wanted to laugh out of sheer happiness at the craziness of it. Dimly lit but still visible through the murk, it sat down there, its huge trunk and the sloping fins just a bit green in the algae-colored light. This is a joke, I thought, a practical joke meant to confuse the fish. I could see the car well enough to notice its radio-antenna, and the windshield wipers halfway up the front window, and I could see the chrome of the front grille reflecting the dull light that ebbed down to it from where we were lying on our stomachs, ten feet above it.

"That is one unhappy automobile," Stephanie said. "Did anyone get caught inside?"

"No," I said, because no one had, and then my brother said, "Maybe."

I looked at him quickly. As usual, he wasn't looking back at me. "They aren't sure yet," he said. "They won't be able to tell until they bring the tow truck out here and pull it up."

Stephanie said, "Well, either they know or they don't. Someone's down there or not, right?"

Ben shook his head. "Maybe they don't know. Maybe there's a dead body in the backseat of that car. Or in the trunk."

"Oh, no," she said. She began to edge backward.

"I was just fooling you," my brother said. "There's nobody down there."

"What?" She was behind the area where the ice was smooth, and she stood up.

"I was just teasing you," Ben said. "The guy that was in the car got out. He got out through the window."

"Why did you lie to me?" Stephanie asked. Her arms were crossed in front of her chest.

"I just wanted to give you a thrill," he said. He stood up and walked over to where she was standing. He put his arm around her.

"I don't mind normal," she said. "Something could be normal and I'd like that, too." She glanced at me. Then she whispered into my brother's ear for about fifteen seconds, which is a long time if you're watching. Ben nodded and bent forward and whispered something in return, but I swiveled and looked around the bay at all the houses on the shore, and the old amusement park in the distance. Lights were beginning to go on, and, as if that weren't enough, it was snowing. As far as I was concerned, all those houses were guilty, both the houses and the people in them. The whole state of Michigan was guilty—all the adults, anyway—and I wanted to see them locked up.

"Wait here," my brother said. He turned and went quickly off toward the shore of the bay.

"Where's he going?" I asked.

He's going to get his car," she said.

"What for?"

"He's going to bring it out on the ice. Then he's going to drive me home across the lake."

"That's really stupid!" I said. "That's really one of the dumbest things I ever heard! You'll go through the ice, just like that car down there did."

"No, we won't," she said. "I know we won't."

"How do you know?"

"Your brother understands this lake," she said. "He knows where the pressure ridges are and everything. He just *knows*, Russell. You have to trust him. And he can always get off the ice if he thinks it's not safe. He can always find a road."

"Well, I'm not going with you," I said. She nodded. I looked at her, and

I wondered if she might be crazed with the bad judgment my parents had told me all teenagers had. Bad judgment of this kind was starting to interest me; it was a powerful antidote for boredom, which seemed worse.

"You don't want to come?"

"No," I said. "I'll walk home." I gazed up the hill, and in the distance I could see the lights of our house, a twenty-minute walk across the bay.

"Okay," Stephanie said. "I didn't think you'd want to come along." We waited. "Russell, do you think your brother is interested in me?"

"I guess so," I said. I wasn't sure what she meant by "interested." Anybody interested him, up to a point. "He says he likes you."

"That's funny, because I feel like something in the Lost and Found," she said, scratching her boot into the ice. "You know, one of those gloves that don't match anything." She put her hand on my shoulder. "One glove. One left-handed glove, with the thumb missing."

I could hear Ben's car starting, and then I saw it heading down Gallagher's boat landing. I was glad he was driving out toward us, because I didn't want to talk to her this way anymore.

Stephanie was now watching my brother's car. His headlights were on. It was odd to see a car with headlights on out on the ice, where there was no road. I saw my brother accelerate and fishtail the car, then slam on the brakes and do a 360-degree spin. He floored it, revving the back wheels, which made a high, whining sound on the ice, like a buzz saw working through wood. He was having a thrill and soon would give Stephanie another thrill by driving her home across ice that might break at any time. Thrills did it, whatever it was. Thrills led to other thrills.

"Would you look at that," I said.

She turned. After a moment she made a little sound in her throat. I remember that sound. When I see her now, she still makes it—a sign of impatience or worry. After all, she didn't go through the ice in my brother's car on the way home. She and my brother didn't drown, together or separately. Stephanie had two marriages and several children. Recently, she and her second husband adopted a Korean baby. She has the complex dignity of many small-town people who do not resort to alcohol until well after night has fallen. She continues to live in Five Oaks, Michigan, and she works behind the counter at the post office, where I buy stamps from her and gossip, holding up the line, trying to make her smile. She still has an overbite and she still laughs easily, despite the moody expression that comes over her when she relaxes. She has moved back to the same house she grew up in. Even now the exterior paint on that house blisters in cobweb patterns. I keep track of her. She and my brother certainly didn't get married; in fact, they broke up a few weeks after seeing the Chevrolet under ice.

"What are we doing out here?" Stephanie asked. I shook my head.

"In the middle of winter, out here on this stupid lake? I'll tell you, Russell, I sure don't know. But I do know that your brother doesn't notice me enough, and I can't love him unless he notices me. You know your brother. You know what he pays attention to. What do I have to do to get him to notice me?"

I was twelve years old. I said, "Take off your shoes."

She stood there, thinking about what I had said, and then, quietly, she bent down and took off her boots, and, putting her hand on my shoulder to balance herself, she took off her brown loafers and her white socks. She stood there in front of me with her bare feet on the ice. I saw in the grayish January light that her toenails were painted. Bare feet with painted toenails on the ice—this was a desperate and beautiful sight, and I shivered and felt my fingers curling inside my gloves.

"How does it feel?" I asked.

"You'll know," she said. "You'll know in a few years."

My brother drove up close to us. He rolled down his window and opened the passenger-side door. He didn't say anything. I watched Stephanie get into the car, carrying her shoes and socks and boots, and then I waved goodbye to them before turning to walk back to our house. I heard the car heading north across the ice. My brother would be looking at Stephanie's bare feet on the floor of his car. He would probably not be saying anything just now.

When I reached our front lawn, I stood out in the dark and looked in through the kitchen window. My mother and stepfather were sitting at the kitchen counter; I couldn't be sure if they were speaking to each other, but then I saw my mother raise her arm in one of her can-you-believe-this gestures. I didn't want to go inside. I wanted to feel cold, so cold that the cold itself became permanently interesting. I took off my overcoat and my gloves. Tilting my head back, I felt some snow fall onto my face. I thought of the word "exposure" and of how once or twice a year deer hunters in the Upper Peninsula died of it, and I bent down and stuck my hand into the snow and frozen grass and held it there. The cold rose from my hand to my elbow, and when I had counted to forty and couldn't stand another second of it, I picked up my coat and gloves and walked into the bright heat of the front hallway.

Try This

Write a scene from the point of view of a young character in a setting that is uncomfortable, threatening, dangerous, or fearful. Create the sense of conflict with the surroundings through at least three senses. Use elements of weather, time of day, and time of year as well as place.

POEMS

Joy Harjo

Deer Ghost

1

I hear a deer outside; her glass voice of the invisible
calls to my heart to stand up and weep in this fragile city.
The season changed once more, as if my childhood
was forced from me, stolen during the dream of the lion
fleeing the old-style houses my people used to make of mud
and straw to mother the source of burning. The skeleton
of stars encircling this misty world stares through the roof;
there is no hiding any more, and mystery is a skin that will never
quite fit. This is a night ghosts wander, and in this place
they are as nameless as the nightmare the muscles in my
left hand remember.

2

I have failed once more and let the fire go out. I misunderstood
 and left my world on your musk angel wings. Your fire scorched
my lips, but it was sweet, a bitter poetry. I can taste you
now as I squat on the earth floor of this home I abandoned
for you. On this street named for a warrior people, a street
named after bravery, I am lighting the fire that crawls from my spine
to the gods with a coal from my sister's flame. This is what names
me in the ways of my people, who have called me back.
The deer knows what it is doing wandering the streets of this
city; it has never forgotten the songs.

3

I don't care what you say. The deer is no imaginary tale
I have created to fill this house because you left me.
There is more to this world than I have ever let on
to you, or anyone.

Heather McHugh

Earthmoving Malediction

Bulldoze the bed where we made love,
bulldoze the goddamn room.
Let rubble be our evidence
and wreck our home.

I can't give touching up
by inches, can't give beating up
by heart. So set the comforter
on fire, and turn the dirt

to some advantage—palaces of pigweed,
treasuries of turd. The fist
will vindicate the hand,
and tooth and nail

refuse to burn, and I
must not look back, as Mrs. Lot
was named for such a little—
something in a cemetery,

or a man. Bulldoze the coupled
ploys away, the cute exclusives
in the social mall. We dwell

on earth, where beds
are brown, where swoops
are fell. Bulldoze

the pearly gates:
if paradise comes down
there is no hell.

Rita Dove

Vacation

I love the hour before takeoff,
that stretch of no time, no home
but the gray vinyl seats linked like
unfolding paper dolls. Soon we shall
be summoned to the gate, soon enough
there'll be the clumsy procedure of row numbers
and perforated stubs—but for now
I can look at these ragtag nuclear families
with their cooing and bickering
or the heeled bachelorette trying
to ignore a baby's wail and the baby's
exhausted mother waiting to be called up early
while the athlete, one monstrous hand
asleep on his duffel bag, listens,
perched like a seal trained for the plunge.
Even the lone executive
who has wandered this far into summer
with his lasered itinerary, briefcase
knocking his knees—even he
has worked for the pleasure of bearing
no more than a scrap of himself
into this hall. He'll dine out, she'll sleep late,
they'll let the sun burn them happy all morning
—a little hope, a little whimsy
before the loudspeaker blurts
and we leap up to become
Flight 828, now boarding at gate 17.

Yusef Komunyakaa

Nude Interrogation

Did you kill anyone over there? Angela shifts her gaze from the Janis Joplin poster to the Jimi Hendrix, lifting the pale muslin blouse over her head. The blacklight deepens the blues when the needle drops into the first groove of "All

Along the Watchtower." I don't want to look at the floor. *Did you kill anyone?* *Did you dig a hole, crawl inside, and wait for your target?* Her miniskirt drops into a rainbow at her feet. Sandalwood incense hangs a slow comet of perfume over the room. I shake my head. She unhooks her bra and flings it against a bookcase made of plywood and cinderblocks. *Did you use an M-16, a handgrenade, a bayonet, or your own two strong hands, both thumbs pressed against that little bird in the throat?* She stands with her left thumb hooked into the elastic of her sky-blue panties. When she flicks off the blacklight, snowy hills rush up to the windows. *Did you kill anyone over there? Are you right-handed or left-handed? Did you drop your gun afterwards? Did you kneel beside the corpse and turn it over?* She's nude against the falling snow. *Yes.* The record spins like a bull's-eye on the far wall of Xanadu. *Yes, I say. I was scared of the silence. The night was too big. And afterwards, I couldn't stop looking up at the sky.*

George MacBeth
Advice From the Extractor

Good morning.

Lot to be said for getting it all
Out of your system, eh? Plenty of bile here.
Spit in the bowl.
I'd say you've been bad-mouthing
Some woman—as our American
Cousins put it—through too many poems.
Clean up your act. Lie

Back in the chair and look directly
Into the light. There. Is that
Better? See things
More clearly now, do we? My
Own experience, having
Had, as one might say, the sort of
Unassimilated fillings

We're talking here, is that only
Time, the great healer,
Allows a proper connoisseurship
Of spitefulness. Better wait.
Wash your mouth out. Those
Fragments of bone tissue
Get under the tongue. Later on

You can bitch at will
About their inadequacies, whoever
They are. For the present
I'd go easy. Watch
Your bite. Lay off the excess sugar
As well as corrosives. It won't
Help. You'll

Find you're better off
With a bitter detachment. Use
A good rinse, a
Scouring powder on Sundays. Come back
In a month. We'll
take another look. Maybe
Compare notes. Get together for a gargle.

Goodbye.

Try This

Below are some themes to do with setting, suggested by the preceding poems. Pick one, remember or imagine the place it refers to, and brainstorm a list of images. Arrange them into lines. Use the name of the place as your title, perhaps?

- ghosts of the past live here
- I will destroy this place
- this is limbo
- history happened there
- facing the institution

DRAMA

Imamu Amiri Baraka

Dutchman

CHARACTERS

Clay, *twenty-year-old Negro*
Lula, *thirty-year-old white woman*
Riders of Coach, *white and black*
Young Negro
Conductor

SCENE: *In the flying underbelly of the city. Steaming hot, and summer on top, outside. Underground. The subway heaped in modern myth.*

Opening scene is a man sitting in a subway seat, holding a magazine but looking vacantly just above its wilting pages. Occasionally he looks blankly toward the window on his right. Dim lights and darkness whistling by against the glass. (Or paste the lights, as admitted props, right on the subway windows. Have them move, even dim and flicker. But give the sense of speed. Also stations, whether the train is stopped or the glitter and activity of these stations merely flashes by the windows.)

The man is sitting alone. That is, only his seat is visible, though the rest of the car is outfitted as a complete subway car. But only his seat is shown. There might be, for a time, as the play begins, a loud scream of the actual train. And it can recur throughout the play, or continue on a lower key once the dialogue starts.

The train slows after a time, pulling to a brief stop at one of the stations. The man looks idly up, until he sees a woman's face staring at him through the window; when it realizes that the man has noticed the face, it begins very premeditatedly to smile. The man smiles too, for a moment, without a trace of self-consciousness. Almost an instinctive though undesirable response. Then a kind of awkwardness or embarrassment sets in, and the man makes to look away, is further embarrassed, so he brings back his eyes to where the face was, but by now the train is moving again, and the face would seem to be left behind by the way the man turns his head to look back through the other windows at the slowly fading platform. He smiles then; more comfortably confident, hoping perhaps that his memory of this brief encounter will be pleasant. And then he is idle again.

Scene 1

(Train roars. Lights flash outside the windows.

Lula enters from the rear of the car in bright, skimpy summer clothes and sandals. She carries a net bag full of paper books, fruit, and other anonymous articles. She is wearing sunglasses, which she pushes up on on her forehead from time to time. Lula is a tall, slender, beautiful woman with long red hair hanging straight down her back, wearing only loud lipstick in somebody's good taste. She is eating an apple, very daintily. Coming down the car toward Clay.

She stops beside Clay's seat and hangs languidly from the strap, still managing to eat the apple. It is apparent that she is going to sit in the seat next to Clay, and that she is only waiting for him to notice her before she sits.

Clay sits as before, looking just beyond his magazine, now and again pulling the magazine slowly back and forth in front of his face in a hopeless effort to fan himself. Then he sees the woman hanging there beside him and he looks up into her face, smiling quizzically.)

LULA: Hello.

CLAY: Uh, hi're you?

LULA: I'm going to sit down . . . O.K.?

CLAY: Sure.

LULA: *(swings down onto the seat, pushing her legs straight out as if she is very weary)* Oooof! Too much weight.

CLAY: Ha, doesn't look like much to me.

(Leaning back against the window, a little surprised and maybe stiff.)

LULA: It's so anyway.

(And she moves her toes in the sandals, then pulls her right leg up on the left knee, better to inspect the bottoms of the sandals and the back of her heel. She appears for a second not to notice that Clay is sitting next to her or that she has spoken to him just a second before. Clay looks at the magazine, then out the black window. As he does this, she turns very quickly toward him.)

Weren't you staring at me through the window?

CLAY: *(wheeling around and very much stiffened)*: What?

LULA: Weren't you staring at me through the window? At the last stop?

CLAY: Staring at you? What do you mean?

LULA: Don't you know what staring means?

CLAY: I saw you through the window . . . if that's what it means. I don't know if I was staring. Seems to me you were staring through the window at me.

LULA: I was. But only after I'd turned around and saw you staring through the window down in the vicinity of my ass and legs.

CLAY: Really?

LULA: Really. I guess you were just taking those idle potshots. Nothing else to do. Run your mind over people's flesh.

CLAY: Oh boy. Wow, now I admit I was looking in your direction. But the rest of that weight is yours.

LULA: I suppose.

CLAY: Staring through train windows is weird business. Much weirder than staring very sedately at abstract asses.

LULA: That's why I came looking through the window . . . so you'd have more than that to go on. I even smiled at you.

CLAY: That's right.

LULA: I even got into this train, going some other way than mine. Walked down the aisle . . . searching you out.

CLAY: Really? That's pretty funny.

LULA: That's pretty funny . . . .God, you're dull.

CLAY: Well, I'm sorry, lady, but I really wasn't prepared for party talk.

LULA: No, you're not. What are you prepared for?

(Wrapping the apple core in a Kleenex and dropping it on the floor.)

CLAY *(takes her conversation as pure sex talk. He turns to confront her squarely with this idea):* I'm prepared for anything. How about you?

LULA *(laughing loudly and cutting it off abruptly):* What do you think you're doing?

CLAY: What?

LULA: You think I want to pick you up, get you to take me somewhere and screw me, huh?

CLAY: Is that the way I look?

LULA: You look like you been trying to grow a beard. That's exactly what you look like. You look like you live in New Jersey with your parents and are trying to grow a beard. That's what. You look like you've been reading Chinese poetry and drinking lukewarm sugarless tea. *(Laughs, uncrossing and recrossing her legs.)* You look like death eating a soda cracker.

CLAY *(cocking his head from one side to the other, embarrassed and trying to make some comeback, but also intrigued by what the woman is saying . . . even the sharp city coarseness of her voice, which is still a kind of gentle sidewalk throb):* Really? I look like all that?

LULA: Not all of it.

(she feints a seriousness to cover an actual somber tone.)

I lie a lot. *(Smiling.)* It helps me control the world.

CLAY *(relieved and laughing louder than the humor):* Yeah, I bet.

LULA: But it's true, most of it, right? Jersey? Your bumpy neck?

CLAY: How'd you know all that? Huh? Really, I mean about Jersey . . . and even the beard. I met you before? You know Warren Enright?

LULA: You tried to make it with your sister when you were ten. (Clay *leans back hard against the back of the seat, his eyes opening now, still trying to look amused.)* But I succeeded a few weeks ago. *(She starts to laugh again.)*

CLAY: What're you talking about? Warren tell you that? You're a friend of Georgia's?

LULA: I told you I lie. I don't know your sister. I don't know Warren Enright.

CLAY: You mean you're just picking up these things out of the air?

LULA: Is Warren Enright a tall skinny black black boy with a phony English accent?

CLAY: I figured you knew him.

LULA: But I don't. I just figured you would know somebody like that. *(Laughs.)*

CLAY: Yeah, yeah.

LULA: You're probably on your way to his house now.

CLAY: That's right.

LULA *(putting her hand on* Clay's *closest knee, drawing it from the knee up to the thigh's hinge, then removing it, watching his face very closely, and continuing to laugh, perhaps more gently than before):* Dull, dull, dull. I bet you think I'm exciting.

CLAY: You're O.K.

LULA: Am I exciting you now?

CLAY: Right. That's not what's supposed to happen?

LULA: How do I know? *(She returns her hand, without moving it, then takes it away and plunges it in her bag to draw out an apple.)* You want this?

CLAY: Sure.

LULA *(she gets one out of the bag for herself):* Eating apples together is always the first step. Or walking up uninhabited Seventh Avenue in the twenties on weekends. *(Bites and giggles, glancing at* Clay *and speaking in loose sing-song.)* Can get you involved . . . boy! Get us involved. Um-huh. *(Mock seriousness.)* Would you like to get involved with me, Mister Man?

CLAY *(trying to be as flippant as* Lula, *whacking happily at the apple):* Sure. Why not? A beautiful woman like you. Huh, I'd be a fool not to.

LULA: And I bet you're sure you know what you're talking about. *(Taking him a little roughly by the wrist, so he cannot eat the apple, then shaking the wrist.)* I bet you're sure of almost everything anybody ever asked you . . . right? *(Shakes his wrist harder.)* Right?

CLAY: Yeah, right . . . . Wow, you're pretty strong, you know? Whatta you, a lady wrestler or something?

LULA What's wrong with lady wrestlers? And don't answer because you never knew any. Huh. *(Cynically.)* That's for sure. They don't have any lady wrestlers in that part of Jersey. That's for sure.

CLAY: Hey, you still haven't told me how you know so much about me.

LULA: I told you I didn't know anything about *you* . . . you're a well-known type.

CLAY: Really?

LULA: Or at least I know the type very well. And your skinny English friend too.

CLAY: Anonymously?

LULA *(settles back in seat, single-mindedly finishing her apple and humming snatches of rhythm and blues song):* What?

CLAY: Without knowing us specifically?

LULA: Oh boy. *(Looking quickly at* Clay.*)* What a face. You know, you could be a handsome man.

CLAY: I can't argue with you.

LULA *(vague, off-center response):* What?

CLAY *(raising his voice, thinking the train noise has drowned part of his sentence):* I can't argue with you.

LULA: My hair is turning gray. A gray hair for each year and type I've come through.

CLAY: Why do you want to sound so old?

LULA: But it's always gentle when it starts. *(Attention drifting.)* Hugged against tenements, day or night.

CLAY: What?

LULA *(refocusing):* Hey, why don't you take me to that party you're going to?

CLAY: You must be a friend of Warren's to know about the party.

LULA: Wouldn't you like to take me to the party? *(Imitates clinging vine.)* Oh, come on, ask me to your party.

CLAY: Of course I'll ask you to come with me to the party. And I'll bet you're a friend of Warren's.

LULA: Why not be a friend of Warren's? Why not? *(Taking his arm.)* Have you asked me yet?

CLAY: How can I ask you when I don't know your name?

LULA: Are you talking to my name?

CLAY: What is it, a secret?

LULA: I'm Lena the Hyena.

CLAY: The famous woman poet?

LULA: Poetess! The same!

CLAY: Well, you know so much about me . . . what's my name?

LULA: Morris the Hyena.

CLAY: The famous woman poet?

LULA: The same. *(Laughing and going into her bag.)* You want another apple?

CLAY: Can't make it, lady. I only have to keep one doctor away a day.

LULA: I bet your name is . . . something like . . . uh, Gerald or Walter. Huh?

CLAY: God, no.

LULA: Lloyd, Norman? One of those hopeless colored names creeping out of New Jersey. Leonard? Gag . . . .

CLAY: Like Warren?

LULA: Definitely. Just exactly like Warren. Or Everett.

CLAY: Gag . . . .

LULA: Well, for sure, it's not Willie.

CLAY: It's Clay.

LULA: Clay? Really? Clay what?

CLAY: Take your pick. Jackson, Johnson, or Williams.

LULA: Oh, really? Good for you. But it's got to be Williams. You're too pretentious to be a Jackson or Johnson.

CLAY: Thass right.

LULA: But Clay's O.K.

CLAY: So's Lena.

LULA: It's Lula.

CLAY: Oh?

LULA: Lula the Hyena.

CLAY: Very good.

LULA   *(starts laughing again):* Now you say to me, "Lula, Lula, why don't you go to this party with me tonight?" It's your turn, and let those be your lines.

CLAY: Lula, why don't you go to this party with me tonight, Huh?

LULA: Say my name twice before you ask, and no huh's.

CLAY: Lula, Lula, why don't you go to this party with me tonight?

LULA: I'd like to go, Clay, but how can you ask me to go when you barely know me?

CLAY: That is strange, isn't it?

LULA: What kind of reaction is that? You're supposed to say, "Aw, come on, we'll get to know each other better at the party."

CLAY: That's pretty corny.

LULA: What are you into anyway? *(Looking at him half sullenly but still amused.)* What thing are you playing at, Mister? Mister Clay Williams? *(Grabs his thigh, up near the crotch.)* What are *you* thinking about?

CLAY: Watch it now, you're gonna excite me for real.

LULA   *(taking her hand away and throwing her apple core through the window):* I bet. *(She slumps in the seat and is heavily silent.)*

CLAY: I thought you know everything about me? What happened? (Lula *looks at him, then looks slowly away, then over where the other aisle* *would be. Noise of the train. She reaches in her bag and pulls out one of the paper books. She puts it on her leg and thumbs the pages list-lessly.* Clay *cocks his head to see the title of the book. Noise of the train.* Lula *flips pages and her eyes drift. Both remain silent.)* Are you going to the party with me, Lula?

LULA *(bored and not even looking):* I don't even know you.

CLAY: You said you know my type.

LULA *(strangely irritated):* Don't get smart with me, Buster. I know you like the palm of my hand.

CLAY: The one you eat the apples with?

LULA: Yeh. And the one I open doors late Saturday evening with. That's my door. Up at the top of the stairs. Five flights. Above a lot of Italians and lying Americans. And scrape carrots with. Also . . . *(Looks at him.)* the same hand I unbutton my dress with, or let my skirt fall down. Same hand. Lover.

CLAY: Are you angry about something? Did I say something wrong?

LULA: Everything you say is wrong. *(Mock smile.)* That's what makes you so attractive. Ha. In that funnybook jacket with all the buttons. *(More animate, taking hold of his jacket.)* What've you got that jacket and tie on in all this heat for? And why're you wearing a jacket and tie like that? Did your people ever burn witches or start revolutions over the price of tea? Boy, those narrow-shoulder clothes come from a tra-dition you ought to feel oppressed by. A three-button suit. What right do you have to be wearing a three-button suit and striped tie? Your father was a slave, he didn't go to Harvard.

CLAY: My grandfather was a night watchman.

LULA: And you went to a colored college where everybody thought they were Averell Harriman.

CLAY: All except me.

LULA: And who did you think you were? Who do you think you are now?

CLAY *(laughs as if to make light of the whole trend of the conversation):* Well, in college I thought I was Baudelaire. But I've slowed down since.

LULA: I bet you never once thought you were a black nigger. *(Mock serious, then she howls with laughter.* Clay *is stunned but after initial reaction, he quickly tries to appreciate the humor.* Lula *almost shrieks.)* A black Baudelaire.

CLAY: That's right.

LULA: Boy, are you corny. I take back what I said before. Everything you say is not wrong. It's perfect. You should be on television.

CLAY: You act like you're on television already.

LULA: That's because I'm an actress.

CLAY: I thought so.

LULA: Well, you're wrong. I'm no actress. I told you I always lie. I'm nothing, honey, and don't you ever forget it. *(Lighter.)* Although my
mother was a Communist. The only person in my family ever to
amount to anything.

CLAY: My mother was a Republican.

LULA: And your father voted for the man rather than the party.

CLAY: Right!

LULA: Yea for him. Yea, yea for him.

CLAY: Yea!

LULA: And yea for America where he is free to vote for the mediocrity of his
choice! Yea!

CLAY: Yea!

LULA: And yea for both your parents who even though they differ about so
crucial a matter as the body politic still forged a union of love and
sacrifice that was destined to flower at the birth of the noble Clay . . .
what's your middle name?

CLAY: Clay.

LULA: A union of love and sacrifice that was destined to flower at the birth
of the noble Clay Clay Williams. Yea! And most of all yea yea for you,
Clay Clay. The Black Baudelaire! Yes! *(And with knifelike cynicism.)*
My Christ. My Christ.

CLAY: Thank you, ma'am.

LULA: May the people accept you as a ghost of the future. And love you,
that you might not kill them when you can.

CLAY: What?

LULA: You're a murderer, Clay, and you know it. *(Her voice darkening with
significance.)* You know goddamn well what I mean.

CLAY: I do?

LULA: So we'll pretend the air is light and full of perfume.

CLAY   *(sniffing at her blouse):* It is.

LULA: And we'll pretend the people cannot see you. That is, the citizens.
And that you are free of your own history. And I am free of my history. We'll pretend that we are both anonymous beauties smashing
along through the city's entrails. *(She yells as loud as she can.)*
GROOVE!

Scene 2

*(Scene is the same as before, though now there are other seats visible in the
car. And throughout the scene other people get on the subway. There are
maybe one or two seated in the car as the scene opens, though neither Clay or
Lula notices them. Clay's tie is open. Lula is hugging his arm.)*

CLAY: The party!

LULA: I know it'll be something good. You can come in with me, looking casual and significant. I'll be strange, haughty, and silent, and walk with long slow strides.

CLAY: Right.

LULA: When you get drunk, pat me once, very lovingly on the flanks, and I'll look at you cryptically, licking my lips.

CLAY: It sounds like something we can do.

LULA: You'll go around talking to young men about your mind, and to old men about your plans. If you meet a very close friend who is also with someone like me, we can stand together, sipping our drinks and exchanging codes of lust. The atmosphere will be slithering in love and half-love and very open moral decision.

CLAY: Great. Great.

LULA: And everyone will pretend they don't know your name, and then . . . *(She pauses heavily.)* later, when they have to, they'll claim a friend-ship that denies your sterling character.

CLAY   *(kissing her neck and fingers):* And then what?

LULA: Then? Well, then we'll go down the street, late night, eating apples and winding very deliberately toward my house.

CLAY: Deliberately?

LULA: I mean, we'll look in all the shopwindows, and make fun of the queers. Maybe we'll meet a Jewish Buddhist and flatten his conceits over some very pretentious coffee.

CLAY: In honor of whose God?

LULA: Mine.

CLAY: Who is . . . ?

LULA: Me . . . and you?

CLAY: A corporate Godhead.

LULA: Exactly. Exactly. *(Notices one of the other people entering.)*

CLAY: Go on with the chronicle. Then what happens to us?

LULA   *(a mild depression, but she still makes her description triumphant and increasingly direct):* To my house, of course.

CLAY: Of course.

LULA: And up the narrow steps of the tenement.

CLAY: You live in a tenement?

LULA: Wouldn't live anywhere else. Reminds me specifically of my novel form of insanity.

CLAY: Up the tenement stairs.

LULA: And with my apple-eating hand I push open the door and lead you, my tender big-eyed prey, into my . . . God, what can I call it . . . into my hovel.

CLAY: Then what happens?

LULA: After the dancing and games, after the long drinks and long walks, the real fun begins.

CLAY: Ah, the real fun. *(Embarrassed, in spite of himself.)* Which is . . . ?

LULA *(laughs at him):* Real fun in the dark house. Hah! Real fun in the dark house, high up above the street and the ignorant cowboys. I lead you in, holding your wet hand gently in my hand . . .

CLAY: Which is not wet?

LULA: Which is dry as ashes.

CLAY: And cold?

LULA: Don't think you'll get out of your responsibility that way. It's not cold at all. You Rascist! Into my dark living room. Where we'll sit and talk endlessly, endlessly.

CLAY: About what?

LULA: About what? About your manhood, what do you think? What do you think we've been talking about all this time?

CLAY: Well, I didn't know it was that. That's for sure. Every other thing in the world but that. *(Notices another person entering, looks quickly, almost involuntarily up and down the car, seeing the other people in the car.)* Hey, I didn't even notice when those people got on.

LULA: Yeah, I know.

CLAY: Man, this subway is slow.

LULA: Yeah, I know.

CLAY: Well, go on. We were talking about my manhood.

LULA: We still are. All the time.

CLAY: We were in your living room.

LULA: My dark living room. Talking endlessly.

CLAY: About my manhood.

LULA: I'll make you a map of it. Just as soon as we get to my house.

CLAY: Well, that's great.

LULA: One of the things we do while we talk. And screw.

CLAY: *(trying to make his smile broader and less shaky):* We finally got there.

LULA: And you'll call my rooms black as a grave. You'll say, "This place is like Juliet's tomb."

CLAY *(laughs):* I might.

LULA: I know. You've probably said it before.

CLAY: And is that all? The whole grand tour?

LULA: Not all. You'll say to me very close to my face, many, many times, you'll say, even whisper, that you love me.

CLAY: Maybe I will.

LULA: And you'll be lying.

CLAY: I wouldn't lie about something like that.

LULA: Hah. It's the only kind of thing you will lie about. Especially if you think it'll keep me alive.

CLAY: Keep you alive? I don't understand.

LULA *(bursting out laughing, but too shrilly):* Don't understand? Well, don't look at me. It's the path I take, that's all. Where both feet take me when I set them down. One in front of the other.

CLAY: Morbid. Morbid. You sure you're not an actress? All that self-aggrandizement.

LULA: Well, I told you I wasn't an actress . . . but I also told you I lie all the time. Draw your own conclusions.

CLAY: Morbid. Morbid. You sure you're not an actress. All scribed? There's no more?

LULA: I've told you all I know. Or almost all.

CLAY: There's no funny parts?

LULA: I thought it was all funny.

CLAY: But you mean peculiar, not ha-ha.

LULA: You don't know what I mean.

CLAY: Well, tell me the almost part then. You said almost all. What else? I want the whole story.

LULA *(searching aimlessly through her bag. She begins to talk breathlessly, with a light and silly tone):* All stories are whole stories. All of 'em. Our whole story . . . nothing but change. How could things go on like that forever? Huh? *(Slaps him on the shoulder, begins finding things in her bag, taking them out and throwing them over her shoulder into the aisle.)* Except I do go on as I do. Apples and long walks with deathless intelligent lovers. But you mix it up. Look out the window, all the time. Turning pages. Change change change. Till, shit, I don't know you. Wouldn't, for that matter. You're too serious. I bet you're even too serious to be psychoanalyzed. Like all those Jewish poets from Yonkers, who leave their mothers looking for other mothers, or others' mothers, on whose baggy tits they lay their fumbling heads. Their poems are always funny, and all about sex.

CLAY: They sound great. Like movies.

LULA: But you change. *(Blankly.)* And things work on you till you hate them.

(More people come into the train. They come closer to the couple, some of them not sitting, but swinging drearily on the straps, staring at the two with uncertain interest.)

CLAY: Wow. All these people, so suddenly. They must all come from the same place.

LULA: Right. That they do.

CLAY: Oh? You know about them too?

LULA: Oh yeah. About them more than I know about you. Do they frighten you?

CLAY: Frighten me? Why should they frighten me?

LULA: 'Cause you're an escaped nigger.

CLAY: Yeah?

LULA: 'Cause you crawled through the wire and made tracks to my side.

CLAY: Wire?

LULA: Don't they have wire around plantations?

CLAY: You must be Jewish. All you can think about is wire. Plantations didn't have any wire. Plantations were big open whitewashed places like heaven, and everybody on 'em was grooved to be there. Just strummin' and hummin' all day.

LULA: Yes, yes.

CLAY: And that's how the blues was born.

LULA: Yes, yes. And that's how the blues was born. *(Begins to make up a song that becomes quickly hysterical. As she sings she rises from her seat, still throwing things out of her bag into the aisle, beginning a rhythmical shudder and twistlike wiggle, which she continues up and down the aisle, bumping into many of the standing people and tripping over the feet of those sitting. Each time she runs into a person she lets out a very vicious piece of profanity, wiggling and stepping all the time.)* And that's how the blues was born. Yes. Yes. Son of a bitch, get out of the way. Yes. Quack. Yes. Yes. And that's how the blues was born. Ten little niggers sitting on a limb, but none of them ever looked like him. *(Points to Clay, returns toward the seat, with her hands extended for him to rise and dance with her.)* And that's how the blues was born. Yes, Come on, Clay. Let's do the nasty. Rub bellies. Rub bellies.

CLAY *(waves his hands to refuse. He is embarrassed, but determined to get a kick out of the proceedings):* Hey, what was in those apples? Mirror, mirror on the wall, who's the fairest one of all? Snow White, baby, and don't you forget it.

LULA   *(grabbing for his hands, which he draws away):* Come on, Clay. Let's rub bellies on the train. The nasty. The nasty. Do the gritty grind, like your ol' rag-head mammy. Grind till you your mind. Shake it, shake it, shake it, shake it! OOOOweeee! Come on, Clay. Let's do the choo-choo train shuffle, the navel scratcher.

CLAY: Hey, you coming on like the lady who smoked up her grass skirt.

LULA   *(becoming annoyed that he will not dance, and becoming more animated as if to embarrass him still further):* Come on, Clay . . . let's do the thing. Uhh! Uhh! Clay! Clay! You middle-class black bastard. Forget your social-working mother for a few seconds and let's knock stomachs. Clay, you liver-lipped white man. You would-be Christian. You ain't no nigger, you're just a dirty white man. Get up, Clay. Dance with me, Clay.

CLAY: Lula! Sit down, now. Be cool.

LULA   *(mocking him, in wild dance):* Be cool. Be cool. That's all you know . . . shaking that wildroot cream-oil on your knotty head, jackets buttoning up to your chin, so full of white man's words. Christ. God. Get up and scream at these people. Like scream meaningless shit in these hopeless faces. *(She screams at people in train, still dancing.)* Red trains cough Jewish underwear for keeps! Expanding smells of silence. Gravy snot whistling like sea birds. Clay, Clay, you got to break out. Don't sit there dying the way they want you to die. Get up.

CLAY: Oh, sit the fuck down. *(He moves to restrain her.)* Sit down, goddamn it.

LULA   *(twisting out of his reach):* Screw yourself, Uncle Tom. Thomas Woolly-head. *(Begins to dance a kind of jig, mocking* Clay *with loud forced humor.)* There is Uncle Tom . . . I mean. Uncle Thomas' Woolly-Head. With old white matted mane. He hobbles on his wooden cane. Old Tom. Old Tom. Let the white man hump his ol' mama and he jes' shuffle off in the woods and hide his gentle gray head. Ol' Thomas Woolly-Head.

(Some of the other riders are laughing now. A drunk gets up and joins Lula in her dance, singing, as best he can, her "song." Clay gets up out of his seat and visibly scans the faces of the other riders.)

CLAY: Lula! Lula! *(She is dancing and turning, still shouting as loud as she can. The drunk too is shouting, and waving his hands wildly.)* Lula . . . you dumb bitch. Why don't you stop it? *(He rushes half stumbling from his seat, and grabs one of her flailing arms.)*

LULA: Let me go! You black son of a bitch. *(She struggles against him.)* Let me go! Help!

(Clay is dragging her toward her seat, and the drunk seeks to interfere. He grabs Clay around the shoulders and begins wrestling with him. Clay clubs the drunk to the floor without releasing Lula, who is still screaming. Clay finally gets her to the seat and throws her into it.)

CLAY: Now you shut the hell up. *(Grabbing her shoulders.)* Just shut up. You don't know what you're talking about. You don't know anything. So just keep your stupid mouth closed.

LULA: You're afraid of white people. And your father was. Uncle Tom Big Lip!

CLAY *(slaps her as hard as he can, across the mouth. Lula's head bangs against the back of the seat. When she raises it again,* Clay *slaps her again):* Now shut up and let me talk. *(He turns toward the other riders, some of whom are sitting on the edge of their seats. The drunk is on one knee, rubbing his head, and singing softly the same song. He shuts up too when he sees* Clay *watching him. The others go back to newspapers or stare out the window)* Shit, you don't have any sense, Lula, nor feelings either. I could murder you now. Such a tiny ugly throat. I could squeeze it flat, and watch you turn blue, on a humble. For dull kicks. And all these weak-faced ofays squatting around here, staring over their papers at me. Murder them too. Even if they expected it. That man there . . . *(Points to well-dressed man.)* I could rip that *Times* right out of his hand, as skinny and middle-classed as I am, I could rip that paper out of his hand and just as easily rip out his throat. It takes no great effort. For what? To kill you soft idiots? You don't understand anything but luxury.

LULA: You fool!

CLAY *(pushing her against the seat):* I'm not telling you again, Tallulah Bankhead! Luxury. In your face and your fingers. You telling me what I ought to do. *(Sudden scream frightening the whole coach.)* Well, don't! Don't you tell me anything! If I'm a middle-class fake white man . . . let me be. And let me be in the way I want. *(Through his teeth.)* I'll rip your lousy breasts off! Let me be who I feel like being. Uncle Tom. Thomas. Whoever. It's none of your business. You don't know anything except what's there for you to see. An act. Lies. Device. Not the pure heart, the pumping black heart. You don't ever know that. And I sit here, in this buttoned-up suit, to keep myself from cutting all your throats. I mean wantonly. You great liberated whore! You fuck some black man and right away you're an expert on black people. What a lotta shit that is. The only thing you know is that you come if he bangs you hard enough. And that's all. The belly rub? You wanted me to do the belly rub? Shit, you don't even know how. You don't know that. That ol' dipty-dip shit you do, rolling your ass like an elephant. That's not my kind of belly rub. Belly rub is not Queens. Belly rub is dark places, with big hats and overcoats held up with one arm. Belly rub hates you. Old bald-headed four-eyed ofays popping their fingers . . . and don't know yet what they're doing. They say, "I love Bessie Smith." And don't even understand that Bessie Smith is saying, "Kiss my ass, kiss my black unruly ass." Before love, suffering, desire, anything you can explain, she's saying, and very plainly, "Kiss my black ass." And if you don't know that, it's you that's doing the kissing.

Charlie Parker? Charlie Parker. All the hip white boys scream for Bird. And Bird saying, "Up your ass, feeble-minded ofay! Up your ass." And they sit there talking about the tortured genius of Charlie Parker. Bird would've played not a note of music if he just walked up to East Sixty-seventh Street and killed the first ten white people he saw. Not a note! And I'm the great would-be poet. Yes. That's right! Poet. Some kind of bastard literature . . . all it needs is a simple knife thrust. Just let me bleed you, you loud whore, and one poem vanished. A whole people of neurotics, struggling to keep from being sane. And the only thing that would cure the neurosis would be your murder. Simple as that. I mean if I murdered you, then other white people would begin to understand me. You understand? No. I guess not. If Bessie Smith had killed some white people she wouldn't have needed that music. She could have talked very straight and plain about the world. No metaphors. No grunts. No wiggles in the dark of her soul. Just straight two and two are four. Money. Power. Luxury. Like that. All of them. Crazy niggers turning their backs on sanity. When all it needs is that simple act. Murder. Just murder! Would make us all sane. *(Suddenly weary.)* Ahhh. Shit. But who needs it? I'd rather be a fool. Insane. Safe with my words, and no deaths, and clean, hard thoughts, urging me to new conquests. My people's madness. Hah! That's a laugh. My people. They don't need me to claim them. They got legs and arms of their own. Personal insanities. Mirrors. They don't need all those words. They don't need any defense. But listen, though, one more thing. And you tell this to your father, who's probably the kind of man who needs to know at once. So he can plan ahead. Tell him not to preach so much rationalism and cold logic to these niggers. Let them alone. Let them sing curses at you in code, and see your filth as simple lack of style. Don't make the mistake, through some irresponsible surge of Christian charity, of talking too much about the advantages of Western rationalism, or the great intellectual legacy of the white man, or maybe they'll begin to listen.

And then, maybe one day, you'll find they actually do understand exactly what you are talking about, all these fantasy people. All these blues people. And on that day, as sure as shit, when you really believe you can "accept" them into your fold, as half-white trusties late of the subject peoples. With no more blues, except the very old ones, and not a watermelon in sight, the great missionary heart will have triumphed, and all of those ex-coons will be stand-up Western men, with eyes for clean hard useful lives, sober, pious and sane, and they'll murder you. They'll murder you, and have very rational explanations. Very much like your own. They'll cut your throats, and drag you out to the edge of your cities so the flesh can fall away from your bones, in sanitary isolation.

LULA   *(her voice takes on a different, more businesslike quality):* I've heard enough.

CLAY   *(reaching for his books):* I bet you have. I guess I better collect my stuff and get off this train. Looks like we won't be acting out that little pageant you outlined before.

LULA: No. We won't. You're right about that, at least.

(She turns to look quickly around the rest of the car.) All right! *(The others respond.)*

CLAY   *(bending across the girl to retrieve his belongings):* Sorry, baby, I don't think we could make it.

(As he is bending over her, the girl brings up a small knife and plunges it into Clay's chest. Twice. He slumps across her knees, his mouth working stupidly.)

LULA: Sorry is right. *(Turning to the others in the car who have already gotten up from their seats.)* Sorry is the rightest thing you've said. Get this man off me! Hurry, now! *(The others come and drag* Clay's *body down the aisle.)* Open the door and throw his body out. *(They throw him off.)* And all of you get off at the next stop.

(Lula busies herself straightening her things. Getting everything in order. She takes out a notebook and makes a quick scribbling note. Drops it in her bag. The train apparently stops and all the others get off, leaving her alone in the coach. Very soon a young Negro of about twenty comes into the coach, with a couple of books under his arms. He sits a few seats in back of Lula. When he is seated she turns and gives him a long slow look. He looks up from his book and drops the book on his lap. Then an old Negro conductor comes into the car, doing a sort of restrained soft shoe, and half mumbling the words of some song. He looks at the young man, briefly, with a quick greeting.)

CONDUCTOR: Hey, brother!
YOUNG MAN: Hey.

(The conductor continues down the aisle with his little dance and the mumbled song. Lula turns to stare at him and follows his movements down the aisle. The conductor tips his hat when he reaches her seat, and continues out the car.)

Curtain

Try This

Write a stage direction, using no more than five elements (furniture, objects, hangings) onstage to set the scene. See how much you can tell us about the place and time and the characters who are likely to enter there.

or:

Write a stage direction for a symbolic setting: the place itself stands for an abstraction, the theme of the play you would set there. Choose and describe the place in such a way that a stage designer would be able to translate your meaning into paint and flats.

Warm-up

Are these people traveling, seeing someone off, or waiting for a traveler? Who is arriving or departing? What is the occasion? Holiday? Duty? Tragedy? Is the couple united or in conflict? Decide and write.

CHAPTER FIVE

STORY

As a Journey
As a Power Struggle
As Connection/Disconnection

Act I, get your guy up a tree. Act II, throw rocks at him.
Act III, get your guy outta the tree.

Julius Epstein

Story as a Journey

The late great novelist and teacher John Gardner used to say that there are only two stories: *someone went on a journey* and *a stranger came to town.* I once ran into a poet at the Yaddo writers' colony who reduced the formula still further. "You fiction writers," he said. "Everything you write is the same: two worlds collide; a love story."

You could do worse, for a definition of a story—for when worlds (cultures, generations, genders, hoods) encounter each other there is bound to be conflict, and when human beings make connection, some form of love occurs.

In Chapter 3, I said that that a character is someone capable of change. Story is the process of that change. The change may be from alive to dead, from ugly to beautiful, from ignorant to wise, callous to compassionate, from certain to uncertain or vice versa. But the change occurs because the character confronts a situation that will challenge her/his assumptions and somehow shake up the easy beliefs—hence the prevalence, in such a formulation, of strangers, journeys, and worlds. I like the metaphor of the two worlds, too, because it suggests both the importance of setting and the necessity of discovery. The new world that the character discovers may be the house next door, it may be a different set of assumptions or the next stage of life (puberty is a foreign country, marriage is an undiscovered planet)—but the story will always end in an altered state in at least the character whose point of view we share. Usually the character will have his or her scope enlarged—but not always. Usually the story will result in greater wisdom, compassion, or understanding—though it can end in diminishment or narrowing. As *readers*, however, we will *always*, if the story succeeds, have our capacity for empathy enlarged by having lived in the character's skin for the duration. Every story is in this important human sense a "love story."

A story is a journey is only one of many useful metaphors for the shape of a story, but it is the one almost always used by actors and directors when they set out to produce a play. Where does the protagonist want to go (what does she/he desire)? What are the obstacles encountered (what discoveries are made, what conflicts arise)? What does she/he do to overcome these obstacles (what decisions are made)? Is the goal reached? Is it as expected? Sometimes the journey of the story ends in fulfillment, sometimes not; sometimes the goal is reached and proves not worth the trip; sometimes a detour leads to paradise.

Here is a **short-short story** (only 101 words) about a long journey. Written in the diction of a five-year-old, it manages to give a panorama in space and time, as well as details that particularize both the setting and the characters. What change takes place in the character? How does the single line of dialogue at the end show this change?

> I've never been this far from home. I've never stayed up this late. I'm out west.
>
> We rode the train. I slept upstairs. You put your clothes in a hammock. They have Dixie cups.
>
> The world has mountains on the edge, where the sun sets, big black things, and that's where we're going.
>
> I'm in the front seat with my mother. I'm five. We're going to a dude ranch. There will be cowboys.
>
> There's a soft green glow on the dash board. My mother wears perfume.
>
> I'm traveling. I've never been this old.
>
> "The stars are ablaze," I tell my mother.
>
> *"Frontiers," John M. Daniel*

Try This

Write a memoir or short-short story, in either case no more than 101 words long, about a journey. Give us the setting, at least two characters, at least three characterizing details. Let the main character be changed by the journey.

or:

Write about a time that you started out on a trip but failed to arrive at your destination. Make yourself the hero or central consciousness in this telling. What was the

continued

obstacle—weather, accident, mechanical failure, human failure, human conflict? Characterize both the people involved and the setting through significant detail; give us a sense of the trip itself. What changed from the beginning expectations? How did you change?

Story as a Power Struggle

Another, perhaps the most common, way of looking at story structure is in terms of **conflict, crisis,** and **resolution,** a shape that comes from Aristotle's insistence on *a beginning, a middle,* and *an end.*

This model acknowledges that, in literature, only trouble is interesting. *Only* trouble is interesting. This is not so in life. Life offers periods of comfortable communication, peaceful pleasure, and productive work, all of which are extremely interesting to those involved. But passages about such times make for dull reading; they cannot be used as a plot.

Suppose, for example, you go on a picnic. You find a beautiful deserted meadow with a lake nearby. The weather is splendid and so is the company. The food's delicious, the water's fine, and the insects have taken the day off. Afterward, someone asks you how your picnic was. "Terrific," you reply, "really perfect." No story.

But suppose the next week you go back for a rerun. You set your picnic blanket on an anthill. You all race for the lake to get cold water on the bites, and one of your friends goes too far out on the plastic raft, which deflates. He can't swim and you have to save him. On the way in you gash your foot on a broken bottle. When you get back to the picnic, the ants have taken over the cake and a possum has demolished the chicken. Just then the sky opens up. When you gather your things to race for the car, you notice a bull has broken through the fence. The others run for it, but because of your bleeding heel the best you can do is hobble. You have two choices: try to outrun him or stand perfectly still and hope he's interested only in a moving target. At this point, you don't know if your friends can be counted on for help, even the nerd whose life you saved. You don't know if it's true that a bull is attracted by the smell of blood.

A year later, assuming you're around to tell about it, you are still saying, "Let me *tell* you what happened last year." And your listeners are saying, "What a story!"

This pattern of trouble and the effort to overcome it is repeated in every story on a larger or smaller scale. It may seem, for example, that the five-year-old in the short-short above is not in much trouble. But look at the huge dangers he faces: *never been this far from home, never up this late; mountains on the edge, big black things where we're going.* The clear and intense desire to get to the dude ranch is countered by the awesome strangeness of the adventure. Two worlds collide, in fact.

In the conflict-crisis-resolution model, story is seen as a power struggle between two nearly equal forces, a **protagonist** or central character and an **antagonist**, who represents the obstacles to the protagonist's desires and may be another human being or some other force—God, nature, the self, and so forth. If the antagonist is some abstract force, then, like the character's desire, it will also have a very specific manifestation: not "nature" but "seven miles of white water rapids on the lower Colorado;" not "the supernatural" but "a mutant reptile embryo capable of hatching in a human middle ear."

It is crucial that the opposing forces have approximately equal force, so that our uncertainty about the outcome keeps us reading. We begin with a situation in which the power is with the protagonist or the antagonist. Something happens, and the power shifts to the other. Something else, and it shifts back again. Each time the power shifts, the stakes are raised, each battle is bigger, more intense than the last, until (at the crisis moment), one of the two opposing forces manifests its power in a way that the other cannot match.

Here is another short-short story (a lavish 232 words this time), also in a child's voice, in which the conflict-crisis-resolution pattern is intense.

> Watching Joey pop the red berries into his mouth like Ju-Ju Bees and Mags only licking them at first, then chewing, so both of their smiles look bloody and I laugh though I don't eat even one . . . then suddenly our moms are all around us (although mine doesn't panic till she looks at the others, then screams along with them things like *God dammit did you eat these?* and shakes me so my "No" sounds like "oh-oh-oh") and then we're being yanked toward the house, me for once not resisting as my mother scoops me into her arms, and inside the moms shove medicine, thick and purple, down our throats in the bathroom; Joey in the toilet, Mags in the sink, me staring at the hair in the tub drain as my mom pushes my head down, and there is red vomit everywhere, splashing on the mirror and powder-blue rugs, everywhere except the tub where mine is coming out yellow, the color of corn muffins from lunch, not a speck of red, *I told you,* I want to scream, and then it is over and I turn to my mother for a touch or a stroke on the head like the other moms (but she has moved to the doorway and lights a cigarette, pushes hair out of her eyes) and there is only her smeared lips saying, *This will teach you anyway.*
>
> "This Is How I Remember It," Betsy Kemper

In this classical pattern, the story begins with an **exposition**, or statement of the situation at the beginning of the action, which is typically, as here, a state of unstable equilibrium (*I laugh, though I don't eat even one* . . .). **Conflict** arrives with the mothers, and that conflict undergoes a series of **complications** involving force, blame, mistake, submission, anger, and so forth. The power struggle between mother and daughter escalates through a change of setting. Details build the contrast between the kinds of *mom* and the kinds of vomit. The **crisis action** occurs as a moment of martyred triumph for the narrator (*I told you*) and then there is a **falling action** or **denouement** in which the mother and daughter retreat to their respective corners and settle back into what (we know by now) is their habit of being. This is the **resolution**. Some questions to consider: Why did the author choose to tell this story in a single sentence? What does the narrator want? Who wins? Is it worth it?

This very short story is very much of the twentieth century, in that the crisis occurs in the mind of the narrator and the "resolution" does not offer a "solution." The completion of the action has changed the characters not by a dramatic reversal, but by moving them deeper into their *impasse.*

Order is a major value that literature offers us, and order implies that the subject has been brought to closure. In life this never quite happens. Even the natural "happy endings," marriage and birth, leave domesticity and childrearing to be dealt with; the natural "tragic endings," separation and death, leave trauma and bereavement in their wake. Literature absolves us of these nuisances. Whether or not the lives of the characters end, the story does, and we are left with a satisfying sense of completion. This is one reason we enjoy crying or feeling terrified or even nauseated by fiction; we know in advance that it's going to be over, and by contrast with the continual struggle of living, all that ends, ends well.

Try This

Write a short story on a postcard. (Write small.) Make sure it has a conflict, a crisis, and a resolution. Send it to a friend in another place (meaning you have published it), or to yourself (when it arrives you will be able to see it fresh).

or:

A story, a memoir, or a play: Place two characters in a dangerous setting. Each has half of something that is no good without the other half. Neither wants to give up his/her half. What happens?

> Connection is human substance, the substance of story. Its gain and loss provides the emotional power.
>
> *Claudia Johnson*

Story as Connection and Disconnection

Every story presents some sort of journey, literal or psychological or both, that results in a change in the central character. Every story shows a pattern of conflict between approximately equal forces, which leads to a crisis and a resolution. Every story also offers a pattern of connection and disconnection between human beings, which is the source of meaning and significance in the story. Conflict is exciting; it keeps the reader wondering what will happen next. But conflict itself is sterile unless it is given human dimension through the connections and disconnections of the characters.

Therefore, boy meets girl, boy loses girl, boy gets girl (connection, disconnection, connection). Therefore Hamlet's father dies (disconnects), but comes back (connects) as a ghost, Hamlet rages against his mother (disconnects), welcomes his schoolfriends (connects), breaks off with Ophelia (disconnects), kills her father (disconnects), betrays his schoolfriends (disconnects), kills his stepfather (disconnects) and, in the arms (connects) of his best friend, dies (disconnects). It will be evident that a story that ends in disconnection, especially death, tends toward tragedy, and one that ends in connection, traditionally marriage, is a comedy. Examine any story that makes you care, and you will see that people *who matter to each other* perform, as in life, patterns of love and hate, alienation and community, anger and forgiveness, connection and disconnection. As Claudia Johnson puts it, "The conflict and surface events are like waves, but underneath is an emotional tide—the ebb and flow of human connection."

Even in the very short compass of the two short-short stories above, these patterns occur. In "Frontiers," the boy is frighteningly separated from home, but his mother is there with him, to take him to the glamorous and grown-up connection with *cowboys*. In "This Is How I Remember It," the girl is connected to her friends, but not so close that she will dare the blood-red berries; the moms arrive to connect, each with her own child; but the heroine deeply disconnects from her punitive and unjust mother.

Try This

Write down a memory of a time you seriously disconnected from someone close to you. Know that the person will never read it.

or:

Write a poem about a death, a breakup, a divorce, a house moving, a quarrel. Find some small positive aspect of the disconnection.

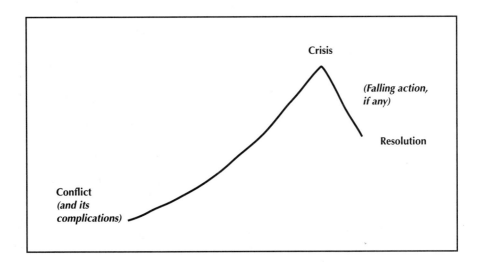

It is useful to think of story shape as an inverted check mark, rising from left to right and ending in a short downswing. The story begins with an *exposition* of the opening situation, develops a conflict through a series of complications in which the power changes back and forth, and culminates in a crisis. Then there is a brief walking-away (falling action or denouement), leading to resolution.

If we take the familiar tale of Cinderella, we can see how even this simple children's story relates to each of the models—as journey, as power struggle, and as pattern of connection/disconnection.

At the opening of the tale we're given the basic conflict: Cinderella's mother has died, and her father has married a brutal woman with two waspish daughters. Cinderella is made to do all the dirtiest and most menial work, and she weeps among the cinders. Cinderella's desire is to be treated equally, or treated well. Her journey is on the literal level from the hearth to the palace, and on the mythic level from slave to Princess. Along the way she encounters the obstacles of powerlessness, evil, short-lived magic, and chance. With the aid of goodness, beauty, magic and chance, she also reaches her goal.

Next consider the story in relation to the "checkmark" diagram in terms of the power struggle. The Stepmother has on her side the strength of ugliness and evil (two very powerful qualities in literature as in life). With her daughters she also has the strength of numbers, and she has parental authority. Cinderella has only beauty and goodness, but (in literature and life) these are also very powerful.

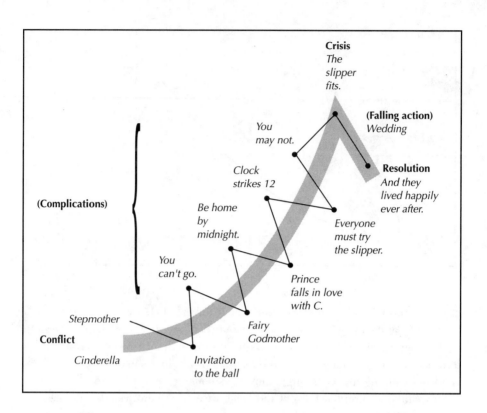

At the beginning of the struggle in "Cinderella," the power is very clearly on the Stepmother's side. But the first event of the story is that an invitation arrives from the Prince, which explicitly states that *all* the ladies of the land are invited to a ball. Notice that Cinderella's desire is not to triumph over her Stepmother (though she eventually will, much to our satisfaction); such a desire would diminish her goodness. She simply wants to be relieved of her mistreatment. She wants equality, so that the Prince's invitation, which specifically gives her a right equal to the Stepmother's and Stepdaughters' rights, shifts the power to her.

The Stepmother takes the power back by blunt force: You may not go; you must get us ready to go. Cinderella does so, and the three leave for the ball.

Then what happens? The Fairy Godmother appears. It is very powerful to have magic on your side. The Fairy Godmother offers Cinderella a gown, glass slippers, and a coach with horses and footmen, giving her more force than she has yet had.

But the magic is not all-potent. It has a qualification that portends bad luck. It will last only until midnight (unlike the Stepmother's authority), and Cinderella must leave the ball before the clock strikes twelve or risk exposure and defeat.

What happens next? She goes to the ball and the Prince falls in love with her—and love is an even more powerful weapon than magic in a literary war. In some versions of the tale, the Stepmother and Stepsisters are made to marvel at the beauty of the princess they don't recognize, pointing to the irony of Cinderella's new power.

And then? The magic quits. The clock strikes twelve, and Cinderella runs down the steps in her rags to her rats and pumpkin, losing a slipper, bereft of her power in every way.

But after that, the Prince sends out a messenger with the glass slipper and a dictum (a dramatic repetition of the original invitation in which all ladies were invited to the ball) that every female in the land is to try on the slipper. Cinderella is given her rights again by royal decree.

What happens then? In most good retellings of the tale, the Stepmother also repeats her assumption of brute authority by hiding Cinderella away, while our expectation of triumph is tantalizingly delayed with grotesque comedy: one sister cuts off a toe, the other a heel, trying to fit into the heroine's rightful slipper.

After that, Cinderella tries on the slipper and it fits. *This is the crisis action.* Magic, love, and royalty join to recognize the heroine's true self; evil, numbers, and authority are powerless against them. At this point, the power struggle has been decided; the outcome is inevitable. When the slipper fits, no further action can occur that will deprive Cinderella of her desire. The change in the lives of all concerned is significant and permanent.

In many of the finest modern short stories and novels, the true territory of struggle is the main character's mind, and so the real crisis action must occur there. Yet it is important to grasp that any mental reversal that takes place in the crisis of a story must be triggered or shown by an action. The slipper must fit. It would not do if the Stepmother just happened to change her mind and give up the struggle; it would not do if the Prince just happened to notice that Cinderella looked like his love. The moment of recognition must be manifested in an action.

The tale has a brief "falling action": the Prince sweeps Cinderella up on his white horse and gallops away to their wedding. The story comes to closure with the classic resolution of all comedy: They lived happily ever after.

If we look at "Cinderella" in terms of connection/disconnection we see a pattern as clear as that represented by the power struggle. The first painful disconnection is that Cinderella's mother has died; her father has married (connected with) a woman who spurns (disconnects from) her; the Prince's invitation offers connection, the Stepmother's cruelty alienates again. The Fairy Godmother connects as a magical friend, but the disappearance of the coach and gown disconnect Cinderella temporarily from that grand and glorious fairy-tale union, marriage to the Prince. If we consult the emotions that this tale engenders— pity, anger, hope, fear, romance, anticipation, disappointment, triumph—we

see that both the struggle between antagonist/protagonist and the pattern of
alienation/connectedness is necessary to ensure, not only that there is an action,
but also that we care about its outcome.

Forms of imaginative writing are not mutually exclusive. Often a memoir is
dramatic, dialogue can be lyrical, narrative turns to poetry. Above all, many
essays, poems, and plays have the fundamental form of story. Here is a familiar poem that is also a story and a monologue:

> Scene: Ferrara
>
> That's my last Duchess painted on the wall,
> Looking as if she were alive. I call
> That piece a wonder, now: Fra Pandolph's hands
> Worked busily a day, and there she stands.
> Will't please you sit and look at her? I said
> "Fra Pandolph" by design, for never read
> Strangers like you that pictured countenance,
> The depth and passion of its earnest glance
> But to myself they turned (since none puts by
> The curtain I have drawn for you, but I)
> And seemed as they would ask me, if they durst,
> How such a glance came there; so, not the first
> Are you to turn and ask thus. Sir, 'twas not
> Her husband's presence only, called that spot
> Of joy into the Duchess' cheek: perhaps
> Fra Pandolph chanced to say, "Her mantle laps
> Over my lady's wrist too much," or "Paint
> Must never hope to reproduce the faint
> Half-flush that dies along her throat"; such stuff
> Was courtesy, she thought, and cause enough
> For calling up that spot of joy. She had
> A heart . . . how shall I say? . . . too soon made glad,
> Too easily impressed; she liked whate'er
> She looked on, and her looks went everywhere.
> Sir, 'twas all one! My favour at her breast,
> The drooping of the daylight in the West,
> The bough of cherries some officious fool
> Broke in the orchard for her, the white mule
> She rode with round the terrace—all and each
> Would draw from her alike the approving speech,
> Or blush, at least. She thanked men,—good, but thanked
> Somehow . . . I know not how . . . as if she ranked
> My gift of a nine hundred years old name
> With anybody's gift. Who'd stoop to blame
> This sort of trifling? Even had you skill
> In speech—(which I have not)—to make your will

Quite clear to such an one, and say, "Just this
Or that in you disgusts me; here you miss,
Or there exceed the mark"—and if she let
Herself be lessoned so, nor plainly set
Her wits to yours, forsooth, and made excuse,
—E'en then would be some stooping, and I choose
Never to stoop. Oh, Sir, she smiled no doubt,
Whene'er I passed her; but who passed without
Much the same smile? This grew; I gave commands;
Then all smiles stopped together. There she stands
As if alive. Will't please you rise? We'll meet
The company below, then. I repeat,
The Count your Master's known munificence
Is ample warrant that no just pretence
Of mine for dowry will be disallowed;
Though his fair daughter's self, as I avowed
At starting, is my object. Nay, we'll go
Together down, Sir! Notice Neptune, tho,'
Taming a sea-horse, thought a rarity,
Which Claus of Innsbruck cast in bronze for me.

"My Last Duchess," Robert Browning

This piece is clearly not an essay, though it makes a persuasive argument for feminism, and many essays have been written to elucidate its contemporary message. It is, however, a poem, in the traditional form of heroic couplets—that is, five feet (repetitions) of a pattern of iambic (unstressed/stressed) syllables, every two lines consecutively rhymed (these terms are discussed in Chapter 9, on Poetry). It is also a dramatic monologue, in the voice of a Duke of Ferrara presenting his case to an envoy of another nobleman, who does not speak. It could easily be staged with either one or two actors, the implied setting externalized as props and scenery. It is also a story—or rather two stories. The first, the *back story* (that is, the events of the past that are necessary to know what is happening in the present) is something like this: the Duke married a young girl whose generous spirit made her happy but aroused his jealousy, his displeasure, and finally his rage. She died; we are not told whether she was murdered or psychologically broken, but we do know that it was his fault. In the story Browning chooses to present—the plot (the distinction between story and plot will be further discussed in Chapter 8 on Fiction)—the Duke is negotiating another marriage with an envoy of a second girl's father. What he desires is a profitable marriage; the power he has is no doubt his dukedom, yet the envoy holds the power to negotiate the girl's hand. As the story unfolds we learn that the Duke is an unreliable narrator, one whose values we don't share and whose word we don't trust. Does the envoy also recoil; will he advise against the marriage? We don't know. But we do know by the resolution of the scene what *our* judgment of the Duke is, and that a wife is not only an object to him, but worth less than an *objet d'art*.

The form of story—in its incarnations as journey, conflict-crisis-resolution, and connection-disconnection—is so prevalent in human culture that scarcely any communication is free of it. The most casual conversation includes anecdotes of destination and detour. The company report boasts of obstacles overcome. The trip to school shapes up as power struggle between protagonist child and antagonist mom, resolved with a connecting hug or a parting blast. Awareness of these shapes can inform any genre of writing and help to bridge the gap between mind and mind, helping to achieve the first desire of any writer: connection with that intimate stranger, the reader.

Try This
Write an essay that tells a story.

or:

Write a story that can be performed dramatically.

or:

Write a dialogue that is a poem.

More to Read

Burroway, Janet. *Writing Fiction: a Guide to Narrative Craft.* New York: Longman,

2003.

Forster, E.M. *Aspects of the Novel.* New York: Harcourt Brace Jovanovich, 1972.

ESSAY

Patricia Hampl
Red Sky in the Morning

Years ago, in another life, I woke to look out the smeared window of a Greyhound bus I had been riding all night, and in the still-dark morning of a small Missouri river town where the driver had made a scheduled stop at a grimy diner, I saw below me a stout middle-aged woman in a flowered housedress turn and kiss full on the mouth a godlike young man with golden curls. But I've got that wrong: *he* was kissing *her*. Passionately, without regard for the world and its incomprehension. He had abandoned himself to his love, and she, stolid, matronly, received this adoration with simple grandeur, like a socialist-realist statue of a woman taking up sheaves of wheat.

Their ages dictated that he must be her son, but I had just come out of the cramped, ruinous half sleep of a night on a Greyhound and I was clairvoyant: This was that thing called love. The morning light cracked blood red along the river.

Of course, when she lumbered onto the bus a moment later, lurching forward with her two bulging bags, she chose the empty aisle seat next to me as her own. She pitched one bag onto the overhead rack, and then heaved herself into the seat as if she were used to hoisting sacks of potatoes onto the flatbed of a pickup. She held the other bag on her lap, and leaned toward the window. The beautiful boy was blowing kisses. He couldn't see where she was in the dark interior, so he blew kisses up and down the side of the bus, gazing ardently at the blank windows. "Pardon me," the woman said without looking at me, and leaned over, bag and all, to rap the glass. Her beautiful boy ran back to our window and kissed and kissed, and finally hugged himself, shutting his eyes in an ecstatic pantomime of love-sweet-love. She smiled and waved back.

Then the bus was moving. She slumped back in her seat, and I turned to her. I suppose I looked transfixed. As our eyes met she said, "Everybody thinks he's my son. But he's not. He's my husband." She let that sink in. She was a farm woman with hands that could have been a man's; I was a university student, hair down to my waist. It was long ago, as I said, in another life. It was even another life for the country. The Vietnam War was the time we were living through, and I was traveling, as I did every three weeks, to visit my boyfriend who was in a federal prison. "Draft dodger," my brother said. "Draft resister," I piously retorted. I had never been kissed the way this woman had been kissed. I was living in a tattered corner of a romantic idyll, the one where the hero is willing to suffer for his beliefs. I was the girlfriend. I lived on pride, not love.

My neighbor patted her short cap of hair, and settled in for the long haul as we pulled onto the highway along the river, heading south. "We been married five years and we're happy," she said with a penetrating satisfaction, the satisfaction that passeth understanding. "Oh," she let out a profound sigh as if she mined her truths from the bountiful, bulky earth, "Oh, I could tell you stories." She put her arms snugly around her bag, gazed for a moment, apparently made pensive by her remark. Then she closed her eyes and fell asleep.

I looked out the window smudged by my nose which had been pressed against it at the bus stop to see the face of true love reveal itself. Beyond the bus the sky, instead of becoming paler with the dawn, drew itself out of a black line along the Mississippi into an alarming red flare. It was very beautiful. The old caution—*Red sky in the morning, sailor take warning*—darted through my mind and fell away. Remember this, I remember telling myself, hang on to this. I could feel it all skittering away, whatever conjunction of beauty and improbability I had stumbled upon.

It is hard to describe the indelible bittersweetness of that moment. Which is why, no doubt, it had to be remembered. The very word—*Remember!*—spiraled up like a snake out of a basket, a magic catch in its sound, the doubling of the m—*re memmemem*—setting up a low murmur full of inchoate associations as if a loved voice were speaking into my ear alone, occultly.

Whether it was the unguarded face of love, or the red gash down the middle of the warring country I was traveling through, or this exhausted farm woman's promise of untold tales that bewitched me, I couldn't say. Over it all rose and remains only the injunction to remember. This, the most impossible command we lay upon ourselves, claimed me and then perversely disappeared, trailing an illusive silken tissue of meaning, without giving a story, refusing to leave me in peace.

Because everyone "has" a memoir, we all have a stake in how such stories are told. For we do not, after all, simply *have* experience; we are entrusted with it. We must do something—make something—with it. A story, we sense, is the only possible habitation for the burden of our witnessing.

The tantalizing formula of my companion on the Greyhound—*oh, I could tell you stories*—is the memoirist's opening line, but it has none of the delicious promise of the storyteller's "Once upon a time . . . " In fact, it is a perverse statement. The woman on the bus told me nothing—she fell asleep and escaped to her dreams. For the little sentence inaugurates nothing, and leads nowhere after its *dot dot dot* of expectation. Whatever experience lies tangled within its seductive promise remains forever balled up in the woolly impossibility of telling the-truth-the-whole-truth of life, any life.

Memoirists, unlike fiction writers, do not really want to "tell a story." They want to tell it *all*—the all of personal experience, of consciousness itself. That includes a story, but also the whole expanding universe of sensation and thought that flows beyond the confines of narrative and proves every life to be not only an isolated story line but a bit of the cosmos, spinning and streaming into the great, ungraspable pattern of existence. Memoirists wish to tell their mind, not their story.

The wistfulness implicit in that conditional verb—*I could tell*—conveys an urge more primitive than a storyteller's search for an audience. It betrays not a loneliness for someone who will listen but a hopelessness about language itself and a sad recognition of its limitations. How much reality can subject-verb-object bear on the frail shoulders of the sentence? The sigh within the statement is more like this: I could tell you stories—if only stories could tell what I have in me to tell.

For this reason, autobiographical writing is bedeviled. It is caught in a self which must become a world—and not, please, a narcissistic world. The memoir, once considered a marginal literary form, has emerged in the past decade as the signature genre of the age. "The triumph of memoir is now established fact," James Atlas trumpeted in a cover story on "The Age of the Literary Memoir" in the *New York Times Magazine.* "Fiction," he claimed, "isn't delivering the news. Memoir is."

With its "triumph," the memoir has, of course, not denied the truth and necessity of fiction. In fact, it leans heavily on novelistic assumptions. But the contemporary memoir has reaffirmed the primacy of the first person voice in American imaginative writing established by Whitman's "Song of Myself." Maybe a reader's love of memoir is less an intrusive lust for confession than a hankering for the intimacy of this first-person voice, the deeply satisfying sense of being spoken to privately. More than a story, we want a voice speaking softly, urgently, in our ear. Which is to say, to our heart. The voice carries its implacable command, the ancient murmur that called out to me in the middle of the country in the middle of a war—remember, remember (*I dare you, I tempt you*).

Looking out the Greyhound window that red morning all those years ago, I saw the improbable face of love. But even more puzzling was the cryptic remark of the beloved as she sat next to me. I think of her more often than makes sense. Though he was the beauty, she was the one who comes back. How faint his golden curls have become (he also had a smile, crooked and charming, but I can only remember the idea of it—the image is gone). It is she, stout and unbeautiful, wearing her flowery cotton housedress with a zipper down the middle, who has taken up residence with her canny eye and her acceptance of adoration. To be loved like that, loved improbably: of course, she had stories to tell. She took it for granted in some unapologetic way, like being born to wealth. Take the money and run.

But that moment before she fell asleep, when she looked pensive, the red morning rising over the Mississippi, was a wistful moment. *I could tell you stories*—but she could not. What she had to tell was too big, too much, too *something*, for her to place in the small shrine that a story is.

When we met—if what happened between us was a meeting—I felt nothing had ever happened to me and nothing ever would. I didn't understand that riding this filthy Greyhound down the middle of bloodied America in the middle of a mutinous war was itself a story and that something *was* happening to me. I thought if something was happening to anybody around me it was happening to people like my boyfriend: They were the heroes, according to the lights that shined for me then. I was just riding shotgun in my own life. I could not have imagined containing, as the farm woman slumped next to me did, the sheer narrative bulk to say, "I could tell you stories," and then drifting off with the secret heaviness of experience into the silence where stories live their real lives, crumbling into the loss we call remembrance.

The boastful little declaration, pathetically conditional (not "I'll tell you a story" but "I could") wavered wistfully for an instant between us. The stranger's remark, launched in the dark of the Greyhound, floated across the human landscape like the lingering tone of a struck bell from a village church, and joined all the silence that ever was, as I turned my face to the window where the world was rushing by along the slow river.

FICTION

Robert Olen Butler

Missing

It was me you saw in that photo across a sugarcane field. I was smoking by the edge of the jungle and some French journalist, I think it was, took that photo with a long lens, and you couldn't even see the cigarette in my hand but you could see my blond hair, even blonder now than when I leaned my rifle against a star apple tree with my unit on up the road in a terrible fight and I put my pack and steel pot beside it and I walked into the trees. My hair got blonder from the sun that even up here in the highlands crouches on us like a mama-san with her feet flat and going nowhere. Though my hair should've gone black, by rights. It should have gone as black as the hair of my wife.

Somebody from the village went into Da Lat and came back with an American newspaper that found its way there from Saigon, probably, brought by some Aussie businessman or maybe even an American GI come back to figure out what it was he left over here in Vietnam. There are lots of them come these days, I'm told, the GIs, and it makes things hard for me, worrying about keeping out of their sight. I've got nothing to do with them, and that's why the photo pissed me off. As soon as I saw it, I knew it was me. I knew the field. I knew my own head of hair. And because you can't see the cigarette; my hand coming down from my face looks like some puny little wave, like I'm saying come help me. And that's the last goddamn thing I want.

I grew the tobacco myself. That's what we do in my village. And up here we grow coffee, too. The first time I saw the girl who would be my wife she was by the side of a road spreading the coffee beans out to dry. Spreading them with her bare feet. And when her family finally let me marry her and we lay down at last in our little house—with wood walls and a wood ceiling in this place in Vietnam where there are hardwood trees and cool nights— she rubbed her hands through my hair, calling it sunlight, and I held her feet in my hands and kissed them and they tasted of coffee.

I'm not missing, I'm here. I know the smell of the wood fires and the incense my wife burns for the dead father and mother who gave her to me and the smell of my daughter's hair washed from the big pot in our back- yard to catch the rainwater, and instead, the "USA Today" has got me on the run, waving pitifully across a field at a photographer to put the word out to the world, but they don't wonder why I'm apparently not smart enough to walk on across that field and say, Take me back to my mama and papa and my brothers and my sisters who are living ruined lives in America because I'm missing in action. I don't even have the sense to get close enough to the road so I can be identified, so I'm the lost child of every family in the coun- try with someone whose body was never found.

But I walked away. I just walked away. And there were a thousand of them like me. Two thousand. More, I heard, a lot more. In the back alleys of Saigon, the little villages in the highlands and along the sea, trying to keep out of the way of the killing just like these people who took us in and didn't ask any questions.

Though I could see the questions all come back in the faces of my people when the newspaper showed up. We all went out to see it. It's the way here. The village is small and our elder is Binh and he knew me from the first, he was the first man I saw when I walked in here in 1970 unarmed and bareheaded and I said in the little bit of Vietnamese I had that I was a friend, I wanted to lie down and sleep. He knew what I was doing.

It was yesterday that we sat on mats in front of Tiên's house and she brought us tea and we looked at the paper.

"It's you, I think," Binh said, and he curved his lower lip upward, lifting the little wisp of a Hồ Chí Minh beard, a beard that he wore not from approval of the man but with a kind of irony.

Tri, who had brought the paper, put it before me again now, and the dozen faces around watched me for the final word. I nodded. Thào, my wife, touched my shoulder. She could see it, too. "Yes," I said.

"What does it say about you?" Binh asked.

"Nothing," I said. "They don't know who I am."

Binh nodded and he did it slow enough that I knew he wanted me to say more. I waited, though, looking away beyond the circle, across the dirt street to the tobacco-drying racks, and some kids were there, two of Tiên's boys squatting and looking back at me and Tri's little girl, who stood staring at a dragon head set on a table in the sun. Tiên had been working on the head, repainting the green and red ridges in its face, getting it ready for Têt, the new year. When I looked away from Binh, I thought my daughter, Hoa, might be there, but she wasn't. And I didn't want to cast my gaze farther with Binh waiting for me to say more.

But I'd waited a little too long already. Binh asked, "Does it speak of some other man?"

"Not one particular man. No. It says some people in America have seen the photo and think it's proof that Americans are still alive over here, men being held by the communists."

"MIA," Binh said, pronouncing each letter with a flat American inflection that he'd picked up from me long ago.

"Yes," I said.

At this, Binh turned his face, in respect, away from Quang who sat next to him. Quang was almost as old as Binh, clean-shaven, with skin the color of this dirt street moments after a rain. But I glanced at him briefly, and there were others from our little circle who did, too. He was holding the newspaper spread tight in his two hands as if trying to stretch any wrinkles out of it. He was looking at my image there, and I think his mind now was on his own lost son. Most of the people of a certain age in my village have dead children from the war. But Quang's boy is missing, still, after more than twenty years, and he worries about where the body might be, the spirit lost and hovering around it waiting for rites that would never come.

My village believes in spirits. Last night we all burned incense in our kitchens for the god of the hearth. Such a god lives in each of our houses, and seven days before Têt he goes up to heaven to report on the family. A family is very important in Vietnam. We work and we care for each other and we live under one roof and there is no ending for such a thing. My wife's mother and father slept on straw mats in our house until the day that each of them died. I will sleep on a straw mat in the house of my daughter until I die. That is my wish.

Perhaps that's why I'm so frightened now to see this image of myself in an American newspaper. Why I looked again across to where the children were, more of them now, gathering to watch us and wonder, and I looked for my daughter and I wanted to see her in that moment, a brief glance even. We are meant to protect our families in all their linked parts like we protect our bodies. And the god of the hearth takes special note in his report of how careful we are about that. And how we respect the spirits, the spirits of our family gone to the afterlife before us and the spirits of all the others in the air around us. And we must respect the gods, as well. The minds and wills that animate the universe. Look where they have brought me.

And Hoa appeared. My daughter is tall now, her body changing from a girl to a woman, and her hair is the brown of the dried tobacco, not black but the color of what we grow and prepare here, and I don't know why I was caught by her hair at that moment but it is long and it has this color that belongs to no one else here, not my wife, not me. And she stepped behind Tri's daughter and she looked to me, briefly, and then at the little girl staring at the dragon.

Binh still had something on his mind. "Do you think some people in America will look at this picture and remember?"

"There will be many who do that," I said, and my eyes moved to Quang, and I was thinking of the grief he was drawing from the paper in his hands even then, and Binh knew what I was saying. But I also understood him. He meant: Do you have other people in that past life of yours who will recognize this son or husband or brother of theirs and suffer from this?

I felt my wife stir beside me. She heard this beneath Binh's words as well, and grew angry at him, I think. It made her fear another woman. I should speak, I knew. But I looked again at Hoa and she was bending to the table and she picked up the dragon head and turned to face Tri's daughter and I could see Hoa's face for a moment there, caught full in the sunlight, and in this light the parts of her body that she had because of me seemed very clear, the highness of her brow, the half-expressed roundness of the lids of her eyes, the length of her nose, the wideness of her mouth, her hair neither dark nor light. And I had a twist of sadness for her, as if she had gotten from me imperfect cells that had made a club foot or an open spine or a weak heart.

She lifted the dragon high with both hands and raised it over her, and she slowly brought it down; her hair, her brow disappeared into the dragon, her eyes and her nose and her mouth, my daughter's face disappeared into great bright eyes, flared nostrils, cheeks of blood red and a brow of green. And Tri's daughter clapped her hands and laughed and the dragon head angled and opened its mouth to her as if to cry out.

I looked at Binh and he was waiting for me to speak and I looked at the others and then at Thào. Her face was slightly turned to me but her eyes were lowered. I thought, It's been nearly twenty years since I first lay down with you and touched those places on your body that were smooth and soft and that are coarser now, and I love them still, I love them more for their very coarseness. I do not wish to open the past either, my wife. But this is my village and I was seen across a field by millions and the eyes of that other country turn this way.

I let a little of the past back into me then, and I did not know what to say. A house with a wraparound porch and maple trees and a grass yard cut close and edged each week in a perfect line along a sidewalk; things unknown in this place. Things that I could see without pain only when they sat unpeopled in my head. Things of a family that were worth keeping only from a summer day when the maple leaves did not stir and when no one from inside this house was visible, no sounds could be heard from inside. How to say that for these Vietnamese who sensed–always–even the dead spirits of a family? Who in this circle could imagine that only this was good in that past life of mine: a maple tree and the smell of fresh paint on the porch, just dried into a Victorian green and smelling like something new, and the creak of a chain on a swing there, my feet touching and pushing, lifting me as if I was flying away.

And these thoughts frightened me. I was thinking about these Vietnamese now from a distance, how they could not know me, and I wanted to blame this distance on that other self that was creeping back in, but it was hard now entirely to do that. After all, this was my past and the haunches it crept on could find strength only from me. And Tri's daughter shrieked and laughed across the way and there was a faint, muffled roaring that I recognized as my daughter's voice and I knew not to look. I could not look at that.

And I rose up from where I crouched and I said, "I'm sorry," and I stepped out of the circle and I did not look at my wife and I did not look at my daughter and I hesitated only for a moment and I knew that no one here would ask me again to speak of this and that was their way and I looked along our village street, down a little slope to a closing of the trees, the road I had followed when Binh first saw me weary and ready to sleep. And I took one step now in that direction, toward the trees, and another step, and I walked away.

I walked for a long time and went up, into a piney wood, and this was an American smell, as American as it was Vietnamese. There were two tall pine trees in the yard behind the house with the wraparound porch and it smelled just like this and there was a chill that made me tremble briefly, tremble in the chest, in the heart, right then, passing through the shadow of a great isolated pine in a little clearing and open to the wind, and the nights in the highlands could be American, too, it could be cold at times here in Vietnam, even in this country of rice paddies and water buffalo.

And I stopped and I sat on a knoll and I looked at my hands darkened by the sun, not as dark as my wife's skin or Binh's or any of the others in the circle I'd broken but as dark as the skin of a Vietnamese child, that dark. This could be the skin of a Vietnamese child. Except for the blond hairs on my knuckles, and I looked at my arms and there was a forest of blond hair on this dark arm, and I was on the porch swing, in the very center, and my arms were taut, my legs were just long enough now to touch and push and lift and my arms were rigid grasping the lip of the seat, and for a moment there was only the cry of the chain above me: I pushed and the chain cried out, over and over, and it seemed painful to this thing for it to carry me, and I rose but always came down again and I never did move from the porch, and I stopped and I sat and still there was silence from the house but I knew I would go in. Against all that I desperately desired, I would go in.

Binh was asking me to go in. They all asked me that now. Just to have me speak. I was to walk into the great bland jaws of that house and what I feared was this: perhaps a family scattered even to the other side of the earth did not truly cease. Once I went in again, perhaps I could never return to Vietnam. I sat now and waited and trembled and nothing came to me to do.

But I could not sit in the woods and I rose and I went back down to the path and I walked again into the village and I went past the vegetable garden and there were three women there in conical straw hats and I knew their names and I knew their children and I passed the house of Tri and the house of Quang and the houses of others whose names I knew, whose children I knew, and I stopped in front of Tiên's house and there was the smell of wood fire from her kitchen and the smell of incense and the dragon's head was sitting in her doorway now and smelling of paint. There was the smell of fresh paint in her doorway and they all came, gradually. Tiên first and then Binh and then the others, all of them came, and my wife came and Hoa was with her and about to go away and I shook my head no and then nodded her to the circle that was forming.

Hoa crouched beside me and Thào next to her, anxious still, I knew, and my daughter turned her face up to me and then away and I leaned near and her hair smelled of the rain, smelled of the water that we gathered in a great stone pot, as is our way here, and we believe that the spirits of our ancestors come close to us and need our prayers, the prayers in our houses with the smoke of incense rising, and I understood how odd and wonderful the air of this village was now because I came here and married and made this child. The air here was filled with the spirits of Thào's coffee farmers and tobacco farmers and woodcutters but also filled with the spirits of my clothiers and newspapermen and bankers, all drawn into this place, into my house, by our incense and our prayers, all brought together by my child, the confluence of families who were, in that invisible realm, astonished to find themselves together.

And I said, "Each new year when I was a child, the god of the hearth went to heaven from my house in America. He came to the council of the gods and he said, There are children in this house and they sleep each night in great fear and they have places on their bodies that are the color of the sky in the highlands of Vietnam just after the sun has disappeared. And they pray, even the youngest of them, a boy, for escape and when they love each other, these children, it is to pray that each of the others escapes. And they know that this will happen for them, if at all, one at a time. And this house is empty of incense. And this house sees no spirits in the world."

And I stopped speaking and the faces in the circle lowered their eyes in deference to me and they understood and they said no more and we all rose and we went away and that night I lay in the dark on a straw mat and my wife lay awake next to me. I could hear her faintly jagged breath and I said, "There was no woman in that life." And my wife sighed softly and her breathing grew as smooth as her body when I first touched her and I closed my eyes.

And I thought of this place in Vietnam where I lay and how it grows coffee and it grows tobacco, and in that other life there was time in the morning when I could slip out of the house and there was no one around but me and I knew that one day I would escape, and inside they drank coffee and smoked cigarettes and read the newspaper.

Try This

Recall an experience that changed you. Write about it with one of the traditional openings of story:

• Once upon a time
• Long ago and far away
• In the beginning
• Let me tell you a story
• Listen!
• It all began

The readings following Chapters 2 and 4 of this book include "**prose poems**," poems that are not written in lines but continue to the margins of the page like prose. These are "A Mown Lawn" on page 79, and "Nude Interrogation" on page 158. This chapter contains two "**short-short**" stories within the text— "Frontier" and "This Is How I Remember It." "Worry," which follows, appeared in the short-short story collection *Microfiction*, but the piece that follows *it*, "A Story About the Body," appeared in the poetry collection *Human Wishes*.

The borderline between a prose poem and a short-short story is very fine, and you could (probably not very fruitfully) argue about whether any given piece is one or the other. In a general way, you could say that a prose poem will pay central attention to the language and its pattern of sound, whereas a short-short story will be first of all structured on the narrative arc conflict-crisis-resolution. You will find many exceptions to this general—not even rule, but—observation. If you contrast "A Mown Lawn" to "This Is How I Remember It," you will see the contrast relatively clearly.

Try This
Write either a prose poem or a short-short story such that no one would claim it was the other. If a poem, dwell on the language but tell *no story*. If a story, plain-speak a plot.

Ron Wallace
Worry

She worried about people; he worried about things. And between them, that about covered it.

"What would you think of our daughter sleeping around?" she said.

"The porch steps are rotting," he replied. "Someone's going to fall through."

They were lying in bed together, talking. They had been lying in bed together talking these twenty-five years. First about whether to have children, he wanted to (although the roof was going fast); she didn't (Down's syndrome, leukemia, microcephaly, mumps). Then, after their daughter was born, a healthy seven pounds eleven ounces ("She's not eating enough"; "The furnace is failing"), they talked about family matters, mostly ("Her friends are hoodlums, her room is a disaster"; "There's something about the brakes, the water heater's rusting out").

Worry grew between them like a son, with his own small insistencies and then more pressing demands. They stroked and coddled him; they set a place for him at the table; they sent him to kindergarten, private school, and college. Because he failed at nearly everything and always returned home, they loved him. After all, he was their son.

"I've been reading her diary. She does drugs. She sleeps around."

"I just don't think I can fix them myself. Where will we find a carpenter?"

Their daughter married her high school sweetheart, had a family, and started a health food store in a distant town. Although she recalled her childhood as fondly as anyone—how good her parents had been and how they worried for her, how old and infirm they must be growing, their house going to ruin—she rarely called or visited. She had worries of her own.

POEMS

Robert Hass
A Story About the Body

The young composer, working that summer at an artist's colony, had watched her for a week. She was Japanese, a painter, almost sixty, and he thought he was in love with her. He loved her work, and her work was like the way she moved her body, used her hands, looked at him directly when she made amused and considered answers to his questions. One night, walking back from a concert, they came to her door and she turned to him and said, "I think you would like to have me. I would like that too, but I must tell you that I have had a double mastectomy," and when he didn't understand, "I've lost both my breasts." The radiance that he had carried around in his belly and chest cavity—like music—withered very quickly, and he made himself look at her when he said, "I'm sorry. I don't think I could." He walked back to his own cabin through the pines, and in the morning he found a small blue bowl on the porch outside his door. It looked to be full of rose petals, but he found when he picked it up that the rose petals were on top; the rest of the bowl—she must have swept them from the corners of her studio—was full of dead bees.

Richard Wilbur
Digging for China

"Far enough down is China," somebody said.
"Dig deep enough and you might see the sky
As clear as at the bottom of a well.
Except it would be real—a different sky.
Then you could burrow down until you came

To China! Oh, it's nothing like New Jersey.
There's people, trees, and houses, and all that,
But much, much different. Nothing looks the same."

I went and got the trowel out of the shed
And sweated like a coolie all that morning,
Digging a hole beside the lilac-bush,
Down on my hands and knees. It was a sort
Of praying, I suspect. I watched my hand
Dig deep and darker, and I tried and tried
To dream a place where nothing was the same.
The trowel never did break through to blue.

Before the dream could weary of itself
My eyes were tired of looking into darkness,
My sunbaked head of hanging down a hole.
I stood up in a place I had forgotten,
Blinking and staggering while the earth went round
And showed me silver barns, the fields dozing
in palls of brightness, patens growing and gone
In the tides of leaves, and the whole sky china blue.
Until I got my balance back again
All that I saw was China, China, China.

Ellen Bryant Voigt

Short Story

My grandfather killed a mule with a hammer,
or maybe with a plank, or a stick, maybe
it was a horse—the story varied
in the telling. If he was planting corn
when it happened, it was a mule, and he was plowing
the upper slope, west of the house, his overalls
stiff to the knees with red dirt, the lines
draped behind his neck.
He must have been glad to rest
when the mule first stopped mid-furrow;
looked back at where he'd come, then down
to the brush along the creek he meant to clear.
No doubt he noticed the hawk's great leisure
over the field, the crows lumped
in the biggest elm on the opposite hill.

After he'd wiped his hatbrim with his sleeve,
he called to the mule as he slapped the line
along its rump, clicked and whistled.

My grandfather was a slight, quiet man,
smaller than most women, smaller
than his wife. Had she been in the yard,
seen him heading toward the pump now,
she'd pump for him a dipper of cold water.
Walking back to the field, past the corncrib,
he took an ear of corn to start the mule,
but the mule was planted. He never cursed
or shouted, only whipped it, the mule
rippling its backside each time
the switch fell, and when that didn't work
whipped it low on its side, where it's tender,
then cross-hatched the welts he'd made already.
The mule went down on one knee,
and that was when he reached for the blown limb,
or walked to the pile of seasoning lumber; or else,
unhooked the plow and took his own time to the shed
to get the hammer.
                      By the time I was born,
he couldn't even lift a stick. He lived
another fifteen years in a chair,
but now he's dead, and so is his son,
who never meant to speak a word against him,
and whom I never asked what his father
was planting and in which field,
and whether it happened before he married,
before his children came in quick succession,
before his wife died of the last one.
And only a few of us are left
who ever heard that story.

Maxine Kumin

Woodchucks

Gassing the woodchucks didn't turn out right.
The knockout bomb from the Feed and Grain Exchange
was featured as merciful, quick at the bone

and the case we had against them was airtight,
both exits shoehorned shut with puddingstone,
but they had a sub-sub-basement out of range.

Next morning they turned up again, no worse
for the cyanide than we for our cigarettes
and state-store Scotch, all of us up to scratch.
They brought down the marigolds as a matter of course
and then took over the vegetable patch
nipping the broccoli shoots, beheading the carrots.

The food from our mouths, I said, righteously thrilling
to the feel of the .22, the bullets' neat noses.
I, a lapsed pacifist fallen from grace
puffed with Darwinian pieties for killing,
now drew a bead on the littlest woodchuck's face.
He died down in the everbearing roses.

Ten minutes later I dropped the mother. She
flipflopped in the air and fell, her needle teeth
still hooked in a leaf of early Swiss chard.
Another baby next. O one-two-three
the murderer inside me rose up hard,
the hawkeye killer came on stage forthwith.

There's one chuck left. Old wily fellow, he keeps
me cocked and ready day after day after day.
All night I hunt his humped-up form. I dream

I sight along the barrel in my sleep.
If only they'd all consented to die unseen
gassed underground the quiet Nazi way.

Li-Young Lee
The Hammock

When I lay my head in my mother's lap
I think how day hides the stars,
the way I lay hidden once, waiting
inside my mother's laughter. And I remember
how she carried me on her back

between home and the kindergarten,
once each morning and once each afternoon.
I don't know what my mother's thinking.

When my son lays his head in my lap, I worry
his lips, swollen with his father's kisses,
won't keep his father's worries from becoming
his. I think, *Dear God*, and remember
there are stars we haven't heard from yet
they have so far to arrive: *Amen,*
and I think, and I feel almost comforted.
I've no idea what my child is thinking.

Between two unknowns, I live my life.
And what's it like? Between my mother's hopes,
older than me by coming before me,
and my child's wishes, older than me
by outliving me, what's it like?
Is it a door, and good-bye on either side?
Is it a window, and eternity on either side?
Yes, Yes, and a little singing between two great rests.

Louise Glück
Vita Nova

In the splitting up dream
we were fighting over who would keep
the dog,
Blizzard. You tell me
what the name means. He was
a cross between
something big and fluffy
and a dachshund. Does this have to be
the male and female
genitalia? Poor Blizzard,
why was he a dog? He barely touched
the hummus in his dogfood dish.
Then there was something else,
a sound. Like

gravel being moved. Or sand?
The sands of time? Then it was
Erica with her maracas,
like the sands of time
personified. Who will
explain this to
the dog? Blizzard,
Daddy needs you; Daddy's heart is empty,
not because he's leaving Mommy but because
the kind of love he wants Mommy
doesn't have, Mommy's
too ironic—Mommy wouldn't do
the rhumba in the driveway. Or
is this wrong. Supposing
I'm the dog, as in
my child-self, unconsolable because
completely pre-verbal? With
anorexia! O Blizzard,
be a brave dog—this is
all material; you'll wake up
in a different world,
you will eat again, you will grow up into a poet!
Life is very weird, no matter how it ends,
very filled with dreams. Never
will I forget your face, your frantic human eyes
swollen with tears.
I thought my life was over and my heart was broken.
Then I moved to Cambridge.

Try This

Several of the preceding poems are also memoirs. All of them are stories. Write a poem of no more than a dozen lines with the title of one of the traditional tales below. Make it contemporary. Can you base it on your own experience?

- Beauty and the Beast
- Ugly Duckling
- Mulan
- Baba Yaga
- Humpty Dumpty
- Noah's Ark
- Three Little Pigs
- Aladdin's Lamp

DRAMA

Carole Real

The Battle of Bull Run Always Makes Me Cry

CHARACTERS

Donna: 34, single, successful, lonely, funny.
Linda: Donna's friend, married, with a toddler.
Amy: Donna's friend, also married, practical.
Patrick: 35, Irish American, single, well dressed, attractive.

(A coffee shop. Linda and Amy are awaiting Donna, who enters, frazzled.)

DONNA: Hi, I'm sorry, I just, oh God what a thing. I got pulled over! By a cop! And he noticed my emissions sticker was expired and I'm like oh God what's that going to be, like another seventy-five-dollar thing? So I started crying!

LINDA: You did?

AMY: Good move.

DONNA: Yeah, I know. But it wasn't even like I had to try.

LINDA: Was he cute?

DONNA: *(Disappointed.)* No.

LINDA: *(Disappointed.)* Oh, too bad.

DONNA: So I said to him that I was on my way to pick up my little girl, Enid. It just came out of my mouth. So, of course he knows I'm lying. I can tell. Because no one has a little girl named Enid.

AMY: Right.

LINDA: What'd he do?

DONNA: He softened.

AMY: Oh good.

DONNA: Yeah, and told me that I should get the emissions thing done and that he'd let me go this time.

AMY: Great!

DONNA: But it freaked me out, let me tell you. That and . . . you know I keep having dreams about Sai Baba.

LINDA: Who?

DONNA: Sai Baba. He's a guru of some sort. They chant for him in Norwalk and places. The guy, who came to clean my rug, Gary? I assumed he was, you know, a pod, and then he picked up one of my Alan Watts books and started talking about it and kundalini and stuff and then he mentioned Sai Baba. But the weird thing is . . . they think he's God. Really God. "The avatar" is what Gary said, which I guess means God. And every night since then, I've had these dreams where I'm someplace, doing something, then all of a sudden people are chanting or talking about Sai Baba. I tried to get one of his books, but they were out.

LINDA: Oh for God's sake!

DONNA: Well, I'm not saying I'll convert . . .

LINDA: For God's sake, for God's sake, for God's sake! Tell us about your date!

DONNA: Oh . . . my date . . .

LINDA: Yes, your . . .

DONNA: My . . . You want to hear . . . ?

LINDA: My God, yes! I got a babysitter so I could meet you!

AMY: We want to hear . . . we're here to hear.

DONNA: Well, it's a thing, let me tell you.

LINDA: What happened?

(Patrick crosses to opposite Donna, Amy, and Linda. He is good-looking and well dressed. He stands, waiting to meet someone. During the play, Donna, Amy, and Linda can see Patrick, and he can see them, though he interacts only with Donna.)

DONNA: Well! We met at the movie theater. And he looked really cute.

AMY: Yeah?

LINDA: No, he's really cute.

DONNA: Right. So, he was there, really cute. And I thought, "Oh God." You know?

AMY and **LINDA:** (three syllables) Yeaaaaah.

DONNA: So we saw the movie, and then we went . . .

LINDA: Wait wait wait. I did not get a babysitter to hear a summary. Start from the beginning. Did you have popcorn. Did he pay for it.

DONNA: I had popcorn. He did not pay for it.

(Linda and Amy react visably negatively.)

He had bought the tickets.

(Linda and Amy take this in and give him a few points.)

So we saw the movie . . .

LINDA: Which movie.

DONNA: Dark Rain.

(We see Patrick seated at the movie.)

AMY: That's supposed to be really sad . . .

DONNA: Oh, it is. It's really really sad.

LINDA: Is it sad?

DONNA: No, it's sad.

LINDA: It has that really cute, that . . .

DONNA: Yes. And he *dies*.

AMY: Oh

DONNA: Alone, in a prison in Istanbul, like a thousand miles from his girlfriend, who really loves him. I was like, distraught.

(Patrick hands a napkin to an invisible person next to him.)

AMY: Did you cry?

DONNA: Yes! Plus I was so tense, from the date thing.

LINDA: Did he cry?

DONNA: No. Actually. He was sort of smirking.

LINDA: Oh, I don't like that. Did he notice you were crying?

DONNA: Yes, he gave me a napkin.

LINDA: That's good.

DONNA: Then after the movie as we were walking to the restaurant he
started talking about politics.

AMY *and* **LINDA**:   *(sympathetic, been there.)* Oh . . .

DONNA: And then, over dinner? The Civil War.

*(Patrick is now at dinner, holding forth about the Civil War. We see his lips
move, but we cannot hear him.)*

AMY: The whole war?

DONNA: One battle in particular.

LINDA: Well, he was probably trying to impress you.

DONNA: Don't people understand how totally unimpressed I am with people
trying to impress me?

LINDA: He probably wanted you to think he's smart.

DONNA: Would I be eating with him if he weren't smart? Have I eaten with
a man who is not smart?

LINDA: Well, he doesn't know that.

AMY: So, what happened?

DONNA: He talked for about forty-five minutes about this one particular
battle.

LINDA: Which one?

DONNA: Oh, like it would mean something to you.

LINDA: Well . . .

DONNA: Anyway, I can't really say which battle. I was feigning. I was sittin'
there thinkin' "Cat food, kitty litter, broccoli, I'd like to fuck this guy
. . ."

(Patrick and Donna lock eyes for a moment.)

DONNA: And he's like blah blah blah Shiloh, blah blah blah Lee.

*(During Patrick's speech, Donna crosses to him and joins him
at a dinner table.)*

PATRICK: . . . then Chamberlain, who was really a remarkable person, a
professor of classical language at Bowdoin . . . he had asked for leave
to go fight, they said no, so he asked to go to England to study and
then joined the army instead . . . he served throughout the war, and at
Gettysburg had the job of holding the flank at Little Round Top. This
is all in Shelby Foote's book.

DONNA: *(to Amy and Linda)* Like I'm gonna read Shelby Foote's book, you
know?

PATRICK: The Union had set up artillery on the ridge. Of course if you can
turn the flank and get behind the Yankees . . .

DONNA: *(feigning)* Right . . .

PATRICK: Anyway, Chamberlain had withstood several charges, he was
running out of men and ammunition, but at the next charge he made
a countercharge with bayonets and the South freaked and didn't try to
take Round Hill after that. He got the Congressional Medal of Honor.
One person *can* make a difference.

DONNA: *(to Linda and Amy)* Why do they do that? Why do they talk to me
about the Civil War?

AMY: Did you see that documentary?

DONNA: Are you talking about the Civil War?

LINDA: *(to Amy)* Yes.

AMY: Did you see that part, that letter . . .

LINDA: Please, I'll go hysterical crying.

AMY: This army officer knows he's going to die in the next battle, and he
writes his wife . . .

LINDA: I can't listen to this! I'll start sobbing!

AMY: The most beautiful letter . . . I cried.

LINDA: I sobbed.

AMY: I boo-hooed. I couldn't watch the rest of the show, I had to lie down.

DONNA: Well, why couldn't he talk about something like that about the
Civil War? Why did he have to go on and on about a battle?

AMY: Because men think *out (makes a gesture with her hands indicating
the outside world)* . . . *in (gesture meaning inner life)*. Women think *in
(gesture)* . . . *out (gesture)*

DONNA: Oh . . .

LINDA: No, that's true.

AMY: So the reason they think of you last, after all the stuff that's out there
in the world, is because they think of themselves last, and you and
your relationship with them is part of them.

DONNA: That's why they like military history.

AMY: Right.

DONNA: Because it's all *out*. *(gestures)*

AMY: Right.

LINDA: What happened next? I have a two-year-old, I need to live vicariously here.

DONNA: So then I said to him . . . *(to Patrick)* Are you nervous because you know I want to sleep with you?

(Patrick stares at her)

AMY *and* **LINDA**: *(They turn towards one another and squeal, at once horrified and thrilled.)* AAAAAAAHHHHHH!

LINDA: You didn't.

AMY: Oh my God.

DONNA: Naah, I didn't have the balls. What I really wanted to say was. *(To Patrick')* Shut up and kiss me! Just please *God* shut the *fuck* up and kiss me! *(To Linda and Amy)* But instead I just said *(to Patrick)* I'm not really a Civil War fan. Per se.

(Patrick looks hurt, and moves the food around on his plate with his fork. To Linda and Amy.)

> Then he was sort of hurt, I could tell, and he sort of moved the food around on his plate. And I started to think, I'm such an asshole, you know, here's this guy taking me out, trying to talk to me, okay, so it's about the battle of Bull Run, whatever, but I can't even be nice to him. And here I am, I'm thirty-four, I haven't had a boyfriend since . . .

LINDA: Ron . . .

DONNA: Ron, who was . . .

LINDA: Unkind.

DONNA: Unkind . . . I need to be more . . . I need . . . I don't know.

AMY: Now, why do you want to date Patrick?

DONNA: What?

AMY: I mean, aside from that he's cute.

DONNA: Well. He looks like my father. A *lot*.

(Linda and Amy take this in.)

> And we have a lot in common. Weird things. And, when I look in his eyes I feel like I'm falling down a long tunnel towards ancient Celtic mysteries.

AMY: Wow. Okay. That's a good reason.

LINDA: Did you tell him that thing? That we talked about? About how you've got all this stuff going for you, a career, and a nice place to live, and now you're really ready for a serious relationship, and looking forward to it? You know, really strong and confident and knowing what you want, but letting him know that you want something more than just a fling?

DONNA: Oh, right. The thing. Right. Okay. (*to Patrick*) You know, Patrick, actually, over the past year it's become sort of clear to me that, well, I have this career, that is going well, and I have a nice home and friends, but the truth is that, without, you know, someone to share it with, it can be really . . . really . . .

(She starts tearing up.)

. . . lonely and . . . empty.

(She cries outright.)

Really lonely.

(She sobs. Patrick, a little stunned, hands her a napkin.)

I'm sorry.

(She wipes her eyes.)

I have to go to the ladies room.

(She gets up and crosses back to the table with Linda and Amy. She sits between them, resting her elbows on the table, and crying into the napkin. To Linda.)

It didn't really go how we planned.

AMY:	**LINDA**:

(Amy and Linda both rub/pat her back.)

Ooooh.	No.

DONNA: It just gets very lonely when they talk about the Civil War.

AMY	**LINDA**:

(Amy and Linda both rub/pat her back.)

Ooooh.	I know.

DONNA: Or politics.

AMY	**LINDA**:

(Amy and Linda both rub/pat her back.)

Ooooh.	I know.

DONNA: Or books.

AMY	**LINDA**:

(Amy and Linda both rub/pat her back.)

Ooooh.	I know.

DONNA: Because they're lecturing! And you don't want a lecture. You want back and forth.

(She makes a back and forth gesture.)

LINDA: I know. That's the thing.

DONNA: That's the thing. You want the back and forth.

AMY: You want back and forth.

DONNA: That's the thing.

LINDA: Then what happened?

DONNA: I stayed in the ladies room a while. There were some other women there and we chatted, you know, about the toilet paper.

AMY: That must have been a nice break.

DONNA: It was.

(She crosses back to Patrick's table.)

The Battle of Bull Run always makes me cry.

PATRICK: That's all right. Do you want to go for a walk?

DONNA: *(Noticing that he's paid the check.)* Yes.

(They leave the restaurant and start to stroll.)

Do you ever think there's just so much that we don't understand? Like, my cat? Kitty? She's been staring at this cat next door, for like two years. But I never let her out, so all she can do is stare at him from the deck. Sometimes I sing the theme from *Romeo and Juliet* when I see them doing this. Anyway, I had problems with her, pee problems. It's a long story, but I decided it was time for her to be able to go outdoors. So I got her all her shots, which cost like two hundred dollars. And then I had to keep her in till the shots kicked in and then the very day she was finally okay to go outside, I came home from work, thinking, okay this is *the* day Kitty gets to go outside and I see Woody, the cat from next door, on my path. And what's at my door but a tiny little freshly killed bird. Like a present. Which he had never done before, in the whole two years I've been there. But my question is, how did he know? How did he know that this was the day, the first day in the two years I've been there that she could come out? Then I realized this is *much much* bigger than we think.

PATRICK: What is.

DONNA: Courtship. I mean, forget trying to analyze it. Because most of it will always remain completely . . . mysterious. And we should just honor the mystery. *(To Linda and Amy.)* Do you think men do that, and women sort of don't? Honor the mystery?

AMY: *(thinking about it)* Maybe.

DONNA: Why is that?

LINDA: What'd he do then?

DONNA: He . . .

PATRICK: *(Thinks it's funny.)* Where's your coat?

DONNA: *(Knows it was dumb.)* I didn't wear one. I always do that.

PATRICK: *(takes his raincoat off)* Here.

(puts the raincoat on her, and buttons it)

DONNA: You'll get wet.

PATRICK: It's okay.

DONNA: Thanks.

PATRICK: My pleasure.

LINDA: What'd he do?

DONNA: He . . .

PATRICK: *(Offers her his arm)*

LINDA: What?

DONNA: It's hard to describe.

(She takes his arm.)

AMY:	**LINDA**:
Tell us!	Tell!

DONNA: He gave me his coat. And he buttoned it up.

AMY:	**LINDA**:
Oooooo.	Oooooooh.

LINDA: That is so hot.

DONNA: And then he gave me his arm, and he walked me home. And he was quiet the whole way.

LINDA: Uncomfortable quiet, or nice like you're in a bubble together quiet?

DONNA: Bubble together.

LINDA: Then, when you got to your place, what did he do?

PATRICK: Goodnight.

(He kisses her.)

DONNA: He said, "goodnight" and kissed me.

LINDA: How was the kiss?

(Donna taps Patrick on the shoulder. Patrick kisses her again.)

DONNA: Very nice. It was a very nice kiss.

LINDA: You had a nice date.

DONNA: Did I?

AMY: Yes.

LINDA: No, you did.

DONNA: I did. I had a nice date.

End

Try This

Write a dialogue between yourself and two friends in which you tell about something that happened to you. How do the friends' comments affect the way you tell the tale? You might think of the telling as a journey and the friends' comments as detours.

Warm-up

One of these people is a respected, accomplished, and successful writer; you decide which one. Write a brief description of the sort of thing he or she writes. Visualize him or her wherever that writing takes place—desk, table, plane, park…what does it feel like to be this person, in this place, writing? Now: somewhere in your journal is a piece you care about, but you don't know how to develop or enrich it; you don't know where it's going. Hand it over to this person. For the next fifteen minutes she or he is going to write it for you.

CHAPTER SIX

DEVELOPMENT AND REVISION

Developing a Draft
Revision and Editing
The Workshop

Ultimately my hope is to amaze myself.

Jerry Uelsmann

Imaginative writing has its source in dream, risk, mystery, and play. But if you are to be a good—and perhaps a professional—writer, you will need discipline, care, and ultimately even an obsessive perfectionism. As poet Paul Engle famously said, "Writing is rewriting what you have rewritten."

Just as a good metaphor must be both apt and surprising, so every piece of literary work must have both unity and variety, both craft and risk, both form and the unpredictable. Having dreamt and played a possibility into being, you will need to sharpen and refine it in action, character, and language, in a continual process of selection and arrangement. This will involve both disciplined work and further play, but it won't always be that easy to tell one from the other. Alice Munro describes the duality of a process in which seeking order remains both mysterious and a struggle:

> So when I write a story, I want to make a certain kind of structure, and I know
> the feeling I want to get from being inside that structure...There is no blueprint
> for this structure . . . It seems to be already there, and some unlikely clue, such as
> a shop window or a bit of conversation, makes me aware of it. Then I start accu-
> mulating the material and putting it together. Some of the material I may have
> lying around already, in memories and observations, and some I invent, and
> some I have to go diligently looking for (factual details), while some is dumped in
> my lap (anecdotes, bits of speech). I see how this material might go together to

make the shape I need, and I try it. I keep trying and seeing where I went wrong and trying again . . . I feel a part that's wrong, like a soggy weight; then I pay attention to the story, as if it were happening somewhere.

Developing a Draft

Your journal is now a warehouse of possibilities, and you probably already have a sense of the direction in which many of its entries might be developed.

- If you wrote of a memory or an event that seems to you to contain a point or to lead toward reflection, if you came up with ideas that mattered to you and that you wanted both to illustrate and to state, then you probably have a memoir or personal essay in the works.

- If a journal entry has a strong setting, with characters who engage each other in action and dialogue, whose thoughts and desires may lead them into conflict and toward change, perhaps a short story is brewing.

- If the sound and rhythm of the language seem integral to the thought, if the images seem dense and urgent, if the idea clusters around imagery and sound rather than playing itself out in a sequence of events, then a poem is probably forming.

- If you have characters who confront each other in dialogue, especially if they are concealing things that they sometimes betray in word or action, and if they face discovery and decision that will lead to change in one or more of their lives, then you very likely have a play.

Chapters 7 through 10 of this book will discuss the techniques peculiar to each of these four forms, and you'll want to look at those chapters as you work toward a finished draft. In the meantime there are a number of ways to develop your ideas in order to find your direction. Some of these are repetitions or adaptations of ideas you have already used for play.

Try This

Take a journal entry you like and highlight any word that seems particularly evocative, that seems to capture the spirit of the whole. Cluster that word. Freewrite.

"Befriend" another journal piece. Read it over, set it aside, and begin writing, starting every thought with the words "it's like . . . it's like . . . it's like . . . " Some of the thoughts will suggest colors, some memories, some metaphors, and so forth. Keep writing, fast, until you're moderately tired.

Pick a journal entry that does not depend on setting, and give it a setting; describe the place and atmosphere in detail. Think of "setting" loosely. Perhaps the setting of a piece is someone's face. Perhaps the weather is internal.

When I was eight or nine, my brother, who was four years older, made up wonderful stories with which he used to pass the hot boring afternoons of Arizona summer. I would whine and beg for another episode. At some point he got tired of it and decided I should make up stories on my own. Then he would drill me by rapping out three nouns. "Oleanders, wastebasket, cocker spaniel!" "Factory, monkey bars, chop suey!" I was supposed to start talking immediately, making up as I went along a story about a dog who used to scrounge around in the garbage until one day he made the mistake of eating a poison flower . . . or a tool and die worker who went to a Chinese restaurant and left his son on the playground . . . My brother was the expert writer (and eventually went on to become an editor at the *Los Angeles Times*). I myself had not considered storytelling—I wrote ill-advised love letters and inspirational verse—and was amazed that I could—almost always—think of some way to include his three arbitrary things in a tale of mystery, disaster, or romance.

Neither of us knew that my brother had stumbled on a principle of literary invention, which is that creativity occurs when things not usually connected are seen as connected. It is the *unexpected* juxtaposition that generates literature. A more sophisticated version of this game is used in film writing. Screen writer Claudia Johnson tells me that she and collaborator Pam Ball once went to a restaurant to celebrate the finishing of a film script. They had no idea what they were going to write next and decided to test the nimbleness of their plotting by outlining a film based on the next three things they overheard. The three conversations turned out to concern a cigarette, a suicide in Chicago, and origami. By the time they had their coffee they had a treatment for the next film.

Novelist Margaret Drabble describes the same process as organic and largely unconscious. "It's an accumulation of ideas. Things that have been in the back of my mind suddenly start to swim together and to stick together, and I think, 'Ah, that's a novel beginning.'"

Try This

Pick, without too much thought about it—random would be fine—three short entries in your writing journal. Take one element from each (a character, an image, a theme, a line of dialogue; again, don't think about it too hard) and write a new passage that combines these three elements. Does it suggest any way that the three entries might in fact be fused into a single piece and be enriched by the fusion?

or:

Take one of your journal entries and rewrite it in the form of one of the following: an instruction pamphlet; a letter to the complaints department; a newspaper item; a television ad; a love song. Does the new juxtaposition of form and content offer any way you can enrich your idea?

Basically, there are two ways to go about structuring a piece of writing, though they are always in some way used in combination.

At one extreme is the outline. You think through the sequence of events of a story or drama; the points of an essay; the verse form of a poem. Then when you have an outline roughly in mind (or written down in detail), you start at the beginning and write through to the end of a draft.

Do not underestimate the power and usefulness of this method. However amorphous the vision of the whole may be, most writers begin with the first sentence and proceed to the last. Though fiction writer/essayist Charles Baxter has mourned the "tyranny of narrative," his stories and novels show the most careful attention to narrative sequence. (That one of them, *First Light*, presents its events in reverse order makes precise sequencing all the more necessary.) E. M. Forster spoke of writing a novel as moving toward some imagined event that loomed as a distant mountain. Eudora Welty advised a story writer to take walks pondering the story until it seemed whole, and then to try to write the first draft at one sitting. Though playwrights may first envision a climactic event and poets may start with the gift of a line that ends up last in the finished poem, still, the pull is strong to write from left to right and top to bottom.

Try This

Bring your research skills to your imaginative work. Identify something in a piece that you aren't sure about. You don't know the facts, don't understand the process or the equipment, aren't clear on the history or the statistics, don't know the definition. Find out. Consult books, reference works, newspapers, the internet; interview someone, email someone, ask the experts.

At the opposite end of the spectrum from the outline is quilting, or "piece work," in which you carry on writing without attention to shape or structure. To use this method, you decide that this paragraph or verse or incident is the kernel of the thing you're going to write, and you continue to doodle and noodle around it, seeing what will emerge. You freewrite a dialogue passage, sketch in a description of the setting, try it in this character's voice and then in the omniscient, let yourself go with a cascade of images. Two or three time a day, sit down and dash out a potential section of such a piece—a few lines, a paragraph, a monologue, images, a character sketch. Talk to yourself in your journal about what theme or idea matters to you, what you'd like to accomplish, what you fear will go wrong. If you do this for several days, you will have roughed out a sizeable portion of your project.

When you have a small mountain of material (I like to write or copy it into a single computer file I label a "ruff," then identify each paragraph by page number so I can find it easily), you print it, chop it into sections, spread it out on a large surface, and start moving pieces around till you seem to have a composition. Tape the sections together and make notes on them, discarding what seems extraneous, indicating what's missing, what needs rewriting, where a transition is in order, and so forth. Then cut-and-paste on the computer to put them in that order, noting the needed changes. When you print out this version, you have a rough shape of your piece.

Try This

Doodle a series of lists—of the characteristics of someone you have written about, or of phrases and idioms that character would use; or of objects associated with a person, place, profession, or memory you have written about. Generate, rapidly, a list of metaphors for some central object in a piece you want to develop.

This cut-jot-and-sort system can work for any genre, and it's worth getting used to the process. However, sometimes it works better than others, and sometimes it just isn't the best way. The advantages of the outline method tend to be clarity, unity, and drive; of the cut-and-paste method richness, originality, and surprise. The problem with writing from an outline is that the piece may seem thin and contrived; the trouble with piece work is that it can end up formless, diffuse, and dull.

You will already have a sense of which method is your natural tendency, and I'd urge you, whichever it is, to work in the opposite direction. The methods are not mutually exclusive, and each can benefit from the particular discipline of the other.

If you start with a clear sense of direction, a determination to follow a plan, then detour from time to time. Too tight a rein on the author's part, too rigid a control of where the imagery is headed, what the protagonist will do next, how the remembered event exactly happened—any of these can squeeze the life out of the work. When you feel the action or the language becoming mechanical, stop and freewrite a monologue, a list of images, an exploration of character, or conflict, or the weather. One freeing trick, if you find your piece flat, is to go through and put some arbitrary line or sentence in each paragraph or verse, something that absolutely does not belong and that you would never put there. Then go away from it for a while, and when you go back, see if there's anything in the nonsense that might in fact improve the sense.

If, on the other hand, you can generate lovely stuff but have trouble finding a through-line for it, if you find yourself in successive drafts generating new possibilities and never settling on a form or sequence, then you probably need to focus on a plan and push yourself through one draft based on it. Set your quilt aside and consider the questions of unity and shape: What is the heart of this piece? What is its emotional core? What, in one word, is it *about?* How can I focus on that, make each part illuminate it, raise the intensity, and get rid of the extraneous?

And don't give up. "The big secret," says fiction writer Ron Carlson, "is the ability to stay in the room. The writer is the person who stays in the room . . . People have accused me . . . 'You're talking Zen here.' And I just say, 'Zen this: The secret is to stay in the room.'"

Try This

Practice in brief form each of the methods above. Pick an entry in your journal—not one you intend to make into a finished work. Before lunch, write an outline of a piece based on that entry. In late afternoon or evening, take *no more than one hour* to write a draft of the piece that covers the whole outline. Your work will have holes, cracks, and sloppy writing. Never mind; get through to the end. Leave it for a day or two, then make marginal notes on what you would want to do in the next draft.

Pick another entry and over the next two or three days, freewrite something or other about it every four hours. Print, cut, and arrange into a sequence or shape. Print out the result and make marginal notes on what the next draft would need.

Discuss in class what you learned from the two methods. Which would suit you best when you come to write an essay, a story, a poem, a play?

Interviewer: Was there some technical problem? What was
it that had stumped you?
Hemingway: Getting the words right.

Revision and Editing

Most people dread revision and put it off; and most find it the most satisfying part of writing once they are engaged in it and engaged by it. The vague feelings of self-dissatisfaction and distress that accompany an imperfect draft are smoothed away as the pleasure of small perfections and improvements come.

To write your first draft, you banished the internal critic. Now make the critic welcome. The first round of rewrites is probably a matter of letting your misgivings surface. Focus for a while on what seems awkward, overlong, undeveloped, flat, or flowery. Tinker. Tighten. Sharpen. Let that small unease surface and look at it squarely. More important at this stage than finishing any given page or phrase is that you're getting to know your story in order to open it to new possibilities.

Development and revision are not really two separate processes but a continuum of invention and improvement, re-seeing and chiseling. Sometimes the mere altering of punctuation will flash forth a necessary insight. Sometimes inspiration will necessitate a change of tense or person. To find the best way of proceeding, you may have to "see again" more than once. The process involves external and internal insight; you'll need your conscious critic, your creative instinct, and readers you trust. You may need each of them several times, not necessarily in that order. Writing gets better not just by polishing and refurbishing, not only by improving a word choice here and image there, but by taking risks with the structure, re-envisioning, being open to new meaning itself. Sometimes, Annie Dillard advises in *The Writing Life*, what you must do is knock out "a bearing wall." "The part you jettison," she says, "is not only the best written part; it is also, oddly, that part which was to have been the very point. It is the original key passage, the passage on which the rest was to hang, and from which you yourself drew the courage to begin."

There are many kinds of work and play that go under the name of "rewriting." It would be useful to go back to the film metaphor—long shot, middle shot, close-up—in order to think of ways of re-visioning your work. You will at some point early or late need to step back and view the project as a whole, its structure and composition, the panorama of its tones: does it need fundamental change, reversal of parts, a different shape or a different sweep? At some point you will be working in obsessive close-up, changing a word to alter the coloration of a mood, finding a fresher metaphor or a more exact verb, even changing a comma to a semicolon and changing it back again. Often you'll be working in middle shot, moving this paragraph from page one to page three, chopping out an unnecessary description, adding a passage of dialogue to intensify the atmosphere. Read each draft of your piece aloud and listen for rhythm, word choice, unintended repetition. You'll move many times back and forth among these methods, also walking away from the piece in order to come back to it with fresh eyes.

Try This

Make a list of things a character or persona in your piece might fear. Add a scene, line, or image in which a character or persona is in great fear.

or:

Show the character doing something genuinely dangerous. But the character/persona is not afraid. Why not?

If you feel stuck on a project, put it away. Don't look at it for a matter of days or weeks, until you feel fresh again. In addition to getting some distance on your work, you're mailing it to your unconscious. You may even discover that in the course of developing a piece, you have mistaken its nature. I once spent a year writing a screenplay—which I suppose I thought was the right form because the story was set in an Arizona cow town in 1914—finally to realize that I couldn't even *find out* what the story was until I got inside the characters' heads. Once I understood this, that story became a novel.

As you plan your revisions and as you rewrite, you will know (and your critics will tell you) what problems are unique to your piece. You may also be able to focus your own critique by asking yourself these questions:

What is this piece about?

Try This

State your idea in a single sentence. Reduce it to a word. Express it in an image. Express it in a line of dialogue that one of your characters might say. Probably none of these things will appear in your finished piece, but they will help you focus. Are you clear about what you're writing about? Does it need thinking and feeling through again?

Is the language fresh?

Try This

Go through your work and highlight generalizations in one color, abstractions in another, clichés in a third. Replace each of them with something specific, wild, inappropriate, far-fetched. Go back later to see if any of these work, in fact. Replace the others, working toward the specific, the precise, and the concrete.

Is it clear?

Try This

Go through your manuscript and highlight the answers to these questions: *Where are we? When are we? Who are they? How do things look? What period, time of year, day or night is it? What's the weather? What's happening?* If you can't find the answers in your text, the reader won't find them either. Not all of this information may be necessary, but you need to be aware of what's left out.

Where is it too long?

Try This

Carefully save the current draft of your piece. Then copy it into a new document on which you play a cutting game—make your own rules in advance. Cut all the adjectives and adverbs. Or remove one line from every verse of a poem. Delete a minor character. Fuse two scenes into one. Cut half of every line of dialogue. Or simply require yourself to shorten it somehow by a third. You will have some sense of what tightening might improve your work. Compare the two drafts. Does the shortened version have any virtues that the longer one does not?

Where is it underdeveloped?

Try This

In any first, second, or third draft of a manuscript there are likely to be necessary lines, images, or passages that you have skipped or left skeletal. Make notes in your margins wherever you feel your piece is underdeveloped. Then go back and quickly freewrite each missing piece. At this point, just paste the freewrites in. Then read over the manuscript (long shot) to get a feel for how these additions change, add, or distort. Are some unnecessary after all? Do some need still fuller expanding? Should this or that one be reduced to a sentence or image? Do some suggest a new direction?

Is your copy clean?

Spelling, grammar, and punctuation are a kind of magic; their purpose is to be invisible. If the sleight of hand works, we will not notice a comma or a quotation mark but will translate each instantly into a pause or an awareness of voice; we will not focus on the individual letters of a word but extract its sense whole. When the mechanics are incorrectly used, the trick is revealed and the magic fails; the reader's focus is shifted from the story to its surface. The reader is irritated at the author, and of all the emotions the reader is willing to experience, irritation at the author is not one.

There is no intrinsic virtue in standardized mechanics, and you can depart from them whenever you produce an effect that adequately compensates for the attention called to the surface. But only then. Unlike the techniques of narrative, the rules of spelling, grammar, and punctuation can be coldly learned anywhere in the English-speaking world—and they should be learned by anyone who aspires to write.

Try This

Your manuscript as you present it to your workshop, an agent, or an editor, is dressed for interview. If it's sloppy it'll be hard to see how brilliant it really is. Groom it. Consult Appendix B for the traditional and professional formats for each genre.

then:

Line Edit: Check through for faulty grammar, inconsistent tenses, unintended repetitions of words, any awkwardness that makes you feel uneasy. Fix them.

and:

Proofread: Run a spellcheck (but don't rely on it entirely). Read through for typos, punctuation errors, any of those goblins that slip into a manuscript. If you are in doubt about the spelling or meaning of a word, look it up.

> Whatever can't be taught, there is a great deal that can,
> and must, be learned.
>
> *Mary Oliver*

The Workshop

Once you have a draft of a piece and have worked on it to the best of your ability, someone else's eyes can help refresh the vision of your own. That's where the workshop can help. Professionals rely on their editors and agents in this process, and as Kurt Vonnegut has pointed out, "A creative writing course provides experienced editors for inspired amateurs. What could be simpler or more dignified?"

In preparation for the workshop, each class member should read the piece twice, once for its content, a second time with pen in hand to make marginal comments, observations, suggestions. A summarizing end note is usual and helpful. This should be done with the understanding that the work at hand is *by definition* a work in progress. If it were finished then there would be no reason to bring it into workshop.

Keep in mind that the goal of the workshop is to make the piece under consideration *the best that it can be.* The group should continue to deal, first, in neutral and inquiring ways with each piece before going on to discuss what does and doesn't "work." It's often a good idea to begin with a detailed summary of what the poetry, story, essay, or drama actually says—useful because if class members understand the characters or events differently, find the imagery confusing, or miss an irony, this is important information for the author, a signal that she has not revealed what, or all, she meant. The exploratory questions suggested in the introduction may still be useful. In addition, the class might address such questions as:

- *What kind of piece is this?*
- *What other works does it remind you of?*
- *How is it structured?*
- *What is it about?*
- *What does it say about what it is about?*
- *What degree of identification does it invite?*
- *How does its imagery relate to its theme?*
- *How is persona or point of view employed?*
- *What effect on the reader does it seem to want to produce?*

Only then should the critique begin to deal with whether the work under consideration is successful in its effects: *is the language fresh, the action clear, the point of view consistent, the rhythm interesting, the characters fully drawn, the imagery vivid?* Now and again it is well to pause and return to more substantive matters: *what's the spirit of this piece, what is it trying to say, what does it make me feel?*

If this process is respectfully and attentively addressed, it can be of genuine value not only to the writer but to the writer-critics, who can learn, through the articulation of their own and others' responses, "what works" and what doesn't, and how to face similar authorial problems. In workshop discussion, disagreements are as often as instructive as consensus; lack of clarity often teaches what clarity is.

For the writer, the process is emotionally strenuous, because the piece under discussion is a sort of baby on the block. Its parent may have a strong impulse to explain and plead. Most of us feel not only committed to what we have put on the page, but also defensive on its behalf—wanting, really, only to be told that it is a work of genius or, failing that, to find out that we have gotten away with it. We may even want to blame the reader. If the criticism is: *this isn't clear,* it's hard not to feel: *you didn't read it right*—even if you understand that although the workshop members have an obligation to read with special care, it is not up to them to "get it" but up to the author to be clear. If the complaint is: *this isn't credible,* it's very hard not to respond: *but it really happened!*—even though you know perfectly well that credibility is a different sort of fish than fact. There is also a self-preservative impulse to keep from changing the core of what you've done: *why should I put in all that effort?*

The most important part of being a writer in a workshop is to learn this: be still, be greedy for suggestions, take everything in, and don't defend. The trick to making good use of criticism is to be utterly selfish about it. Ultimately you are the laborer, the arbiter, and the boss in any dispute about your story, so you can afford to consider any problem and any solution. Therefore, the first step toward successful revision is learning to hear, absorb, and accept criticism.

It *is* difficult. But only the effort of complete receptivity will make the workshop work for you. The chances are that your draft really does not say the most meaningful thing inherent in it, and that most meaningful thing may announce itself sideways, in a detail, a parenthesis, an afterthought, a slip. Somebody else may spot it before you do. Sometimes the best advice comes from the most surprising source. The thing you resist the hardest may be exactly what you need.

After the workshop, the writer's obligation alters slightly. It's important to take the written critiques and take them seriously, let them sink in with as good a will as you brought to workshop. But part of the need is also not to let them sink in too far. Reject without regret whatever seems on reflection wrong-headed, dull, destructive, or irrelevant to your vision. Resist the impulse to write "for the workshop" what you think your peers or teacher will praise. It's just as important to be able to discriminate between helpful and unhelpful criticism as it is to be able to write. It is in fact the same thing as being able to write. So listen to everything and receive all criticism as if it is golden. Then listen to yourself and toss the dross.

More to Read

Aitchity, Kenneth. *A Writer's Time*. New York: W.W. Norton, 1986.

Kaplan, David Michael. *Revision: A Creative Approach to Writing and Rewriting Fiction*. Cincinnati: Story Press, 1997.

Strunk, William Jr. and E.B. White. *The Elements of Style*. Boston: Allyn and Bacon, 1979.

Woodruff, Jay, ed. *A Piece of Work: Five Writers Discuss Their Revisions*. Iowa City: University of Iowa Press, 1993.

HOW TO LOSE THINGS /? / THE GIFT OF LOSING THINGS?

[Draft 1]

One might begin by losing one's reading glasses
oh 2 or 3 times a day - or one's favorite pen.

THE ART OF LOSING THINGS
The thing to do is to begin by "mislaying".

Mostly, one begins by "mislaying":
keys, reading-glasses, fountain pens
- these are almost too easy to be mentioned,
and "mislaying" means that they usually turn up
in the most obvious place, although when one
is making progress, the places grow more unlikely
- This is by way of introduction. I really
want to introduce myself - I am such a
fantastic lly good at losing things
I think everyone shd. profit from my experiences.

You may find it hard to believe, but I have actually lost
I mean lost, and forever two whole houses,
one a very big one. A third house, also big, is
at present, I think, "mislaid" - but
maybe it's lost, too. I won't know for sure for some time.
I have lost one/long peninsula and one island.
I have lost - it can never be has never been found -
a small-sized town on that same island.
I've lost smaller bits of geography, like   and many smaller bits of geography or scenery
a splendid beach , and a good-sized bay.
Two whole cities, two of the
world's biggest citiies (two of the most beautiful
although that's beside the point)
A piece of one continent
and one entire continent.   All gone, gone forever and ever.

One might think this would have prepared me
for losing one average-sized not especially------- exceptionally
beautiful or dazzlingly intelligent person
(except for blue eyes)   (only the eyes were exceptionally beautiful and
But it doesn't seem to have, at all...   the hands looked intelligent)
                         the fine hands

a good piece of one continent
and another continent - the whole damned thing!
He who loseth his life, etc. - but he who
loses his love - neever, no never never never again -

A
 x
B

EXAMPLES

The first and final drafts of Elizabeth Bishop's poem "One Art" show an evolution from a focused freewrite toward the very intricate poetic form of a **villanelle**, in which the first and third lines are repeated at the end of alternating successive verses and as a couplet at the end. In spite of this very demanding scheme, the finished version is about half the length of the freewrite. Notice how the ideas are increasingly simply stated, the tone of the final version calm and detached until the burst of emotion in the last line. In these two drafts, Bishop plays with various points of view, trying "one" and "I" and "you" before settling on the final combination of instruction and confession. The title too works toward simplicity, from "How to Lose Things," "The Gift of Losing Things," and "The Art of Losing Things" to the most concise and understated "One Art."

The finished poem:

Elizabeth Bishop

One Art

The art of losing isn't hard to master;
so many things seem filled with the intent
to be lost that their loss is no disaster.

Lose something every day. Accept the fluster
of lost door keys, the hour badly spent.
The art of losing isn't hard to master.

Then practice losing farther, losing faster:
places, and names, and where it was you meant
to travel. None of these will bring disaster.

I lost my mother's watch. And look! my last, or
next-to-last, of three loved houses went.
The art of losing isn't hard to master.

I lost two cities, lovely ones. And, vaster,
some realms I owned, two rivers, a continent.
I miss them, but it wasn't a disaster.

—Even losing you (the joking voice, a gesture
I love) I shan't have lied. It's evident
the art of losing's not too hard to master
though it may look like (*Write it!*) like disaster.

A detailed comparison of the many drafts of this poem appears in the fine essay "A Moment's Thought" in Ellen Bryant Voigt's The Flexible Lyric *(Athens and London, The University of Georgia Press, 1999).*

Notice also that this is a "list poem" or "catalogue poem," built on a list of things that can be lost. It's almost impossible to overstate the importance of the list in literature. You can use lists of images to build a description or a portrait, extend a metaphor by listing the aspects of a comparison, or structure an essay as a list of ways to look at your subject. (Margaret Atwood's "The Female Body" (p. 254) is structured in such a way.) It could even be argued that a story is based on a list of events one after the other.

Try This

Choose one of the lists in your journal and play around with it, extending each item on the list into a sentence or two, adding an image, an idea, a memory. When you have a page or so, look it over and see what repeated images or ideas emerge. What do the parts have in common? What do you seem to be saying? Can you give it a title? If so, you may have a theme. Try arranging the parts into lines. Now try cutting whatever seems extraneous to your theme. Are you part way to a poem?

The Opening of *Time Lapse:*
a revision narrative.

As I write this, I am still in the process of revising a new novel, *Time Lapse*. The novel tells the story of a girl born in Belgium in 1930, who escapes to England during the second world war and later emigrates to America. Most of the novel deals with her adolescent and adult life, but after I had written many of the later scenes, it seemed to me that the novel should begin with an image of that childhood escape, which affects everything she later does. I felt "inspired" when I woke up one morning and tapped out this:

> Always,
> she retained one image from the boat, too fleeting for a memory but too substantial for a dream, like a few frames clipped from a kinetoscope. She was standing in the stern, embraced from behind by a woman who was wrapping her in rough blanket stuff. Her shoes and the hem of her coat above her knees were wet. She knew that the woman was kind, but the smell of anxiety and too many nights' sweat filled her with dark judgment. There was no moon at all, which was the point, but all the same she could watch the wake of the boat widening behind them. She also knew, in a cold, numbed way, that her father was bleeding on the shore, but what presented itself as monstrous was the wake, dark and glutinous, ever spreading toward the land, as if she herself were a speck being washed

from a wound. *I will never go back. I will never.* This was experienced as grief, not yet a vow.

After a day or so I felt this was melodramatic—that "dark judgment," her father "bleeding on the shore," the "monstrous" and "glutinous" sea. I noticed that "kinetoscope" stuck out like a piece of show-off research. I thought there should be more sense of the woman trying to help her, and of the others on the boat. The past tense also troubled me. If she "always retained," then wouldn't the memory be in the present?

Always,

also, she is standing in the stern, embraced from behind by a woman who swaddles her in coarse blanket stuff. Her shoes and the hem of her coat above her knees are wet. There is no moon—which is the point—but all the same she can see the wake widening in the Channel, and close beside her on the deck the boy who broke his shin, the bone stub moving under the flesh like a tongue in a cheek. The man—his father?—still has the boy's mouth stuffed with a forearm of loden coat to keep him from crying out, although they are far enough from shore that the oars have been shipped and the motor roped into life. It sputters like a heart. Behind her the people huddle—you can't tell heroes from refugees—over flasks of tea and Calvados whose fireapple smell flings up on the smell of sea. She will never see any of these people again. The woman's armpit cups her chin, old wet wool and fear. She knows unflinchingly that her father has been left behind. What presents itself as monstrous is the wake—dark, glutinous—which seems to be driving them from the land on its slubbed point as if the boat is a clot being washed from a wound.

    I will never go back. I will never. This is experienced as grief, not yet a vow.

I fiddled with this a lot, still dissatisfied with its tone, which seemed to set the book on a loftier course than I intended, but it was several months before it struck me that *the woman should tell this scene.* I think it was the image of the boy's broken bone "like a tongue in a cheek" that gave me the first hint of the woman's voice. She was a British woman; I imagined her as working class, one of the accidental heroes of the Resistance, a practical, solid sort. This revelation must have occurred to me on an airplane (the disembodied feeling of airplanes *always* sets me writing) because I scribbled on a page of a yellow pad:

[handwritten manuscript draft with numerous revisions and crossings-out]

Now I started over, putting the scene back in chronological order but always chasing the woman's voice, also reading up on the period and the events of the war, checking out British expressions with my son who lives in London:

This must have been about 'forty, the Vicar and I were coming down from Teddington maybe once a month to make the crossing from Dover to Ostend and back again. We had the use of Duck Henley's trawler and half a dozen meeting points along the coast, underground runners all through that part of Flanders setting up the times. ~~Usually~~ they ~~came on foot, talk about misery and scared, and~~ they mostly run together, only it's the children that stick out in your mind.

~~Sometimes they were that dumb brave. There were babies never made a peep, and~~ I remember one boy landed squeejaw off the dock and broke his shin so the bone rolled under his skin like a tongue in a cheek. It was maybe the same trip we was expecting a girl and her father and nearly pushed off without, when we saw her running ~~all by herself~~ down the rocks, straight into the water up to her coat hem. O'Hannaughy swung his arm signalling her to go round the dock and lowered her down with her shoes full of water. I wrapped her up and she says po-faced, "My Father sends me to come ahead." She says, "My fah-zer."

What I remember ~~about her~~ is, we had a little bunsen and usually when you got out far enough to rope the motors alive, they were glad to hunker down over a cuppa. But this one didn't leave the stern six, maybe eight hours of crossing, looking back where we'd come from. ~~It was black dark—we always picked nights with no moon—but all the same you could see the wake.~~ Very polite she was in her soggy shoes, but couldn't be budged. ~~I knew not to ask about her father.~~ And I remember I tucked the blanket around her, which she let me, and I thought the way we must have looked to God, that greasy little trawler in the black ~~water~~, like a clot being washed ~~out of~~ a wound.

[handwritten marginalia:] They came in all sorts, talk about misery & scared,) · I never saw one of them again. · or maybe another · from wake, · in the dark. · arrives not. He is not able to

Over the course of several months I kept coming back to this scene, trying to imagine it more fully, to heighten the sense of danger as the little boat flees the mines and U-boats, but to keep it in the chatty, down-to-earth voice of the woman who was—when? I asked myself suddenly; why?—telling this story—to whom? At some point, having spent perhaps a couple of full-time work weeks on this tiny but crucial scene, it came to me that the woman was being interviewed on television, for one of those anniversary documentaries of the war. At once, though I do not describe the scene of the interview, I could see and hear her more clearly.

The book now begins this way:

Janet Burroway
Transit: Ostend—Dover

All that spring and summer we brought back boatloads of the refugees. The Vicar organized us. They didn't mind I was a woman because I was able-bodied. We traveled down from Teddington once a month to make the crossing, and we had the use of Duck Henley's trawler and half a dozen meeting points along the Flemish coast. Underground runners all through Belgium setting up the rendezvous.

It's a wonder what you remember. Great swollen blanks, and then some daft thing bobs up like flotsam. Such as, I'd never worn a pair of trousers, and what I couldn't get used to was the twill going swish between my thighs. Is that camera running? Don't show me saying *thighs*, will you? Anyway, that and the smells. Tar, old fish in the wet boards. Seasick, of course. And off your own skin a bit of metal smell, with a sourness like fireworks. When they say "sweating bullets" I expect that's what they mean.

The ones we ferried came in every sort—rich man, poor man, tinker, tailor. I never saw a one of them again. Now and then I cross via Newhaven over to Normandy for the shopping, and I look around and think: they're not so different, take away their pocket books and their sunburn. What struck me, in Teddington everybody got raw noses from the cold and spider veins from the fire, but those ones were always drained-looking like they hadn't been out of doors, although most had been living rough or walking nights. You probably think I misremember it from a newsreel—not that we ever made it into the Movietone—but I said it at the time: every one of them gray, and eyes like drain holes that the color washed right down.

It's the children stick in your mind—a wee tiddler with its eyes wide open and its mouth tight shut. I remember one boy landed crooked off the dock and broke his shin, so the bone stub rolled under the skin like a tongue in a cheek. Somebody gave him a mouthful of coat sleeve to keep him quiet.

It was that same trip we were expecting a father and daughter that didn't show up, and we about pushed off without them. We'd heard dogs, and you never knew the meaning of dogs—it could be the patrols, or just somebody's mutt in a furore. One thing I've never understood, you pick a night with no moon and a piece of shore without a light—a disused lighthouse this was, great dark lump in the dark—and you can't see a whit, *can not see*. And then there's a click, like, in the back of your eyes, and you can. Sandiford was pressing off the piling, and the Vicar said, *no, steady on*. Duck was reluctant—you couldn't know when the boy would yell out—and then he felt it too and had them put up the oars. The waves were thick as black custard, and the black shore, and now, click! there's this girl, maybe ten or twelve, gawky little tyke, slogging straight into the water up to her coat hem. Sandiford swung his arm signaling her to go round the dock and fetched her down with her shoes full of water. She's got one hand done up in a fist against her collar bone. I wrapped her up, and she says po-faced, "My father arrives not. I arrive alone." She says, "My fah-zer." I knew better than to ask.

From there across—you understand, nobody said *U-boats*. Nobody said *mines*. Mostly you didn't keep an eye out, except for Duck and Sandiford whose job it was, because you were superstitious you would call them up. All the same that's what was in everybody's mind. You just hoped the kiddies didn't know the odds.

What I remember is, we had a little paraffin stove, and usually when you got out far enough to rope the motors into life, they were all glad to settle down over a cuppa. But this one didn't leave the stern maybe eight hours of rough crossing, looking back where we'd come from in the dark. She held that one hand tight as lockjaw, and I thought she had some money in there, maybe, or a bit of jewelry, something she'd been told to keep from harm. You'd think you wouldn't be curious under the circumstances, but eight hours is a long time to be standing, your mind must be doing something. I remember I tucked the blanket tighter around her and held it there, which she let me, and for most of the way we just stood till it was lightening a little down by the horizon. She dozed, I thought. She sagged against me and bit by bit her hand relaxed over the top of the blanket. There was nothing in it. Not a thing. I cupped it in my own and chafed it back to life a little. And I thought the way we must have looked to God, that greasy little trawler in the black wake, like a clot being washed from a wound.

My folder of drafts of this passage now runs to forty pages, excessive and obsessive perhaps, but it is after all the beginning of the book and must be right. I have noticed over the years that my digging at, fiddling with, scratching away at a scene will often turn up something much more fundamental than a new image or a livelier verb. In this case, I gradually realized that the reason the scene must be in somebody else's voice is that *the heroine does not remember it*. Traumatized by her flight, she cannot recall witnessing her father's death until she is nearly fifty years old. When I realized that, I understood much better what story I was telling and how the plot could be shaped and resolved. I had the delicious chance to let my heroine see the television documentary in the 1980s—in a twenty-year-old rerun—and let that chunk of interview, which contained the reader's first view of her, finally jog her memory.

Try This

Choose a scene in your journal, either of fiction or memoir, and rewrite it from another point of view, in another voice. Try to choose a character as different from the original voice as possible, so that we get not just a change of "person" (from *he* or *she* to *I*), but a different set of attitudes, a different take on the events. Under what circumstances would this character be telling the story? To whom? Set the scene if you like.

or:

Interview one of your characters. Write the questions out as if you were in fact conducting a radio, television, or newspaper interview, and then answer them.

or:

Trade brief character descriptions with another writer. Make up a list of questions for that writer's character, then trade lists and write your own character's answers to the questions.

Developing Scene

Here is a paragraph from a student journal:

> I woke up late this morning—as usual. I had no clean clothes and the fridge was next to bare. Traffic was heavy as I sped to work. Some jerk cut me off and I almost had a wreck. At work I went to my desk and there was a note to go and see the boss. I waited outside her office for a while before she called me in. I couldn't figure out why she wanted to see me. I went inside and sat down. My boss handed me an envelope. She told me that my services were no longer needed and that I was free to go. I got my belongings from my desk and left. The drive home was quick. I am now unemployed.

This is a summary paragraph in which any one of the sentences could be made into a scene. Challenged to pick one of the sentences and turn it into a scene, one student chose "Some jerk cut me off and I almost had a wreck"—because, he said, it had "the most voice." This was the scene he imagined:

> Some old geezer in a ball cap cut me off and I almost had a wreck on the way to work. I hate people who think they can drive but can't. I hate them especially while commuting to my daily humiliation and I decided to teach this guy a little lesson by playing near bumper cars with his bright red 300 ZX which he probably bought with his social security retirement checks, money I was paying in each month so he can be a horse's butt on the highway. I passed him and pulled in front of him and kept hitting my brakes, until I saw him jumping up and down in his

seat, his mouth open in screams I couldn't hear. Finally, he rolled down his window and shot me the bird, letting all his good AC back into the hot summer morning. Suddenly I was feeling much better, like that lady in Fried Green Tomatoes who repeatedly rear-ended the car of the person who had stolen her parking space, smashing both vehicles into one ugly mass, both of us knowing life is tough, that self-defense is what it's all about.

Try This
Pick another sentence from the paragraph and turn it into a scene.

or:

Identify a summary in your own journal. Pick a sentence and turn it into a scene.

Un-drafting

One effective way to teach yourself almost any technique is to take a published work and "un-draft" it, or move it back toward a rough draft by taking out its strengths. For instance, here is a paragraph of a fine student short story, "Watertables," by Adam Marshall Johnson:

> Inside the No Show Tavern, I order three tenderloins, slaw, a six of Coors and a draft. Willert's youngest, Winston, sets the beer before me and I suck the cool foam. The glasses have gotten smaller. I rent Dad's land to Willert for a third of the futures and Winston rolls up once in a while in a million-dollar Steiger to watch game shows in a climate-controlled cab as he cultivates the rows. He has walked into the cooler and I can see him looking out into the bar through frosted glass. I put a handful of plastic forks in my shirt pocket and I can see him stare at me through rows of brown bottles. He wipes the white from the glass with his hand, to see what else I may take. Sweat drips from my nose onto the bar. Even the beer tastes salty in this heat.

If I highlight the concrete details in this passage, and then remove them, replacing them with generalizations, I have a very clear idea of the value of the details. The paragraph stripped of its specificity might read:

Inside the bar, I order food and drink. The bartender gives me the drink and I drink it. The glasses seem smaller than the last time I was here. I rent my father's land to this bartender's father in exchange for a percentage of the profit, and sometimes this bartender arrives in his expensive farm equipment to watch television as he works. . . .

Likewise, if I take a passage full of active verbs and reduce them to passivity, it becomes clear how active verbs invigorate prose.

"We have provisions." Linda rummaged noisily in her grocery bag, interrupting poetry. "Yes indeed we do, even if some of them are raw. Christopher Columbus wouldn't have minded raw, so why should we? And then there's those little noodle stands everywhere." She plunked a five-hundred-yen coin down on the table. She crumpled up her napkin, threw it on her plate, and made for the door. I folded my napkin neatly, just as I'd seen the Japanese do, placed it on the table, and hastened after her bobbing grocery bag, hugging my own to my chest and making sure to nod at the waiter over the cabbage head I was going to use to make stew if I ever got back home.

"Come again," the waiter said.

"The Priest," Kim Garcia

Denuded of its energetic verbs, the passage becomes:

"We have provisions." Linda was noisily going through her grocery bag, so the poetry was interrupted . . . A five-hundred-yen coin was placed by her on the table. Also her napkin was crumpled and thrown on her plate while she herself went to the door . . .

Try This
Pick a passage you like and *spoil it* by replacing specific details with generalizations and judgments.

Pick another and spoil it by replacing active verbs with passive or bland ones.

Choose a poem that seems to say a lot in just a very few lines. Spoil it by "spelling out" all the meanings in the images. Try to imagine what the original freewrite would have been like, loose and meandering. Can you now write a different poem from this "undraft"?

Line Editing

No one really has an eagle eye for her own writing. It's harder to keep your attention on the mechanics of your own words than any other—for which reason a friend or a copy editor with the skill is invaluable. In the meantime, however, try to become a good surface editor of your work. Reading aloud always helps.

What follows is a passage with at least three punctuation mistakes, three spelling mistakes, one grammatical mistake, four typos, two awkward repetitions, one unclear antecedent, two misused words, and a cliché (though some may fit more than one category and a few may cause disagreement—that is the nature of proofreading). Spot and correct them. Make any necessary judgment calls. Then take a passage of your own and give it the same scrutiny.

Together, Lisel and Drakov wondered through Spartanvilles noisy, squalid streets. Goats clogged the noisy streets and the venders cursed them. The factory generater seemed to send it's roar overhead at the level of a low plane.

A homeless man leared up at them crazy as a cuckoo. They were astonished to see the the local police had put up a barrier at the end of Main Street, plus the government were making random passport checks at the barrier.

"What could they be looking for on a georgeous day like this"? Lisel wondered.

Drakov said, "Us, Maybe."

Warm-up

Write down the first answer that comes into your mind: What emotion, quality, or idea is demonstrated by this scene? Set the picture aside. Consult your memory. What incidents in your own life connect you to that emotion, quality, or idea? List them quickly. Write about *one* of those incidents.

CHAPTER SEVEN

ESSAY

Kinds of Essay
Essay Techniques
Fact and Truth

The essay is a pair of baggy pants into which nearly anyone and anything can fit.

Joseph Epstein

The word **essay** comes from the French for "try," and no other designation so
well captures the modest and partial nature of the form. Anything in the world
is potential subject matter, and anything you say about it is merely a try—an
attempt to be accurate, to be meaningful, to be interesting, to offer a perspective.

The tradition of the essay is that it is based in fact, and that the reader has
a right to expect that the facts presented will be accurate and truthful. This is
at present an enormously interesting issue, partly because in the latter half of the
twentieth century readers became intensely interested in "what really happened,"
and memoirs, personal experience, biography, and autobiography are now more
easily marketable than fiction or poetry. No doubt television is partly responsible for the shift toward the essay as hot property, both because TV has accustomed us to having the facts of any human drama instantly and live, and because
we have been overfed with formulaic dramatic plots.

Not that it's altogether clear what is fact and what is fiction. News can be and
is manipulated; television raises the question of how much "entertainment" enters
journalistic decisions. Is a docudrama document or drama? If a memoir "remembers" dialogue from forty years ago, is it memory or fiction? If a living person
is shielded from recognition in a biography, is the piece dishonest? If you have
taken seven trips in a fishing boat and you want to write about it as personal
experience, do you have to go through seven trips, or can you conflate them

243

into one trip and still call it fact? How much dramatizing may be said to reveal rather than distort the truth?

At some point every writer of memoir and personal essay has to grapple with these issues. Luckily, they don't have to be grappled with in first draft. Having accepted that the mere fact of putting something into words *changes* it, begin by putting into words as clearly and vividly as you can something that you know about, care about, or that has happened to you. Then begin to look for particular purpose. Consider how to raise the tension and the drama. There will inevitably be changes of emphasis and balance in the shaping of both rough draft and revisions. You can take advantage of the gentle permission of the essay form: you may tell as well as show; you may say in so many words what the significance is for you. Often the effect of an essay rests precisely in this, that it begins in personal experience but reaches out to a larger idea or area of thought about the human condition. As authors Carol Burke and Molly Best Tinsley put it in their book *The Creative Process*, "The continuous movement back and forth from specific instance to general significance, from fact to meaning, from the sensory and emotional to the intellectual—such is the art of the essay."

Given its qualities of fact and forthrightness, the essay is a capacious, malleable, and forgiving form. Not only does it *not* have to have the thesis–topic-sentence–conclusion form of outline we were all taught, but it can easily borrow from any form you choose: story, monologue, lesson, list, rondel, collage. The trick is to find the right shape for the idea you have to present.

Kinds of Essay

Just about anyone who gets through high school in America becomes familiar with basic forms of the essay: the **expository** that imparts information; the **narrative** that recounts events in their order; the **descriptive** that adds sense impressions; the **persuasive** that wants to influence us. An **article** is usually an essay that purports to be "objective," that de-emphasizes the perspective and personality of the writer to concentrate on the subject matter; publication in a newspaper or magazine is implied. A **feature** is a human interest story, also bound for a newspaper. An article that concentrates on a person or place may be called a **profile**.

But any or all of these purposes may be mixed, freed, and enlivened through greater attention to stylistic and dramatic devices, personal voice, and a search for range and resonance. Such essays may be called **literary nonfiction** or **creative nonfiction**, the latter being a popular (if slightly cumbersome) term to describe essays that include the personal but don't necessarily stay there. Lee Gutkind, an important practitioner and champion of the form, sees creative nonfiction as allowing the writer "to employ the diligence of a reporter, the shifting voices and viewpoints of a novelist, the refined wordplay of a poet, and the analytical modes of the essayist," and he sees as a requirement that the essays should "have purpose and meaning beyond the experiences related." The techniques Gutkind describes are akin to those that Tom Wolfe co-opted in the 1960s for what he termed **new journalism**, a kind of reporting in which the reporter became a character in his report, and which relied on all the techniques of a novelist including—importantly, for Wolfe—the details of dress, gesture, speech, and ownership that reveal social status.

Creative nonfiction encompasses two sorts of essay that differ more in emphasis than in kind—but may differ radically in emphasis—and that will be the focus of this chapter. A *memoir* is a story retrieved from the writer's memory, with the writer as protagonist—the *I* remembering. Memoir tends to place the emphasis on the story, and the "point" is likely to emerge, as it does in fiction, largely from the events and characters themselves, rather than through the author's speculation or reflection. The *personal essay*, on the other hand, usually has its origin in something that has happened in the writer's life, but it may have happened yesterday afternoon, or it may represent an area of interest deliberately explored, and it is likely to give rise to a meditation on some subject that the experience suggests.

Example: I took a photograph out of an old frame to put in a picture of my new husband and stepdaughter. Because the frame was constructed in an amazingly solid way, I thought about the man whose photo I was displacing, his assumptions about permanence, how we use frames to try to capture and hang onto moments, memories, families, selves that are in fact always in flux; how we frame our cities with roads, our shoreline with resorts, our dead with coffins—marking our territory, claiming possession. In this instance a very small task led me to write about the nature of impermanence and enclosure.

Both memoir and personal essay grow out of some degree of autobiographical experience and are usually (though there are exceptions) written in the first person. The distinction between them is not always clear, although it may be said that the memoir sets up a conversation or dialectic between the writer and his/her past, while the emphasis of the personal essay is likely to be conversational, an implied or sought relationship between the writer and the reader. Philip Lopate, in the brilliant introduction to his anthology *The Art of the Personal Essay*, dissects the tone in terms of its intimacy, its "drive toward candor and self-exposure," the conversational dynamic and the struggle for honesty.

The personal essay is a form that allows maximum mobility from the small, the daily, the domestic to the universal and significant. Essayist Philip Gerard says, "The subject has to carry itself and also be an elegant vehicle for larger meanings." What makes it "creative" is that though you may take the subject matter of research or journalism, there is "an apparent subject and a deeper subject. The apparent subject . . . is only part of what we are interested in." Whereas you might write a newspaper article about the Little Miss Blue Crab Festival of Franklin County, naming the contestants, the organizers, and the judges, describing the contest, announcing the winner—if you undertook this same subject matter as a piece of creative nonfiction, your main focus would not be the event itself but the revelation of something essential about the nature of beauty contests, or children in competition, or the character of the fishing village, or coastal society, or rural festivals. In a first-person essay, the focus might be on how you personally fit or don't fit into this milieu, what memories of your own childhood it calls up, how it relates to your experience of competition in general, or other structures in your life and, by extension, life in general. You would have "distance on it," a perspective that embraces not just the immediate event but its place in a human, social, historical, even cosmic context. Because creative nonfiction has this deeper (or wider, or more universal, or significant) subject, it won't necessarily date in the manner of yesterday's newspaper.

Try This

Begin with the conventional notion of titling an essay:
On _____.

- Make a list of at least six titles that represent things you might like to write about; things that interest you and that you feel confident you know something about. These may be either abstractions or specifics, *On Liberty* or *On Uncle Ernie's Saddle.*
- Then make a list of six subjects you do *not* want to write about, and wouldn't show to anybody if you did. (*On _____*).
- Make a list of six titles in which the preposition "on" could be a pun: *On Speed. On the Net. On My Feet.*
- Make a list of six titles dealing with subjects about which you know "nothing at all." For me such a list might include: *On Brain Surgery. On Refrigerator Repair. On Tasmania.*

If you choose to write an essay from the first list, you are embarking on an honorable enterprise. If you choose from the second list, you are very courageous. If you choose from list three, you'll probably have a good time—and remember that such an essay should deal with both aspects of the pun: *On My Feet* should deal with toenails, calluses, pain or podiatry, and also with courage or persistence. The last list offers the wildest ride and may turn up something original, comic (Dave Barry makes a living in this territory), or unexpectedly true. Remember that your intent is not to deceive: signal or confess your ignorance when appropriate. When I think about my short list above, I think that if I were to write about brain surgery, I could write about how certain clichés—"Well, it's not brain surgery"—come into fashion. If I were to write about "refrigerator repair," it would have to be about cleaning out the moldy leftovers, including those in my mind. "On Tasmania" would start with the confession, "I get Tasmania and Tanzania mixed up"—and go on about dreams of the travel I will certainly never undertake.

Any of the four lists may, like focused freewrites, unlock subject matter that you didn't know you had in you. Although the perennial advice "write what you know" still holds, the essay is a good place for honest exploration of your ignorance, and to find out what you know about what you don't know about.

> Memory has its own story to tell.
>
> *Tim O'Brien*

Essay Techniques

Creative nonfiction tells a true story. How does it tell a story? (I'll deal with the "true" part below.)

Every writerly technique that has been discussed in these pages can be used in the essay form, and just as a character will be most richly drawn when presented by more than one method, so a variety of techniques will enrich the texture of nonfiction. As an essayist you may (and should) employ image, metaphor, voice, dialogue, point of view, character, setting, scene, conflict, human connection—and you are also free to speak your mind directly, to "tell" what you mean and what matters. The success of your essay may very well depend on whether you achieve a balance between the imaginative and the reflective. Often, the story and its drama (the showing) will fill most of the sentences—that is what keeps a reader reading; but the startling or revelatory or thoughtful nature of your insight about it (the telling) will have equal impact.

Try This

Take two sheets of paper and sit in front of a mirror. On one sheet, draw a self portrait. Keep adding details. As you do so, jot on the other paper anything that comes to mind about your body, your self, your picture, the memories it evokes. Use any of these things as the trigger for an essay about your relationship with your self (what could be more personal?) Be daring: what do you love about yourself, hate, fear; what makes you proud, preen, gag?

Like a story, creative nonfiction needs scenes. If you are working from a remembered period of your life, it may present itself as summary, and summary will have its place in your essay; but when you get to what mattered—what changed you, what moves us—it will need the immediacy of detailed action, of discovery and decision.

> Just down from the mountains, early August. Lugging my youngest child from the car, I noticed that his perfectly relaxed body was getting heavier every year. When I undressed his slack limbs, he woke up enough to mumble, "I like my own bed," then fell back down, all the way down, into sleep. The sensation of his weight was still in my arms as I shut the door.
>
> "Images," Robert Hass

Notice that Hass begins with a brief summary (or longshot) of the situation, then moves at once into the sensual apprehension of the action, the boy's body relaxed, heavy, slack, while the father takes care of him.

Like a story, creative nonfiction depends on character, and the creation of character depends on both detail and dialogue. Dialogue is tricky because the memory does its own editing, but you can re-create a voice from memory no less than from imagination. Write, remembering as truly as you can, then test in your mind whether the other person involved would agree: *what we said was like this.*

> Whatever looks I had were hidden behind thick cat-eyed glasses and a hearing aid that was strapped to my body like a dog halter. My hallucinatory visions would sometimes lift me up and carry me through the air. When I told my mother that I was afraid of the sky, she considered it a reasonable fear, even though she said, "Well, the sky isn't something I could ever be afraid of."
>
> "Falling in Love Again," Terry Galloway

Like a story, creative nonfiction needs the context and texture of setting. Frequently an encounter with setting is the point and purpose of the piece, whether that encounter is with an exotic foreign country or your own backyard. If you're stuck for a way to begin, you might remember the longshot–middle shot–closeup pattern.

> It's past eleven on a Friday night in the spring of 1955. Here comes a kid down the length of Eighteenth Street in the Midwood section of Flatbush, in Brooklyn, New York. He passes the kept lawns and tidy hedges under big leafy sycamores and maples. The middle class is asleep, and most of the houses attached to the lawns are dark, though an occasional window pulses with blue-gray television light. Streetlamps shine benignly, and Mars is red in the sky. The kid is on his way home from the weekly meeting of Troop 8, Boy Scouts of America . . .
>
> "For the Love of a Princess of Mars," Frederick Busch

Unlike a story, creative nonfiction involves a balance of dramatization and overt reflection. This doesn't mean that the balance needs to be the same in all essays. On the contrary, a memoir that leaves us with a vivid image of an aging relative or a revelation of an error in judgment may be absolutely appropriate, whereas a piece on a walk in the woods may need half its space to analyze and elucidate the discoveries you have made. Sometimes an essay will convey its personal intensity precisely through the force of its abstractions.

> I have had with my friend Wes Jackson a number of useful conversations about the necessity of getting out of movements—even movements that have seemed necessary and dear to us—when they have lapsed into self-righteousness and self-betrayal, as movements seem almost invariably to do. People in movements too readily learn to deny to others the rights and privileges they demand for themselves. They too easily become unable to mean their own language, as when a "peace movement" becomes violent.
>
> *"In Distrust of Movements," Wendell Berry*

One part of the purpose of an essay will always be to inform or teach, either by presenting new knowledge or by combining old facts in a new way. Often the essay seduces the reader with a personal note into an educational enterprise. The nature essayist Barry Lopez demonstrates the technique again and again; he places himself in relation to the landscape, and later in the piece slips in the history, archeology, or biology. So a typical essay will begin "I am standing at the margin of the sea ice called the floe edge at the mouth of Admiralty Inlet . . ." or "We left our camp on Pingok Island one morning knowing a storm was moving in from the Southwest . . ." Later in each piece, more factual or speculative paragraphs begin, "Three million colonial seabirds, mostly northern fulmars, kittiwakes, and guillemots, nest and feed here in the summer," and, "Desire for wealth, for spiritual or emotional ecstasy, for recognition—strains of all three are found in nearly every arctic expedition." Lopez immediately involves the reader in the human drama, but he also wants to teach us what he knows. He exhibits the range of the impulse toward the personal essay: involvement and intellectual enlargement, both operating at full stretch. He wants to have and to offer both the experience and the knowledge.

Try This

Write a personal essay about a building you care about. Choose one of which you have strong memories, then do at least a little research about the place itself. This research might, if it's a house or school in your home town, consist of calling people to interview them. If it's a church or municipal building of some sort, it might be archival or library research. You will know what's appropriate. How does your memory of the place

continued

contrast with, or how is it qualified by, what you have learned? Is there an idea to be mined in the difference between them?

If your essay asks for research, it may be very different, and vastly more inclusive, than what you usually mean by research. Taking a walk in your old neighborhood or getting on a surfboard for the first time, phoning or e-mailing friends and family members, reading old letters including your own, digging among photographs or mementos or recipes—any of these may be exactly what you need to research a memoir. If your subject takes you into areas you need to know more about, you may spend as much time in interview and legwork as on the Internet or in the library.

When it comes to the writing, an essay may be researched and still be "personal," either by making the research (including interview, observation, and detective work) part of the essay, or by allowing the reader to share the emotions you as writer experienced in the process. How does it *feel* to watch a kidney operation? What emotions pass among the athletes in the locker room? How did your interview of Aunt Lena change your view of your family?

Try This

Interview several members of your family, several members of your neighborhood, and/or several acquaintances about a historical event that took place before you were born. Research the event well enough to know its facts and sequence, but put the emphasis of your piece on the composite memory of the people who were alive. You are not trying to write history, but to capture the flavor of a certain time, a certain kind of memory, a group of people in relation to that history.

Although the personal essay offers an insight into the writer's life and thought, that doesn't necessarily mean that it must be written in the first person. It may be that the story you have to tell or the drama you have witnessed can be best conveyed (as in a short story) by focusing on that experience, implying rather than spelling out how it has moved you. George Plimpton writes sports stories in the first person because his point is to expose the emotions of an amateur among the pros; whereas Roger Angell writes occasionally in the first person, and sometimes in the collective "we," but most often in the third person, focusing on the players but putting on their stories the stamp of his style. If in doubt, try a few paragraphs in first and then in third person; fool around with the perspective of fly-on-the-wall and with myself-as-participant. Usually the material will reveal its own best slant, and the experiment may help you find out what you have to say.

Transitions are particularly important in the essay because of the needed rhythm back and forth between scene and summary, abstraction and detail. In the essay we expect a degree of direction and interpretation that in fiction would be called **authorial intrusion**. An essayist is allowed and encouraged to employ intrusion to a degree, and we expect and ask for the generalization that says, in effect: *this is what I think*. I find it useful, when I find myself getting a little wound up or mixed up in the writing, to type in "What's my point?" and try to answer the question right then. The question can come out later. Often the answer can, in some form or other, stay. Even if you end up cutting it, it may help you find your way.

In the past, when writing a critical or research essay, you've been told to pick a confined and specific subject and explore it thoroughly. The same advice holds for creative nonfiction. Don't try to write about "my family," which will overwhelm you with vagaries and contradictions, just as if your subject was "Shakespeare." Write about one afternoon when things changed. Focus on one kid in the fifth grade who didn't fit in. Write about your first encounter with language, oysters, God, hypocrisy, race, or betrayal. A memoir is a story, and like a story it will describe a journey and a change; it will be written in a scene or scenes; it will characterize through detail and dialogue. The difference is not only that it is based on the facts as your memory can dredge them up, but that you may interpret it for us as you go along or at the end or both: *this is what I learned, this is how I changed, this is how I relate my experience to the experience of the world, and of my readers.*

> I never want to discover, after reading a piece of nonfiction, that I have not read a piece of nonfiction.
>
> *Joe Mackall*

Fact and Truth

"Essays," says novelist and travel writer Edward Hoagland, "are how we speak to one another in print—caroming thoughts not merely in order to convey a certain packet of information but with a special edge or bounce of personal character in a kind of public letter . . . More than being instructive, as a magazine article is, an essay has a slant . . ."

How do you balance the information against the slant? How, in that *caroming*, do you judge when edge or bounce has overwhelmed instruction?

The best you can do is to be scrupulously exact about facts, and, beyond that, to explore and test the essential truth of what you have to say.

But the distance between "facts" and "essential truth" can be troubling. What and how much is it fair to make up? Let's say I'm writing a piece about my mother, and I want to give an accurate image of her. When I try to remember the things she wore, what stands out are the unusual things, the embroidered yellow wedding coat she kept for special occasions, the pink satin housecoat that was too precious to wear often. These are in my memory precisely because they were uncharacteristic of her, whereas the kind of housedress she wore every day is a blur of composite images, a mnemonic generalization. As a writer I concentrate on this vagueness and bring it into focus in my imagination *as if* it were fiction. *She wore a cap-sleeve cotton house dress, a plaid of lavender and yellow crisscrossing on faded gray.* Or: *She wore a cotton housedress with piping around the collar, sprigs of lily-of-the-valley tied with a pink bow on a pale gray ground.* I don't know whether these images came from somewhere deep in my memory, or whether I "made them up." They are true to the image of my mother I am trying to capture, and therefore they partake of "essential truth," whereas if I said she wore bikinis or Armani, I would be honoring neither fact nor truth.

Fiction writers also grapple with the level of historical or regional fact that is necessary to their truth, and like essayists, they answer it differently. James Joyce wanted every Dublin bus route and ticket price accurate in *Ulysses*; E. L. Doctorow invented the events of several famous real lives in *Ragtime.* In the only historical novel I have written, I decided that I could harmlessly put an ice house in a rural Arizona town seven years before there was actually such a thing, but that I couldn't blow off the arm of a famous Mexican General two years before, historically, it happened.

The delicacy of this issue is slightly augmented for an essayist, and I think the touchstone is: an absence of the intent to deceive. A fiction writer is in the clear to the extent that a reader understands from the beginning that the story is "made up"—yet must on whatever level of reality convince us to suspend disbelief. Since a reader of essays expects factual truth, you are under some obligation to signal its absence. It can add to both the authenticity and the interest of a piece (as long as it isn't too repetitive), to say in effect: I don't remember exactly, but I seem to see . . . or: So-and-so says it was this way, but I think . . . or: I am imagining that it must have been . . .

I know nothing about how they meet. She is a schoolgirl. He is at work, probably a government clerk in a building near her school. At the hour when the school and the office are out for lunch their lives intersect at sandwich counters, soft-drink stands, traffic lights, market squares. Their eyes meet or their bodies collide at one of these food queues. He says something suggestive, complimentary. She suppresses a smile or traps one beneath her hands.

"A Son in Shadow," Fred D'Aguilar

> **Try This**
> Write a personal essay about your parents' courtship. It may be totally imaginary (in which case, that you are making it up becomes part of the subject matter and the truth of your essay); or you may write it from facts you already know (acknowledging where you fill in, leave out, or speculate); or you may "research" it by interviewing family members (in which case your research may become the subject of the essay, the family members become characters, and their interviews become dialogue). You may choose any method you like, based on whatever quantity of information you have or choose to use; but it must remain an essay; that is, with a basis in fact, so that where you invent, you acknowledge "I imagine . . . I guess . . . I'm inventing here."

"When you use memories as a source," says E. L. Doctorow, "they're no different from any other source—the composition still has to be made." Memory is imperfect; that is its nature, and you are responsible only for the honest attempt and the honest presentation. No two siblings will remember their mother, or even Christmas dinner, in the same way. One of the leaps of faith you must make to write from memory is that the process of writing itself will yield that essential truth. Sometimes clarifying a quotation, compressing several conversations or events into one, exaggerating one physical detail while omitting another, or transposing a scene from one locale to another—any of these can honor (and reveal) an essential truth when the literal truth would distort. If you get the color of your childhood wagon wrong, it will not damage that truth. If you sentimentalize an emotion, it will.

It is likely that the most troubling conflict you face as a writer of memoir and personal essay will be between your essential truth and obligation to those you know. When does honesty require that you reveal an ugly fact? Is it arrogance to suppose that anything you write is worth wounding someone else? There is no answer to this dilemma, or there are as many answers as there are works in a lifetime or paragraphs in a work. As a rough rule of thumb, I would say that the cost of honesty might be the loss of your own labor. That is: write your truth. You are under no obligation to publish it, and you may find yourself under the pressure of personal integrity not to. If you need to alter details in order to conceal a living person, let it be later. It may or may not work, but it will be easier to alter identifying details than to censor yourself as you write.

> **Try This**
> Write an anonymous memoir about someone you dislike or someone you are afraid of. The surer you are that nobody is going to know who wrote it, the freer you are to write;
> *continued*

but also, strangely! the more freely you write, the less likely anybody is to know who wrote it. You have angers and fears that nobody has ever suspected, right? Write.

Tell your life story in three incidents involving hair.

Pick the five photographs that you would want to illustrate your life so far. Choose one of them to write about.

More to Read

Gutkind, Lee. *The Art of Creative Nonfiction.* New York: John Wiley & Sons, 1997.

Zinsser, William. *On Writing Well.* New York: HarperCollins, 1998.

READINGS

Margaret Atwood

The Female Body

From Michigan Quarterly Review

> . . . entirely devoted to the subject of "The Female Body."
> Knowing how well you have written on this topic . . . this
> capacious topic . . .
> —*letter from Michigan Quarterly Review*

1.

I agree, it's a hot topic. But only one? Look around, there's a wide range. Take my own, for instance.

I get up in the morning. My topic feels like hell. I sprinkle it with water, brush parts of it, rub it with towels, powder it, add lubricant. I dump in the fuel and away goes my topic, my topical topic, my controversial topic, my capacious topic, my limping topic, my nearsighted topic, my topic with back problems, my badly behaved topic, my vulgar topic, my outrageous topic, my aging topic, my topic that is out of the question and anyway still can't spell, in its oversized coat and worn winter boots, scuttling along the sidewalk as if it were flesh and blood, hunting for what's out there, an avocado, an alderman, an adjective, hungry as ever.

2.

The basic Female Body comes with the following accessories: garter belt, panti-girdle, crinoline, camisole, bustle, brassiere, stomacher, chemise, virgin zone, spike heels, nose ring, veil, kid gloves, fishnet stockings, fichu, bandeau, Merry Widow, weepers, chokers, barrettes, bangles, beads, lorgnette, feather boa, basic black, compact, Lycra stretch one-piece with modesty panel, designer peignoir, flannel nightie, lace teddy, bed, head.

3.

The Female Body is made of transparent plastic that lights up when you plug it in. You press a button to illuminate the different systems. The circulatory system is red, for the heart and arteries, purple for the veins; the respiratory system is blue; the lymphatic system is yellow; the digestive system is green, with liver and kidneys in aqua. The nerves are done in orange and the brain is pink. The skeleton, as you might expect, is white.

The reproductive system is optional, and can be removed. It comes with or without a miniature embryo. Parental judgment can thereby be exercised. We do not wish to frighten or offend.

4.

He said, I won't have one of those things in the house. It gives a young girl a false notion of beauty, not to mention anatomy. If a real woman was built like that she'd fall on her face.

She said, If we don't let her have one like all the other girls she'll feel singled out. It'll become an issue. She'll long for one and she'll long to turn into one. Repression breeds sublimation. You know that.

He said, It's not just the pointy plastic tits, it's the wardrobes. The wardrobes and that stupid male doll, what's his name, the one with the underwear glued on.

She said, Better to get it over with when she's young. He said, All right, but don't let me see it.

She came whizzing down the stairs, thrown like a dart. She was stark naked. Her hair had been chopped off, her head was turned back to front, she was missing some toes and she'd been tattooed all over her body with purple ink in a scrollwork design. She hit the potted azalea, trembled there for a moment like a botched angel, and fell.

He said, I guess we're safe.

5.

The Female Body has many uses. It's been used as a door knocker, a bottle opener, as a clock with a ticking belly, as something to hold up lampshades, as a nutcracker, just squeeze the brass legs together and out comes your nut. It bears torches, lifts victorious wreaths, grows copper wings and raises aloft a ring of neon stars; whole buildings rest on its marble heads.

It sells cars, beer, shaving lotion, cigarettes, hard liquor; it sells diet plans and diamonds, and desire in tiny crystal bottles. Is this the face that launched a thousand products? You bet it is, but don't get any funny big ideas, honey, that smile is a dime a dozen.

It does not merely sell, it is sold. Money flows into this country or that country, flies in, practically crawls in, suitful after suitful, lured by all those hairless pre-teen legs. Listen, you want to reduce the national debt, don't you? Aren't you patriotic? That's the spirit. That's my girl.

She's a natural resource, a renewable one luckily, because those things wear out so quickly. They don't make 'em like they used to. Shoddy goods.

6.

One and one equals another one. Pleasure in the female is not a requirement. Pair-bonding is stronger in geese. We're not talking about love, we're talking about biology. That's how we all got here, daughter.

Snails do it differently. They're hermaphrodites, and work in threes.

7.

Each Female Body contains a female brain. Handy. Makes things work. Stick pins in it and you get amazing results. Old popular songs. Short circuits. Bad dreams.

Anyway: each of these brains has two halves. They're joined together by a thick cord; neural pathways flow from one to the other, sparkles of electric information washing to and fro. Like light on waves. Like a conversation. How does a woman know? She listens. She listens in.

The male brain, now, that's a different matter. Only a thin connection. Space over here, time over there, music and arithmetic in their own sealed compartments. The right brain doesn't know what the left brain is doing. Good for aiming though, for hitting the target when you pull the trigger. What's the target? Who's the target? Who cares? What matters is hitting it. That's the male brain for you. Objective.

This is why men are so sad, why they feel so cut off, why they think of them-selves as orphans cast adrift, footloose and stringless in the deep void. What void? she asks. What are you talking about? The void of the universe, he says, and she says Oh and looks out the window and tries to get a handle on it, but it's no use, there's too much going on, too many rustlings in the leaves, too many voices, so she says, Would you like a cheese sandwich, a piece of cake, a cup of tea? And he grinds his teeth because she doesn't understand, and wanders off, not just alone but Alone, lost in the dark, lost in the skull, searching for the other half, the twin who could complete him.

Then it comes to him: he's lost the Female Body! Look, it shines in the gloom, far ahead, a vision of wholeness, ripeness, like a giant melon, like an apple, like a metaphor for "breast" in a bad sex novel; it shines like a balloon, like a foggy noon, a watery moon, shimmering in its egg of light.

Catch it. Put it in a pumpkin, in a high tower, in a compound, in a chamber, in a house, in a room. Quick, stick a leash on it, a lock, a chain, some pain, settle it down, so it can never get away from you again.

Try This
You have by this time generated a number of lists in your journal. Pick one of them and add to it. See if your list has room for a memory, a song, a metaphor, a fantasy, a machine, a sarcasm, a dream, a grand idea. Pick seven items on the list and write a paragraph about each. Do they add up to a rough draft of an essay?

Jamaica Kincaid
Those Words That Echo . . . Echo . . . Echo Through Life

How do I write? Why do I write? What do I write? This is what I am writing: I am writing "Mr. Potter." It begins in this way; this is its first sentence: "Mr. Potter was my father, my father's name was Mr. Potter." So much went into that one sentence; much happened before I settled on those eleven words.

Walking up and down in the little room in which I write, sitting down and then getting up out of the chair that is in the little room in which I write, I wanted to go to the bathroom. In the bathroom Mr. Potter vanished from my mind; I examined the tiles on the floor in front of me and found them ugly, worn out.

I looked at the faucet and the sink in front of me, but not too closely; I did not examine those. I flushed the toilet and I thought: Will the plumbing now just back up? Does the septic need pumping? Should I call Mr. A. Aaron? But Mr. A. Aaron's name is not that at all. His real name is something quite far from that. His real name is something like Mr. Christian or Mr. Zenith, though I cannot remember exactly. He only calls himself A. Aaron so he can be the first listing in the telephone book under the heading "Septic Tanks & Systems—Cleaning." I come back and look at Mr. Potter.

"Mr. Potter," I write, and I put clothes on him, even though I do not see him naked, for he was my father, and just now he is not yet dead. He is a young man, and I am not yet born. Oh, I believe I am seeing him as a little boy; as a little boy he has clothes, but he has not shoes. I do not place him in shoes until he is—I have not decided when exactly I shall allow him to wear shoes.

And then after many days of this and that and back and forth, I wrote, with a certainty that I did not necessarily intend to last, "Mr. Potter was my father, my father's name was Mr. Potter." And Mr. Potter remained my father, and Mr. Potter remained my father's name for a long time, even up to now.

And then? I grew tired of that sentence and those eleven words just sitting there all alone followed by all that blank space. I grew sad at seeing that sentence and those eleven words just sitting there followed by nothing, nothing, and nothing again. After many days it frightened me to see nothing but that one sentence and those eleven words and nothing, nothing, and nothing again came after them. "Say something," I said to Mr. Potter. To myself I had nothing to say.

Speaking no longer to Mr. Potter, speaking no longer to myself in regard to Mr. Potter, I got up at five o'clock in the morning and at half-past five o'clock went running with my friend Meg and a man named Dennis Murray; he builds houses of every kind in the city of Bennington in the state of Vermont.

"My father is dead," I said to Dennis one morning as we were just past the Mahar funeral parlor on Main Street. I never make an effort to speak before the funeral parlor. I despise death and consider it a humiliation and in any case much overdone and so plan never to do it myself and plan never to have anything at all to do with it, for it is so contagious. I have noticed that when you know people who die, you catch it and end up dead too.

"My father is dead," I said to Dennis, but he could not hear me for he was far ahead. He runs at a faster pace than I do, and he thought I was agreeing with something he had just said about the weekend he had just spent hiking into the woods and spending the night and fishing with a friend whose name I cannot remember and catching many trout and cooking them and eating them and going to sleep in a tent while there was a great downpour of rain outside and waking up the next morning and having the best pancakes and fishing again and doing everything again and all of it as perfect as it had been before and then coming home to his wife who loves him very much.

And the perfect narrative of Dennis's life, uninterrupted by any feelings of approaching and then leaving behind the Mahar funeral parlor, did not make me envious or make me grieve that Mr. Potter's life remained frozen in the vault that was his name and the vault of being only my father.

The days then rapidly grew thick into all darkness with only small spaces of light (that is autumn) and then remained solidly all darkness with only small patches of light (that is winter), and then the darkness slowly thinned out (that is spring), but the light was never as overwhelming in its way as the darkness was overwhelmingly dark in its way (that is summer). So too was the night dark except for when the moon was full and the day bright with light except for when clouds blocked out the sun. And Mr. Potter remained my father, and my father's name remained Mr. Potter for a very long time.

One day when I seemed uncertain about which foot to put first, the one in front of the other, my husband said to me, "Mrs. S., Mrs. S., how are you doing?" and "Are you okay?" The first letter in his family's chosen name is S. Our children go to school every day on a great big bus that was painted yellow and driven by a woman named Verta. A man named Mr. Sweet came and picked up our rubbish.

In the American way we have much rubbish, and Mr. Sweet is hard of hearing. Saying to him, as I feel I must if I see him, I must say to him, "Hallo, Mr. Sweet." And since he cannot hear me, he is deaf, he looks at me and then holds his ear forward, cupping it in the palm of his hand, as if it were a receptacle, for he wants it to receive the sounds that I am making.

"What?" says Mr. Sweet. "Hallo," I say again, and Mr. Sweet is then very nice and sincerely so, and he asks if I could pay him for the eight weeks he has picked up the rubbish without being paid.

"But no," I say to him, and then I explain that I am not allowed to write checks because I never put the debits and balances in their proper columns, and I make a mess of the household accounts. Mr. Sweet says, "Yep, yep," and then Mr. Sweet says he will see me next week. Mr. Sweet does not know about Mr. Potter, not in the way of my writing about him, not in the way of Mr. Potter as a real person.

And one day, after all sorts of ups and downs and many travails that are interesting, especially to me, Mr. Potter was driving a motorcar and dressing in a way imitative of men who had enormous amounts of money. And of course Mr. Potter was right to imitate the wardrobe of men who had enormous amounts of money, for without the existence of Mr. Potter and people like him, working very hard and being paid a mere pittance, there can be no enormous amounts of money. And I am Mr. Potter's daughter, so I know this.

But that "and one day" left me bereft and exhausted and feeling empty; and that "and one day" is just what I want when in the process of encountering a certain aspect of my world.

And then that one day, that one day after Mr. Potter's life advanced and exploded on the page, I had to have my lunch, but I could not eat too much of anything, not even plain green leaves. I could only eat very small amounts of anything, for I wanted to fit into my nice blue (tilting to lavender) silk taffeta skirt, a skirt that has box pleats. And I so love my nice blue (tilting to lavender) silk taffeta skirt with the box pleats and will not eat too much of anything, even just plain green leaves, for I look very beautiful in it. I look most beautiful in it when I am in a room all by myself, just alone with only my reflection, no one at all there to observe me.

In the early afternoon, just after I have eaten my lunch, I look at Mr. Potter, in my own way, a way I am imagining, a way that is most certainly true and real. (His name really was Roderick Potter; he really was my father.) He cannot look back at me unless I make him do so, and I shall never make him do so.

The telephone rings, and I do not answer it. The telephone rings, and I do not answer it. The telephone rings, I answer it, and on the other end is someone employed by one of my many creditors asking me to satisfy my debt. I promise to do so in a given time, but I have no money. I like having no money. I do not like having no money. I only like to have contempt for people who have a great deal of money and are unhappy even so, or are happy with money in a way that I find contemptible.

Driving past a sign that says YIELD, driving past the house where a dentist lives, driving past the house where the chiropractor I see from time to time lives, swiftly I pass by a sloping moist field that in spring is filled up with marsh marigolds. Swiftly I go past the home for delinquent children. Swiftly I go to await my children getting off the bus with Verta.

My children will soon get off the schoolbus, the one painted a harsh yellow, and it is driven by Verta. "Mr. Shoul," I say to myself, for I am all alone in the car, having driven so swiftly. "Mr. Shoul," I say, for I now can see that I have saddled Mr. Potter with this personality, Mr. Shoul. And Mr. Shoul is a merchant, an ordinary merchant, specializing in nothing particular; he sells anything. Mr. Shoul sells everything. Mr. Shoul might sell Mr. Potter; on the other hand, he might draw the line at selling Mr. Potter. And I have saddled Mr. Potter with Mr. Shoul.

Mr. Potter does not know the world. He is produced by the world, but he is not familiar with the world. He does not know its parameters. Mr. Potter was my father, my father's name was Mr. Potter. My children pour out of the bus. My daughter (she is fourteen) hurls an insult at my son (he is ten). His small self (the self that is not seen) crumbles to the ground; I rush to pick up his self that is not seen but has fallen to the ground and bring it back together again with his self that I can see.

I look at her, my daughter. What should I do? For her selves (one or two or three or more) are not all in one bundle, tied up together, either.

"Mr. Shoul" I say to myself, for I am at the bus stop and can tell no one what I am really thinking. "Mr. Shoul," I say. What to tell Mr. Potter about Mr. Shoul, where to begin?

"Mr. Shoul!" I shout at Mr. Potter, but Mr. Potter cannot hear me. I have left him at home on the page, the white page, the clean white page, all alone with Mr. Shoul. "Mr. Shoul," I write, "Mr. Shoul," I will tell Mr. Potter, "Mr. Shoul comes from Lebanon."

Try This

The "apparent subject" of Jamaica Kinkaid's essay is a sequence of more or less banal events. What is the deep subject? Write an essay "in denial"—that is, write about a troubling or traumatic incident without mentioning it directly.

Richard Selzer
The Knife

One holds the knife as one holds the bow of a cello or a tulip—by the stem. Not palmed nor gripped nor grasped, but lightly, with the tips of the fingers. The knife is not for pressing. It is for drawing across the field of skin. Like a slender fish, it waits, at the ready, then, go! It darts, followed by a fine wake of red. The flesh parts, falling away to yellow globules of fat. Even now, after so many times, I still marvel at its power—cold, gleaming, silent. More, I am still struck with a kind of dread that it is I in whose hand the blade travels, that my hand is its vehicle, that yet again this terrible steel-bellied thing and I have conspired for a most unnatural purpose, the laying open of the body of a human being.

A stillness settles in my heart and is carried to my hand. It is the quietude of resolve layered over fear. And it is this resolve that lowers us, my knife and me, deeper and deeper into the person beneath. It is an entry into the body that is nothing like a caress; still, it is among the gentlest of acts.

Then stroke and stroke again, and we are joined by other instruments, hemo-stats and forceps, until the wound blooms with strange flowers whose looped handles fall to the sides in steely array.

There is sound, the tight click of clamps fixing teeth into severed blood vessels, the snuffle and gargle of the suction machine clearing the field of blood for the next stroke, the litany of monosyllables with which one prays his way down and in: *clamp, sponge, suture, tie, cut.* And there is color. The green of the cloth, the white of the sponges, the red and yellow of the body. Beneath the fat lies the fascia, the tough fibrous sheet encasing the muscles. It must be sliced and the red beef of the muscles separated. Now there are retractors to hold apart the wound. Hands move together, part, weave. We are fully engaged, like children absorbed in a game or the craftsman of some place like Damascus.

Deeper still. The peritoneum, pink and gleaming and membranous, bulges into the wound. It is grasped with forceps, and opened. For the first time we can see into the cavity of the abdomen. Such a primitive place. One expects to find drawings of buffalo on the walls. The sense of trespassing is keener now, heightened by the world's light illuminating the organs, their secret colors revealed—maroon and salmon and yellow. The vista is sweetly vulnerable at this moment, a kind of welcoming. An arc of the liver shines high and on the right, like a dark sun. It laps over the pink sweep of the stom-ach, from whose lower border the gauzy omentum is draped, and through which veil one sees, sinuous, slow as just-fed snakes, the indolent coils of the intestine.

You turn aside to wash your gloves. It is a ritual cleansing. One enters this temple doubly washed. Here is man as microcosm, representing in all his parts the earth, perhaps the universe.

I must confess that the priestliness of my profession has ever been impressed on me. In the beginning there are vows, taken with all solemnity. Then there is the endless harsh novitiate of training, much fatigue, much sac-rifice. At last one emerges as celebrant, standing close to the truth lying cur-tained in the Ark of the body. Not surplice and cassock but mask and gown are your regalia. You hold no chalice, but a knife. There is no wine, no wafer. There are only the facts of blood and flesh.

And if the surgeon is like a poet, then the scars you have made on countless bodies are like verses into the fashioning of which you have poured your soul. I think that if years later I were to see the trace from an old inci-sion of mine, I should know it at once, as one recognizes his pet expressions.

But mostly you are a traveler in a dangerous country, advancing into the moist and jungly cleft your hands have made. Eyes and ears are shuttered from the land you left behind; mind empties itself of all other thought. You are the root of groping fingers. It is a fine hour for the fingers, their sense of touch so enhanced. The blind must know this feeling. Oh, there is risk everywhere. One goes lightly. The spleen. No! No! Do not touch the spleen that lurks below the left leaf of the diaphragm, a manta ray in a coral cave, its bloody tongue protruding. One poke and it might rupture, exploding with sudden hemorrhage. The filmy omentum must not be torn, the intestine scraped or denuded. The hand finds the liver, palms it, fingers running along its sharp lower edge, admiring. Here are the twin mounds of the kidneys, the apron of the omentum hanging in front of the intestinal coils. One lifts it aside and the fingers dip among the loops, searching, mapping territory, establishing boundaries. Deeper still, and the womb is touched, then held like a small muscular bottle—the womb and its earlike appendages, the ovaries. How they do nestle in the cup of a man's hand, their power all dormant. They are frailty itself.

There is a hush in the room. Speech stops. The hands of the others, assistants and nurses, are still. Only the voice of the patient's respiration remains. It is the rhythm of a quiet sea, the sound of waiting. Then you speak, slowly, the terse entries of a Himalayan climber reporting back.

"The stomach is okay. Greater curvature clean. No sign of ulcer. Pylorus, duodenum fine. Now comes the gall-bladder. No stones. Right kidney, left, all right. Liver . . . uh-oh."

Your speech lowers to a whisper, falters, stops for a long, long moment, then picks up again at the end of a sigh that comes through your mask like a last exhalation.

"Three big hard ones in the left lobe, one on the right. Metastatic deposits. Bad, bad. Where's the primary? Got to be coming from somewhere."

The arm shifts direction and the fingers drop lower and lower into the pelvis—the body impaled now upon the arm of the surgeon to the hilt of the elbow.

"Here it is."

The voice goes flat, all business now.

"Tumor in the sigmoid colon, wrapped all around it, pretty tight. We'll take out a sleeve of the bowel. No colostomy. Not that, anyway. But, God, there's a lot of it down there. Here, you take a feel."

You step back from the table, and lean into a sterile basin of water, resting on stiff arms, while the others locate the cancer.

When I was a small boy, I was taken by my father, a general practioner in Troy, New York, to St. Mary's Hospital, to wait while he made his rounds. The solarium where I sat was all sunlight and large plants. It smelled of soap and starch and clean linen. In the spring, clouds of lilac billowed from the vases; and in the fall, chrysanthemums crowded the magazine tables. At one end of the great high-ceilinged, glass-walled room was a huge cage where colored finches streaked and sang. Even from the first, I sensed the nearness of that other place, the Operating Room, knew that somewhere on these premises was that secret dreadful enclosure where *surgery* was at that moment happening. I sat among the cut flowers, half drunk on the scent, listening to the robes of the nuns brush the walls of the corridor, and felt the awful presence of *surgery*.

Oh, the pageantry! I longed to go there. I feared to go there. I imagined surgeons bent like storks over the body of the patient, a circle of red painted across the abdomen. Silence and dignity and awe enveloped them, these surgeons; it was the bubble in which they bent and straightened. Ah, it was a place I would never see, a place from whose walls the hung and suffering Christ turned his affliction to highest purpose. It is thirty years since I yearned for that old Surgery. And now I merely break the beam of an electric eye, and double doors swing open to let me enter, and as I enter, always, I feel the surging of a force that I feel in no other place. It is as though I am suddenly stronger and larger, heroic. Yes, that's it!

The operating room is called a theatre. One walks onto a set where the cupboards hold tanks of oxygen and other gases. The cabinets store steel cutlery of unimagined versatility, and the refrigerators are filled with bags of blood. Bodies are stroked and penetrated here, but no love is made. Nor is it ever allowed to grow dark, but must always gleam with a grotesque brightness. For the special congress into which patient and surgeon enter, the one must have his senses deadened, the other his sensibilities restrained. One lies naked, blind, offering; the other stands masked and gloved. One yields; the other does his will.

I said no love is made here, but love happens. I have stood aside with lowered gaze while a priest, wearing the purple scarf of office, administers Last Rites to the man I shall operate upon. I try not to listen to those terrible last questions, the answers, but hear, with scorching clarity, the words that formalize the expectation of death. For a moment my resolve falters before the resignation, the *attentiveness*, of the other two. I am like an executioner who hears the cleric comforting the prisoner. For the moment I am excluded from the centrality of the event, a mere technician standing by. But it is only for the moment.

The priest leaves, and we are ready. Let it begin.

Later, I am repairing the strangulated hernia of an old man. Because of his age and frailty, I am using local anesthesia. He is awake. His name is Abe Kaufman, and he is a Russian Jew. A nurse sits by his head, murmuring to him. She wipes his forehead. I know her very well. Her name is Alexandria, and she is the daughter of Ukrainian peasants. She has a flat steppe of a face and slanting eyes. Nurse and patient are speaking of blintzes, borscht, piroshki—Russian food that they both love. I listen, and think that it may have been her grandfather who raided the shtetl where the old man lived long ago, and in his high boots and his blouse and his fury this grandfather pulled Abe by his side curls to the ground and stomped his face and kicked his groin. Perhaps it was that ancient kick that caused the hernia I am fixing. I listen to them whispering behind the screen at the head of the table. I listen with breath held before the prism of history.

"Tovarich," she says, her head bent close to his.

He smiles up at her, and forgets that his body is being laid open.

"You are an angel," the old man says.

One can count on absurdity. There, in the midst of our solemnities, appears, small and black and crawling, an insect: The Ant of the Absurd. The belly is open; one has seen and felt the catastrophe within. It seems the patient is already vaporizing into angelhood in the heat escaping therefrom. One could warm one's hands in that fever. All at once that ant is there, emerging from beneath one of the sterile towels that border the operating field. For a moment one does not really see it, or else denies the sight, so impossible it is, marching precisely, heading briskly toward the open wound.

Drawn from its linen lair, where it snuggled in the steam of the great sterilizer, and survived, it comes. Closer and closer, it hurries toward the incision. Ant, art thou in the grip of some fatal *ivresse*? Wouldst hurtle over these scarlet cliffs into the very boil of the guts? Art mad for the reek we handle? Or in some secret act of formication engaged?

The alarm is sounded. An ant! An ant! And we are unnerved. Our fear of defilement is near to frenzy. It is not the mere physical contamination that we loathe. It is the evil of the interloper, that he scurries across our holy place, and filthies our altar. He *is* disease—that for whose destruction we have gathered. Powerless to destroy the sickness before us, we turn to its incarnation with a vengeance, and pluck it from the lip of the incision in the nick of time. Who would have thought an ant could move so fast?

Between thumb and forefinger, the intruder is crushed. It dies as quietly as it lived. Ah, but now there is death in the room. It is a perversion of our purpose. Albert Schweitzer would have spared it, scooped it tenderly into his hand, and lowered it to the ground.

The corpselet is flicked into the specimen basin. The gloves are changed. New towels and sheets are placed where it walked. We are pleased to have done something, if only a small killing. The operation resumes, and we draw upon ourselves once more the sleeves of office and rank. Is our reverence for life in question?

In the room the instruments lie on trays and tables. They are arranged precisely by the scrub nurse, in an order that never changes, so that you can reach blindly for a forceps or hemostat without looking away from the operating field. The instruments lie *thus*! Even at the beginning, when all is clean and tidy and no blood has been spilled, it is the scalpel that dominates. It has a figure the others do not have, the retractors and the scissors. The scalpel is all grace and line, a fierceness. It grins. It is like a cat—to be respected, deferred to, but which returns no amiability. To hold it above a belly is to know the knife's force—as though were you to give it slightest rein, it would pursue an intent of its own, driving into the flesh, a wild energy.

In a story by Borges, a deadly knife fight between two rivals is depicted. It is not, however, the men who are fighting. It is the knives themselves that are settling their own old score. The men who hold the knives are mere adjuncts to the weapons. The unguarded knife is like the unbridled war-horse that not only carries its helpless rider to his death, but tramples all beneath its hooves. The hand of the surgeon must tame this savage thing. He is a rider reining to capture a pace.

So close is the joining of knife and surgeon that they are like the Centaur—the knife, below, all equine energy, the surgeon, above, with his delicate art. One holds the knife back as much as advances it to purpose. One is master of the scissors. One is partner, sometimes rival, to the knife. In a moment it is like the long red fingernail of the Dragon Lady. Thus does the surgeon curb in order to create, restraining the scalpel, governing it shrewdly, setting the action of the operation into a pattern, giving it form and purpose.

It is the nature of creatures to live within a tight cuirass that is both their constriction and their protection. The carapace of the turtle is his fortress and retreat, yet keeps him writhing on his back in the sand. So is the surgeon rendered impotent by his own empathy and compassion. The surgeon cannot weep. When he cuts the flesh, his own must not bleed. Here it is all work. Like an asthmatic hungering for air, longing to take just one deep breath, the surgeon struggles not to feel. It is suffocating to press the feeling out. It would be easier to weep or mourn—for you know that the lovely precise world of proportion contains, just beneath, *there*, all disaster, all disorder. In a surgical operation, a risk may flash into reality: the patient dies . . . of *complication*. The patient knows this too, in a more direct and personal way, and he is afraid.

And what of that *other*, the patient, you, who are brought to the operating room on a stretcher, having been washed and purged and dressed in a white gown? Fluid drips from a bottle into your arm, diluting you, leaching your body of its personal brine. As you wait in the corridor, you hear from behind the closed door the angry clang of steel upon steel, as though a battle were being waged. There is the odor of antiseptic and ether, and masked women hurry up and down the halls, in and out of rooms. There is the watery sound of strange machinery, the tinny beeping that is the transmitted heartbeat of yet another *human being*. And all the while the dreadful knowledge that soon you will be taken, laid beneath great lamps that will reveal the secret linings of your body. In the very act of lying down, you have made a declaration of surrender. One lies down gladly for sleep or for love. But to give over one's body and will for surgery, to *lie down* for it, is a yielding of more than we can bear.

Soon a man will stand over you, gowned and hooded. In time the man will take up a knife and crack open your flesh like a ripe melon. Fingers will rummage among your viscera. Parts of you will be cut out. Blood will run free. Your blood. All the night before you have turned with the presentiment of death upon you. You have attended your funeral, wept with your mourners. You think, "I should never have had surgery in the springtime." It is too cruel. Or on a Thursday. It is an unlucky day.

Now it is time. You are wheeled in and moved to the table. An injection is given. "Let yourself go," I say. "It's a pleasant sensation," I say. "Give in," I say.

Let go? Give in? When you know that you are being tricked into the hereafter, that you will end when consciousness ends? As the monstrous silence of anesthesia falls discourteously across your brain, you watch your soul drift off.

Later, in the recovery room, you awaken and gaze through the thickness of drugs at the world returning, and you guess, at first dimly, then surely, that you have not died. In pain and nausea you will know the exultation of death averted, of life restored.

What is it, then, this thing, the knife, whose shape is virtually the same as it was three thousand years ago, but now with its head grown detachable? Before steel, it was bronze. Before bronze, stone—then back into unremembered time. Did man invent it or did the knife precede him here, hidden under ages of vegetation and hoofprints, lying in wait to be discovered, picked up, used?

The scalpel is in two parts, the handle and the blade. Joined, it is six inches from tip to tip. At one end of the handle is a narrow notched prong upon which the blade is slid, then snapped into place. Without the blade, the handle has a blind, decapitated look. It is helpless as a trussed maniac. But slide on the blade, click it home, and the knife springs instantly to life. It is headed now, edgy, leaping to mount the fingers for the gallop to its feast.

Now is the moment from which you have turned aside, from which you have averted your gaze, yet toward which you have been hastened. Now the scalpel sings along the flesh again, its brute run unimpeded by germs or other frictions. It is a slick slide home, a barracuda spurt, a rip of embedded talon. One listens, and almost hears the whine—nasal, high, delivered through that gleaming metallic snout. The flesh splits with its own kind of moan. It is like the penetration of rape.

The breasts of women are cut off, arms and legs sliced to the bone to make ready for the saw, eyes freed from sockets, intestines lopped. The hand of the surgeon rebels. Tension boils through his pores, like sweat. The flesh of the patient retaliates with hemorrhage, and the blood chases the knife wherever it is withdrawn.

Within the belly a tumor squats, toadish, fungoid. A gray mother and her brood. The only thing it does not do is croak. It too is hacked from its bed as the carnivore knife lips the blood, turning in it in a kind of ecstasy of plenty, a gluttony after the long fast. It is just for this that the knife was created, tempered, heated, its violence beaten into paper-thin force.

At last a little thread is passed into the wound and tied. The monstrous booming fury is stilled by a tiny thread. The tempest is silenced. The operation is over. On the table, the knife lies spent, on its side, the bloody meal smear-dried upon its flanks. The knife rests.

And waits.

Try This

You are probably not a surgeon, but several times in your journal you have written about something at which you are in fact an expert. Focus on that expertise—its difficulties, dangers, and rewards, but also its equipment, the look of it, the setting, how it affects the body. Write a personal essay about your experience that will also teach those who have no such skill or knowledge.

Susan Lester

Belongings

At twenty, he has square feet and wide bones and thick coarse hair; a smile that, while slow, is generous. You want to pet him. From all the bulk and fur of him you wouldn't expect his hands, magician hands. Quick. He draws caricatures in charcoal, plays Bach on guitar, juggles beanbags, and folds colored papers into deer and mice, cuts perfect stars with scissors in one snip, hiding, always hiding the effort.

"Ancient Oriental secret," he tells you when you ask. Understand that he drills himself in skills, wrests them painfully from nothingness, trains his hands as if they are wild animals.

Maybe it was night and cold. (According to almanacs, it snows in Seoul). Concealed by darkness she took him to the orphanage, laid him on a table cunningly designed to revolve, outside to in, accepting infants without revealing mothers. She walked home, still tender from the birthing.

He is seven months old when they send him to us on an airplane. We wait at the terminal to receive him, our son. Thirty babies are carried from the jumbo jet by men and women with dark hair, dark eyes. He is among them, asleep, full head of black hair sticking straight up, skin warm as a fever, voice deep when he murmurs. He doesn't cry. They pass him to me. I cry. I undress him in the airport bathroom like a gift I can't wait to open. His diaper is dry. My hands are shaking.

Maybe it was daylight and, unashamed, she strode to the orphanage to deposit him. She had meant the conception to be a tool with which she would pry open a distinguished place for herself. Too late, she saw it was her censure. She wiped her hands on her clothing going home.

His brother is inside my belly, a quick little fetus seven months old, conceived on the day we decided to adopt. Magic decision. He turns in my womb, taps at me from inside as if curious. I laugh. The Korean men smile for politeness when I laugh, not knowing the joke that is passing between my children.

Maybe she was charmed by a stranger, felt his love like the sun's light and opened herself, morning flower that broke laws with its tenderness. That night when she walked to the orphanage, there were stars above her, stars whose light had begun many hundreds of years before. She knew about stars, she understood that many hundreds of years hence, this moment would be seen by the stars she saw now. Pure light.

They hand him to me, asleep, then bow. Two men. I look at them covertly. This is how my son will look someday, this tall, this dark, this broad of face.

Bewildered, he opens his eyes, dark eyes, so dark I can't see pupils in them. He comes to me nuzzling his forehead in my neck, moving his head back and forth, back and forth, as if saying, "No, no, no, no, no." He lays his head against me then sleeps again. Once more, the men bow. They don't know my tongue. We smile. We compare the name bands on our wrists. Mine. His. Theirs. Yes, they match. We smile.

Maybe this was the punishment she meted out to her lover: to dispose of the object created by his passion and thus make all his passion negligible. Maybe on the way home she ate chocolate.

He is five and in school. He hates school. He says he fears he will fall out of line. On his first day, he asks me to pray to God to see if God can change his eyes. A child told him God could.

I pray a curse on the child who inaugurated this hope in him. I rake leaves in the yard for a week, turn soil, prune branches, master anger. I brush aside pebbles and branches and sticks to discover an anthill from which emerge a thousand ants. Within seconds they have filed themselves into lines. I shift a stone to divert them. I uncover, with a start, a lemon-colored toy car in a square hole, a small pebbled driveway for its entrance, a pinecone roof. I kneel and look, intrigued, my heart opened like a flower to the sunlight.

Maybe she was a New Woman, one who stepped away from the governing social order in which, antlike, individuals served as cells of a greater organism. She was warned that when isolated, one died; when shamed, one lost her place. But she stood brave against it, loved a man despite it, bore a child because of it. In anger she conceived, in triumph gave birth; in hope she gave away her son to live where she believed he would be free.

He is a mewling infant with moist, soft skin, infected navel, self-containment. I do not know him yet. A foster family keeps him. Five sons. They carry him on their backs and feed him rice milk. They sleep with him on their heated floors and tease him so he moved his head back and forth, back and forth, as if saying, "No, no, no, no, no." Outdoors, the country smells of minerals and earth, inside, of boiled rice and tea and garlic.

Maybe she hid herself, magician girl, appeared always to be obedient, all the while breaking with the order that sustained her. She bowed as if she obeyed, but broke, then feared the law. She hid the hot fetus within her, the fetus that would cut her, like a sword, from her mother and her father and her husband-to-be. Isolated, she would die. She crept, terrified, to the orphanage's turntable, hoping to abandon there fear. But fear went home with her, and with it, grief.

He hoards things. I call him a pack rat, though he knows I'm intrigued by the things he keeps. He refused to cut his thick horse-mane of hair. "Are you saving it for something?" I try to show reason.

"It's only peach fuzz," he answers. "Ancient Oriental peach fuzz."

His room is a labyrinth of beautiful things: guitar, girlfriend's pillow, drawing board, the *I Ching*, broken clock parts, Holy Bible, plastic jars, blue glass bits, stuffed dogs, burnt-edge corks, wooden boxes, rolls of tape, his baby blanket.

I kneel and look. This, I say, is because, at seven months, he knew that a person could lose everything, his people, his belongings, the smell of his ground, the hot floor where he sleeps, the white robes of ceremony, even the sound of his language. He does not know he remembers these things, or remember that he lost them. I do not remind him, but I let him hoard; I let him explain.

"What happened to your real mother?" asks Clark, blond four-year-old living next door.

"She died," he says.

"So," I say. And maybe she did. I would have.

Try This
Write an essay composed of scenes that are at least fifty percent invented—letting us as readers understand they are not fact—but that represent a sort of truth we can also understand.

Warm-up

What is going on in this girl's mind? What has happened in the last two hours? What has happened in the last two years? How much of this can you let us know without leaving this room, this chair, her thoughts?

CHAPTER EIGHT

FICTION

Story and Plot
Scene and Summary
Backstory and Flashback
Text and Subtext

The writer of any work . . . must decide two crucial points:
what to put in and what to leave out.

Annie Dillard

You have a story to write. You have a character in mind. The character has a desire. A situation presents itself. That the situation will lead to fulfillment of the desire is possible, but uncertain. How do you proceed?

Aristotle, the Greek philosopher who was also the first critic in Western literature, famously said that a story must have a beginning, a middle, and an end. This is less obvious than it looks. As the author, the questions you must answer are: Where shall I begin? Where will I end? What is in between? When you have made these decisions, you have made a choice between *story* and *plot*.

Story and Plot

Humphry House, in his commentaries on Aristotle, defines **story** as everything the reader needs to know to make coherent sense of the plot, and **plot** as the particular portion of the story the author chooses to present—the "present tense" of the narrative. The story of *Oedipus Rex*, for example, begins before Oedipus's birth with the oracle predicting that he will murder his father and marry his mother. It includes his birth, his abandonment with hobbled ankles, his childhood with his foster parents, his flight from them, his murder of the stranger at the crossroads, his triumph over the Sphinx, his marriage to Jocasta and his reign in Thebes, his fatherhood, the Theban plague, his discovery of the truth, and his self-blinding and self-banishment. When Sophocles set out to plot a play on this story, he began the action at dawn on the very last day of it. All the information about Oedipus's life is necessary to understand the plot, but the plot begins with the conflict: How can Oedipus get rid of the plague in Thebes? Because the plot is so arranged, it is the revelation of the past that makes up the action of the play, a process of discovery that gives rise to the significant theme: Who am I? Had Sophocles begun with the oracle before Oedipus's birth, no such theme and no such significance could have been explored.

E. M. Forster, in *Aspects of the Novel*, makes substantially the same distinction between plot and story. A story, he says, is:

> . . . the chopped off length of the tape worm of time . . . a narrative of events arranged in their time sequence. A plot is also a narrative of events, the emphasis falling on causality. "The king died, and then the queen died," is a story. "The king died, and then the queen died of grief," is a plot. The time sequence is preserved, but the sense of causality overshadows it. Or again: "The queen died, no one knew why, until it was discovered that it was through grief at the death of the king." This is a plot with a mystery in it, a form capable of high development. It suspends the time sequence, it moves as far away from the story as its limitations will allow. Consider the death of the queen. If it is in a story we say, "and then?" If it is in a plot we ask, "why?"

The human desire to know why is as powerful as the desire to know what happened next, and it is a desire of a higher order. Once we have the facts, we inevitably look for the links between them, and only when we find such links are we satisfied that we "understand." Rote memorization in a science bores almost everyone. Grasp and a sense of discovery begin only when we perceive *why* "a body in motion tends to remain in motion" and what an immense effect this actuality has on the phenomena of our lives. The same is true of the events of a story. Random incidents neither move nor illuminate; we want to know why one thing leads to another and to feel the inevitability of cause and effect.

A *story* is a series of events recorded in their chronological order. A *plot* is a series of events deliberately arranged so as to reveal their dramatic, thematic, and emotional significance.

Here, for example, is a series of uninteresting events chronologically arranged.

Ariadne had a bad dream.
She woke up tired and cross.
She ate breakfast.
She headed for class.
She saw Leroy.
She fell on the steps and broke her ankle.

Leroy offered to take notes for her.
She went to a hospital.

This series of events does not constitute a plot, and if you wish to fashion it into a plot, you can do so only by letting us know the meaningful relations among the events. We first assume that Ariadne woke in a temper because of her bad dream, and that Leroy offered to take notes for her because she broke her ankle. But why did she fall? Perhaps because she saw Leroy? Does that suggest that her bad dream was about him? Was she, then, thinking about his dream-rejection as she broke her egg irritably on the edge of the frying pan? What is the effect of his offer? Is it a triumph or just another polite form of rejection when, really, he could have missed class once to drive her to the x-ray lab? All the emotional and dramatic significance of these ordinary events emerges in the relation of cause to effect, and where such relation can be shown, a possible plot comes into existence.

Ariadne's is a story you might very well choose to tell chronologically: it needs to cover only an hour or two, and that much can be handled in the compressed form of the short story. But such a choice of plot is not inevitable even in this short compass. Might it be more gripping to begin with the wince of pain as she stumbles? Leroy comes to help her up and the yolk yellow of his T-shirt fills her field of vision. In the shock of pain she is immediately back in her dream. . . .

Here is another example, of a quite standard story: A girl grows up bossed by her older sister, who always tells her she's fat and a nerd. She ends up with "low self-esteem," poor grades, and a stutter. She has "social anxiety;" she stays at her computer most of the time. Her mother takes her to a series of therapists, but nothing brings her out of her shell. She's not asked to the big basketball dance, and won't go alone, but on the night of the game the computer system that runs the gym lighting system breaks down, and the coach, who knows she's a computer whiz, gives her a call. She fixes the program and catches the eye of the handsome Center (who probably takes off her glasses and lets down her hair, right?) And they live happily ever after.

This Cinderella story line shows up over and over again in film and print. The question is, how can you make it fresh and interesting? Where should your *plot* begin?

You may start, if you like, with the immigration of the heroine's grandparents from Lithuania. But if you do, it's going to be a very long story and we may close the book before she's born. You may begin it, like your childhood tale of Cinderella, with the background situation of the family, but then you must summarize, generalize, and focus on minor characters; and you may have a hard time holding our attention. Begin with the announcement of the dance? Better. If so, you'll somehow have to let us know all that has gone before, either through dialogue or through the girl's memory; but you have only a few days to cover and you have an opportunity to show the sisters in conflict. Suppose you begin with the telephone call from the coach? Is that perhaps best of all? An urgent dramatic scene, an immediate conflict that must lead to a quick and striking crisis?

It is a cliché of critical reaction—and not just for the work of beginners!—that "your story actually begins on page three." I think there is good reason that this failure of technique afflicts even professional writers. When you begin a story you are very properly feeling your way, getting to know your characters, bringing the setting into focus, testing the sorts of voice and action that will work. Since you're a little unsteady on your literary feet at this point, it's a temptation to fiddle with the dialogue, alter this phrase, perfect that image. The writing, thus polished, starts to look valuable—so it's hard to see that the reader doesn't need the same extended orientation that you did. Sometimes you need a few weeks' distance, or somebody else's insight, to recognize that you can move farther faster.

Try This

By now you have from your journal entries an idea for a short story. Take fifteen minutes to list all the events of this story in their chronological order. List *everything* we will need to know in order to make sense of it. If Seth's fear of water results from the time his cruel half-brother held him under when he was five, and we will need to know this is order to understand why he won't go out in a boat at twenty—then list the bullying incident in its chronological place.

- Find the item exactly halfway down your list. Write the first paragraph of your story beginning it there.
- Take the last item on your list. Write the first paragraph of the story beginning it there.
- Pick the *right* item on your list for the beginning of the story. Try these: Begin with a line of dialogue. Begin with an action. Begin with an image of danger. Begin with the weather. Begin with the protagonist's thought. Begin with a long shot. Begin with a closeup.
- Try tossing out page one.

> A child in a tantrum screams, throws toys, lies on the floor, and kicks in the air. The parents say, "You're making a scene!"
>
> *Jerome Stern*

Scene and Summary

Summary and **scene** are methods of treating time in fiction. A summary covers a relatively long period of time in relatively short compass; a scene deals at length with a relatively short period of time.

Summary is a useful and often necessary device: to give information, fill in a character's background, let us understand a motive, alter pace, create a transition, leap moments or years.

Scene is *always* necessary to fiction. Scene is to time what concrete detail is to the senses; that is, it is the crucial means of allowing your reader to experience the story with the characters. A confrontation, a turning point, or a crisis occurs at given moments that take on significance as moments and cannot be summarized. The form of a story requires confrontation, turning points, and crises, and therefore requires scenes. As Jerome Stern points out in *Making Shapely Fiction*, when you want everyone's full attention you "make a scene" like a child in a tantrum, using the writer's full complement of "dialogue, physical reactions, gestures, smells, sounds, and thoughts."

It is quite possible to write a short story in a single scene, without any summary at all. It is not possible to write a successful story entirely in summary. One of the most common errors beginning fiction writers make is to summarize events rather than to realize them as moments.

In the following paragraphs from Margaret Atwood's *Lady Oracle*, the narrator has been walking home from her Brownie troop with older girls who tease and terrify her with threats of a bad man.

> The snow finally changed to slush and then to water, which trickled down the hill of the bridge in two rivulets, one on either side of the path; the path itself turned to mud. The bridge was damp, it smelled rotten, the willow branches turned yellow, the skipping ropes came out. It was light again in the afternoons, and on one of them, when for a change Elizabeth hadn't run off but was merely discussing the possibilities with the others, a real man actually appeared.
>
> He was standing at the far side of the bridge, a little off the path, holding a bunch of daffodils in front of him. He was a nice-looking man, neither old nor young, wearing a good tweed coat, not at all shabby or disreputable. He didn't have a hat on, his taffy-colored hair was receding and the sunlight gleamed on his high forehead.

The first paragraph of this quotation covers the way things changed over a period of a few months and then makes a transition to one of the afternoons; the second paragraph specifies a particular moment. Notice that although summary sets us at a distance from the action, sense details remain necessary to its life: *snow, path, bridge, willow branches, skipping ropes*. The scene is introduced when an element of conflict and confrontation occurs. That the threatened bad man does appear and that he is surprisingly innocuous promises a turn of events and a change in the relationship among the girls. We need to see the moment when this change occurs.

Throughout *Lady Oracle*, which is by no means unusual in this respect, the pattern recurs: a summary leading up to, and followed by, a scene that represents a turning point.

My own job was fairly simple. I stood at the back of the archery range, wearing a red leather change apron, and rented out the arrows. When the barrels of arrows were almost used up, I'd go down to the straw targets. The difficulty was that we couldn't make sure all the arrows had actually been shot before we went down to clear the targets. Rob would shout, Bows DOWN, please, arrows OFF the string, but occasionally someone would let an arrow go, on purpose or by accident. This was how I got shot. We'd pulled the arrows and the men were carrying the barrels back to the line; I was replacing a target face, and I'd just bent over.

The summary in the second excerpt describes the general circumstances during a period of time—this is how things were, this is what usually or frequently happened: *I'd go down to the straw targets. Rob would shout.* Again, when the narrator arrives at an event that changes her circumstance (*I got shot*), she focuses on a particular moment: *I was replacing a target face, and I'd just bent over.* Notice that the pattern summary-to-scene parallels in time the spatial pattern of longshot-to-closeup.

Since the changes in your story will take place in fully developed scenes, it's important to limit the *number* of scenes, and summary can be useful to get you from one to another. Frequently, the function of summary is precisely to heighten scene. It is in the scene, the "present" of the story, that the drama, the discovery, the decision, the potential for change, engage our attention.

Try This
Look at the list of your story's events. How many of them belong in summary? Which of them involve moments of discovery or decision and should be scenes? How *few* scenes would it be possible to use and still tell the story? Those three dinners with dad—could they be conflated to one? The quarrel on the morning after—could it happen the same night? List the events of the story that represent its essential scenes.

Start writing one of these scenes with a method or a mood you've never used before. Begin with a cliché. Begin with an angry line of dialogue. Begin with a death. Begin tenderly. Begin with an action no bigger than a breadbox. Begin with the outcome of the scene and then go back to get us there.

Backstory and Flashback

Clearly, if you are going to begin *in medias res*, or in the middle of the action, then parts of your story will have to be brought in later. **Backstory** is a relatively new term, which started out in film meaning a *prequel*, but has come to refer to any information about the past—whatever has occurred before the plot begins and is necessary to make the story coherent. Such information can be revealed in dialogue, or in the character's thoughts, or in the narrative itself. When the narrative actually travels back from its current action to present the past in scenes, it is called a **flashback**—also a term borrowed from film.

There is, I think, one cardinal rule about the past in fiction: don't give us more than we need. As with opening paragraphs, so with backstory: as author you need to know so much about your characters in order to make them real and complex that you may think we readers need as much. But if your characters are interesting and credible, we probably don't. Especially in the twenty-first century—accustomed to the quick cuts of film, inundated with the lessons of psychology—we will understand causal connections, accept odd behavior, and tolerate a degree of inconsistency without needing a whole lot of psychological explanation. On the other hand, our primal desire to get on with the story is as powerful as it was in the cave, and we are likely to be impatient with too much background information.

When intrusive passages of childhood, motivation, and explanation tend to come early in the story, before we are caught up in the action, we wonder whether there is any story on its way. Dialogue, brief summary, a reference or detail can often tell us all we need to know, and when that is the case, a flashback becomes cumbersome and overlong. If, four pages into your story, you find there is more action happening in the character's memory than in the present action, you may not yet have found where the story lies.

If you are tempted to use flashback to fill in the whole past, try using your journal for exploring background. Write down everything, fast. Then take a hard look at it to decide just how little of it you can use, how much of it the reader can infer, how you can sharpen an image to imply a past incident or condense a grief into a line of dialogue. Trust the reader's experience of life to understand events from action and attitude. And keep the present of the story moving.

That said, flashback is one of the most magical of fiction's contrivances, because the reader's mind is a swifter mechanism for getting into the past than anything that has been devised for stage or even film. All you must do is to give the reader smooth passage into the past, and the force of the story will be time-warped to whenever and wherever you want it.

Flashback is effectively used in fiction to *reveal* at the *right time*. It does not so much take us from, as contribute to, the central action of the story, so that as readers we suspend the forward motion of the narrative in our minds as our understanding of it deepens.

If you find that you need an excursion into the past, provide some sort of transition. A connection between what's happening in the present and what happened in the past will often best transport the reader, just as it does the character. Avoid blatant transitions, such as "Henry thought back to the time" and "I drifted back in memory." Assume the reader's intelligence and ability to follow a leap back.

A graceful transition to the past allows you to summarize necessary background quickly, as in this excerpt from William Trevor's "*Le Visiteur*":

> "And now what else?" she enquired when *les amuse-geueles* were finished.
>
> Guy talked about Club 14 because he could think of nothing else. It was odd, it seemed to him, what was said and what was not; and not just here, not only by the Buissonnets. His mother had never asked a single thing about the island, or even mentioned the Buissonnets except, in his childhood, to say when September was half over that it was time for him to visit them again. Once he had tried to tell her of the acre or two Monsieur Buissonnet and his labourers had reclaimed for cultivation during the year that had passed, how *oliviers* or vines had been planted where only scrub had grown before, how a few more metres had been marked out for irrigation. His mother never displayed an interest. "Oh, it is because they have no children of their own," she said when he asked why it was that the Buissonnets invited him. "It is so sometimes."

Notice how deftly Trevor moves from current dialogue to a general reflection—*It was odd . . . and not just here*—to a summary of the past—*His mother had never*—to a specific moment of flashback with the mother's dialogue—"*Oh, it is because . . .*"

When you end a flashback, make it clear that you are catching up to the present again. Repeat an action or image that the reader will remember belongs to the basic time period of the story. Often simply beginning the paragraph with "Now . . ." will accomplish the reorientation. Trevor accomplishes it, after a paragraph more of childhood reminiscence, by returning to the next course of the restaurant lunch. This transition also has the nature of an interruption, as if the waiter intrudes on his memories.

> . . . The accompaniments of the *soupe de langoustines* came, the waiter unfamiliar, new this season as the waiters often were.

Try This

Put your character in motion. On foot, or on a vehicle, on a quest. What does he or she need urgently? Why so urgently? Let us know in a flashback of no more than three sentences. Avoid the words *remembered, recalled, thought back to*, and others of their ilk.

Add a character. In dialogue, let us know some important thing from the past.

Add music. Let the music trigger a memory good or bad, in thought or dialogue. Let the memory reveal something we didn't know before.

Text and Subtext

As a writer you are always trying to mean more than you say. You want dialogue to convey information and character, you want setting to convey mood and
propel the action, you want clothing to indicate politics, and gesture to betray
thought.

You can do this, and your reader can understand it, because people operate
this way in their daily lives. We express ourselves in many ways besides words,
sometimes by choice and sometimes in self-betrayal, sometimes trying to conceal
for the sake of friendship and sometimes in fear or contempt. How many times
have you sat through a meal in which the dialogue was all polite, anecdotal,
and bland, but everybody was *desperate* with boredom, anger, anxiety, or the
need to control?

The *text* is what is stated in any situation; the *subtext* is whatever remains
unstated—with the usual implication that the unstated is what's really going on.

Imagine a restaurant scene in which Bill asks his friend Lex to pass the
shrimp. Lex passes them by way of his wife, Sara, who takes a handful on the
way. There are none left for Bill's wife, Jane, who says she didn't want any
more anyway. Imagine how the dialogue, gestures, glances, facial expressions,
tones of voice differ in this scene if Lex suspects that Bill is having an affair with
Sara; and/or Jane is pregnant, which Sara knows but her husband doesn't;
and/or Jane feels herself to be superior to the rest of them, including her husband; and/or Sara and Lex had a quarrel just before they left home in which
Lex accused her of selfishness; and/or Jane is trying to get home early to intercept a phone call from Bill's mother, who may have cancer; and/or Bill wrote
a report that he suspects will get Lex fired. Any combination of these complications probably means that all four of them are sick of the friendship anyway, and looking for a way to end it. Yet they may not. Situations of this complexity occur every day.

Here is a passage from Barbara Kingsolver's *Poisonwood Bible*, in which an
American Baptist minister and his family sit with a Bantu council in the Bel-
gian Congo:

> Father tried to interrupt the proceedings by loudly explaining that Jesus is
> exempt from popular elections. But people were excited, having just recently got
> the hang of democratic elections. The citizens of Kilanga were ready to cast their
> stones . . .
>
> Anatole, who'd sat down in his chair a little distance from the pulpit, leaned
> over and said quietly to Father, "They say you thatched your roof and now you
> must not run out of your house if it rains."
>
> Father ignored this parable. "Matters of the spirit are not decided at the mar-
> ketplace," he shouted sternly. Anatole translated.

"*Á bu, kwe?*" Where, then?" asked Tat Nguza, standing up boldly. In his opinion, he said, a white man who has never even killed a bushbuck for his family was not the expert on which god can protect our village.

When Anatole translated that one, Father looked taken aback. Where we come from, it's hard to see the connection.

Father spoke slowly, as if to a half-wit, "Elections are good, and Christianity is good. Both are good." We in his family recognized the danger in his extremely calm speech, and the rising color creeping toward his hairline.

In this passage, while a controlled form of political negotiation goes on, the participants vie for status, and we have a dozen or more clues to the political and personal subtext. The contrast between the Congolese's parables and the American's abstractions, the conflicting logic, the gestures, bodily movements and expressions, the genuine calm of the translator as opposed to the bottled-fury calm of the father—all these reveal the unspoken meanings. In addition, they are interpreted through the point of view of a daughter who, in spite of her youth and relative innocence, has reason to understand the signs.

Try This

Put two characters of your story in a situation in which they must say less or other than they mean. Reveal the protagonist's true feeling through thoughts, and the other character's through gesture, expression, or other external sign.

Subtext is a necessary result and cost of civilization—if everyone went around saying what they meant all the time there would be fewer friends and a lot more pain—but it offers a glorious opportunity for art. When your characters let us know by action, tone, thought, gesture, hesitation, slip of the tongue, contradiction, or backtracking that they are leaving an iceberg's worth of the truth submerged, the reader reads their truth as well as the words.

Try This

All of the following are the opening lines of published short stories, some of them famous. Pick one and write the first few paragraphs of a story. Write fast.
- She stood with her black face some six inches from the moist window-pane and wondered would it ever stop raining.
- It was Sunday—not a day, but rather a gap between two other days.
- Mother says that when I start talking I never know when to stop.
- He wasn't pretty unless you were in love with him.
- Once upon a time, I was dissatisfied with how I used my brains and with how Sam used his.

continued

- He had no body hair.
- I wasn't his friend, but I wasn't one of the main kids who hounded him up onto the shed roof, either.

More to Read

Gardner, John. *The Art of Fiction.* New York: Vintage Books, 1985.

Stern, Jerome. *Making Shapely Fiction.* New York: W.W. Norton, 1991.

READINGS

Nadine Gordimer

The Diamond Mine

Love during wartime.

I'll call her Tilla. You may call her by another name. You might think you knew her. You might have been the one. It's not by some simple colloquial habit that we "call" someone instead of naming: call him up.

It is during the war, your war, the forties, that has sunk as far away into the century as the grandfathers' 1914. He is blond, stocky in khaki, attractively nearsighted, so that the eyes, which are actually having difficulty with focus, seem to be concentrating attentively on her. This impression is emphasized by his lashes, blond and curly as his hair. He is completely different from the men she knows in the life of films—the only men she knows, apart from her father—and whom she expected to come along one day not too far off, Robert Taylor or even the foreigner, Charles Boyer. He is different because—at last—he is real. She is sixteen. He is no foreigner, no materialization of projection from Hollywood. He's the son of friends of her maternal grandmother, detailed to a military training camp in the province where the girl and her parents live. Some people even take in strangers from the camp for the respite of weekend leave; with a young daughter in the house, this family would not go so far as to risk that, but when the man of the family is beyond call-up age an easy way to fulfill patriotic duty is to offer hospitality to a man vouched for by connections. He's almost to be thought of as an elective grandson of the old lady. In war these strangers, remember, are Our Boys.

When he comes on Friday night and stays until Sunday his presence makes a nice change for the three, mother, father, and daughter, who live a quiet life, not given to socializing. That presence is a pleasant element in the closeness between parents and daughter: he is old enough to be an adult like them and, only eight years ahead of her, young enough to be her contemporary. The mother cooks a substantial lunch on the Sundays he's there; you can imagine what the food must be like in a military camp. The father suggests a game of golf—welcome to borrow clubs—but it turns out the soldier doesn't play. What's his game, then? He likes to fish. But his hospitality is four hundred miles from the sea; the soldier laughs along in manly recognition that there must be a game. The daughter: for her, she could never tell anyone, his weekend presence is a pervasion that fills the house, displaces all its familiar odors of home, is fresh and pungent—he's here. It's the emanation of khaki washed with strong soap and fixed—as in perfume the essence of flowers is fixed by alcohol—by the pressure of a hot iron.

The parents are reluctant cinema-goers, so it is thoughtful of this visiting friend of the family to invite the daughter of the house to choose a film she'd like to see on a Saturday night. She has no driving license yet (seventeen was the qualifying age in those days) and the father does not offer his car to the soldier. So the pair walk down the road from streetlight to streetlight, under the trees, all that autumn, to the small town's center, where only the cinema and the pub in the hotel are awake. She is aware of window dummies, in the closed shops that her mother's friends patronize, observing her as she walks past with a man. If she is invited to a party given by a school friend, she must be home strictly by eleven, usually fetched by her father. But now she is with a responsible friend, a family connection, not among unknown youths on the loose; if the film is a nine-o'clock showing, the pair are not home before midnight, and the lights are already extinguished in the parents' bedroom. It is then that, schoolgirlish, knowing nothing else to offer, she makes cocoa in the kitchen, and it is then that he tells her about fishing. The kitchen is locked up for the night, the windows are closed, and it is amazing how strong that presence of a man can be, that stiff-clean clothing warmed—not a scent, not a breath but, as he moves his arms graphically in description of playing a catch, it comes from the inner crease of his bare elbows, where the sun on Maneuvers hasn't got at the secret fold, from that center of being, the pliant hollow that vibrates between his collarbones as he speaks, the breastplate rosy down to where a few brownish-blond hairs disappear into the open neck of the khaki shirt. He will never turn dark, his skin retains the sun, glows. Him.

Tilla has never gone fishing. Her father doesn't fish. Four hundred miles from the sea, the boys at school kick and throw balls around—they know about, talk about football and cricket. The father knows about, talks about golf. Fishing. It opens the sea before her, the salt wind gets in her narrowed eyes, conveying to her whole nights passed alone on the rocks. He walks from headland to headland on dawn-wet sand, the tide is out—sometimes in midsentence there's a check, half smile, half breath, because he's thinking of something this child couldn't know. This is his incantation; it shuts out the parade-ground march toward killing and blinds the sights that the gun trains on sawdust-stuffed figures on which he is being drilled to see the face of the enemy, to whom he himself is the enemy, with guts (he pulls the intricately perfect innards out of the fish he's caught, a fisherman's simple skill) in place of sawdust. The sleeping parents are right: he will not touch her innocence of what this century claims, commands from him.

As they walk home where she used to race her bicycle up and down under the trees, the clothing on their arms—the khaki sleeve, the sweater her mother has handed her as a condition of permission to be out in the chill night air—brushes by proximity, not intention. The strap of her sandal slips, and as she pauses to right it, hopping on one leg, he steadies her by the forearm and then they walk on hand in hand. He's taking care of her. The next weekend, they kiss in one of the tree-dark intervals between streetlights. Boys have kissed her; it happened only to her mouth. The next Saturday, her arms went around him, his around her, her face approached, was pressed, breathed in, and breathed against the hollow of neck where the pendulum of heartbeat can be felt, the living place above the breastplate from which the incense of his presence had come. She was there.

In the kitchen there was no talk. The cocoa rose to the top of the pot, made ready. All the sources of warmth that her palms had extended to, everywhere in the house, as a domestic animal senses the warmth of a fire to approach, were in this body against hers, in the current of arms, the contact of chest, belly muscles, the deep strange heat from between his thighs. But he took care of her. Gently loosened her while she was discovering that a man has breasts, too, even if made of muscle, and that to press her own against them was an urgent exchange, walking on the wet sands with the fisherman.

The next weekend leave—but the next weekend leave is cancelled. Instead there's a call from the public phone at the canteen bar. The mother happened to answer and there were expressions of bright and encouraging regret that the daughter tried to piece into what they were responding to. The family was at supper. The father's mouth bunched stoically: Marching orders. Embarkation. The mother nodded round the table, confirming. She—the one I call Tilla—stood up, appalled at the strength to strike the receiver from her mother and the inability of a good girl to do so. Then her mother was saying, but of course we'll take a drive out on Sunday, say goodbye and Godspeed. Grandma'd never forgive me if she thought . . . Now, can you tell me how to get there, beyond Pretoria, I know . . . I didn't catch it, what mine? And after the turnoff at the main road? Oh, don't bother, I suppose we can ask at a petrol station if we get lost, everyone must know where that camp is. Is there something we can bring you, anything you'll need . . .

It seems they're to make an outing of it. Out of her stun: that essence, ironed khaki and soap, has been swept from the house, from the kitchen, by something that's got nothing to do with a fisherman, except that he is a man and, as her father has stated—embarkation—men go to war. Her mother makes picnic preparations: Do you think a chicken or pickled ox tongue, hard-boiled eggs . . . Don't know where one can sit to eat in a military camp, there must be somewhere for visitors. Her father selects from his stack of travel brochures a map of the local area to place on the shelf below the windshield. Petrol is rationed, but he has been frugal with coupons; there are enough to provide a full tank. Because of this, plans for the picnic are abandoned—no picnic—her mother thinks, Wouldn't it be a nice gesture to take the soldier out for a restaurant lunch in the nearest city? There won't be many such luxuries for the young man on his way to war in the North African desert.

They have never shown her the mine, the diamond mine, although ever since she was a small child they have taken her to places of interest as part of her education. They must have talked about it—her father is a mining-company official himself, but his exploitation is gold, not precious stones—or more likely it has been cited in a general-knowledge text at school: some famous diamond was dug up there.

The camp is on part of the vast mine property, commandeered by the Defense Force. Over the veld there are tents to the horizon, roped and staked, dun as the scuffed and dried grass and the earth scoured by boots—boots tramping everywhere, khaki everywhere, the wearers replicating one another, him. Where will they find him? He did give a tent number. The numbers don't seem to be consecutive. Her father is called to a halt by a replica with a gun, slow-spoken and polite. The car follows given directions retained differently by the mother and the father; the car turns, backs up, take it slowly for heaven's sake.

She is the one: There. There he is.

Of course, when you find him you see that there is no one like him, no bewilderment. They are all laughing in the conventions of greeting, but his eyes have their concentrated attention for her. It is his greeting of the intervals between streetlights, and of the kitchen. This weekend that ends weekends seems also to be the first of winter; it's suddenly cold, wind bellies and whips at that tent where he must have slept, remote, between weekends. It's the weather for hot food, shelter. At the restaurant, he chooses curry and rice for this last meal. He sprinkles grated coconut and she catches his eye and he smiles for her as he adds dollops of chutney. The smile is that of a greedy boy caught out and is also as if it were a hand squeezed under the table. No wine—the father has to drive, and young men oughtn't to be encouraged to drink, enough of that in the Army—but there is ice cream with canned peaches, coffee served, and peppermints with the compliments of the management.

It was too warm in the restaurant. Outside, high-altitude winds carry the breath of what must be early snow on the mountains, far away, unseen, as this drive back to the camp carries the breath of war, far away, unseen, where all the replicas in khaki are going to be shipped. No heating in the family car of those days, the soldier has only his thin, well-pressed khaki and the daughter, of course, like all young girls, has taken no precaution against a change in the weather—she is wearing a skimpy flounced cotton dress (secretly chosen, although he, being older, and a disciple of the sea's mysteries, probably won't even notice) that she was wearing the first time they walked to the cinema. The mother, concealing, she believes, irritation at the fecklessness of the young—next thing she'll have bronchitis and miss school—fortunately keeps a rug handy and insists that the passengers in the back seat put it over their knees.

It was easy to chat in the preoccupations of food along with the budgerigar chitter of other patrons in the restaurant. In the car, headed back for that final place, the camp, the outing is over. The father feels an obligation: at least, he can tell something about the diamond mine that's of interest, and soon they'll actually be passing the site of operations again, though you can't see much from the road.

The rug is like the pelt of some dusty pet animal settled over them. The warmth of the meal inside them is bringing it to life, a life they share, one body. It's pleasant to put their hands beneath it; the hands, his right, her left, find one another.

. . . You know what a diamond is, of course, although you look at it as something pretty a woman wears on her finger, hmm? Well, actually it consists of pure carbon crystallized . . .

He doesn't like to be interrupted, so there's no need to make any response, even if you still hear him. The right hand and the left hand become so tightly clasped that the pad of muscle at the base of each thumb is flattened against the bone and interlaced fingers are jammed down between the joints. It isn't a clasp against imminent parting, it's got nothing to do with any future, it belongs in the urgent purity of this present.

. . . The crystallization in regular octahedrons, that's to say eight-sided, and in allied forms and the cut and polished ones you see in jewelry more or less follow . . .

The hands lay together, simply happened, on the skirt over her left thigh, because that is where she had slipped her hand beneath the woolly comfort of the rug. Now he slowly released, first fingers, then palms—at once awareness signalled between them, that the rug was their tender accomplice, it must not be seen to be stirred by something—he released himself from her and for one bereft moment she thought he had left her behind, his eight-year advantage prevailed against such fusion of palms as it had done, so gently (oh, but why), when they were in the dark between trees, when they were in the kitchen.

   . . . colorless or they may be tinted occasionally yellow, pink, even black . . .

The hand had not emerged from the rug. She followed as if her eyes were closed or she were in the dark; it went as if it were playing—looking for a place to tickle, as children do to make one another wriggle and laugh—where her skirt ended at her knee, going under her knee without displacing the skirt and touching the tendons and the hollow there. She didn't want to laugh (what would her father make of such a response to his knowledgeable commentary), so she glided her hand to his and put it back with hers where it had been before.

   . . . one of the biggest diamonds in the world after the Koh-i-noor's hundred and nine carats, but that was found in India . . .

The hand, his hand, pressed fingers into her thigh through the cotton flounce, as if testing to see what was real about her, and stopped, and then out of the hesitation went down and, under the rug, up under the gauze of skirt, moved over her flesh. She did not look at him and he did not look at her.

   . . . and there are industrial gems you can cut glass with, make bits for certain drills, the hardest substance known . . .

At the taut lip of her panties he hesitated again, no hurry, all something she was learning, he was teaching, the anticipation in his fingertips, he stroked along one of the veins in there in the delicate membranelike skin that is at the crevice between leg and body (like the skin that the sun on Maneuvers couldn't reach in the crook of his elbow), just before the hair begins. And then he went in under the elastic edge and his hand was soft on soft hair, his fingers like eyes attentive to her.

   . . . Look at this veld—nothing suggests one of the greatest ever, anywhere, down there, down in what we call Blue Earth, the diamondiferous core . . .

She has no clear idea of where his hand is now, what she feels is that they are kissing, they are in each other's mouths although they cannot look at one another.

Are you asleep back there? The mother is remarking her own boredom with the mine. He is eight years older, able to speak: Just listening. His finger explores deep down in the dark, the hidden entrance to some sort of cave with its slippery walls and smooth stalagmite. She's found, he's found her.

The car is passing the mine processing plant.

. . . product of the death and decay of forests millennia ago, just as coal is, but down there the ultimate alchemy, you might say . . .

Those others, the parents, they have no way of knowing. It has happened, it is happening under the old woolly rug that was all they could provide for her. She is free of them. Found, and they don't know where she is.

At the camp, the father shakes the soldier's hand longer than in the usual grip. The mother for a moment looks as if she might give him a peck on the cheek, Godspeed, but it is not her way to be familiar.

Aren't you going to say goodbye? She's not a child, good heavens, a mother shouldn't have to remind of manners.

He's standing outside one of the tents with his hands hanging open at his sides as the car is driven away, and his attention is upon her until, with his furry narrowed sight, he'll cease to be able to make her out, while she can still see him, see him until he is made one with all the others in khaki, replicated, crossing and crowding, in preparation to embark.

If he had been killed in that war they would have heard through the grandmother's connections.

Is it still you, somewhere, old.

Try This

"The Diamond Mine" makes unusual use of the second person, in that the *you* seems sometimes to be the reader and sometimes the character otherwise called *he*.

Take a few paragraphs of the story you are writing and recast them as if they were addressed to one of the characters.

Rick DeMarinis
Your Fears Are Justified

There's a bomb on this plane. I offer no proof. And yet I know. Panic constricts my breathing. My heart can be heard, I'm sure of that. It ticks in my ear like an egg timer. I get out of my seat slowly so as not to alarm the others. In the rest room I splash my face with cold water. The bomb is with the cargo. We're approaching Clinic City. The plane touches down. The bomb, though armed, does not explode.

In the Clinic City hospital I have to share a room with a heart patient. "What are you here for?" he asks. "Brain tumor," I say. He perks up, interested. "How's your ticker?" he says. His wife, large and phlegmatic, visits twice a day. They whisper. "You're terminal?" she asks, coyly. It's as if she's asked me about the weather in Des Moines. "Not that I know of," I say. "Brain tumor," her husband whispers, nudging her. They exchange loving glances. I know what they are thinking. It's clear: *They want my heart.* "Macroadenoma," I say. "Nonmalignant." They wink at each other. She consoles me with a ladyfinger. After the operation I fly home, weak but still sensitive to threats.

I appreciate your interest. I honor your adrenalized state. Your fears are justified. I'm sorry. I will sit here in my living room and decide what to tell you. Yes, there is no hope. But remember, some fuses are duds, some tumors are benign, some heart patients recover on their own. You have time to change your life.

Laurie Berry

Mockingbird

Peter has just returned from Mexico, where his face turned the chalky pink color of Pepto Bismol. Rachel is at that swooning stage of love, stupid with happiness at his return.

That evening they drink cold vodka and gossip about a child-laden couple they know, who rise at dawn for work and return home at seven to bathe the three-year-old, console the eight-year-old, and struggle through dinner in time to collapse in bed by ten.

"Even so they have a great house," she says. "And nice things. They make a lot of money."

Peter shakes his head and says, offhandedly: "I'd rather inherit it."

They are both shocked by the statement. An island of silence bobs to the surface. Rachel swallows the last of her vodka, and with it the realization that she is in love with a man who has just traveled to a third world nation to play tennis.

"By the way—" He looks up guiltily, making a game of it. "Promise me you'll never tell anyone I said that."

This makes her laugh, freshens her love. They laugh some more. Talk their slow way toward dinner. Spy on the remarkable albino Mexican boy playing in the yard next door. Make love with windows open and then lie there listening to the mariachi music that pumps through her Houston barrio neighborhood.

Everything is soft, very soft. And luck abundant as Johnson grass. The Mimosa trees' green canopy. And the mockingbirds, not yet vicious, waiting for the fierce end of summer.

Try This

Write the short story you are working on as a short-short. If you had to condense it into 250–300 words, what would you retain? This exercise may help you whenever a story seems amorphous or sprawling—when you don't, in fact, quite know what it's about.

Heather Sellers
It's Water, It's Not Going to Kill You

In the good days, my family lived in a condo, on the twenty-third floor of Pleasure Towers in Ormond Beach, overlooking the Atlantic Ocean.

One afternoon, when we got home from school, my mother was up against the stove, her hands behind her, fingers laced across the cool burners. My father rifled through my mother's orderly Tupperwared leftovers in the fridge, yelling at her, "Why can't you have fun? Why?"

Since I had turned twelve, they'd been fighting. And actually, I noticed, they'd always been fighting. Whenever one walked in the room, the other one was already mad. "I think our parents might be mental cases," I confided to Sid. "I hope no one ever finds out."

Sid thought no one would find out. "They never go anywhere," he reminded me.

"Well, I wish they would," I'd said. "We'd be better off on our own." I had in mind Austrian get-ups. Sid sporting a green pointed felt hat, a cute little house in the woods, lots of pets, newspaper articles on Sid and Geor-

gia Jackson, the amazing fairy tale of two children making it on their own!
Here in the heart of Daytona Beach in the middle of 1976!

I stood in the doorway to our galley kitchen, leaning in. But my body
was out. I was in. I swung my hips to the side to keep Sid from entering the
kitchen, and bent myself into a C in the doorway. They did not see me, their
flexible daughter, their daughter in the shape of a good letter.

Sid scooted between my legs and went to the fridge. "'Scuse," he said.

I could see the ocean between my mother and my father.

I thought he was about to wheel around and hit her.

Get out, I wanted to say.

I realized I was talking to myself.

My brother—Sid—and I were wet in those days, always something of
us was wet. Well, me anyway. Sid was dark; he dried faster. My long planks
of yellow hair held water like seaweed does—and it was nearly down to the
small of my back, where I wanted it—my palms sweated, balls of juice came
out of my armpits, and the soles of my feet felt sweet and squishy. Welp, I
thought, I'm a girl. Such is my lot.

At night, in the room we shared, Sid would feel the back of my neck,
and the wet mats of hair under my topcoat of hair.

"You'll mildew before you're forty," he said. "Your hair is going to
rot, you know. You're going to get that crud on your neck, like old people."

"Well, at least I have a brain."

"We should be nice to each other," he said.

"You start first," I said.

Every day, we went from the condo to the pool to the ocean to school,
and back, through the pool, up to the condo for cheese and water, and to
the ocean, and back for dinner, and then back to the sea until dark.

To Sid, my dark bristly brother, I said, "People will think you're a
vermin, and shoot you."

We'd tussle, embarrassed, rolling around on the long white shag carpet; we were too old to be sharing a room, too old to be fighting like dogs, like
that.

In my family, the father wasn't supposed to get out of bed before the
kids were off to school.

"But don't dads go to work in the morning?" I asked, eating my
favorite breakfast, shrimp on toast.

"I get him off after you two are processed," my mother said. She woke
us up at six in the morning; we had time to race the elevators (Pleasure
Towers had two) down to the Pool Level, dive in, then run down to the beach,

and throw ourselves into the cold green sea. Then, we ran across the hard sand, always on the eye-out for shark teeth, raced the waiting elevators, back upstairs, and put our school clothes on.

Our skin could rot off, I thought. But that's the only really bad thing I thought could happen. Or, sometimes, because we never showered, rarely bathed, I thought we might—me and Sid—dissolve. Like maybe it was too much swimming, too much salt drying to powder on our skin, too much lying on the bottom of the pool and watching the sun become a free kaleidoscope, a little too much pulsing with the waves. As though we might stop being children at all.

On Friday at 11:00 a.m. there was another space launch down the road at Canaveral. School was canceled so we could go with our families to see the launch.

"Why not us?" Sid said. We were sitting in the condo. It was late morning, and odd to be on the sofa with my mother. My father's snoring came from their bedroom. My mother's nest of blue blankets was still on the white circular sofa, where she'd slept, curled in the curve of the rented sofa.

"We aren't the kind of family all that interested in *space*," my mother said.

I said, "I'm very interested in space. I am studying the galaxy."

"You aren't," Sid said.

"I want to someday. I want to be a deep-sea diver."

"Then study the ocean, which you don't know anything about."

"It's all related, Sid. Mom, tell him, it's all related."

"Georgia, honey."

"It's all related." I flung myself to the floor and executed a perfect backbend. My shorts pulled up, and I let them, I let the seam tighten between my legs, like I was inside a rubber band. "Tell him!" I felt good and strange, too.

Sid was playing the spoons at the table. My mother drifted to the floor, slunk down. She sprawled out on her side, like a nursery schooler at nap. She put her head down. I sprang onto her.

"Honey," she said softly, not kindly. "I am utterly exhausted. Play with Sid?"

I could see she was exhausted. I could taste her exhaustion. She put her hands over her ears, like I was a shout, just being on her. "I'm too old to play with him," I said.

We'd already been swimming. My braid lay on my back like a wet horse tail. I looked out the sliding glass doors: these were our walls, all along the front and side of the condo—glass walls! I didn't belong here at all. I belonged at the space launch, and not with the kids. I belonged in the rocket. I vowed to start studying the sky. Forget jockeying for the position of keeper of the homonym bulletin board—why was I wasting my time on fifth grade?

"I think we'll go back to Orlando today, use the day to look for housing." My mother was sorting through dozens of paper slips stuffed in her awkward white purse. Her lists.

"No," I said. "Terrible."

"We don't want to move," Sid said. He rubbed her arm. He was nice, like a butler. Like something from *Wind in the Willows*, a beaver or wee weasel of a butler.

"Children," she said. "Please. I need your support."

"Well, what's happening?" I said. I was back on the floor, trying a headstand. "Does he have a new job? Did he get fired, Mom?"

We heard my father clear his throat, or his nostrils, his entire being. Then he launched into a fit of coughing.

My father was between jobs. My mother said we were moving back to Orlando; foreclosure, equity, top-heavy, overdrawn.

"I thought Bethune Cookman was paying for the condo, and he was a teacher now?"

"Ask him, kids. Explain it to your children, Buck."

My dad held his drink in front of her face like a citation.

"Explain it again, please," I said. "You have this money, but you don't?" I didn't feel they were great explainers, even though my mother had been a teacher and my father had been many things.

"Haven't you had this in school? Don't they teach you anything at that goddamn school?"

"Ah," I said. "Yes. Yes. We learn a lot. But you know, it's fifth grade. What can I say?"

"We don't really learn," Sid said. He got a slap on the cheek from my dad. I started sweating between my legs and behind my knees; these were new zones of productivity for me. "Fourth grade isn't really learning." Sid ducked my father's arm this time, and went and sat at the piano, and he pretended to play, dramatically wheeling his hands up and down the keys like a tiny weasel genius.

Mother marched into the dining room and braced herself on the glass table with her arms, as if she were holding that plate of glass down, keeping it from slipping off.

"Yikes," I said.

"You still won't listen," my father said. He kept coming toward her, right up to her face.

"I don't to want to listen," my mother said. She pushed her hair back and quickly circled behind the table.

I fell out of my chair. Something I had practiced, fun, like magic tricks or pretending to be drowning, my two other passions in life.

"Georgia," Sid said. He was chewing his hand.

I crawled past them, across the white shag, and folded myself in the credenza.

Sid knocked on the door. Then he stood up and turned his back on the credenza. I felt like I was sailing off.

I sat there crunched up among the tablecloths, the board games, Battleship, Scrabble, Trouble. Usually I felt extremely slender, smart, and small for a twelve-year-old. Sid was eleven, and exponentially smaller. Now I felt huge, an explosion of person.

Hot and huge.

I opened the door to the exact right place. From this vantage point, I had a new view of my family's legs. My father's, bare, because he was in his usual outfit, black dress shoes, thin white socks, and green golfer shorts. It seemed to me his legs were missing a lot of their hair. They were bare, skinny, and shiny, as if he were a woman, or diseased. The skin was pink and spotty, like a leopard shell.

My mother's legs were cricked up under her on the dining room chair. She had her head on the glass; I could see the face of my mother through the glass, crying, squashed, like a sea creature in a too-small tank at the aquarium. My poor mom.

She wore support hose because carrying us two kids inside her body for a total of eighteen months (that's almost two years) caused a serious problem with varicose veins, and she could never again stand for long periods of time. Her legs were hidden in khakis, wrinkled and thick.

Kelly the bird was on top of me, on the credenza. I could hear her eating. I could imagine her tiny legs, those green scales, her knees bending backward as she scratched her back.

"I'm leaving," my father said. In his fed up voice. I heard him pouring a drink.

"Threaten away," my mother said. "You don't scare me. You simply don't." She was up now, looking right at the credenza, not seeing me.

I scratched the inside of the wood. *Grand Rapids, Mich.*, the sticker said. I peeled it off. It was hard to breathe. I ate the sticker.

Sid was on the floor, picking the scab on his knee, making it bleed. He had the pale yellow legs of a blue-eyed person, the skin translucent, and to me—a blonde person with green-brown tan skin—Sid, all pale with dark hair and watery eyes, was creepy. Like a pond at night.

Sid also had white hairs sticking out of his legs. Some like baby hairs and more and more like goat hairs—thick, coarse wires. His legs were noodle-like and difficult to look at for a length of time. He had the scab off in a perfect sheet—I could just feel it between my own fingers like a mat from Mars, a wonderful strange alive/dead thing to pick apart, taste, multiply, save, bury, plant, drop over the edge of the balcony. He had the scab off completely, and he was going around the edge with his mouth, that hard edge. And then the soft middle part would be free. We liked them, scabs.

My father left the room.

"What was that woman doing here?" my mother said through her teeth. Her feet were planted hard in the white carpeting under the inch-thick dining room glass table. "What was she doing here? What was she doing in my house? My house," my mother said.

"Condo," Sid said.

I saw my father's legs reappear.

"MC, you know damn well. You insist on making misery. You fuck-ing insist!" He swatted the chandelier, and one of the teardrop crystals flew into the sliding glass doors. Kelly Green went nuts. I slammed my cupboard door shut and wished I had a pillow in with me, a bolster cushion from the sectional. Then the front door to our condo slammed behind my dad.

I crawled out and had a fit.

I knew I was way too old. I didn't know—something was wrong with me.

Sid brought me a cold washcloth and said he was going down to find shark teeth.

"Wait up," I said. I was trying to breathe again. I had the cold wash-cloth on my face. I was curled up in a sweaty mess, looking up at the bottom of the dining room table, the smudge mark, where my mother's face had been.

The next night, when my dad told us he was leaving, he put it like he'd been month-to-month the whole time. Like we were leased, and he was mov-ing on.

"I'm giving you my notice," he said. I looked at his watch. It was only 5:00 p.m. My mom and Sid and I were sitting at the table picking the skins of shrimp and drenching them in ketchup. Even my mom liked her shrimp that way, the pink completely dunked in ketchup before she put it in her mouth.

Suddenly there he was, standing behind me, with a lit cigarette, and the dining room—*poof*—silvery with smoke.

I sat at the head of the table, in his seat, by the bowl of shrimp on their big bed of ice cubes in my mom's mixing bowl. Now that we lived at the beach, shrimp was a regular dinner, not such a dressy dinner.

"What about the children, Buck. What about them? I can see why you hate me, and that's fine, that's fine, of course you hate me, but what about them?" My mother kept peeling her shrimp. Now she had a village of them, naked, stranded, small pink hooks all along the edge of her plate.

She wasn't eating. She wasn't moving her lips. Those words—*the children, the children*—came out and hovered with the white and pink shrimpers and the pyramids of translucent shells. And then she toweled her hands, squirted the lemon on them, folded her hands, and seemed to simply put herself away.

I started screaming.

My mother was turning to wax.

Sid said, "We don't need him anyway. He's never here." Sid had popped a shrimp with its shell and tail on in his maw. He was crunching away, and I was so afraid. I was afraid the shrimp would come back to life and swim inside of him. I was afraid my dad was going to wallop him, I was afraid my father would want to marry me and take me with him because my housekeeping skills were so useful and polished, I was afraid I was going to throw up and never like shrimp again.

"Everyone hates you," Sid said.

My dad started to go after Sid with his fist, but Sid was out on the balcony, through the open sliding glass doors, and in about a half a second he was crawling over the railing, hanging there like a monkey on the outside of the railing—I am not kidding. Twenty-three floors up. It wasn't the first time he'd done it, but it was the first time he'd done it real showy like this.

And my mother started screaming, and I thought this was pretty scary, because it was Safety Week and we had learned so much.

If you are on fire, drop and roll. If someone is drowning, don't save them; call someone. One drowning is better than two.

"You all hate me, you hate me," she kept saying without moving a single facial muscle. Then, she did move—she dug at her hair with her hands, pushed her poor hair into one big tall gray fan around her face. I was thinking Madame Tussaud's.

"Honey, come in, come in," she said to Sid. "Get some candy, Georgia," she said. She wouldn't step out there onto the balcony, into the wind. She had never set foot on the balcony.

My dad stood there, his hand in the bowl of shrimp, sloshing them around, sort of stirring the shrimp, the ice.

Sid did banshee screaming. He dropped himself from the balcony, over the other side, and hung on with just his hands. I tried to see if his knuckles were white. Behind him, the Camelot sign was flashing way up the beach, the hotels looked fake like in *Godzilla*, and the sky was wrecked with clouds.

I couldn't believe it. "Sid, come in! Don't mess around!" I yelled.

"*Sh*, you will scare him to his death!" my mother screamed.

"You are the ones making him do this," I yelled right back at her. I wanted to push her. I had to grab my own hands; I had to bite them.

"Shut up!" Sid yelled, and he scooted along the edge, hand over hand, his body hanging over the balcony.

"Fool kid," my father said quietly.

"We should call the fire department," I said. I was frozen, though, to my spot. I looked at the bird. She had her eyes closed. I was envisioning a net, ten men, a bull's-eye, Sid floating, Sid doing somersaults, me on the six o'clock news. "The pressure cooker that is our family home life got to be too much for him," I could say to the anchorman. People could call and adopt us. We could sleep at the television station and talk to the childless couples who wanted to rescue adorable Georgia and tormented-but-promisingly-sweet Sidley.

My dad made himself another drink in the kitchen, while Mother stood by the sliding glass doors, not going too close to Sid, who still hung. He had his head back, looking up into the dark crazy blue-black sky.

"Mom, don't *push* him. Don't go out there," I said. "That's just what he wants you to do."

"I'm leaving, MC, and you know it's best. There's nothing you can do." My dad spoke from the kitchen. He jangled the car keys. In his other hand, his glass was full and curled close to his chest.

"You are not leaving me, mister. You are not leaving these children. You are not. I will not let you." She shouted this to the balcony.

"I'll come in, Mom. When he goes." Sid faked like he was crawling back over the balcony, and my mom made the sign of the cross and ran through the kitchen and grabbed the car keys straight out of my dad's hands, and ran to the front door and slammed it shut, with her on the inside. She braced herself against the door, a big X.

Sid didn't come in, but I could tell he wanted to. He peered in at us, over the balcony railing. He still dangled, twenty-three floors up. He wanted to see our parents, and he couldn't.

I ran up to my mom, who was gripping her purse and keys in an unnatural way, and the whole time I was hoping my own brother would fall, so at least my parents would have to stay together for my sake, for the sake of the memory of the smushed Sid-man.

I reached for her hand, for the car keys—it seemed to me no one should have them right now. My dad threw his drink down on the carpeting and ripped her off the door, grabbing her behind her neck, and prying her head and back right off. It was like she was wrapping paper. He just threw her down. She landed like pick-up sticks, against the hall table, and the mail there fluttered to the floor.

"You are going about this in the wrong way, MC." She still had the keys. I ducked as my dad swung around, sloshing his drink on my leg, my side, the carpeting, and my mother was up. She took a pouncelike stance. Her eyes were blazing violet. I felt blood in my throat.

"I'll wrong way you, mister."

Then she grabbed her purse from behind the silk bougainvillea, where it was lodged, and she ran out the door for real this time. My dad went out into the hall where we were only supposed to use our whisper voices. He bellowed after her, "There's nothing you can do, MC. I am leaving this cracker factory once and for all!"

But she was the one leaving. She was like a football player running down the red-carpet hall, running to the elevator, her purse tucked deep into her gut.

"You haven't seen anything yet, mister. Let me tell you." The elevator came, and she flung herself in. "You don't know who you are dealing with, buster. If anything happens to these children."

My dad and I tentatively walked halfway down the hall. I wondered if Sid had come in yet. The bronze elevator doors closed around her, and you could see my dad and me reflected all the way down that hall in those elevator doors, only we were tall and thin and wavering, not like real people at all.

"For pity's sake," Dad said. "All hell's broken loose and there's no reason for it to be like this."

I grabbed his leg and cried, *Please please please please please.*

He kicked me. He actually kicked me with his shoe and left a black mark on my thigh. I couldn't believe it.

"Daddy," I was crying. I cried and cried and cried. I couldn't believe how our lives were turning out. I couldn't believe this was my family. I felt this enormous crushing sense. It was never going to be any different. It was never going to be any better. It was never going to be a good family. Suddenly we sprawled in all directions, my family, like a man-o-war after you poured sugar on it in the sea. Tearing itself apart, as its only way to survive.

I hated Pleasure Towers and the beach, and I was the kind of person who loved the beach. In the hall, slumped up against the stucco-sharp wall, I cried and cried and cried. I hadn't ever cried like that before. I could tell my face would be permanently altered after this cry. I wished people would come out of their condos and rescue me, intervene, but no one did.

"You guys, come quick," Sid yelled. We could hear him way out in the hallway, the tomblike hall of the Towers, and we ran back into the condo, over the thrown-down drink in the hallway, and into the dining room. Sid, firmly anchored on the balcony, chowed down on a super-size bag of M&M's

that were supposed to be for baking, not eating. He stood there, popping them in, staring down at the beach, like he was at the races.

"Look," he said, and pointed toward the beach.

At the edge of the water, our aqua blue Plymouth was about to be launched.

My mother was driving it into the water. Some flares glowed on the beach behind her; I don't know how they got there.

Our family's car was slowly drifting into the Atlantic Ocean, my favorite body of water.

"Daddy," I whispered. "Oh, no."

Then it stopped in the sand that is soft right before the wave sand. She hopped out. Her ankles were in the breakers, her support hose would be getting wet, carrying that water up her legs—it was too awful to imagine. Beside her, the station wagon bobbled, nosed, settled.

"For God's sake," my dad said. "You don't get an engine wet. Is she out of her mind?" He threw his cigarette over the edge. Sid watched it float down and made bomb noises the whole way.

"*Sh*," I said. I didn't want a lot of freak-out movement up here. I didn't think we should be distracting my mother. Pushing her over the edge. She motioned the people clustering behind her on the beach to get back, get back, her white vinyl purse clutched like the space capsule she was taking to Atlantis, the lost city, and she hopped back in and hit the gas; the Plymouth lurched and launched and went out, farther, into the water.

"Oh Jesus Christ, she has to do everything the goddamn hard way," my dad said. He wasn't going to be able to leave us, though; you have to give my mom credit for that. What could he do, walk?

"Sid, son, get your ass off the railing, son." He slammed his drink down his throat. Now that Sid stood with us, inside the balcony, his upper body flopped over it, my dad suddenly got parental. I wanted to say that, but I knew I'd get hit. Plus, I had the altered face from my big cry a few minutes ago, and it hurt to talk. And, my mother had just driven our car into the Atlantic Ocean. I didn't want to get sent to my room at this juncture.

People gathered in greater numbers to watch our ocean-borne Plymouth. Buffy from the twelfth floor of our building, and Angie, the gate man's daughter, were there. A few dog walkers and the usual retired men in sweaters and brown bathing trunks clustered in small groups. The car kept going out. Bobbing like a toy. The ocean, I pretended, was a bulletin board, and my mother, a friendly felt object, and we could pin her anywhere; the ocean was tiny. "Okay," I said cheerily. "She'll come back now. She'll come back. It's getting dark, almost." Mentally, I pasted her and the wagon onto the sand, like felt pieces on a pale fabric board.

"We should go help her out, man," Sid said. "It's a scene."

A man with white hair, a guy who looked like Santa, waded in after the car and waved his arms in the *rescue me rescue me* SOS signal.

When the breakers hit, the car nosed up, then down. Angling down, it lost ground—that is, from our point of view. It came back toward shore—a good two waves' worth. Everything seemed about to be okay; the car easing back to the beach, the windows rolled down. She could get out. I knew she wouldn't leave her purse.

"She won't leave her purse," said Sid.

Sid peeled fronds off the palm on the balcony, my dad drank deeply, and I just sat there, bars of the railing between my toes. I felt like I was watching television.

"Could I have a sip of that?" Sid asked our dad. Sid stood fully planted inside the balcony now. Not hanging over. Now I had the urge to push him over. My mode made me angry: when Sid got into danger, I wanted to rescue him. I wanted the wind to be perfectly still when he hung over the edge of the balcony, or sat on the rail, barely balancing. I couldn't even breathe. But when he stood all military-proper on the AstroTurf, begging my dad for a sip of his liquor, not even watching Mom in the Plymouth, I wanted to shove him off the twenty-third floor. I wanted Sid to be arrested and for us to visit him at Boy's Town. There would be organized activities, and I would visit so often I would become the Dean of Boys when I grew up, and kids everywhere would want to come to this place, to be in my command, to be safe from their parents. I could learn to sew, I thought, and I wanted to jump off the balcony. Why did I have a brain like that? Who wanted to save their family and kill their family at the same time?

But when we were all scattered like this, I wanted us to be back like we were, although I couldn't remember what that would have been.

Some of the men on the beach had waded in, but they stood way off, leeward, out of the way. You couldn't tell if the men were talking or not. You couldn't tell if they had a plan. And she was still in the car; at least I think she was. Had she swum away? Had she somehow slipped into the water and swum to the bottom of the sea? The light was getting shifty and blue-black, most of the peach streaks all gone, and I couldn't see my mother anymore. Was she lying down on the front seat?

Two dogs broke loose and raced each other to the car. But the light looked different, and everything was flat and unreal, like a movie, though I had never actually seen a movie. My mother would not be rescued because this was not an accident. It was on purpose.

Sid was now back to straddling the balcony like it was a horse. My dad pretended to shove him.

"Jesus, Dad, kill me why don't you."

"Are we going down there?" What are we going to do, Daddy?" I asked. I tried not to sound whiny. "Shouldn't you—"

"—Fuck her," he said. "We are going to fuck her."

With that the car turned sideways and lunged back to us, back to the sand, the shore, the tiny miniature onlookers in their dark bathing suits; all catawampus our family car hooked itself back onto the beach and rested on the sand sideways, listing.

The three of us stood on the balcony like the Swiss Family Robinson without the Swiss part, without the Robinson part. We were just up high. And we huddled by Sid, my dad's glass of vodka gleaming like a steady light, my hands around his waist. I pressed my stomach into his back so my guts wouldn't launch. Slowly, as the seawater turned pink all around the aqua blue Plymouth in the last streaks of sunset, she climbed out of the window on the driver's side and came back at us.

Try This

Write the story you're not allowed to write—the story that would get you into trouble.

Ian Frazier
Tomorrow's Bird

Since January, I've been working for the crows, and so far it's the best job I ever had. I kind of fell into it by a combination of preparedness and luck. I'd been casting around a bit, looking for a new direction in my career, and one afternoon when I was out on my walk I happened to see some crows fly by. One of them landed on a telephone wire just above my head. I looked at him for a moment, and then on impulse I made a *skchhh* noise with my teeth and lips. He seemed to like that; I saw his tail make a quick upward bobbing motion at the sound. Encouraged, I made the noise again, and again his tail bobbed. He looked at me closely with one eye, then turned his beak and looked at me with the other, meanwhile readjusting his feet on the wire. After a few minutes, he cawed and flew off to join his companions. I had a good feeling I couldn't put into words. Basically, I thought the meeting had gone well, and as it turned out I was right. When I got home there was a message from the crows saying I had the job.

The first interview proved indicative of the crows' business style.

They are very informal and relaxed, unlike their public persona, and mostly they leave me alone. I'm given a general direction of what they want done, but the specifics of how to do it are up to me. For example, the crows have long been unhappy about public misperceptions of them: that they raid other birds' nests, drive songbirds away, eat garbage and dead things, can't sing, etc.—all of which are completely untrue once you know them. My first task was to take these misperceptions and turn them into a more positive image. I decided the crows needed a slogan that emphasized their strengths as a species. The slogan I came up with was "Crows: We Want to Be Your Only Bird™." I told this to the crows, they loved it, and we've been using it ever since.

Crows speak a dialect of English rather like that of the remote hill people of the Alleghenies. If you're not accustomed to it, it can be hard to understand. In their formal speech they are as measured and clear as a radio announcer from the Midwest—though, as I say, they are seldom formal with me. (For everyday needs, of course, they caw.) Their unit of money is the empty soda bottle, which trades at a rate of about twenty to the dollar. In the recent years of economic boom, the crows have quietly amassed great power. With investment capital based on their nationwide control of everything that gets run over on the roads, they have bought a number of major companies. Pepsi-Cola is now owned by the crows, as well as Knight Ridder Newspapers and the company that makes Tombstone Frozen Pizzas. The New York Metropolitan Opera is now wholly crow-owned.

In order to stay competitive, as most people know, the crows recently merged with the ravens. This was done not only for reasons of growth but also to better serve those millions who live and work near crows. In the future, both crows and ravens will be known by the group name of Crows, so if you see a bird and wonder which it is, you don't have to waste any time; officially and legally, it's a crow. The net result of this, of course, is that now there are a lot more crows—which is exactly what the crows want. Studies they've sponsored show that there could be anywhere from ten to a thousand times more crows than there already are, with no strain on carrying capacity. A healthy increase in crow numbers would make basic services like cawing loudly outside your bedroom window at six in the morning available to all. In this area, as in many others, the crows are thinking very long-term.

If more people in the future get a chance to know crows as I have done, they are in for a real treat. Because I must say, the crows have been absolutely wonderful to me. I like them not just as highly profitable business associates but as friends. Their aggressive side, admittedly quite strong in disputes with scarlet tanagers, etc., has been nowhere in evidence around me. I could not wish for any companions more charming. The other day I was having lunch with an important crow in the park, me sipping from a drinking fountain while he ate peanuts taken from a squirrel. In between sharp downward raps of his bill on the peanut shell to poke it open, he drew me out with seemingly artless questions. Sometimes the wind would push the shell to one side, and he would steady it with one large foot while continuing the raps with his beak. And all the while, he kept up his attentive questioning, making me feel that, business considerations aside, he was truly interested in what I had to say.

"Crows: We Want to Be Your Only Bird™." I think this slogan is worth repeating, because there's a lot behind it. Of course, the crows don't literally want (or expect) to be the only species of bird left on the planet. They admire and enjoy other kinds of birds and even hope that there will still be some remaining in limited numbers out of doors as well as in zoos and museums. But in terms of daily usage, the crows hope that you will think of them first when you're looking for those quality-of-life intangibles usually associated with birds. Singing, for example: crows actually can sing, and beautifully, too; so far, however, they have not been given the chance. In the future, with fewer other birds around, they feel that they will be.

Whether they're good-naturedly harassing an owl caught out in daylight, or carrying bits of sticks and used gauze bandage in their beaks to make their colorful free-form nests, or simply landing on the sidewalk in front of you with their characteristic double hop, the crows have become a part of the fabric of our days. When you had your first kiss, the crows were there, flying around nearby. They were cawing overhead at your college graduation, and worrying a hamburger wrapper through the wire mesh of a trash container in front of the building when you went in for your first job interview, and flapping past the door of the hospital where you held your first-born child. The crows have always been with us, and they promise that, by growing the species at a predicted rate of 17 percent a year, in the future they'll be around even more.

The crows aren't the last Siberian tigers, and they don't pretend to be. They're not interested in being a part of anybody's dying tradition. But then how many of us deal with Siberian tigers on a regular basis? Usually, the nontech stuff we deal with, besides humans, is squirrels, pigeons, raccoons, rats, mice, and a few kinds of bugs. The crows are confident enough to claim that they will be able to compete effectively even with these familiar and well-entrenched providers. Indeed, they have already begun to displace pigeons in the category of walking around under park benches with chewing gum stuck to their feet. Scampering nervously in attics, sneaking through pet doors, and gnawing little holes in things are all in the crow's expansion plans.

I would not have taken this job if I did not believe, strongly and deeply, in the crows myself. And I do. I could go on and on about the crows' generosity, taste in music, sense of family values; the "buddy system" they invented to use against other birds, the work they do for the Shriners, and more. But they're paying me a lot of bottles to say this—I can't expect everybody to believe me. I do ask, if you're unconvinced, that you take this simple test: Next time you're looking out a window or driving in a car, notice if there's a crow in sight. Then multiply that one crow by lots and lots of crows, and you'll get an idea of what the next few years will bring. In the bird department, no matter what, the future is going to be almost all crows, almost all the time. That's just a fact.

So why not just accept it, and learn to appreciate it, as so many of us have already? The crows are going to influence our culture and our world in beneficial ways we can't even imagine today. Much of what they envision I am not yet at liberty to disclose, but I can tell you that it is magnificent. They are going to be birds like we've never seen. In their dark, jewel-like eyes burns an ambition to be more and better and to fly around all over the place constantly. They're smart, they're driven, and they're comin' at us. The crows: let's get ready to welcome tomorrow's only bird.

Try This

Take a few paragraphs of the story you are writing and substitute an animal for one of the characters. What animal will it be? How will it behave? What can this teach you about your character?

Try This

The following are the opening phrases from the stories you have just read. Pick one and use it to begin the story you have been planning. Write the first page without pause.

- I'll call her . . .
- There's a bomb . . .
- (_____) has just returned from . . .
- In the good days, my family lived in . . .
- Since (_____), I've been working for . . .

CHAPTER NINE

POETRY

Free Verse and Formal Verse
Imagery, Connotation, and Metaphor
Density and Intensity
Prosody, Rhythm, and Rhyme

Good poems are the best teachers.

Mary Oliver

There are hundreds of definitions of poetry, ranging from the religious to the flippant by way of sentiment and psychology. Poetry is "the natural language of all worship," "devil's wine," "an imitation of an imitation," "more philosophic than history," "painting that speaks," "a criticism of life," "fine-spun from a mind at peace," "a way of taking life by the throat," "the language of an act of attention," "an escape from emotion," "the antithesis to science," "the bill and coo of sex," "a pause before death."

Unlike the essay or drama, poetry can take shapes that bear little or no resemblance to each other. Individual poems may aspire to freeze a single image like a painting or to spin off musical variations like a jazz riff. Unlike the novel or the short story, length has nothing at all to do with whether a thing may be called poetry; epics may cover many hundreds of pages or take hours to recite, while the haiku is seventeen syllables.

In *The Creative Process*, teachers Carol Burke and Molly Best Tinsley observe that poems "obey no absolute rules and serve no single purpose; rather they adapt to the distinct needs of specific times and individual poets . . . Any definition we formulate precludes others and imprisons us prematurely in a partial understanding of poetry."

Considering the difficulty, perhaps the most comprehensive and least confining definition is W. H. Auden's: *Poetry is memorable speech.*

This memorably succinct sentence contains the two essentials. Poetry is meant to be heard aloud in the human voice, and it is meant to be remembered. All of the techniques that belong to this genre aid speech or memory or both. **Rhyme**, for example, is a memory aid that pleases the ear. **Rhythm** and **meter** augment both the memory and the music of the spoken voice; so do similarities of sound such as **alliteration** and **assonance**. Image and story are powerfully mnemonic, as are **figures of speech** including simile and metaphor.

Memory is crucial because poetry predates writing. One early purpose of form—rhyme, rhythm, alliteration, and so forth—was to make it possible to remember and tell long histories of peoples, their trials and heroic battles. Now we have print, film, tape, disk, digital recording, and other technologies for the preservation of ideas, but poetry still startles and stays in the mind through its manipulation of sound and figures of speech, which have also evolved into myriad ways of intensifying and compressing meaning.

Free Verse and Formal Verse

Learning to be a poet in the twenty-first century presents difficulties unlike any of the other genres, and the problem is this: up until the twentieth century the great bulk of poetry in English was written in **formal verse**, set patterns of rhythm and rhyme. From *Beowulf* in Old English with its lines of interlocking alliteration, through the intricate official meters of the Welsh Bards, in the burgeoning verse patterns of the Renaissance, to the measured couplets of the Enlightenment, the passionate craft of the Romantics and the sophisticated subtleties of the Victorians—all was based on formal **scansion** and set verse pattern. But though there had been rebellions against the **stanza** and experiments with looser rhythms—notably Emily Dickinson and Walt Whitman in America—it was only in the twentieth century that English poetry generally loosened its forms, set its rhymes askew, took on the rhythms of ordinary speech, and settled into **free verse**.

Poet Mary Oliver suggests that there may have been larger social forces at work, such that in an increasingly classless society, the poet's lofty traditional role was democratized. Those drawn to the looser rhythms of free verse also saw every subject, no matter how homely or mundane, as legitimate territory for their work. (Poet Caroline Kizer recounts how she once quit a workshop because she was told that pigs were not a proper subject for poetry.) A close parallel might be seen here in the way that the prescribed movements and structures of the classical ballet gave way to modern dance. In ballet, a central aspiration was to deny gravity; to extend, lift, leap, and soar beyond the limitations of the human body. Modern dance, by contrast, accepted, celebrated, and exploited the earthbound, and gravity became a partner in the physical exploration of our condition. Just so, human limitation including the bluntness and jaggedness of ordinary speech became part of the subject matter and the mode of verse.

All the great new practitioners of free verse taught themselves the rigors of the earlier periods, but those rigors are buried deep in the speech patterns of their poetry. Although many poets in the latter part of the century returned with enthusiasm to the stricter structures of "New Formalism," you have not grown up reading formal contemporary verse. If you begin by writing in closed forms, you are likely to turn out archaic-sounding stanzas, cliché rhymes, and the singsong rhythms of greeting cards. Yet if you begin with free verse, which often disguises itself to the uninitiated ear as prose, you may develop sloppy patterns in which you fail to understand and learn the craft of sound.

Poetry is not chopped prose. The Bloomsburg poet and novelist Vita Sackville West scathingly put down people who "think they may mumble inanities which would make them blush if written in good common English, but which they think fit to print if split up into lines." Mary Oliver in *A Poetry Handbook* more gently chides that a student unschooled in verse forms "quickly, then . . . falls into a *manner* of writing, which is not a style but only a chance thing, vaguely felt and not understood . . ."

There is no easy solution to this difficulty, but since writing is learned first of all in the doing, I propose that you go about writing poems by borrowing from other genres in which you are more practiced and adept, and at the same time begin to *play* with the permutations of sound and rhythm. This chapter will suggest some possibilities for such play, and the "Basic Prosody" in Appendix C will lead you to invent others of your own. Meanwhile, read widely in both formal (rhymed and metered) and **informal** (free) verse, with particular attention to metaphor and patterns of sound. Imitate what you like; imitation, which has been called the sincerest form of flattery, is also the most teaching form of play.

Begin by writing poems about the subjects that matter to you, based on patterns you have already used in your journal and other writing.

Try This

Write a poem:

- that presents an image in more than one sense
- that is a single metaphor, extended and elaborated
- about a memory
- in a voice other than your own
- in dialogue
- about a particular instance of weather
- about a place
- about a person you know

continued

- about a person you invent
- that is a story
- in which two people disconnect
- in the form of a letter
- in the form of a list.

Imagery, Connotation, and Metaphor

Because poetry attempts to produce an emotional response through heightened evocation of the senses, imagery holds a central place among its techniques.

Remember that not all images are metaphors. Sometimes, as Robert Hass puts it, "they do not say *this is that*, they say *this is*."

> O Western wind, when wilt thou blow,
> That the small rain down can rain?
> Christ, that my love were in my arms
> And I in my bed again!

This most famous of anonymous poems, disputedly from the thirteenth to the fifteenth centuries, contains no metaphors. Its simple images are wind, rain, lover, arms, and bed. The poem says, "I am stuck here in an ugly climate with no chance of getting out any time soon, and I'm lonely and miserable and miss my girl." But it says all that with a good deal more force partly because of the way the first line evokes the sound of the wind (all those *w*'s, the breath of *wh*, the vowel length of blow-oh-oh) and partly because it uses images rich in connotation.

Words have **denotation**—a primary meaning—and also **connotation**, which refers to the layers of suggestion and implication they acquire through usage. Words can be richly encrusted with all we have heard, read, seen, felt, and experienced in their name. *Love*, certainly, implies longing, lust, romance, affection, tenderness, and, for each of us, further images of all these and more. *Bed* evokes sex, but also warmth, safety, comfort, home. *Wind* has connotations of wailing and loneliness and, in this poem, in combination with its sounds, becomes a lament, a cry of yearning. The "small rain" evokes gentleness by contrast with both the implied harshness of the climate and the force of the exclamation, "*Christ! That my love . . .*" The word *Christ* itself, its implicit gentleness and faith set against its use as a curse, offers a high tension of contradictory connotation.

Connotation is partly personal, which means that no two readers ever read exactly the same poem. Since I grew up in the desert, the first image that comes to my mind in the poet's plea for "small rain" is a parched barren landscape. Someone who grew up in New England might think of long winter and the gentler promise of spring.

Imagery is necessary to poetry for the same picture-making reason it is necessary to all literary writing, but poetry also asks for and usually receives the special intensity of metaphor. Metaphor has a strong hold on the imagination because of its dual qualities of surprise and precision. Emily Dickinson described in a letter to a friend how she had studied the Scriptures to learn the "mode of juxtaposing elements of concrete things with equally fundamental ideas and feelings—grass, stone, heart, majesty, despair."

Metaphor (including simile) has as its central function to make concrete, so that even if one member of the comparison is an abstraction it will be realized in the thingness of the comparison ("the purple terricloth robe of nobility," "like a diver into the wretched confusion"), whereas most metaphors compare two sensible images and let the abstraction remain unvoiced but present in the tension between them ("electric eel blink like stringlight," "a surf of blossoms," "rooms cut in half hang like flayed carcasses"). The function of comparison is not to be pretty, but to be exact, evocative, and as concrete as the sidewalk.

Learning to recognize and flee clichés, to find metaphors that are both surprising and apt, can only be learned by attention, trial and error. The ability to spot clichés, as Jerome Stern points out, is "not in the genetic code." But this is one place in your apprenticeship where the practice of brainstorming, free-associating, and clustering can continue to help, because the attention we pay to the poetic image allows for free, extreme, even wild connection. The less you clamp down on your dreaming, the less you concede to logic, the less you allow your internal critic to shut you up, the more likely you are to produce the startling-dead-on comparison. Cut logic loose, focus on what you see, taste, touch. Freewrite, and let the strangeness in you surface.

From time to time you may even come up with a good **conceit**, which is a comparison of two things radically and startlingly unlike—in Samuel Johnson's words, "yoked by violence together." A conceit compares two things that have no evident similarity; so the author must explain to us, sometimes at great length, why these things can be said to be alike. (When John Donne compares a flea to the Holy Trinity, the two images have no areas of reference in common, and we don't understand. He must explain to us that the flea, having bitten both the poet and his lover, now has the blood of three souls in its body.)

Try This

Eat a meal blindfolded. Write a poem in which you describe it literally only in terms of taste and smell. Metaphors may evoke the others senses.

The process of learning what's fresh and what's stale is complicated—and in no language more so than English—by the fact that not all familiar phrases are clichés. Many have settled down into the language as **idioms**, a "manner of speaking." English is so full of idioms that it is notoriously difficult for foreigners to learn. Try explaining to a non-native speaker what we mean by: *put* *'em up, can you put me up?, put 'er there, don't let me put you out, do you put out?, he put it off, I was put off, he put in!*

Moreover, English is full of **dead metaphors**, comparisons so familiar that they have in effect ceased to be metaphors; they have lost the force of the original comparison and acquired a new definition. Fowler's *Modern English Usage* uses the word "sift" to demonstrate the dead metaphor, one that has "been used so often that speaker and hearer have ceased to be aware that the words used are not literal."

> Thus, in *The men were sifting the meal* we have a literal use of *sift*; in *Satan hath desired to have you, that he may sift you as wheat*, *sift* is a live metaphor; in *the sifting of evidence*, the metaphor is so familiar that it is about equal chances whether *sifting* or *examination* will be used, and that a sieve is not present to the thought.

English abounds in dead metaphors. *Abounds* is one, where the overflowing of liquid is not present to the thought. When a person *runs* for office, legs are not present to the thought, nor is an arrow when we speak of someone's *aim*, hot stones when we go through an *ordeal*, headgear when someone *caps* a joke. Unlike clichés, dead metaphors enrich the language. There is a residual resonance from the original metaphor but no pointless effort on the part of the mind to resolve the tension of like and unlike.

Alert yourself to metaphors, idioms, and dead metaphors in your reading and in your writing; eventually the recognition will become second nature, and a powerful background awareness in your craft. Meanwhile *keep your eyes peeled* for *the deafening roar* of *purple prose, keep taking care of business*, and *give it your best shot one word at a time*, because *it's not whether you win or lose, it's how you play the game; that's what it's all about.*

Try This

Go back to the list of clichés you made for Chapter One. Add to it. Make a list of dead metaphors. Then choose a phrase from either list that you find particularly vivid (or detestable) and write a short poem in which you take it *literally*. Focus on, imagine, dream the images as if they were real. Some poor exhausted fellow is *running for office?* What must it feel like to have *a nose to the grindstone? Sifting the evidence? A vale of tears?*

Density and Intensity

The meaning in a poetic line is *compressed*. Whereas a journalist may treat it as a point of honor to present information objectively, and a legal writer may produce pages of jargon in an attempt to rule out any ambiguity, subjectivity and ambiguity are the literary writer's stock in trade; you are at constant pains to mean more than you say. This is why dialogue must do more than one thing at a time, why an image is better than an abstraction, and why an action needs to represent more than mere movement. Especially and to a heightened degree in poetry, this **density**, this more-than-one-thing-at-a-time, raises the **intensity** of feeling. Poet Donald Hall observes that, "In logic no two things can occupy the same point at the same time, and in poetry that happens all the time. This is almost what poetry is for, to be able to embody contrary feelings in the same motion."

Not only imagery but each of the elements discussed in this book—voice, character, setting, and story—will be relevant to achieving this compression, and each in a particular and particularly heightened way. The techniques of good prose make for good poetry—only more so. Active verbs are crucial. Nouns will do more work than adjectives. Specific details will move more than abstractions. Vocabulary, word choice, syntax, and grammar take on added importance; you will spend a good deal of time cutting vague verbiage and looking for the phrases that strike with special vividness or suggest double meaning or vibrate or *resonate* with widening significance.

One way to demonstrate for yourself the density of poetic techniques is to write a "replacement poem." In this form of play, you take any poem you admire and replace all the nouns, verbs, adjectives, and adverbs with other words that are in each case the same part of speech. Other parts of speech—conjunctions, prepositions, articles—you may leave or change as you please. Here for an example is Gerald Stern's "Columbia The Gem":

> I know that body standing in the Low Library,
> the right shoulder lower than the left one, the lotion sea lotion
> his hold is ended
> Now the mouths can slash away in memory
> of his kisses and stupefying lies.
> Now the old Reds can walk with a little spring
> in and around the beloved sarcophagi
> Now the Puerto Ricans can work up another funny America
> and the frightened Germans can open their heavy doors a little.
> Now the River can soften its huge heart
> and move, for the first time, almost like the others
> without silence

This poem is a damning portrait, made forceful by sense images and energetic verbs, compressed in its rhythm to a kind of poignant anger. If I replace all the major parts of speech (and some prepositions and conjunctions), the mood and meaning will change, but the energy will remain. Here is my replacement poem:

They bless this mother bending in her plastic kitchen,
the crooked knee redder than the straight one, the Clorox stink Pine Sol
her shine is glorious
Soon the peppers will leap aloft in celebration
of her moans and hypocritical hypochondria.
Then the fat flowers will jump to the black waters
over and under the hysterical linoleum
Then the giant corporations will buy out another weeping mom-and-pop
and the laughing Coke-folk will crank her rusted icemaker a while.
Then the stove will burst its stinking flame
and collapse, in its last meal, very near the drains,
for reconciliation.

Try This

Write a replacement poem. Choose any poem from anywhere in your reading, but make it one that you truly admire. You needn't worry about making sense; the poem will do it for you. You can fiddle afterward if you want to move it nearer your meaning.

Get together with three or four others and decide on a poem you will all "replace." Discuss how different are your voices and your visions. What do the replacements have in common?

Voice will have a special importance in your poetry not only because of the likelihood or inevitability that you will adopt a persona, but also because in the concentrated attention we pay to the language, diction becomes content. Imamu Amiri Baraka says, "the first thing you look for is the stance." Interestingly, Baraka is here arguing that all poetry is *political*—that poets reveal their way of looking at the world the moment they open their mouths. "Stance" is another way of saying *point of view*, in both the sense of opinion and the sense that the poem reveals who is standing where to watch the scene.

Caroline Kizer voices the perhaps surprising requirement that "in a poem something happens." Her mentor Theodore Roethke even advised thinking of a poem "as a three-act play, where you move from one impulse to the next, and then there is a final breath, which is the summation of the whole." Kizer points out that Roethke's poem "I Knew A Woman" (on p. 115) contains the line "She taught me Turn, and Counter-turn, and Stand," which is "the essence of the dramatic structure. It's what a long poem has to do. It doesn't require physical action, but there has to be some mental or emotional action that carries through the poem." In a poem what happens may be huge, historical, mythical, or it may be mental or microscopic. It need not involve an overt action, it may be a shift of perspective, a movement of the mind—but as in a story it will involve some discovery and also at very least the decision to accept a new perspective. To the extent that the poem involves decision and discovery, it will also tell a story.

There is great poetic potential in all sorts of doubleness: pun, paradox, **oxymoron**, and anomaly, as well as the larger ironies of life. What makes for freshness—the combination of two things not usually combined—also makes for density. Here is a poem by Sharon Olds in which image, voice, character, setting, and story are compressed into vivid and resonant "contrary feelings":

> When I take my girl to the swimming party
> I set her down among the boys. They tower and
> bristle, she stands there smooth and sleek,
> her math scores unfolding in the air around her.
> They will strip to their suits, her body hard and
> indivisible as a prime number,
> they'll plunge in the deep end, she'll subtract
> her height from ten feet, divide it into
> hundreds of gallons of water, the numbers
> bouncing in her mind like molecules of chlorine
> in the bright blue pool. When they climb out,
> her ponytail will hang its pencil lead
> down her back, her narrow silk suit
> with hamburgers and fries printed on it
> will glisten in the brilliant air, and they will
> see her sweet face, solemn and
> sealed, a factor of one, and she will
> see their eyes, two each, and the curves of their sexes,
> one each, and in her head she'll be doing her
> wild multiplying, as the drops
> sparkle and fall to the power of a thousand from her body.
>
> *"The One Girl at the Boys Party"*

This poem marries puberty and mathematics—a conceit, because we can't immediately apprehend any similarity. The strange combination begins prosaically enough, with some tension in the contrast between the boys' bristling and the girl's smoothness, and develops into an extended metaphor as the poem progresses. We are surprised by the image "her math scores unfolding in the air around her" and then the power struggle inherent in the numbers begins to unfold, the "body hard and indivisible, the "plunge in the deep end," the "pencil lead down her back," the "power of a thousand" laying out for us an absolutely generic American scene in terms that render it alive and new. As for "embodying contrary feelings in the same motion," here we have a portrait of a girl who has all the power of refusal—*smooth, sleek, indivisible, sweet, solemn and sealed*. But what is the effect of those hamburgers and fries glistening on her suit? What of her wild multiplying?

And consider the voice. How would this poem be altered if it were in the voice of the girl herself, rather than the mother? If it were from the viewpoint of one of the guys? The poem has very much the tone of personal experience: suppose it were an essay rather than a poem. How would language have to change? What points made by the imagery would be made in explanatory or confessional prose? How *long* would it have to be?

Try This

Write a few paragraphs of the essay this poem would be if it were an essay. Untangle the syntax, supply the missing reasoning and reflection, develop the point of view of the mother.

Write the poem from the daughter's viewpoint.

Write it from a boy's viewpoint.

Write a poem, in exactly one hundred words, about a scene familiar to you, developing a metaphor or conceit.

Cut it to fifty words, leaving in all the sense.

> Make the sound an echo to the sense.
>
> *Alexander Pope*

Prosody, Rhythm, and Rhyme

Good poets are born with innate talent, and the talent shows in the play, the rhythms, the lines and images that "come naturally." But if a child shows talent, for example, for doodling spaceships or horses or fashion models, at some point a teacher will sit her down and say: *Draw this orange. Good. Now, this is how you make it look round; this is how you make it look rough; this is how you make it look as if the light is coming from the left; this is how you make it look as if the surface it sits on is stretching away into the distance.* The student may have no intention of painting in the style called realism; but precisely in order to master the craft that will allow successful imagination, invention, and innovation, it will be necessary to know how to produce on paper the illusion of the ordinary.

Prosody (the study of versification) is the study of drawing oranges in sound.

As a language for poetry, English has possibilities that greatly outweigh its—also considerable—disadvantages. It is a language with many thousands of different **syllables**—the unit of speech that can be uttered with a single breath. This means that it is poor in rhymes, as opposed to Italian, for example, where many words employ the same ending syllables. English poets of the Renaissance, who wanted to emulate the sonnets of Petrarch, felt a little defensive that they couldn't rhyme as densely as he could without repeating themselves. Because of the paucity of similar end-sounds, many rhymes in English have become clichés (*spoon-moon-June, why-die-I, do-blue-you . . .*) and by the early twentieth century most poets in the language had tired of these clichés and launched into **slant rhymes**, also called **off rhymes** (*spoon-main-join; why-play-joy*), thus vastly extending the range of effects.

On the other hand, English is a language rich in *onomatopoeia*. This is true not just of words that literally imitate the sound they designate—words like *buzz, murmur, hum.* There are also a very large number in an intermediate category, which strongly echo their meaning. Try *squeal* or *crash* or *whip.* Beyond that, certain **phonemes** (the smallest unit of distinguishable sound) have an emotive or suggestive quality. *Plosives* explode, *sibilants* hiss, and *gutterals* growl. Contrast the word *stop* with the word *sprawl.* Try pretending that each word means the other. It's hard, because that plosive *p* sound *does* stop you, whereas the long lax dipthong of the other really does sprawl. Beware, however. The "dingdong theory"—that individual words begin in some fundamental sensory reflex—has been thoroughly disproved. *Connotation* also determines our reaction to words and phrases. In terms of pure sound, there is nothing more inherently beautiful in *blooming goldenrod* than in *coronary thrombosis.*

Much of this you already know in a way that, if not instinctive, has come to you by a combination of imitation, context, and repetition, through nursery rhymes, songs, and jingles. But there is a sense in which things only come into existence when they are learned and can't be clearly thought without being defined. For instance, in Alexander Pope's line, "When Ajax strives some rock's vast weight to throw," you can feel the muscularity and effort. But to understand and be able to employ the effect, it helps to know that it's achieved by a combination of **spondees** and **consonant clusters**. Or again: William Butler Yeats' line, "I walk through the long schoolroom questioning." Why is this line so long? Because it uses **long vowels**, many **consonants** and an unusual number of heavy **stresses**.

"Do you really think the poet was so deliberate as all that?" students sometimes ask. Yes. A skilled and proficient poet, if in doubt, will count the syllables. She will wait for the gift of the right words, but might purposely seek a sibilant to suggest a slithering motion, or open vowels for the emotion of awe. Poet Heather McHugh rightly says, "the poet *feels* his way toward the finishedness of the poem." On the other hand, it is reliably reported that Goethe's mistress threw him out of bed when she discovered he was tapping iambs on her bare back.

What follows in the next few pages is a few prosody terms and their mean-ings, and some illustrations. An expanded discussion of these terms, and others related to them, will be found in Appendix C, "A Basic Prosody." As you become familiar with these terms, set yourself short exercises in the play of prosody, but in your prosody play, *do not make sense.* Write with real words in real sen-tences following whatever technique you have set yourself, but *do not try to mean anything.* If you don't aim for sense, you will be free to concentrate on hearing the sound effects, and you won't write clichés or greeting card verse. If you practice long enough and playfully enough, these five-finger exercises will even-tually sharpen your ear, and you will find the effects consciously and uncon-sciously entering your poetry.

> The line, when a poem is alive in its sound, measures: it is
> a proposal about listening.
>
> *Robert Hass*

The **line**, common to nearly all poetry, is a unit of verse ending in a typo-graphical break. It visually represents a slight oral pause or hesitation, what poet Denise Levertov calls "a half-comma," so that both the word at the end of the line and the one at the beginning of the next receive a slight extra emphasis. The line operates *not as a substitute* for the sentence, but in addition to it. The line directs the breath; the rhythm of the line is played off against the rhythm of the sense, and this is one of the ways that poets alter, stress, and redirect their meaning. Here is the famous beginning of Milton's *Paradise Lost*:

Of man's first disobedience, and the Fruit
Of that immortal tree . . .

Notice how that fatal apple is given prominence by its position at the end of the line. In general, it may be said that the end of just about anything—line, paragraph, stanza, story—is the strongest position, and the beginning is the second strongest.

A **caesura** is a pause that occurs within the line (above, after *disobedience*), and can help manipulate the rhythm, as can **enjambment**, the running-on of the sense from one line to another (*and the fruit of that immortal tree . . .*) A line that is **end-stopped**, meaning that the line break coincides with a pause in the sense, ends with greater finality:

An elegy is really about the wilting of a flower,
the passing of the year, the falling of a stone.

William Stafford, "A Lecture on the Elegy"

English is a **stress** language, and any sentence can be marked in a pattern of stressed and unstressed syllables, as here.

Syllabic verse employs a meter in which only the syllables are counted—for instance, in the *cinquain*, where the lines have a syllable count of 2-4-6-8-2, whatever the number of stresses:

> He yells.
> I'm going to
> Be buried in the sea
> Like a pirate and treasure
> Down deep.
>
> *Oscar Ruiz, "Deep"*

But most formal English verse counts both stresses and syllables. **Scansion** is the measuring of a line into stressed (or accented) and unstressed (or unaccented) syllables and the number of repetitions of that pattern, each repetition called a **poetic foot.**

The English line is usually based on one of four poetic feet:

Iamb, unstress-stress: the sky

    They grew / their toes / and fin/gers well / enough.

Trochee, stress-unstress: heav/en

    Ti/ger, ti/ger, burn/ing bright!

Anapest, unstress-unstress-stress in the sky

    From the dark / to the dark / is a sliv/er of gray

Dactyl, stress-unstress-unstress heav/en or

    Go and ask / Sally to / bring the boys / over now.

Try This

Make a quick list of terms that relate to any subject you know well (you can go back and add to it at any time)—kinds of fish or shoes, baseball terms, car parts, fabrics, tools, instruments; whatever falls in your area of expertise. Try to list at least twenty or thirty words. Here for example is a list of some spices on my spice shelf:

ginger	turmeric	parsley
cinnamon	oregano	arrowroot
cardamom	rosemary	cayenne
pepper	cumin	fennel
peppercorns	dill weed	coriander
paprika	poppy seed	curry
cloves	sesame seed	cilantro
bay leaves	thyme	chili

continued

Now mark the scansion of each word on your list:

gínger   túrmĕrĭc   párslĕy, etc.

Can you make any general observations about the scansion of your words? I notice, for example, that a lot of spices happen to be trochees or dactyls, the stress falling on the first syllable. This might suggest that spices would be good for drumming rhythms and incantations, and if I wanted to use them in comic lyrics, I'd have to precede them with unstressed syllables: *So the ginger and sesame said to the salt . . .*

The **meter** of a poem is based on the number of feet in each line. A **monometer** line has only one foot, a **dimeter** line has two feet, a **trimeter** three, **tetrameter** four, **pentameter** five, and **hexameter** six.

An iambic tetrameter line, for example, would have four iambic feet:

Ă bóy / ĭs nót / ă píece / ŏf dírt.

A dactylic hexameter line would consist of six dactyls:

Whý dŏ Ĭ / wánt sŏ mŭch / pléxĭglăss / stúff ĭn mỹ / lúmĭnŏŭs / Cádĭllăc?

Try This
(Remember not to make too much sense . . .)
1. Write a line of iambic dimeter:
(example: *Ĭ gríeve / tŏ gó.*)

. . . of trochaic trimeter
(*Jáck bĕ / nímblĕ, / húmblỹ.*)

. . . of anapestic tetrameter
(*Ĭf thĕ sún / ĭn thĕ ský / hăs ă wón/dĕr ŏf shíne.*)

. . . of iambic pentameter—which is the most common line in English, the meter of Shakespeare and blank verse—(*Whatév/ĕr wóod/ĕn wórld / ĭs bóund / tŏ róll.*)

. . . of dactylic hexameter
(*Béautĭfŭl / Jénnĭfĕr, / wóndĕrfŭl / sócĭalĭte, / féll ŏn hĕr / Pókĕman.*)

In addition to the **true rhymes** (*lean-green-mean*) and **slant rhymes** (*lean-mine-tone*) in English, poets manipulate sound through the use of **alliteration**, the repetition of consonants (*Peter Piper picked a peck of pickled peppers*), and **assonance**, the repetition of vowel sounds (*lady may crave a place*). Rhymes may be **internal**, rhyming within the line, or from the end of one line into the middle of another. Or they may be **end-rhymes**, the pattern that delights children for its musical quality:

Little Miss Muffet	a
Sat on a tuffet	a
Eating her curds and whey.	b
Along came a spider	c
And sat down beside her	c
And frightened Miss Muffet away.	b

The letters at right signal the traditional way of marking a rhyme pattern, each new rhyme sound assigned a succeeding letter of the alphabet.

> Free verse is, of course, not free.
>
> *Mary Oliver*

Free verse determines a pattern of sound and rhythm not at the outset but as the poem develops. The idea or meaning or pattern of imagery comes first, and the pattern of sound and rhythm comes after. It could be said that in the case of formal verse the meaning fills the pattern and in the case of free verse that the pattern fills the meaning. This would, however, seem to imply a superiority of the latter method, whereas many poets glory in the freedom that the restraints of formal verse allow. Just as the rules and equipment of a particular game, basketball or ice hockey, free an athlete to develop a particular set of excellences and stretch skills to the utmost, so the apparent arbitrariness of poetic form can free a poet to leap or flow with particular brilliance within those boundaries. Without such rules and equipment, it's harder to drive toward or develop specific strengths.

The rules of scansion briefly sketched here are reiterated and expanded on in Appendix C, together with some suggestions for stanza form; and at the end of this chapter are some suggestions for still further study. As you become familiar and comfortable with scansion, assonance and alliteration, slant and internal rhyme, caesura, enjambment, and so forth, identify them in your poems; become aware of the possibilities they offer. When you feel skilled in using various devices, you may want to try formal verse, or you may want to employ that skill within the "free" verse that develops its rhythms and sound patterns from within.

In either case, if it is your intention, your calling, and your destiny to be a poet, then you probably drink in this technical trivia with an unslakable thirst, like a sports fan after baseball statistics or a train spotter with a schedule in hand. W. H. Auden observed that the best poets often start out with a passion, not for ideas or people, but for the possibilities of sound. It is surely true that the love of language can be practiced in the throat, the ear, the heartbeat, and the body; and that whatever you have or may in future have to say, the saying of it starts there.

Try This

Write a dozen lines of blank (iambic pentameter) verse, employing some alliteration, some assonance, some internal rhyme. Try varying end-stopped lines with run-on or enjambment lines. Don't make sense. Make music.

More to Read

Addonizio, Kim and Dorianne Laux. *The Poet's Companion: A Guide to the Pleasures of Writing Poetry*. New York: W.W. Norton, 1997.

Bishop, Wendy. *Thirteen Ways of Looking for a Poem*. New York: Longman, 2000.

Fussell, Paul. *Poetic Meter and Poetic Form*. New York: Random House, 1965.

Oliver, Mary. *A Poetry Handbook*. New York: Harcourt Brace, 1994.

READINGS

Sylvia Plath
Stillborn

These poems do not live: it's a sad diagnosis.
They grew their toes and fingers well enough,
Their little foreheads bulged with concentration.
If they missed out on walking about like people
It wasn't for any lack of mother-love.

O I cannot understand what happened to them!
They are proper in shape and number and every part.
They sit so nicely in the pickling fluid!
They smile and smile and smile and smile at me.
And still the lungs won't fill and the heart won't start.

They are not pigs, they are not even fish,
Though they have a piggy and a fishy air—
It would be better if they were alive, and that's what they were.
But they are dead, and their mother near dead with distraction,
And they stupidly stare, and do not speak of her.

Steve Kowit

The Grammar Lesson

A noun's a thing. A verb's the thing it does.
An adjective is what describes the noun.
In "The can of beets is filled with purple fuzz"

of and *with* are prepositions. *The's*
an article, a *can's* a noun,
a noun's a thing. A verb's the thing it does.

A can *can* roll—or not. What isn't was
or might be, *might* meaning not yet known.
"Our can of beets *is* filled with purple fuzz"

is present tense. While words like *our* and *us*
are pronouns—i.e., *it* is moldy, *they* are icky brown.
A noun's a thing; a verb's the thing it does.

Is is a helping verb. It helps because
filled isn't a full verb. *Can's* what *our* owns
in "*Our* can of beets is filled with purple fuzz."

See? There's almost nothing to it. Just
memorize these rules . . . or write them down!
A noun's a thing, a verb's the thing it does.
The can of beets is filled with purple fuzz.

Peter Meinke

The Poet, Trying
to Surprise God

The poet, trying to surprise his God
composed new forms from secret harmonies,
tore from his fiery vision galaxies
of unrelated shapes, both even & odd.
But God just smiled, and gave His know-all nod
saying, "There's no surprising One who sees
the acorn, root, and branch of centuries;
I swallow all things up, like Aaron's rod.

So hold this thought beneath your poet-bonnet;
no matter how free-seeming flows your sample
God is by definition the Unsurprised."
"Then I'll return," the poet sighed, "to sonnets
of which this is a rather pale example."

"Is that right?" said God. "I hadn't realized . . ."

Try This

These first three poems are **self-reflexive**; they are about language and writing, two
of them with the writing of poetry, one of them in the very intricate poetic form of a
villanelle. Write a self-reflexive poem, either about your own poetry or about some
technical point of language. If you like, try making the poem comic, choosing a formal pattern in which to do it.

or:

Try to surprise God. You can't surprise Him with a sonnet—Peter Meinke has already
done that, and God can't be surprised twice. What would surprise Him?

Adrienne Rich

Like This Together

—for A.H.C.

1.
Wind rocks the car.
We sit parked by the river,
silence between our teeth.
Birds scatter across islands
of broken ice. Another time
I'd have said: "Canada geese,"
knowing you love them.
A year, ten years from now
I'll remember this—
this sitting like drugged birds
in a glass case—
not why, only that we
were here like this together.

2.

They're tearing down, tearing up
this city, block by block.
Rooms cut in half
hang like flayed carcasses,
their old roses in rags,
famous streets have forgotten
where they were going. Only
a fact could be so dreamlike.
They're tearing down the houses
we met and lived in,
soon our two bodies will be all
left standing from that era.

3.

We have, as they say,
certain things in common.
I mean: a view
from a bathroom window
over slate to stiff pigeons
huddled every morning; the way
water tastes from our tap,
which you marvel at, letting
it splash into the glass.
Because of you I notice
the taste of water,
a luxury I might
otherwise have missed.

4.

Our words misunderstand us.
Sometimes at night
you are my mother:
old detailed griefs
twitch at my dreams, and I
crawl against you, fighting
for shelter, making you
my cave. Sometimes
you're the wave of birth
that drowns me in my first
nightmare. I suck the air.
Miscarried knowledge twists us
like hot sheets thrown askew.

5.

Dead winter doesn't die,
it wears away, a piece of carrion

picked clean at last,
rained away or burnt dry.
Our desiring does this,
make no mistake, I'm speaking
of fact: through mere indifference
we could prevent it.
Only our fierce attention
gets hyacinths out of those
hard cerebral lumps,
unwraps the wet buds down
the whole length of a stem.

Eni∂ Shomer

Romantic, at Horseshoe Key

All day the light breaks up the waves,
turning them over in dark spadefuls

while I fish from the pier raised
like a spyglass into the Gulf.

There is such eloquence in the factual
that has no name, in all the ways water

is patterned in a boat's wake: Laces
coming undone? A chain slipping its gears?

What should I call the time we ate cherries
by the pound for moisture, the water jug

forgotten on the dock? You said *years
from now our trees will crown this plot*

of water. A surf of blossoms,
our hands branded red as hearts . . .

I can't subtract you from this place,
from the boat basin's curved

embrace, the red channel markers
that ripen all night in my sleep.

My pale purple line enters the water
and deflects like a censored

thought. Now I see you in your boat
moving quickly through the ink

of my poem. Gulls keep turning
the pages of the sky. I write

the way a shore bird prints her words
in sand to be read by water.

I name it romantic, this belief
that pain is only the bad year of an orchard.

Try This

The two preceding poems are about love and loss, with the emphasis of the imagery
not on an elaborated metaphor but on the situation at hand. Take a memory piece from
your journal and heighten and condense the imagery of the setting, the event, the persons, into a poem.

Raymond Carver

Locking Yourself Out, Then Trying to Get Back In

You simply go out and shut the door
without thinking. And when you look back
at what you've done
it's too late. If this sounds
like the story of a life, okay.

It was raining. The neighbors who had
a key were away. I tried and tried
the lower windows. Stared
inside at the sofa, plants, the table
and chairs, the stereo set-up.
My coffee cup and ashtray waited for me
on the glass-topped table, and my heart
went out to them. I said, *Hello, friends,*
or something like that. After all,
this wasn't so bad.
Worse things had happened. This
was even a little funny. I found the ladder.

Took that and leaned it against the house.
Then climbed in the rain to the deck,
swung myself over the railing
and tried the door. Which was locked,
of course. But I looked in just the same
at my desk, some papers, and my chair.
This was the window on the other side
of the desk where I'd raise my eyes
and stare out when I sat at that desk.
This is not like downstairs, I thought.
This is something else.

And it was something to look in like that, unseen,
from the deck. To be there, inside, and not be there.
I don't even think I can talk about it.
I brought my face close to the glass
and imagined myself inside,
sitting at the desk. Looking up
from my work now and again.
Thinking about some other place
and some other time.
The people I had loved then.

I stood there for a minute in the rain.
Considering myself to be the luckiest of men.
Even though a wave of grief passed through me.
Even though I felt violently ashamed
of the injury I'd done back then.
I bashed that beautiful window.
And stepped back in.

James Tate

Prose Poem

I am surrounded by the pieces of this huge
puzzle: here's a piece I call my wife, and
here's an odd one I call convictions, here's
conventions, here's collisions, conflagrations,
congratulations. Such a puzzle this is! I
like to grease up all the pieces and pile
them in the center of the basement after
everyone else is asleep. Then I leap headfirst like a diver into the wretched confusion.
I kick like hell and strangle a few pieces,

bite them, spitting and snarling like a mongoose.
When I wake up in the morning, it's all fixed!
My wife says she would not be caught dead at
that savage resurrection. I say she would.

Try This

Each of the preceding two poems offers an extended metaphor that purports to be "like
the story of a life." Cluster or free-associate the idea of "my life" and pick a single specific image from which to develop a poem with a whole-life metaphor. Comedy is fine;
if you can make us catch breath, so much the better.

Dave Smith

Black Silhouettes of Shrimpers

Grand Isle, Louisiana

Along the flat sand the cupped torsos of trash fish
arch to seek the sun, but the eyes
glaze with thick gray, death's touch
already drifting these jeweled darters.

Back and forth against the horizon slow trawlers
gulp in their bags whatever rises
here with the shrimp they come for.
Boys on deck shovel the fish off

like the clothes of their fathers out of attics.
Who knows what tides beached them,
what lives were lived to arrive just here?
I walk without stepping on any

dead, though it is hard, the sun's many blazes
spattering and blinding the way ahead
where the wildness of water coils
dark in small swamps and smells fiercely of flesh.

If a cloud shadows everything for a moment, cool,
welcome, there is still no end in sight,
body after body, stench, jewels
nothing will wear, roar and fade of engines.

Try This

How many connotations do you feel or find for the word "water?" List them quickly—
a long list, as fast as you can write. Read it over *once*. Set it aside. Write a rough
draft of a poem about water.

Set it aside. Take it out in a week. What will you do with it? What will you keep?
Where is the poem in it?

Ruth Stone

Repetition

It's unbearable and yet, every day
you go to the city. The stench
of the dead mouse entrails
in the entrails of the car.
Or is it a larger thing
like a man's hand?
A rotten joke.
Maybe it's a pound of ground beef
that you forgot to take in
when you got back from the Grand Union
and the phone was ringing.
The flesh is angry and you
cannot drive away from it.
It says, "Get rid of me."
It is not insidious.
Harmless compared to industrial
pollution. But who would want
those vulnerable pink lungs
babies are born with?
On the obstacle course, the big tires
of the tractors, the tricky ruts
of mud and the slow-moving men
under yellow hard hats
and the women with stop signs;
the CAT shovel and finally,
the sad girl with long yellow hair,
holding her red flag
at the end of the line.

Agha Shahid Ali
Ghazal

The only language of loss left in the world is Arabic—
These words were said to me in a language not Arabic.

Ancestors, you've left me a plot in the family graveyard—
Why must I look, in your eyes, for prayers in Arabic?

Majnoon, his clothes ripped, still weeps for Laila.
Oh, this is the madness of the desert, his crazy Arabic.

Who listens to Ishmael? Even now he cries out:
Abraham, throw away your knives, recite a psalm in Arabic.

From exile Mahmoud Darwish writes to the world:
You'll all pass between the fleeting words of Arabic.

The sky is stunned, it's become a ceiling of stone.
I tell you it must weep. So kneel, pray for rain in Arabic.

At an exhibition of Mughal miniatures, such delicate calligraphy:
Kashmiri paisleys tied into the golden hair of Arabic!

The Koran prophesied a fire of men and stones.
Well, it's all now come true, as it was said in the Arabic.

When Lorca died, they left the balconies open and saw:
his qasidas braided, on the horizon, into knots of Arabic.

Memory is no longer confused, it has a homeland—
Says Shammas: Territorialize each confusion in a graceful Arabic.

Where there were homes in Deir Yassein, you'll see dense forests—
That village was razed. There's no sign of Arabic.

I too, Oh Amichai, saw the dresses of beautiful women.
And everything else, just like you, in Death, Hebrew, and Arabic.

They ask me to tell them what "Shahid" means—
Listen: it means "The Beloved" in Persian, "Witness" in Arabic.

Try This

A **ghazal** is a Persian form of verse, usually five to twelve couplets (though Aga Shahid Ali's is thirteen), with the second line of each couplet either rhyming or repeating the same word. The theme is usually romantic—in fact the name of the form comes from the Arabic word for "boy-girl talk," but is also often mystical. Write a ghazal. Use your name in the final stanza.

Sharon Olds
The Language of the Brag

I have wanted excellence in the knife-throw,
I have wanted to use my exceptionally strong and accurate arms
and my straight posture and quick electric muscles
to achieve something at the center of a crowd,
the blade piercing the bark deep,
the haft slowly and heavily vibrating like the cock.

I have wanted some epic use for my excellent body,
some heroism, some American achievement
beyond the ordinary for my extraordinary self,
magnetic and tensile, I have stood by the sandlot
and watched the boys play.

I have wanted courage, I have thought about fire
and the crossing of waterfalls, I have dragged around

my belly big with cowardice and safety,
my stool black with iron pills,
my huge breasts oozing mucus,
my legs swelling, my hands swelling,
my face swelling and darkening, my hair
falling out, my inner sex
stabbed again and again with terrible pain like a knife.
I have lain down.

I have lain down and sweated and shaken
and passed blood and feces and water and
slowly alone in the center of a circle I have
passed the new person out
and they have lifted the new person free of the act
and wiped the new person free of that
language of blood like praise all over the body.

I have done what you wanted to do, Walt Whitman,
Allen Ginsberg, I have done this thing,
I and the other women this exceptional
act with the exceptional heroic body,
this giving birth, this glistening verb,
and I am putting my proud American boast
right here with the others.

Try This
Write a brag. This will be a list poem. Find a refrain line (other than "I have wanted")
to introduce each item on your list of excellences. Believe every boast.

John Berryman
Dream Song 14

Life, friends, is boring. We must not say so.
After all, the sky flashes, the great sea yearns,
we ourselves flash and yearn,
and moreover my mother told me as a boy
(repeatingly) "Ever to confess you're bored
means you have no

Inner Resources." I conclude now I have no
inner resources, because I am heavy bored.
Peoples bore me,
literature bores me, especially great literature,
Henry bores me, with his plight & gripes
as bad as achilles,

who loves people and valiant art, which bores me.
And the tranquil hills, & gin, look like a drag
and somehow a dog
has taken itself & its tail considerably away
into mountains or sea or sky, leaving
behind: me, wag.

Try This

Write a poem that begins with an outrageous general pronouncement—try to make it more outrageous than *"Life, friends, is boring."* Develop a "proof" in imagery. Try using repetition, alliteration, assonance, and/or internal rhyme.

Yvonne Sapia

My Uncle Guillermo Speaks at His Own Funeral

If this is the last sound I may make
I must say something that is true.

LaVida, my wife, I hated
that cock you kept
chained to the stove.
During the yellowed mornings
he crowed out his madness
as if he'd forgotten
who lived there,
so you'd sing compensatory
songs when the kitchen
steamed with the rhythm
of arroz y habichuelas
and the anger of my desire.

When you fell in love
with my brother Miguel,
I covered my ears as you told me.
My arms grew weak
and thin as a boy's.
You were certain to carry
something out from my world
since I could not even
stir the air with my meaning.

Oh, I loved you like the windows
which watched you
and I loved you when
your crotch was a furnace
and I love you now
though you're ugly
with crying.

Try This

Write a poem in the voice of someone you know, speaking publicly—at a birth, funeral, graduation, confirmation, wedding, promotion, retirement, or other significant event. Let the persona say what actually could not or would not be said.

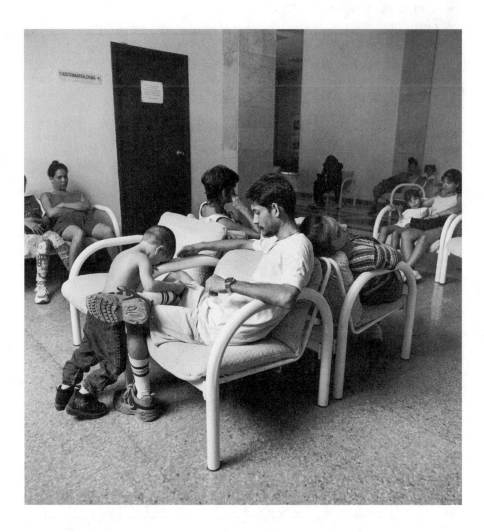

Warm-up

Set a scene in a hospital waiting room. Two characters talk about anything *except* illness, accident, or death.

CHAPTER TEN

DRAMA

The Difference Between Drama and Fiction
Sight: Sets, Action, Costumes, Props
Sound: Verbal and Nonverbal
Some Notes on Screenwriting

Nothing comes close to it—this living experience between
the actor and the audience, sharing the same space at the
same time.

Kevin Spacey

The Difference Between Drama and Fiction

Like fiction, a play tells a story of human change, in which a character goes on
a psychic journey, through a process of discovery and decision, connection and
disconnection, involving a power struggle between protagonist and antagonist,
to arrive at a situation different from that in which he or she began. As with
fiction, it is important to choose the plot you will make from this story, the particular portion that will be dramatized. Why does the action begin in this place,
at this particular time? It might be a good idea, therefore, to go back and re-
familiarize yourself with Chapters 5 and 8, on Story and Fiction.

In stage drama the process of story is condensed and intensified. Usually
something has happened before the curtain opens, called the **inciting incident**,
which creates the situation in which the protagonist finds him/herself: Hamlet's father has died and his mother has remarried. The play will present this
situation through **exposition**: the watchmen reveal that the ghost of Hamlet's
father has been walking near the castle at night. Very soon, the action begins with
a **point of attack**: the ghost speaks to Hamlet, demanding revenge against
Claudius. Now the play has set up its conflict, identified the protagonist and
antagonist, and it is time for the complications to begin.

All of these traditions can also be identified in a story: the inciting incident of "Cinderella" would be that her mother has died and her father has remarried; the exposition tells us that the stepmother and stepsisters mistreat her; the point of attack arrives with the invitation to the ball.

But drama is different from fiction, in fundamental ways that mean you as a writer select and arrange differently if you choose to tell your story in the form of a play. Here, for a start, is a chart:

Fiction	Drama
Takes place in the reader's imagination.	Takes place here, now, on the stage.
Takes place in private, in solitude.	Takes place in public, communally.
All images are in words, transcribed in the brain.	Actors, props, costumes can be seen; dialogue & music can be heard.
Can go into characters' thoughts.	All thoughts must be externalized.
Author may interpret directly.	Only characters express opinions.
Can go into past action.	Past must be made part of present.
Can be any length; room to digress.	Length more or less prescribed; must be focused.
Can be taken up and put down at will.	Continuous performance.
Costs only the text and reading time.	Expensive in time, effort, money.
The writer writes what the reader reads.	The play is interpreted by the cast.

The core fact of theater is that it takes place right now! right here! before your very eyes! Fiction is usually written in past tense, and even when it is not, there is an implied perspective of "looking back" on an action completed. The constant effort of the fiction writer must therefore be to give the imaginative past the immediacy of the present. In drama, the effort is the opposite, to present the necessary information of the past as an integral part of the present drama.

When you write for the stage, you lose a great deal that you may indulge as a fiction writer—the freedom not only to leap from place to place and from past to future, but also to go inside your characters' minds to tell us directly what they are thinking; to interpret for us, telling us what to believe about them or the situation; and to digress on themes or topics that may be of interest but do not add to the action.

What you gain is the live presence of sight and sound—movement, music, props, costumes, sound effects—to be used as inventively as you and your director can devise. You gain the community of people bent on a single venture, their talents put at the service of your script, their interest invested in your success. What you gain above all is the body of the actor, with all the immediacy and expressiveness that implies.

A play is *short*. It takes much longer to say words aloud than to read them silently (test it by timing yourself reading a short story, and then reading it aloud). Whereas it might take five or fifteen hours to read a novel, it's unlikely you will get an audience to sit still for more than a couple of hours (and the current tendency is toward shorter plays)—yet the substance of a short story is unlikely to be rich enough for the effort of a full evening's staging. This means that drama is an *intense* form; the dialogue must be economical and focused. Like a short-short story, a play asks that you throw the audience immediately into the action. Like a poem, it asks for several things to be going on at once. Whereas poetry depends for its density largely on the interplay between sound and meaning, drama depends on the interplay between sight and sound. As poetry plays the rhythm of the line in tension with the rhythm of the sentence, so drama plays the revelation of the verbal in tension with the revelation of the visual.

Try This

Take any paragraph of fiction or memoir in your journal and play with the idea of putting it onstage. Where would it take place; what would the characters say; how would they be dressed, how would they behave?

I take it as my principal that words do not mean everything.

Antonin Artaud

Sight: Sets, Action, Costumes, Props

The drama begins the moment the audience sees the stage, and this first sight sets the tone for everything that follows. The set may represent the extreme of **fourth-wall realism**, the convention that we are spying on what happens through the space where the fourth wall of the room has been removed; or at the opposite extreme of **theatricalism**, the convention that acknowledges the stage is a stage, the actors are actors, and the audience is an audience. It may be anywhere between or a combination of the two. In Arthur Miller's "Death of a Salesman," for example, two floors of a house are realistically represented, but when the characters move into memory or fantasy, they ignore the doors and walk through the walls.

The scenery will set the tone even if you decide on a bare stage, or "no set at all," because the less there is on the stage, the more the audience will read into what is there. Human beings are meaning-making creatures; we love to interpret and conclude. So when scenery, clothing, and objects appear onstage we will read significance at once. If the curtain opens on a maypole or a tribal mask or a backdrop of a bonfire, it's no use telling us that these are mere decoration. We will take them for clues.

This fact is full of rich possibilities for the playwright, and also for the actor. Choose clothes that characterize, objects that reveal. Remember that everything we wear and own bespeaks our desires, choices, background, gender, politics— and make your stage visually vivid with such hints.

If there are elements of familiar exterior or interior space on the stage, give them a distinct meaning. If the play takes place in a college dorm room (and you can probably make a more imaginative choice), then how do the wall hangings, clothes, objects, plants characterize the person who lives here? The playwright has no less an obligation than the poet or story writer to choose revealing specific details. How do you communicate with the readers of your play—and especially with the designer—in order to help them translate your vision either mentally or onto the stage? *"A typical college dorm room"* will *not* do it (in fact, avoid the words *normal*, *typical*, and *ordinary*—they are all copouts). A writer of stage directions is a writer and must paint the picture in the words.

It is even possible to introduce conflict before the actors enter, as in this opening stage direction from Simon Gray's *Butley:*

> An office in a College of London University. About 10 in the morning. The office is badly decorated (white walls, graying, plaster boards) with strip lighting. There are two desks opposite each other, each with a swivel chair. BEN's desk, left, is a chaos of papers, books, detritus. JOEY's desk, right, is almost bare. Behind each desk is a bookcase. Again, BEN's is chaotic with old essays and mimeographed sheets scattered among the books, while JOEY's is neat, not many books on the shelves.

Here, before a single character enters, we know a good deal about the characters of Ben and Joey, and that there will be conflict between them. When Ben enters, other props, his costume, and his way of relating to them further reveal his character, his current state of mind, the tone of the play we are going to see, and again the potential conflict:

> As the curtain rises, BEN enters, in a plastic raincoat, which he takes off and throws into the chair. He has a lump of cotton wool on his chin, from a particularly nasty shaving cut. He goes to his chair, sits down, looks around as if searching for something, shifts uncomfortably, pulls the plastic mac out from under him, searches through its pockets, takes out half a banana, a bit squashed, then throws the raincoat over to JOEY's desk. He takes a bite from the banana...

One important thing to notice about stage directions is that they tell us *what we see* but do not give us any information that we must learn through dialogue. The stage direction above goes far enough to tell us that the cotton is on a bad shaving cut—which is a visual directive to the props and makeup department—but it does not say "Ben has been quarreling with his wife." This is information that we would have to learn through dialogue, and it must wait for dialogue to be revealed. In general, the script reveals information in the order in which it is revealed onstage. What the audience learns through sight or nonverbal sound will appear in the stage directions. What it learns through dialogue will be revealed only when the characters say it.

Frequently, however, what the characters say is at odds with what they wear, handle, or, especially, do. They speak a text but reveal the subtext through these other means. The **stage lie** can be revealed by action, or by slips of the tongue, stumbling, exaggeration—all those verbal clues by which we learn in life that people are not telling the absolute truth. We never trust the frankness of anyone who begins, "To be frank with you . . ."

The sort of information that comes through a stage lie is a major source of understanding to the audience. The actor wears satin flounces and says, "I've always preferred the simple life." He clutches the wallet to his chest and says, "The money doesn't mean a thing to me, it's the principle." She says, "Oh, good, I was just coming to see you," and quickly slips the folder into the drawer. In all these instances, sight is at odds with sound, and we are likely to believe the evidence of our eyes. Here is Ben's first line of dialogue:

The telephone rings.

BEN: Butley, English. Hello, James, have a nice break? (*A pause—he mouths a curse.*) Sorry, James, I can't talk now—I'm right in the middle of a tutorial—'bye.

Because the truth is often revealed in the discrepancies between sight and sound, text and subtext, stage directions are important. But not *all* stage movement is worthy of a stage direction. Most movement is "blocking," that is, a decision on the director's part about where the actors should move and what they should do during a given passage. As playwright, you can make your stage directions count by specifying only the sights and movements that help tell a story— as *"he mouths a curse"* does above. It's fine if you see the play taking place in your mind, but *"She moves left from the chair to the couch and sits again"* is usually not going to help tell the story, and should be left up to the director.

In the chapter on Setting, I said that relationship to place is revealing of character, and that when there is discomfort or conflict in that relationship, a story has already begun. Playwrights productively exploit this fact. The curtain opens on a huge room dominated by a mahogany desk and leather chair. One door opens. A young woman enters clutching her handbag in front of her. She cranes her head forward, peering at the ceiling, the walls. She reaches out gingerly and touches the desk with two fingers. She steps sideways, stops, then perches on the edge of a straight back chair. Another door opens. Another woman enters, shrugging off her coat and hooking it with one motion on the coat rack behind her. She juggles a clipboard through this process, crosses without looking at the first woman, slings herself into the leather chair, and swivels it around. How much do you know about the situation already? More important, how much do you know about the relationship between these people by their relationship to the room? Who belongs here? Who has the power? Who, so far, has your sympathy? (And remember that in literature the sympathy of the reader or the audience is very great power!)

Try This

Choose a setting that seems to you both familiar and slightly dull: that dorm room, a kitchen, a restaurant, or something similar. Then write an opening stage direction of no more than a hundred words that makes it both interesting to look at and revealing of its owner.

Introduce into this setting one character who is familiar with it and comfortable with it, and one who is unfamiliar and uncomfortable. What does each want? Write a page or so of their dialogue (with stage directions as appropriate).

Sound: Nonverbal and Verbal

Dialogue is the most important element of most stage plays, but there are hundreds of nonverbal sounds that are ripe with emotional content. Make yourself aware of them and be alert to ways you can take advantage of them. A baby's cry, a scream, whistling, sobbing, laughing, a howl of pain, a sneeze, a cluck of irritation, fingers drumming, feet tapping—all of these are human sounds that are often clearer indications of mood than speech. But nonhuman sounds also often produce in us immediate reaction: a crash, splintering glass, a ringing telephone, squealing tires, a siren, a gun shot, horse's hooves...

Try This
Make two lists, one of human nonverbal sounds, one of nonhuman sounds with emotional potential in our reaction to them. Make the lists long. Keep adding to the lists. Think about ways to use them.

Music, too, though its choice is often the province of the director, can be incorporated into the written text, as an indicator of mood, period, or character, or can even be made a part of the action by representing a conflict between two characters: the Daughter character plays Britney Spears on the boom box while Dad opts for Schubert on his old LPs. **Diegetic** sound and music, like this example, occurs realistically within the action: someone practices the violin, or the sounds of traffic come through the open window. **Nondiegetic** sound is stylized, not arising from the action but as an accompaniment or background to it: the hero bursts into song at the office water cooler, or a jazz riff covers the blackout between scenes.

In this short excerpt from "Death of a Salesman," dialogue, action, and diegetic sound come together to create a composition of meanings that is almost like the texture of music itself. The aging salesman and his wife are in the bedroom:

> **LINDA** (*timidly*):   Willy, dear, what has he got against you?
> **WILLY:**   I'm so tired. Don't talk any more.
>
> *Biff slowly returns to the kitchen. He stops, stares toward the heater.*
>
> **LINDA:**   Will you ask Howard to let you work in New York?
> **WILLY:**   First thing in the morning. Everything'll be all right.
>
> *Biff reaches behind the heater and draws out a length of rubber tubing. He is horrified and turns his head toward Willy's room, still dimly lit, from which the strains of Linda's desperate but monotonous humming rise.*

Here we have the husband and wife in "no dialogue" (*what has he got against you/Don't talk any more*); their son, in contrasting action, confirms his father's suicide attempt, while the mother hums (nonverbal) and, against Willy's reassurance—*Everything'll be all right*—the lighting symbolically fades. This very small scene, with its interlocking elements, represents **dramatic irony**, which occurs whenever the audience knows more than the characters know. In this instance, we have known for most of the act about the suicide attempt Biff has just learned about, and unlike Linda we already guess what Biff "has against" his father. We know with grim certainty that "everything" won't be all right.

Try This
Rewrite the scene you did for the exercise on page 342, this time for radio. "Translate" your stage direction into sound alone, verbal, nonverbal, and musical, trying to reveal everything through the one sense.

Unlike the other genres, all the dialogue in drama is direct. There is no place for indirect or summary dialogue. With the single exception of "ad lib"—which means that the actors fill in at their discretion with, for instance, greetings to each other or background mumble—you write the words any character speaks. You may not, for example, say in a stage direction, *"Joe calls in from the bathroom, still complaining."* It's the playwright's obligation to produce the words.

The most difficult dialogue to write is often the exposition, in which you must give the audience the necessary information about what has gone on before curtain rise, and what the situation is now. A useful tradition, and probably the most frequently used device, is to have a character who knows explain to a character who doesn't know. But if you don't have a character who is handily ignorant, you can have two characters talk about the situation and make it sound natural as long as they concentrate on how they feel about it, or disagree about it, so that the information comes out incidentally, sideways. If a character says, "My sister's train is due at four o'clock into Union Station," we get the facts, but if he says, "I can't talk now! I've got to make it to Union Station by four—my sister goes bananas if I'm not there to meet her train," we know something about his attitude and the relationship as well as the situation—and it sounds like talk.

A third expository device, if your play is stylized, is to have a character come forward and speak directly to the audience. Ever since film began to prove itself the best medium for realism, this **theatricalist** technique (acknowledging that the play is a play and the audience an audience) has become more and more popular in the theater.

Good dialogue will carry most of its tone as an integral part of the lines, and when this is the case, there is no need to announce the tone of voice in a stage direction—and it can in fact be insulting to the actors. An example:

SHE *(slyly)*: By the way, did you get the rent money from the Smiths?
HE *(suspiciously)*: What makes you ask that?

SHE *(casually)*:   Oh, nothing, I just wondered.

HE *(angrily)*:   You've had all the money you're going to get this week!

Not a single one of these tonal directions is necessary; the tone is inherent in the lines. Contrast with this version:

SHE: By the way, did you get the rent money from the Smiths?

HE: What makes you ask that?

SHE *(slipping the catalogue behind the cushion)*:   Oh, nothing, I just wondered.

HE *(laughing)*:   You've had all the money you're going to get this week! *(He begins to tickle her.)*

Here, actions and tone reveal a contradiction or qualification of what the words suggest, so the stage directions are appropriate.

Here are a few further things to remember about play dialogue, to make it natural and intense:

- The sooner you introduce the conflict, the better. A certain amount of exposition will be necessary, but if you can reveal *at the same time* the point of attack, it's all to the good. *Hamlet* begins with two guards discussing the fact that the ghost has walked (the inciting incident). But they immediately anticipate the conflict: *Will it walk again?*

- Dialogue is action when it contains both conflict and the possibility of change. Keep alert to the possibility that characters discover and decide through the medium of talk. Debate between two firmly decided people is not dramatic, no matter how mad they are. Disagreement between people who must stay in proximity to each other, especially if they care about each other, is inherently more dramatic than if they can walk away.

- Use "no" dialogue, in which people deny, contradict, refuse, qualify, or otherwise say no to each other.

- Dialogue has to be said, so say it aloud and make sure it says easily, allows for breath, sounds like talk.

- Remember that people are not always able or willing to say just what they mean, and that this breaks the flow of the talk. This is especially true when emotions are heating up. People break off, interrupt themselves and each other. They use sentence fragments. Don't always finish their . . .

- Silence can be white hot. The most intense emotions are the ones you can't express in words. When a character spews out an eloquent paragraph of anger, he is probably not as angry as if he stands, breathes hard, and turns away.

- Vary short exchanges with longer ones. A change of pace, from a sharp series of short lines to a longer speech and back again, keeps the rhythm interesting.

- Nearly everybody tries to be funny now and again. You can often reveal character, and also what a character may be hiding, by having her try to make light of it. A joke that falls flat with other characters is a great tension-raiser. Conversely, beware of having the characters too amused by each others' wit; the funnier they find the jokes, the less likely the audience is to be amused.

- Similarly, avoid having the characters comment on each other's dialogue; it's self-conscious. If He says, "That's a clever way to put it!" we'll hear the author in the praise.

There are also several deliberate theatrical traditions for revealing thought. In the **soliloquy** the character simply talks to himself (*To be or not to be . . .*), and the audience accepts that these words take place in the mind. In an **aside**, the character says one line to another character and another to the audience or to thin air. Traditionally, the aside is always the truth of that character's feeling. In a **voiceover**, the thoughts are recorded and play over the live scene. All of these techniques are stylized and can tend to be self-conscious. Use *very sparingly*—especially if your basic mode is realistic.

Crucial events of the past can be difficult to introduce naturally. One useful technique for doing this is the **emotional recall**, in which one character tells another about an incident from the past. But a narrated event is no more inherently dramatic than a debate, and you must not rely on the narration to hold the audience's interest. In order to keep the drama in the here! and now! the narration must hold the potential for change. The important emotion in an emotional recall is not the emotion of the teller but of the listener. Typically, a charged situation exists between one character and one or more others (it can be her mother or a mob). The first character tells a story. The listener(s) change attitude entirely. The dramatic situation is not the one in the story, it is the one on stage, where we see the change.

Try This
Choose one of the characters you have written about in your journal. Write a monologue in that character's voice beginning with one of the following trigger lines:

- I knew right away I'd said the wrong thing.
- What is it this time?
- I didn't hear the doorbell.
- What took you so long?
- You think you know me.
- It started out fine.

continued

Now introduce stage directions into the monologue, describing anything we can see—
what the character is wearing, doing, and so forth—so as to change, contradict, or qualify the meaning of the speech.

The trade-off between fiction and drama requires an act of faith. The audience does not receive what you wrote in the form in which you wrote it, but in
an interpretation of it filtered through director, actors, and designers who may
know less about it than you do. You are in effect handing them your baby to do
with as they please. Moreover, the theater is unforgiving in terms of its cost, so
that practical constraints are always in the way of the imagination, demanding
that you pare down the cast, presenting you with a meager version of your vision.

What you get in return is the thrill of an organic collaboration in which, at its
best, the talents of a dozen or a few dozen people are laid down in tracks along your
own. Because all of these tracks must work together if the project is to succeed,
theater succeeds less often than prose and poetry. Because the show is alive and
has the depth of all that collaboration, when it does work, it works with exhilarating immediacy. You need stamina for such a strong chance of failure. On the other
hand, nothing in an author's experience matches the thrill of sitting in an audience watching the live embodiment of your words, *feeling* the emotions of the audience around you as they laugh or cry with the work of your imagination.

Try This
Write a ten-minute play in which two characters must somehow divide up a quantity of goods. Is it an inheritance? A divorce? A charity sale? Leftovers? What's the
conflict? What particular thing or things represent the conflict? Who wins?

or:

Write a ten-minute play in which two characters are unfailingly polite to each other.
On the last page, one of the characters turns viciously on the other, and the audience
is not surprised.

Some Notes on Screenwriting

My advice to those who want to write for film is that, for the same reason a
painter should begin with a still life, a screenwriter should begin with a stage
play. It isn't easier, but it does reveal the necessary craft more clearly. Film
restores many of the freedoms of the novelist. But filmmakers who rely on these
freedoms do not learn storytelling in images as well as those who grapple with
the stricter discipline of the stage.

In the early days of cinema, most directors and writers naturally considered film the sister-art of the stage, since it involved actors, sets and so forth. (A great exception was D. W. Griffiths, who declared that he had learned everything about film technique from Charles Dickens.) As the cinema developed, it became ever clearer that the camera uses many of the techniques of fiction—the ability to move instantly in space and time, the advantage of point of view, closeups and slow motion for intensity, quick cuts and juxtaposition for revealing meaning and metaphor. At the same time, it became evident that film is a far better medium for realism than the stage, since the camera can go on location. Stage "realism," with painted flats for rooms and plywood cutouts for trees, was no match for the living room and the forest. As a result, although realistic plays still abound, the general direction of the theater in the second half of the twentieth century was toward stylization—theatricalism, the use of minimal stage elements and symbolic exaggeration, the incorporation of costume and set changes into the action. Since one thing the theater has over the movies is the living relationship of actor with audience, playwrights began to exploit this strength. Characters directly address or interact with the audience; the script is **self-reflexive**, calling attention to the fact that it's a play.

This movement has been strangely freeing. Playwrights have been more inclined to borrow elements from other disciplines—dance, mime, puppetry, technology—to break the mold of "the well-made play" and display their psychological or social insights in the context of spectacle.

It may, then, seem paradoxical to say that playwriting is the best first discipline toward film. But just as formal verse can teach you the possibilities of verbal music, so the limitations of this confined space can focus your efforts on the telling of a dramatic story. Many young screenwriters become so seduced by the marvels of what the *camera* can do, that they fail to learn what the writer must do. The delicious vocabulary—*cameo, rack focus, wipe, dolly shot, dissolve*—can mask the simple need that a film, like a story, like a memoir, like a play, must be about these people in this place with this problem. If you can put a man, a woman, a box, and a bottle, say, in a rectangular frame on a bare floor, and make us *care*—then you can *write*, and you can write a film. The imagination must come first. The machine will follow.

More to Read: On Playwriting

Downs, William Missouri, and Lou Anne Wright. *Playwriting: From Formula to Form.*

    Fort Worth: Harcourt Brace, 1998.

Sossaman, Stephen. *Writing Your First Play.* Upper Saddle River, New Jersey: Prentice

    Hall, 2000.

More to Read: On Screenwriting

Field, Syd. *Screenplay: The Foundations of Screenwriting, Third Edition*. New York:
Dell, 1994.

Johnson, Claudia. *Writing Short Screen Plays that Connect*. Boston: Focal Press, 2000.

Readings

Richard Dresser

The Road to Ruin

Commissioned and First Produced by Actors Theatre of Louisville

Characters

CLIFF, a man in his thirties
CONNIE, his wife
FRED, a middle-aged auto mechanic
JIMBO, the proprietor of a Jersey City garage

Setting

The middle of a rainy night at Jimbo's garage. It's in a particularly menacing neighborhood in Jersey City just off the highway. We can see the office of the garage and small part of the parking lot.

RISE: *Darkness. The sound of rain, then two car doors open, a dog barks, and the car doors slam shut. We hear* CLIFF *and* CONNIE's *voices in the lot outside the garage.*

CONNIE: I will never ride in that car again.
CLIFF: Then how do you plan to get home?
CONNIE: That's a very good question. Since nobody seems to be here.
CLIFF: Maybe I'll take a quick look at it myself.
CONNIE: You can't even get the hood up, I've seen you try!
CLIFF: That was one time, before they showed me where the little catch is.
CONNIE: We've had the car for two years and you can't get the hood up.
CLIFF: Well if I got just a little bit of support from you it might be different.
Come on.

(CLIFF opens the door to the office of JIMBO'S garage. It's illuminated by a fluorescent clock on the wall, a Coke machine, and a neon sign. CONNIE follows

CLIFF *in out of the rain. They stand in the ghostly light of the office. It contains a desk with a telephone, a wall-phone, and horrible clutter. Besides the doorway leading outside, there's a closed door leading into the garage.)*

CONNIE: This place better be open.

CLIFF: *(calling out:)* Hello? Anybody here? *(CONNIE sits down. She gets out a small mirror and checks herself out. The door to the garage opens, revealing a blinding white light. FRED Enters. He is covered with grease. He closes the door, switches on the lights in the office, and sits down at the desk, opens the desk drawer, and takes out a sandwich. He eats the sandwich, paying no attention to them. CONNIE looks at CLIFF, challenging him to take charge of the situation. CLIFF tentatively approaches the desk.)* Excuse me, sir. We've got a little problem with our car. We were hoping that you could perhaps take a look at it.

FRED: Can't you see I'm on my break?

CLIFF: Oh, right. Sorry. *(CLIFF crosses to where CONNIE is impatiently sitting. A low voice:)* He's on his break.

CONNIE: *(pained)* For how long?

CLIFF: *(clearing his throat)* Uh, how long would the break be? *(They both watch FRED, but there's no response.)*

CONNIE: Maybe he could give us the key to the ladies room.

CLIFF: Yes, uh, sir? Is there a ladies room key? For my wife?

(Without turning to them, FRED points toward the corner. They follow where he is pointing. CONNIE goes to the corner and gets a cinder block with the ladies room key on it.)

CONNIE: Is this it? *(FRED suddenly puts the sandwich back in the drawer and slams it shut.)*

FRED: People steal, okay? *(CONNIE picks up the cinder block and starts outside where FRED is pointing.)*

CONNIE: *(To CLIFF:)* Would you call Triple A? We haven't got all night and he obviously won't help us. *(CONNIE struggles out with the cinder block. CLIFF takes a quarter from his pocket and goes to the wall-phone.)*

CLIFF: Mind if I . . . *(FRED is intently reading a magazine. CLIFF checks the yellow pages, and dials. As he does this, FRED slowly swivels around in his chair and takes CLIFF's wallet from his back pocket. Then he swivels back into his previous position as CLIFF finishes dialing. CLIFF moves toward the doorway, trying to have some privacy from FRED. The phone on FRED's desk rings. FRED answers it. On phone:)* Yes, is this the Automobile Club?

FRED: *(on phone:)* Uh-huh.

CLIFF: I wonder if you can help me. I'm at a station in Jersey City called Jimbo's and my car is broken down. No one here will help us, and I need to get my car towed. It's very important that I get back to the city because my wife has a job interview tomorrow.

FRED: *(on phone:)* What seems to be the problem?

CLIFF: *(on phone:)* It was going and then it stopped . . . *(He turns around and sees FRED on the phone. CLIFF hangs up the phone. FRED hangs up the phone.)* Why are you talking to me?

FRED: You called. I answered.

CLIFF: Why did it ring here?

FRED: This is the only phone you can call from there. Dial any number and it will ring here. Wanna try again?

CLIFF: Will you fix my car?

FRED: What's wrong with it?

CLIFF: It was running fine and then it started making this sound, like . . . somewhere between a rattle and . . . a . . . moan . . . and then it stopped and we were lucky enough to coast down the ramp and right in here.

FRED: Damn lucky.

CLIFF: We thought you could, what is it—give it a jump start or something.

FRED: It was moaning?

CLIFF: Could you at least look at it?

FRED: Not 'til Jimbo gets here.

CLIFF: You couldn't look at it without him? *(FRED opens another desk drawer and gets out a cup of coffee. He stares at CLIFF. Then he gets out a contract from the desk drawer.)*

FRED: Work order. Sign on the X.

(CLIFF signs. FRED immediately takes a stamp and loudly bangs it down on the contract in several places. Then he tears out the bottom sheet and files it in a file cabinet, puts another in an envelope, stamps the envelope and sends it down a mail slot. He gives another to CLIFF, who puts it in his pocket without looking at it. CONNIE Enters from the garage carrying the cinder block, which she drops in the corner.)

CLIFF: Was it okay? *(No response.)* I mean the bathroom, sometimes in a place like this . . . but of course maybe they do keep it clean. You never know.

CONNIE: Did he look at the car?

CLIFF: He hasn't actually looked at it, no, but we discussed it.

CONNIE: And?

CLIFF: He can't look at it until the boss shows up.

CONNIE: Why not?

CLIFF: You know, union or insurance or something. There must be a good reason.

CONNIE: I want to get my dog and my luggage and go home. *(beat)* When is the boss showing up? *(louder:)* When is he showing up?

FRED: *(swiveling in the chair to face her)* You won't be talking so loud. You'll keep your voice down when he shows up.

CLIFF: My wife is a broadcast journalist. She is one of three candidates to be the week-end weather girl on channel 7. So you had better show a little goddamn respect when addressing her, my man. *(Headlights outside. FRED immediately puts the coffee cup back in the drawer and hides the magazine he was reading.)*

CLIFF: Good. Maybe now we can get a little service here. *(JIMBO Enters. He's soaking wet.)*

FRED: *(very politely:)* How is it out there? *(JIMBO glares at FRED, then turns his attention to CLIFF and CONNIE.)*

JIMBO: Whose car is blocking my driveway?

CLIFF: That's our car. It stalled out and we just coasted in here. We thought maybe we could get help, but no one has lifted a finger. *(JIMBO goes menacingly over to FRED, who cowers.)*

JIMBO: Any telephone calls? *(JIMBO and FRED burst into hysterical laughter.)*

CLIFF: Could it be the spark plugs? I hear that if they get wet it can stall a car.

FRED: *(To JIMBO:)* Don't listen to him. He don't know much. *(confidentially:)* She was moaning before she stopped.

CLIFF: Moaning is not what I meant!

JIMBO: *(turning on CLIFF)* I know what's wrong with your car.

CLIFF: Really? *(beat)* What?

JIMBO: Your car is depressed.

CLIFF: That's not possible.

JIMBO: No? *(To FRED:)* He says it's not possible. *(JIMBO opens the door to the garage and Exits into the white light.)*

CONNIE: Did you call the auto club?

CLIFF: I tried.

CONNIE: Good lord. I'm going to call a cab. I have to start putting on my make-up in...two hours. *(CONNIE goes to the phone.)*

CLIFF: Don't bother. All the calls go through the desk and he stops them. *(CONNIE dials and the phone rings on the desk. CONNIE hangs up the wall-phone and the phone on the desk stops. FRED smiles at her.)*

CONNIE: We never should have come to New Jersey.

FRED: You people think a car can't get depressed? Take a peek out back. The whole lot is full of 'em. Just sittin' there. They gave up.

CLIFF: *(staring out the window)* What do you do with them?

FRED: Talk to 'em. Try to build up their self-esteem. *(JIMBO comes back in. FRED spins around in his chair and studies the papers on his desk.)*

JIMBO: That was a helluva place to leave your car.

CONNIE: We didn't mean to leave it there—

CLIFF: That's where it happened to stop. Believe me, there was absolutely no planning on our part.

JIMBO: *(To FRED:)* Move it.

FRED: We got no room—

JIMBO: Make room! *(FRED jumps up and goes outside.)*

CLIFF: I signed a work order and I'm going to insist that you live up to it.

JIMBO: He got you to sign?

CLIFF: It's right here. I'm a man who respects a contract. *(beat)* How soon can you look at my car?

JIMBO: Depends.

CLIFF: On what?

JIMBO: On how bad it is.

CLIFF: How can you tell how bad it is if you don't look?

JIMBO: You're a wise-guy, aren't you? I could put your nose in a lug wrench. Give it a couple of turns and then we'd see how wise you are.

CLIFF: My wife has to put on her cosmetics. If you can't look at the car tonight, then we'll have to leave it here.

JIMBO: I'm all backed up. No way will your car stay here tonight.

CONNIE: Maybe you'd like to buy it.

CLIFF: Connie!

CONNIE: *(urgent whisper:)* It's a perfect chance to get rid of it!

JIMBO: I don't buy 'em anymore. Too much trouble.

CLIFF: Then what will it cost for you to look at it right now? Fifty bucks?

JIMBO: Put'er on the table. *(CLIFF reaches for his wallet, which is gone.)*

CLIFF: My God, Connie. My wallet—

CONNIE: What?

CLIFF: It's gone—

CONNIE: And I didn't bring my purse—

CLIFF: *(To JIMBO:)* Listen, we seem to have misplaced our money. But we've got every credit card you can name. We have a mortgage, bank cards, securities, mutual funds, IRAs, you name it. We're good for the money.

JIMBO: People like you I see by the hundreds. They never pay up.

CLIFF: Don't judge me by the others! I'll give you my watch! *(CLIFF puts his watch on the desk.)*

CONNIE: Cliff, we can't even take the train if we don't have money.

JIMBO: Let me tell you a story. One of 'em came in here, he could have been your twin. Tried to give me a *personal check. (Pause. CLIFF and CONNIE aren't sure if the story is over.)*

CLIFF: What happened?

JIMBO: He turned out to be a bad credit risk. *(JIMBO presses a buzzer on the desk and makes a violent motion out the window. There is a loud, grating sound.)*

CLIFF: Your jewelry, Connie—

CONNIE: Cliff! *(CONNIE starts taking off her jewelry and putting it on the desk.)*

CLIFF: All of it, Connie! *(CONNIE moans and takes off more. JIMBO slides it into the desk drawer, which he closes.)*

CLIFF: And if that isn't enough, then we'll give him Ramon—

CONNIE: Not Ramon!

CLIFF: *(To JIMBO:)* She's got a dog in the car that's worth six grand. He just won every prize at the show, for Chrissakes this dog could do your taxes if you want. He's yours. You can barbecue the sucker for all I care. I just want you to know that we are people who are as good as our word—

CONNIE: We are not going to give this man Ramon!

CLIFF: Listen to reason, Connie. We are going to give him whatever he wants. We have no car and no money—

(FRED comes in pushing a little hand truck with a cube of compressed metal on it.)

JIMBO: I've changed my mind. You can leave your car here now because we have the room.

FRED: Where do you want it, boss?

CONNIE: *(a small, stricken voice:)* That's our car, isn't it?

CLIFF: What have you done?

CONNIE: My God. Ramon! Where is Ramon? *(To FRED:)* Was there a dog in there?

FRED: *(To the metal block:)* Here boy! Here boy! *(To CONNIE:)* He don't come when you call.

JIMBO: Put'er way in back. They're last in line and they got no money.

CLIFF: I loved that car! *(turning on JIMBO)* How could you do that?

JIMBO: *(turning to FRED)* You can get cleaned up, Fred. *(FRED wheels the hand-truck into the garage.)*

JIMBO: *(To CLIFF:)* See? Take away your money and you're just like every-body else.

CONNIE: Come on, Cliff. We'll walk.

JIMBO: I give you two blocks, maybe three. Then they'll get you.

CONNIE: Nobody's going to "get us."

JIMBO: A healthy pair like you? You get picked up and bought and sold and bought and sold and pretty soon you're on the other side of the world bent over in the hot sun harvesting cocoa plants. *(beat)* The only way to leave this place is in a car. And you ain't got one.

CLIFF: Okay. We'll wait here—

JIMBO: You wait here you gotta work. That way you'll be able to get another car.

CLIFF: Okay, we'll work tonight. I don't mind.

JIMBO: What can you do? Can you fix things? *(beat)* 'Course not. Profes-sionals. Can't do a damn thing and I got three acres of cars turning into scrap iron.

CLIFF: I could talk to the cars . . . try to cheer'em up.

CONNIE: God, Cliff.

JIMBO: Fair enough. And maybe some day one of 'em will be yours. *(beat)* 'Course I gotta charge you rent.

CLIFF: Fine. Take it out of my pay. *(beat)* How much do I get?

JIMBO: It's all in the contract you signed.

CLIFF: What contract? *(CLIFF looks blank. Then he hurriedly gets out the paper he signed.)* My God. I thought it was a work order. I'll never get away . . . Connie . . .

JIMBO: It's already gone to the central office. Try to break a contract with *them* . . .

(FRED Enters, wearing Bermuda shorts, sun-glasses, and sandals with high black socks. He's carrying a work shirt, which he tosses on the chair. He stops at the desk and puts on CLIFF's watch. FRED takes out his wallet—which is CLIFF's wallet—and carefully counts out some bills, which he gives to JIMBO.)

FRED: That's the last of it. I'd say we're square, boss.

JIMBO: *(looks at his watch)* Your shift is done, Fred. *(beat)* Seven years to the day. Now you got your choice of cars. *(FRED goes to the wall where a number of keys are hanging. He selects one.)*

FRED: *(To CLIFF:)* The pay's okay but the rent's worse. *(FRED starts for the door.)*

CLIFF: You're leaving?

FRED: I done my time.

CONNIE: Could you give us a ride? Oh, please, just get us across the bridge—

JIMBO: Not this one. He works here now.

CONNIE: Then take me, please, Manhattan's right over there—

CLIFF: Connie!

FRED: I guess I could do that.

CLIFF: What about me?

JIMBO: You signed up to have your car fixed—

CLIFF: How can you fix it now?

JIMBO: It'll take time. Gotta send out for parts. And there's a whole slew of people in front of you. You'll meet 'em, living in their cars, wandering through the lot out back. Nice folks who ran into some car trouble. You gotta wait your turn, just like everyone else.

CONNIE: I'll come back for you, Cliff. As soon as I get the job—

FRED: That's what they all say. *(beat)* I was coming through here with the wife and kids. A week's holiday at the shore, you know? We get off the highway to look for a place to eat. The car stalls, right out front. We thought we were lucky, a garage right handy. Jimbo put the car out back with the others. We kept waiting for it to get better, but it never did. Months go by, I'm pumping gas, we're living in the car wash. This wasn't much of a place for the kids to grow up, so one morning the wife says she's gonna take the kids and make a break for it, try to get out and get help. That was six and a half years ago. Some vacation.

CONNIE: Cliff, you know I'd stay if it weren't for the job.

CLIFF: I know, darling. *(beat)* Maybe I'll see you on TV.

CONNIE: I sure hope so, Cliff. *(They embrace. Then CONNIE and FRED leave. CLIFF watches them.)*

JIMBO: The sooner you start the sooner you can leave. That's just common sense.

(CLIFF takes off his shirt and puts on the work shirt that FRED brought out. It fits perfectly, and has CLIFF's name over the pocket. CLIFF opens the door to the garage and steps into the white light. Blackout.)

THE END

Try This

Write a scene in which two characters on a journey are interrupted, stopped, stranded, or forced to detour.

Sybil Rosen

Duet For Bear and Dog

For David

CHARACTERS

Woman
Man
Bear
Dog
She

Empty stage. A stepladder can serve as a tree. WOMAN and MAN enter.

WOMAN: *(Two-way radio noises.)* 203, this is 364. What's your 20?
MAN: 209 north above Kerhonkson. What you got?
WOMAN: Bear up a tree on Main Street in Woodstock.
MAN: I'm on my way. How'd it get there?
WOMAN: Would you believe, a little rat dog?

(They exit. DOG chases BEAR onstage. She goes up a ladder.)

BEAR: Oh, shit.
DOG: *(Triumphant.)* Aha! I'm a dog! I'm a dog! *(Pisses on tree.)* Take that, you rottweilers, you shepherds, you labradors! Up yours, you pachyderms and raptors and primates! You can cut off my balls, but I'm still a man! I'm a dog!
BEAR: Ah, the call of the wild. Are you finished?
DOG: *(Over.)* Cousin to the wolf, brother to the jackal, helpmate of the homo sapien—!
BEAR: Oh my God.
DOG: I'm a dog. And you—are mine!
BEAR: You're nuts! *(She growls, takes bluff swipe at him.)* I never ate a dog before, but there's always a first time. I had a pig once. It was a bad year. I'm not scared of you.
DOG: Then what are you doing up a tree?
BEAR: It's called instinct. You wouldn't know about that.
DOG: Very funny. What I lack in instinct, I make up for in finesse. They're coming for you.
BEAR: *(Panicked.)* Who? Who's they?
DOG: I don't know. Some guys got called.
BEAR: Who called them?

DOG: The one I belong to. Who belongs to me. *(Sings.)* "Fish gotta swim, birds gotta fly, I gotta love one man till I die—" She does nails. And facials.

BEAR: That explains the ribbon. *(Laughs as DOG rips ribbon from head.)* You guys have a curious thing with these humans. I bet you have a name.

DOG: *(A sore point.)* What's it to you?

BEAR: I knew it. Look, I got lost. I took a wrong turn. Just let me get down. Who knows what they'll do to me?

DOG: I don't know. Put you in a zoo maybe. *(Finds this hilarious.)*

BEAR: Don't laugh! I have a cousin that was captured by these circus people. Last thing I heard he's walking a tightrope and wearing a tutu.

DOG: You got what you deserve—plundering those garbage cans, sucking up to Dumpsters.

BEAR: Oh? I've seen your handiwork. You and your kind. You're not above delving into garbage.

DOG: I don't do garbage. I'm a lapdog. I get cashews by hand.

BEAR: *(Hungry.)* Cashews?

DOG: Yeah. And chocolates. Potato chips. Raspberries even.

BEAR: Raspberries?

DOG: I'm highly evolved.

BEAR: The little red ones? The nubbly kind you roll around on your tongue?

DOG: Whatever.

BEAR: *(Swoons.)* I love those. It was a dry year for raspberries. Blueberries too. That's why I had to go to Dumpsters. Did you ever eat a diaper?

DOG: What do I look like?

BEAR: Oh, spare me. You guys are notorious shiteaters. Me, I'm basically a herbivore.

DOG: What about the pig?

BEAR: Like I said, it was a bad year. Okay, I admit I'm not above a fish or two. When they're running. How about you? You like fish?

DOG: *(Shrugs.)* Only to roll on. *(Looks around, sees something, growls at BEAR.)*

BEAR: Hey! Quit that! What's the big idea?

DOG: *(Growling.)* She's coming, I gotta make it look good. Could be some cashews in it. *(Growls more.)*

(SHE speaks with a thick Russian accent.)

SHE: Good boy, Boris.

BEAR: Boris?

DOG: Shit!

SHE: Keep up there. They come soon. Good boy, Boris.

BEAR: *(Mocking.)* Good boy, Boris!

DOG: *(To BEAR.)* Shut up!

SHE: My God, that is a big bear! Look at that behind. Is big as Kremlin.

BEAR: I take that as a compliment. And this is just August. I have to put on fifty more pounds before I den and birth my babies.

SHE: Would look good, lying on floor in den, yes?

BEAR: No.

DOG: There's a thought.

BEAR: Shut up, Boris!

SHE: In Russia, we have bears. Brown bears. They drink vodka and come down chimney at Christmas time.

(MAN and WOMAN enter.)

BEAR: Oh God, they're here.

WOMAN: There it is.

MAN: Jesus. Nice bear.

WOMAN: What do you think? One hundred fifty pounds?

MAN: Easy.

SHE: You come for bear?

MAN: Yes ma'am. Garth McGowan. Department of Environmental Conservation. You the woman that called?

(WOMAN walks around ladder, checking out BEAR.)

SHE: Yes.

MAN: That the dog?

SHE: That is Boris.

BEAR: *(To WOMAN.)* What are you looking at?

MAN: What happened?

SHE: I am in shop, making motion circles on face of customer. With cucumber facial. I make myself. And I am telling how I leave in Russia bad husband and mother of rotten heart—

MAN: Ma'am? Excuse me, we—

SHE: Wait! I tell you. So Boris is barking. Yip, yip, yip, yip, yip.

DOG: That's not how I sound.

MAN: *(Appreciatively.)* Damn dog.

WOMAN: I'll get the equipment. *(Exits.)*

SHE: I look. Oh my God. Staring in window—is bear. Standing on legs, with paws on window. Like this. *(Demonstrates.)* First I think is bad husband from Russia, come to finish me. I am shaking in booty—

MAN: These are brown bears, ma'am. They're very docile.

SHE: What means docile?

MAN: Gentle, timid, shy.

(WOMAN returns.)

SHE: I should marry one. You are married?

MAN: Yes ma'am.

SHE: Why do I know that?

WOMAN: *(To MAN.)* Let's go, let's go—

MAN: Ma'am—

SHE: Let me finish story. Please. I jump. *(Demonstrates.)* Bear jumps. *(Demonstrates.)* I go to close door. Out goes Boris. Yip, yip, yip, yip, yip. Bear goes up tree. I make phone call. Customer gives big tip. End of story.

MAN: Got it.

SHE: What you do now?

MAN: First we'll dart the bear. Tranquilize it. Then when it's on the ground, we'll take some data, pull a tooth—

SHE and BEAR: A tooth?

MAN: Yes ma'am. That's how we age them.

BEAR: Ouch.

MAN: Then we'll give it some ear tags, put it in the trap we brought, take it to the mountains, and let it go.

SHE and BEAR and DOG: *(Surprised.)* Oh. That sounds nice.

MAN: Yes ma'am. It'll be a lot happier up there. So if you'll just stand back—You can call your dog off now.

DOG: *(To MAN.)* Wait a second. You don't get it.

SHE: Here, Boris.

DOG: Jeez. I treed that bear.

SHE: Boris. Come, Boris. Come to Momma.

DOG: *(Moping over.)* Times like this I wish I was a dingo.

SHE: *Sit.*

DOG: Shit. *(Sits.)*

BEAR: It's your own fault. You gave in. For the easy bone and winter hearth. For the soft bed and the cashews.

DOG: We didn't give in! It wasn't like that at all. Hell, it was our idea, we thought of it. They had scraps, for God's sake. These human beings. Just laying around. They couldn't eat everything. You know how big a mastodon is? It seemed like a good idea. It *was* a good idea. It still is. I could do without the ribbon.

BEAR: You call that evolutionary? I call it quits. Adaptation? Please. Let's not mince words. You capitulated. You should have been out there with us. In the Pleistocene. Working out the kinks of hibernation. Fine tuning the fecal plug. Learning how to give birth in our sleep.

DOG: So sue me.

(Bam! WOMAN fires the dartgun. MAN sets a stopwatch. BEAR starts. DOG barks.)

WOMAN: Bulls-eye.
MAN: Good shot.
WOMAN: Are you timing?
MAN: *(Nods.)* I give it sixty seconds max.
SHE: Boris. Stop. What is wrong?
BEAR: *(Beginning to slow down.)* What do you know? I have a dart in my
    ass.
SHE: What happen now?
MAN: It'll come down. Watch.

(BEAR begins to get very loose and woozy. Her tongue goes in and out.)

BEAR: I hear bees. Back and forth between nectar and hive. Follow the buzz
    to the succulent grubs, socked away in the waxy comb, swimming in
    sweet honey. Rip the hive, the paper breaks like an egg. Bees zing
    around my head. Sting my nose. I don't feel them. I don't feel any-
    thing. Roll the grubs on my tongue. Stinging berries dipped in
    sugar—

(She falls slowly down ladder to the ground.)

WOMAN: Bingo.
MAN: *(Stopping watch.)* Fifty-two seconds.

(They go to BEAR. SHE and DOG go too. DOG sniffs at BEAR.)

SHE: Is hurt?
WOMAN: No. It makes a big boom, but they're very limber. They have a lot
    of fat to cushion them.
SHE: It and me both. Is sleeping?
WOMAN: Not exactly. More like immobilized. Now if you could just step
    back, ma'am, until we're finished—
SHE: It will wake?
WOMAN: No. We just want to move as quietly as we can around the bear. If
    you could back up ten feet. When we're done, you'll have a chance to
    touch it. If you want. And the dog too, ma'am, please.
SHE: Boris. Come.
DOG: Smells like a dream I had once. One of those where your paws gallop
    and your jowls blow. *(Demonstrates.)* Wish I could remember what I
    was dreaming about. Something about savannahs, and a fire, and
    bones, big as a house.

SHE: *(Sharp.)* Boris! *(Then quietly.)* Boris. Come.

(DOG and SHE go to one side.)

WOMAN: It's a female.
MAN: Wonder if she's pregnant.
WOMAN: Hang on, honey. We're taking you home.

(All freeze except BEAR.)

BEAR: I follow the north side of the mountain, where the sun neither rises nor sets. Under two silver birches, below the sheltering rock, I squeeze myself into crevices an otter couldn't fill. My breath heats the den, steam rises from my fur, making weather under the earth. I sleep the long sleep, in a cradle of soil. And dream of babies, pushing out of me, cubs small as kittens, fat as flesh, eyes awake. They know the continent of my body. They find their way in the dark, to force their mouths upon me, and suck and purr and thrive. Until the unseen days lengthen and the wild crocus pushes through the snow. Then I awaken, newborn and ageless, and take my young into the still white world.

END

Try This

Take a realistic scene you have written and stylize it with a major reversal of some kind: children are played by adult actors, men are played by women, the characters are animals, or something similar. What happens?

José Rivera
GAS

For Juan Carlos Rivera

CAST
Cheo

TIME: Start of the ground offensive of the Persian Gulf War.

PLACE: A gas station.

(A car at a gas station. CHEO stands next to the pump about to fill his car with gas. He is a working-class Latino. Before he pumps gas he speaks to the audience.)

CHEO: His letters were coming once a week. I could feel his fear. It was in his handwriting. He sat in a tank. In the middle of the Saudi Arabian desert. Wrote six, seven, eight hours a day. These brilliant letters of fear. This big Puerto Rican guy! What the fuck's he doing out there? What the fucking hell sense that make? He's out there, in the Saudi sand, writing letters to me about how he's gonna die from an Iraqi fucking missile. And he's got all this time on his hands to think about his own death. And there's nothing to do 'cause of these restrictions on him. No women, no magazines, 'cause the Saudis are afraid of the revolutionary effects of ads for women's lingerie on the population! Allah would have a cow! There's nothing he's allowed to eat even remotely reminds him of home. Nothing but the fucking time to sit and think about what it's gonna be like to have some fucking towel-head—as he calls them—run a bayonet clean through his guts. He's sitting in the tank playing target practice with the fucking camels. Shooting at the wind. The sand in all the food. Sand in his dreaming. He and his buddies got a camel one day. They shaved that mother-fucker clean! Completely shaved its ass! Then they spray-painted the name of their company, in bright American spray-paint, on the side of the camel, and sent it on its way! Scorpion fights in the tents! All those scenes from fucking *Apocalypse Now* in his head. Fucking Mar-lon Brando decapitating that guy and Martin Sheen going fucking nuts. That's what fills my brother's daily dreams as he sits out there in the desert contemplating his own death. The Vietnam Syndrome those people are trying to eradicate. His early letters were all about that. A chronicle. His way of laying it all down, saying it all for me, so I would know what his last days, and months, and seconds were like. So when he got offed by an Iraqi missile, I would at least know what it was like to be in his soul, if just for a little while. He couldn't write to save his life at first. Spelled everything totally, unbelievably wrong. "Enough": e-n-u-f. "Thought": t-h-o-t. "Any": e-n-y. But with time, he started to write beautifully. This angel started to come out of the desert. This singing angel of words. Thoughts I honestly never knew he had. Confessions. Ideas. We started to make plans. We start to be in sync for the first time since I stopped telling him I loved him. I used to kick his fucking ass! It wasn't hard or nothing. That's not bragging, just me telling you a simple truth. He was always sick. Always the first to cry. He played drums in a parade back home. He couldn't even play the fucking instrument, he was so uncoordinated.

Spastic. But they let him march in the parade anyway—without drumsticks. He was the last guy in the parade, out of step, banging make-believe drumsticks, phantom rhythms on this snare drum—playing air drum for thousands of confused spectators! Then he got into uniforms and the scouts. But I knew that bullshit was just a cover anyway. He didn't mean it. Though after he joined the army and was in boot camp, he took particular delight in coming home and demonstrating the fifty neat new ways he learned to kill a guy. One day he forgot he weighed twice my weight and nearly snapped my spine like a fucking cucumber! I thought, in agony, "where's my bro? Where's that peckerhead I used to kick around? The first one to cry when he saw something beautiful. The first one to say 'I love that' or 'I love Mom' or 'I love you.'" He never got embarrassed by that, even after I got too old to deal with my fucking little brother kissing me in front of other people. Even later, he always, always, always ended every conversation with, "I love you bro," and I couldn't say, "I love you" back, 'cause I was too hip to do that shit. But he got deeper in it. The war thing. He wrote to say I'd never understand. He's fighting for my right to say whatever I want. To disagree. And I just fucking love how they tell you on the news the fucking temperature in Riyadh, Saudi Arabia! Like I fucking care! And a couple of times the son-of-a-bitch called me collect from Saudi! *I said collect!* And I told him if Saddam Hussein didn't kill him, I would! He told me about troubles with his wife back home. He'd just gotten married a month before shipping out. He didn't really know her and was wondering if she still loved him. My brother always loved ugly women. It was a thing with him. Low self-esteem or something. Like he couldn't love himself and didn't understand a woman that would. So he sought out the absolute losers of the planet: trucker whores with prison records who liked to tie him up and whip him, stuff like that. I honestly have trouble contemplating my little brother being whipped by some trucker whore in leather. Love! He didn't know another way. Then he met a girl who on their first date confessed she hated spiks—so my brother married her! This racist looked him in the eye, disrespected his whole race to his face, and my brother says, "I do." Last night somebody got on TV to say we shouldn't come down on rich people 'cause rich people are a minority too, and coming down on them was a form of racism! And I thought, they're fucking afraid of class warfare, and they should be! And the news showed some little white punk putting up flags all over this dipshit town in California and this little twirp's story absorbed twenty minutes of the news—this little, blond Nazi kid with a smile full of teeth—and the protests got shit. And this billboard went up in

my town showing Stalin, Hitler, and Hussein, saying we stopped him
twice before we have to stop him again! This billboard was put up by
a local newspaper! The music, the computer graphics, the generals
coming out of retirement to become media stars, public hard ons. And
we gotta fight NAKED AGGRESSION—like his asshole president
should come *to my fucking neighborhood* if he wants to see naked
aggression! I never thought the ideas in the head of some politician
would mean the death of my brother and absolutely kill my mother.
I'm telling you, that woman will not survive the death of my brother
no matter how much she believes in God, no matter how much praying she does. But I keep that from him. I write back about how it's not
going to be another Vietnam. It's not going to be a whole country that
spits on you when you come back. That we don't forget the ones we
love and fight for us. Then his letters stopped. I combed the newspapers trying to figure out what's going on over there, 'cause his letters
said nothing about where he was. He wasn't allowed to talk about
locations, or troop size, or movement, 'cause, like, I was going to personally transmit this information to the Iraqi fucking Ministry of
Defense! I thought about technology. The new shit Iraq has that was
made in the United States, shit that could penetrate a tank's armour
and literally travel through the guts of a tank, immolating every living
human soul inside, turning human Puerto Rican flesh into hot screaming soup, the molecules of my brother's soul mixing with the metal
molecules of the iron coffin he loved so much. I couldn't sleep. My
mother was suicidal. Why wasn't he writing? The air war's continuing.
They're bombing the shit out of that motherfucking country! And I
find myself ashamed. I think, "yeah, bomb it more. Level it. Send it
back to the Stone Age. Make it so every last elite Republican Guard is
dead. So my brother won't get killed." For the first time in my life, I
want a lot of people I don't hate to die 'cause I know one of them
could kill the man I love most in this fucked up world. If my brother is
killed, I will personally take a gun and blow out the brains of George
Herbert Walker Bush. And I'm sick. I'm sick of rooting for the bombs.
Sick of loving every day the air war continues. Sick of every air strike,
every sortie. And being happy another Iraqi tank got taken out and
melted, another Iraqi bunker was bombed, another bridge can't bring
ammunition, can't deliver that one magic bullet that will incapacitate
my brother, bring him back a vegetable, bring him back dead in his
soul, or blinded, or butchered in some Iraqi concentration camp. That
the Iraqi motherfucker that would torture him won't live now 'cause
our smart bombs have killed that towelhead motherfucker in his sleep!
They actually got me wanting this war to be bloody!

(Beat.)

Last night the ground war started. It started. The tanks are rolling. I find my gut empty now. I don't have thoughts. I don't have dreams. My mother is a shell. She has deserted herself and left behind a blathering cadaver, this pathetic creature with rosary beads in her hands looking up to Christ, and CNN, saying words like "Scud," "strategic interests," "collateral damage," "target rich environment"—words this woman from a little town in Puerto Rico has no right to know. So I fight my demons. I think of the cause. Blood for oil. I NEED MY CAR, DON'T I? I NEED MY CAR TO GET TO WORK SO I CAN PAY THE RENT AND NOT END UP A HOMELESS PERSON! DON'T I HAVE A RIGHT TO MY CAR AND MY GAS? AND WHAT ABOUT FREEING DEMOCRATIC KUWAIT?!

(Beat.)

So I wait for a sign, anything, a prayer, any sign. I'll take it. Just tell me he's okay. Tell me my brother's gonna kill well and make it through this alive. He's gonna come home and he's gonna come home the same person he left; the spastic one who couldn't spell . . . the one who couldn't play the drums.

(*CHEO starts to pump gas. As he pumps the gas, he notices something horrifying. He pulls the nozzle out of the car. Blood comes out of the gas pump. CHEO stares and stares at the bloody trickle coming out of the gas pump.*)

BLACKOUT

Try This

Write a monologue in which a physical object or action functions as a symbolic comment on the words.

Lanford Wilson

Eukiah

CHARACTERS
Butch
Eukian

TIME: The Present

SETTING: An abandoned private airplane hangar.

A dark empty stage represents a long abandoned private airplane hangar. The space is vast and almost entirely dark. A streak of light from a crack in the roof stripes the floor.

Butch walks into the light. He is a young powerful, charming man; everybody's best friend. He is also menacing. Nothing he says is introspective. Everything is for a purpose. During the indicated beats of silence he listens; for Eukiah to answer, for the sound of breathing, for the least indication of where Eukiah is. The play is a seduction.

Voices have a slight echo in here.

BUTCH: Eukiah? *(Beat.)* Eukiah? *(Beat.)* Barry saw you run in here, so I know you're here. You're doin' it again, Eukiah, you're jumping to these weird conclusions you jump to just like some half-wit. You don't wanna be called a half-wit, you gotta stop actin' like a half-wit, don't ya? You're getting' to where nobody can joke around you, ya know that? What kind of fun is a person like that to be around, huh? One you can't joke around? We talked about that before, remember? (Beat.) Eukiah? What're you thinkin'? You thinkin' you heard Barry say something, you thought he meant it, didn't you? What did you think you heard? Huh? What'd you think he meant? Eukiah? *(Beat.)* You're gonna have to talk to me, I can't talk to myself here. *(Beat.)* Have you ever known me to lie to you? Eukiah? Have you ever known that? *(Pause. He might walk around some.)* Okay. Boy, this old hangar sure seen better days, hasn't it? Just like everything else on this place, huh? Been pretty much a losing proposition since I've known it, though. Probably you too, hasn't it? Hell, I don't think they have the wherewithal anymore, give even one of those ol' barns a swab a paint. You think? Might paint 'em pink, whattaya think? Or candy stripes. Red and white. Peppermint. You'd like that. *(Beat.)*

This'll remind you of old Mac's heyday, though, won't it? Private airplane hangar. Talk about echoes, this is an echo of the past, huh? Ol' Mac had some winners, I guess, about twenty years ago. That must have been the life, huh? Private planes, keep 'em in your private hangar. You got your luncheons with the dukes and duchesses. Winner's Circle damn near every race. If they wasn't raised by Ol' Mac or their sire or dam one wasn't raised by Ol' Mac, I don't imagine anybody'd bother to bet on 'em, do you? Boy that's all gone, huh? Planes and limos and all, dukes and duchesses—good lookin' horses, though. Damn shame we can't enter 'em in a beauty contest somewhere. I know, you're attached to 'em, but I'll tell you they make damn expensive pets.

What was you? Out by the paddock when Barry was talkin' to me? You think you overheard something, is that it? What do you think you heard? You want to talk about it? I know you'd rather talk to me than talk to Barry, huh? Eukiah? *(Pause.)* Is this where you come? When you run off all temperamental and sulking? Pretty nasty old place to play in. Echoes good though. Gotta keep awful quiet if you're trying to be secret like you always do in a place like this.

Why do you do that? You got any idea? I'm serious, now. Run off like that. They're waitin' supper on you, I guess you know. You know how happy they're gonna be about it, too. *(Beat.)* Eukiah? What was it you think you heard, honey? What? Was it about horses? 'Cause I thought I told you never trust anything anybody says if it's about horses.

EUKIAH: *(Still unseen.)* I heard what Barry said. You said you *would*, too.

BUTCH: *(Relaxes some, smiles.)* Where the dickens have you got to? There's so much echo in here I can't tell where you are. You back in those oil drums? You haven't crawled up in the rafters have you? Watch yourself. We don't want you getting' hurt. I don't think those horses would eat their oats at all, anybody gave 'em to 'em 'cept you. I think they'd flat out go on strike. Don't you figure?

EUKIAH: They wouldn't drink, you couldn't get 'em to.

BUTCH: Don't I know it. Pot-A-Gold, for sure. You're the only one to get him to do anything. I think he'd just dehydrate. He'd blow away, you wasn't leadin' him. We could lead him to water but we couldn't make him to drink, isn't that right? *(Beat.)* What are you hiding about? Nobody's gonna hurt you. Don't I always take up for you? You get the weirdest ideas. What do you think you heard Barry say?

EUKIAH: He's gonna burn the horses.

BUTCH: What? Oh, man. You are just crazy sometimes, these things you dream up. Who is? Barry? What wold he wanna do something crazy like that for?

EUKIAH: I heard you talkin'.

BUTCH: Can you answer me that? Why would he even dream of doin' something like that?

EUKIAH: For the insurance.

BUTCH: No, Eukiah. Just come on to supper, now, I got a date tonight, I can't mess around with you anymore. You really are a half-wit. I'm sorry, but if you think Barry'd do something like that, I'm sorry, that's just flat out half-witted thinkin'. It's not even funny. The way you talk, you yak all day to anybody around, no idea what you're saying half the time; anybody heard something like that there wouldn't be no work for me or you or anybody else around here, 'cause they just lock us all up.

EUKIAH: You said you would.

BUTCH: *I* would? I would what?

EUKIAH: You said it was about time somebody did somethin'.

BUTCH: Eukiah, come out here. I can see you over by that old buggy, my eyes got used to the dark. There ain't no sense in hiding anymore. *(Beat.)* Come on out, damnit, so we can go to supper. I'm not going to play with you anymore. Come on. Well, just answer me one thing. How's burnin' 'em up gonna be any better than maybe splittin' a hoof or somethin' like that? Come on, crazy. The least little thing happens to make a horse not run, it's the same as if he had to be destroyed, you ought to know that. *(Eukiah is just visible now. He is maybe sixteen years old. He is slow and soft; he has the mentality of an eight-year-old.)*

EUKIAH: Yeah, but they already took Pot-A-Gold and Flashy and that gray one, the speckled one, off. They already sold 'em.

BUTCH: Which one do you call Flashy, you mean Go Carmen? The filly? And Old Ironside? Why would they do that?

EUKIAH: 'Cause they're the best ones. Then they put three no good horses in their stalls, so nobody would know. And they're gonna burn 'em and nobody can tell they ain't the horses they're supposed to be, Butchy.

BUTCH: Nobody could run Pot-A-Gold somewhere else, Euky. You know those numbers they tattoo in his mouth? That's gonna identify him no matter where he goes, anybody'll know that's Pot-A-Gold.

EUKIAH: Some other country. They wouldn't care.

BUTCH: Anywhere on earth…

EUKIAH: They got some plan where it'll work, 'cause I heard 'em.

BUTCH: I don't know what you think you heard, but you're really acting half-witted here.

EUKIAH: Don't call me—

BUTCH: Well, I'm sorry, but what would you call it? A person can't burn down a barn full of horses, Euky. What a horrible thing to think. No wonder you get scared, you scare yourself thinking things like that. Those horses are valued, hell I don't even know, millions of dollars probably. Insurance inspectors come around, they take a place apart. You tell me, how would somebody get away with a trick like that?

EUKIAH: What was you talkin' about then?

BUTCH: I don't even know. Where it was you heard what you thought you heard. You're too fast for me. You'll have to go into supper and ask Mac what Barry was talking about, won't you? Would that make you feel better? Instead of jumpin' to your weird conclusions. Now, can you get that out of your head? Huh? So we can go eat and I can take a bath and go on my date? Is that all right with you? Then I'll come back and tell you all about it. Got a date with Mary, you'd like to hear about that, wouldn't you?

(Eukiah begins to grin.)

BUTCH: Yes? That's okay with you, is it?

EUKIAH: I guess. *(He moves into the light, closer to Butch.)*

BUTCH: You guess. You're just going to have to trust me, Eukiah, nobody needs money that bad. Not even on this place. I don't even think nobody could get away tryin' to pull something like that.

(He puts his arm around Eukiah's neck and they start to move off, but Butch has Eukiah in a head lock. He speaks with the strain of exertion.)

BUTCH: Not unless there was some half-wit on the place that got his neck broke being kicked in the head and got burned up in the fire.

(Eukiah goes to his knees. Butch bears down on his neck; it breaks with a dull snap. He lets Eukiah slump to the floor. Butch is breathing hard, standing over Eukiah's body.)

BUTCH: I thought I told you. Never trust anything anybody says if it's about horses.

END

Try This

Villains are most effective when they are also charming, convincing, touching, or otherwise not being villainous. Write a speech for an unsympathetic character that makes us for the moment sympathetic.

David Ives
The Philadelphia

This play is for Greg Pliska, who knows what a Philadelphia can be.

CHARACTERS

Al: California cool; 20s or 30s
MARK: frazzled; 20s or 30s
WAITRESS: weary; as you will

SETTING

A bar/restaurant. A table, red-checkered cloth, two chairs, and a specials board.

AL is at the restaurant, with the WAITRESS.

WAITRESS: Can I help you?

AL: Do you know you would look fantastic on a wide screen?

WAITRESS: Uh-huh.

AL: Seventy millimeters.

WAITRESS: Look. Do you want to see a menu, or what?

AL: Let's negotiate, here. What's the soup du jour today?

WAITRESS: Soup of the day you got a choice of Polish duck blood or cream of kidney.

AL: Beautiful. Beautiful! Kick me in a kidney.

WAITRESS: *(Writes it down.)* You got it.

AL: Any oyster crackers on your seabed?

WAITRESS: Nope. All out.

AL: How about the specials today, spread out your options.

WAITRESS: You got your deep fried gizzards.

AL: Fabulous.

WAITRESS: Calves' brains with okra.

AL: You are a *temptress*.

WAITRESS: And pickled pigs' feet.

AL: Pigs' feet, *I love it*. Put me down for a quadruped.

WAITRESS: If you say so.

AL: Any sprouts to go on those feet?

WAITRESS: Iceberg.

AL: So be it. *(Waitress exits, as MARK enters, looking shaken and bedraggled.)*

MARK: Al!

AL: Hey there, Marcus. What's up?

MARK: Jesus!

AL: What's going on, buddy?

MARK: Oh man...!

AL: What's the matter? Sit down.

MARK: I don't get it, Al. I don't understand it.

AL: You want something? Want a drink? I'll call the waitress—

MARK: *(Desperate.)* No! No! Don't even try. *(Gets a breath.)* I don't know what's going on today, Al. It's really weird.

AL: What, like . . . ?

MARK: Right from the time I got up.

AL: What is it? What's the story?

MARK: Well—just for an example. This morning I stopped off at a drugstore to buy some aspirin. This is at a big drugstore, right?

AL: Yeah . . .

MARK: I go up to the counter, the guy says what can I do for you, I say, Give me a bottle of aspirin. The guy gives me this funny look and he says, "Oh we don't have *that*, sir." I said to him, You're a drugstore and you don't have any aspirin?

AL: Did they have Bufferin?

MARK: Yeah!

AL: Advil?

MARK: Yeah!

AL: Extra-strength Tylenol?

MARK: Yeah!

AL: But no aspirin.

MARK: No!

AL: Wow . . .

MARK: And that's the kind of weird thing that's been happening all day. It's like, I go to a newsstand to buy the *Daily News*, the guy never even *heard* of it.

AL: Could've been a misunderstanding.

MARK: I asked everyplace—*nobody* had the *News*! I had to read the *Toronto Hairdresser*. Or this. I go into a deli at lunch time to buy a sandwich, the guys tells me they don't have any *pastrami*. How can they be a deli if they don't have pastrami?

AL: Was this a Korean deli?

MARK: This was a kosher from *Jerusalem* deli. "Oh we don't carry *that*, sir," he says to me. "Have some tongue."

AL: Mmm.

MARK: I just got into a cab, the guy says he doesn't go to 56th Street! He offers to take me to Newark instead!

AL: Mm-hm.

MARK: Looking at me like I'm an alien or something!

AL: Mark. Settle down.

MARK: "Oh I don't go *there*, sir."

AL: Settle down. Take a breath.

MARK: Do you know what this is?

AL: Sure.

MARK: What is it? What's happening to me?

AL: Don't panic. You're in a Philadelphia.

MARK: I'm in a what?

AL: You're in a Philadelphia. That's all.

MARK: But I'm in—

AL: Yes, physically you are in New York. But *meta*physically you are in a Philadelphia.

MARK: I've never heard of this!

AL: You see, inside of what we know as reality there are these pockets, these black holes called Philadelphias. If you fall into one, you run up against exactly the kinda shit that's been happening to you all day.

MARK: Why?

AL: Because in a Philadelphia, no matter what you ask for, you can't get it. You ask for something, they're not gonna have it. You want to do something, it ain't gonna get done. You want to go somewhere, you can't get there from here.

MARK: Good God. So this is very serious.

AL: Just remember, Marcus. This is a condition named for the town that invented the *cheese steak*. Something that nobody in his right mind would willingly ask for.

MARK: And I thought I was just having a very bad day . . .

AL: Sure. Millions of people have spent entire lifetimes inside a Philadelphia and never even knew it. Look at the city of Philadelphia itself. Hopelessly trapped forever inside a Philadelphia. And do they know it?

MARK: Well what can I do? Should I just kill myself now and get it over with?

AL: You try to kill yourself in a Philadelphia, you're only gonna get hurt, babe.

MARK: So what do I do?

AL: Best thing you can do is wait it out. Someday the great cosmic train will whisk you outa the City of Brotherly Love and off to someplace happier.

MARK: *You're* pretty goddamn mellow today.

AL: Yeah well. Everybody has to be someplace. *(WAITRESS enters.)*

WAITRESS: Is your name Allen Chase?

AL: It is indeed.

WAITRESS: There was a phone call for you. Your boss?

AL: Okay.

WAITRESS: He says you're fired.

AL: Cool! Thanks. *(WAITRESS exits.)* So anyway, you have this problem . . .

MARK: Did she just say you got *fired?*

AL: Yeah. I wonder what happened to my pigs' feet . . .

MARK: Al—!? You *loved* your job!

AL: Hey. No sweat.

MARK: How can you be so calm?

AL: Easy. You're in a Philadelphia? *I* woke up in a Los Angeles. And life is beautiful! You know Susie packed up and left me this morning.

MARK: Susie left you?

AL: And frankly, Scarlett, I don't give a shit. I say, go and God bless and may your dating pool be Olympic-sized.

MARK: But your job? The garment district is your life!

AL: So I'll turn it into a movie script and sell it to Paramount. Toss in some sex, add a little emotional blah-blah-*blah*, pitch it to Jack and Dusty, you got a buddy movie with a garment background. Not relevant enough? We'll throw in the hole in the ozone, make it E.C.

MARK: E.C.?

AL: Environmentally correct. Have you heard about this hole in the ozone?

MARK: Sure.

AL: Marcus, I *love* this concept. I *embrace* this ozone. Sure, some people are gonna get hurt in the process, meantime everybody else'll tan a little faster.

MARK: *(Quiet horror.)* So this is a Los Angeles . . .

AL: Well. Everybody has to be someplace.

MARK: Wow.

AL: You want my advice? *Enjoy your Philadelphia.* Sit back and order yourself a beer and a burger and chill out for a while.

MARK: But I can't order anything. Life is great for you out there on your cosmic beach, but whatever *I* ask for, I'll get a cheese steak or something.

AL: No. There's a very simple rule of thumb in a Philadelphia. *Ask for the opposite.*

MARK: What?

AL: If you can't get what you ask for, ask for the opposite and you'll get what you want. You want the *Daily News*, ask for the *Times*. You want pastrami, ask for tongue.

MARK: Oh.

AL: Works great with women. What is more opposite than the opposite sex?

MARK: Uh-huh.

AL: So. Would you like a Bud?

MARK: I sure could use a—

AL: No. Stop. *(Very deliberately.) Do you want . . . a Bud?*

MARK: *(Also deliberately.)* No. I *don't* want a Bud. *(WAITRESS enters and goes to the specials board.)*

AL: Good. Now there's the waitress. Order yourself a Bud and a burger. But do not *ask* for a Bud and a burger.

MARK: Waitress!

AL: Don't call her. She won't come.

MARK: Oh.

AL: You're in a Philadelphia, so just figure, fuck her.

MARK: Fuck *her.*

AL: You don't need that waitress.

MARK: *Fuck* that waitress.

AL: And everything to do with her.

MARK: *Hey waitress! FUCK YOU!* (*WAITRESS turns to him.)*

WAITRESS: Can I help you, sir?

AL: *That's* how you get service in a Philadelphia.

WAITRESS: Can I help you?

MARK: Uh—no thanks.

WAITRESS: Okay, what'll you have? *(Takes out her pad.)*

AL: Excellent.

MARK: Well—how about some O.J.

WAITRESS: Sorry. Squeezer's broken.

MARK: A glass of milk?

WAITRESS: Cow's dry.

MARK: Egg nog?

WAITRESS: Just ran out.

MARK: Cuppa coffee?

WAITRESS: Oh we don't have *that*, sir. *(MARK and AL exchange a look, and nod. The WAITRESS has spoken the magic words.)*

MARK: Got any ale?

WAITRESS: Nope.

MARK: Stout?

WAITRESS: Nope.

MARK: Porter?

WAITRESS: Just beer.

MARK: That's too bad. How about a Heineken?

WAITRESS: Heineken? Try again.

MARK: Rolling Rock?

WAITRESS: 'Outa stock.

MARK: Schlitz?

WAITRESS: Nix.

MARK: Beck's?

WAITRESS: Next.

MARK: Sapporo?

WAITRESS: Tomorrow.

MARK: Lone Star?

WAITRESS: Hardy-har.

MARK: Bud Lite?

WAITRESS: Just plain Bud is all we got.

MARK: No thanks.

WAITRESS: *(Calls.) Gimme a Bud! (To MARK.)* Anything to eat?

MARK: Nope.

WAITRESS: Name it.

MARK: Pork chops.

WAITRESS: *(Writes down.)* Hamburger . . .

MARK: Medium.

WAITRESS: Well done . . .

MARK: Baked potato.

WAITRESS: Fries . . .

MARK: And some zucchini.

WAITRESS: Slice of raw. *(Exits, calling.)* Burn one!

AL: Marcus, that was excellent.

MARK: Thank you.

AL: *Excellent.* You sure you've never done this before?

MARK: I've spent so much of my life asking for the wrong thing without
knowing it, doing it on purpose comes easy.

AL: I hear you.

MARK: I could've saved myself a lot of trouble if I'd screwed up on purpose
all those years. Maybe I was in a Philadelphia all along and never
knew it!

AL: You might've been in a Baltimore. They're practically the same.
(WAITRESS enters, with a glass of beer and a plate.)

WAITRESS: Okay. Here's your Bud. *(Sets that in front of MARK.)* And one cheese steak. *(She sets that in front of AL, and starts to go.)*

AL: Excuse me. Hey. Wait a minute. What is that?

WAITRESS: It's a cheese steak.

AL: No. I ordered cream of kidney and two pairs of feet.

WAITRESS: Oh we don't have *that*, sir.

AL: I beg your pardon?

WAITRESS: We don't have that, sir. *(Small pause.)*

AL: (To MARK.) You son of a bitch! *I'm in your Philadelphia!*

MARK: I'm sorry, Al.

AL: You brought me into your fucking Philadelphia!

MARK: I didn't know it was contagious.

AL: Oh God, please don't let me be in a Philadelphia! Don't let me be in a—

MARK: Shouldn't you ask for the opposite? I mean, since you're in a Philad—

AL: Don't you tell *me* about life in a Philadelphia.

MARK: Maybe you're not really—

AL: I taught you everything you know about Philly, asshole. Don't tell *me* how to act in a Philadelphia!

MARK: But maybe you're not really in a Philadelphia!

AL: Do you see the cheese on that steak? What do I need for proof? The fucking *Liberty Bell*? Waitress, bring me a glass of water.

WAITRESS: Water? Don't have that, sir.

AL: *(To MARK.)* "We don't have *water*"—? What, you think we're in a sudden drought or something? *(Suddenly realizes.)* Holy shit, I just lost my job . . . ! Susie left me! I gotta make some phone calls! *(To WAITRESS.)* 'Scuse me, where's the pay phone?

WAITRESS: Sorry, we don't have a pay ph—

AL: Of *course* you don't have a pay phone, of *course* you don't! Oh shit, let me outa here! *(Exits.)*

MARK: I don't know. It's not that bad in a Philadelphia.

WAITRESS: Could be worse. I've been in a Cleveland all week.

MARK: A Cleveland. What's that like?

WAITRESS: It's like death, without the advantages.

MARK: Really. Care to stand?

WAITRESS: Don't mind if I do. *(She sits.)*

MARK: I hope you won't reveal your name.

WAITRESS: Sharon.

MARK: *(Holds out his hand.)* Good-bye.

WAITRESS: Hello. *(They shake.)*

MARK: *(Indicating the cheese steak.)* Want to starve?

WAITRESS: Thanks! *(She picks up the cheese steak and starts eating.)*

MARK: Yeah, everybody has to be someplace . . . *(Leans across the table with a smile.)* So.

BLACKOUT

Try This

The Greek and Roman method of comedy was to take an absurd idea and follow it very logically, very precisely and straight-faced to its conclusion. If you have a good, really absurd idea, write a ten-minute comedy. (This is a good place to brainstorm *what if . . . ?*)

Appendix A

Collaborative Exercises

The artistic process—in the visual, plastic, musical, and theatrical arts, but also in literature—is a sensual rather than a mental process. It's not a lot of help to a writer to say: *don't think so much*. But exercises that emphasize the sensual sources of the imagination can often help break down the habits of abstraction that stand in its way.

The exercises that follow come from theater, drawing, physical and psychological therapy, meditation, music, and dance. They sometimes involve writing, but all operate as prewriting prompts. Some are designed to break down linear training of the brain, some to foster a communal sense of the writing process, some to involve the body—eye, ear, limbs, and/or torso—or to introduce spatial or compositional elements into the inventive adventure. They are not a test of *anything*—neither artistic ability nor flexibility nor social skill. *Everybody* who takes part in them risks occasional embarrassment. Discussing when and why such embarrassment occurs is part of the learning process. Indeed, "debriefing" each exercise—discussing what happened, when this or that emotion occurred, whether it hindered or helped the imagination, how one element led to another—is an important part of the exercise.

The First Class
• This exercise can be done at the first class, before the book has been assigned or the roll taken. On a scrap of paper or a 3 × 5 card each student finishes the sentence "Writing is . . ." The instructor or a class member takes away the phrases, sorts them (at random or artfully), and prints them under the title "Writing is." Distribute and discuss the resulting poem at the next class. It is almost inevitable that the piece will:
  - be recognizable as a poem
  - demonstrate a "list" or "catalogue" poem
  - contain abstractions, images, and metaphors
  - contain some alliteration and assonance, and probably rhyme
  - involve some repetition
  - involve some paradox
  - reveal both the fears and the joys class members already experience as writers

Getting Started
These exercises can be used at the beginning of any or all classes:
• Stretch and center your body to improve concentration. Repeat each of these movements three times: Exhale as you let your head hang forward, inhale as you raise it. Look to the left as far as you comfortably can, then to the right. Let your head tilt to the left as far as you can, then to the right. With hands on your waist, bend to the left as far as you can, then to the right. Squat as far as you can, let your head and arms hang forward, then roll up from the hips and stretch your arms high overhead. Now sit and relax; be aware of your back against the chair back, your hips and thighs against the seat, your feet on the floor, your hands at rest. Let gravity center you. Take a deep breath.

- A word-at-a-time story. Someone start with a word. Go around the room, each person adding a word while someone writes them on the board. Keep going until you fill all available space. Use ordinary grammar but don't "write." Just let it flow. The word that comes naturally will be best—sometimes "the," "and," "it," and so forth. Discuss what happened. Where are the connections, repetitions, new directions in the flow of words? What possibilities does it suggest? *Is* it a story? Is there a story in it? A poem? A play? What emotions occurred as the exercise went on—amusement, disappointment, irritation, pleasure? This exercise helps you develop flexibility and flow, since the next word *will* occur to you each time, but it will usually not be the word next written, so you'll have to keep concentrating and adjusting.

- One form of brainstorming—or in Hollywood parlance *spitballing*—that you can play with in class or in a journal is *What if?*
  - What if you turned on all the faucets and Dr. Pepper came out?
  - What if Elvis showed up at the picnic?
  - What if ten-year-old Louise came home and announced she was through with school, and her folks said *great, yeah, ok, whatever?*
  - What if a character (a preacher, a drunk, a locked-out teenager) rents a motel room and finds a corpse in the bed?

And so forth. You can make this into a class game by each making up a *What if?* and putting them all on one sheet. (Somebody could take them home and email them to everybody else.) Then have everyone write a few paragraphs of a *What if* not his or her own.

Do it often. If you think your ideas turn out to be sleazy science fiction or romance, quiet the critic. You're not required to pursue any idea, and generating them will make your mind nimble.

1. Image

- As a group, walk around the periphery of the room at a comfortable pace, relaxing as you walk. Gently shake out your hands, arms, shoulders. When you are ready, start pointing at things and shouting out *the wrong names for them* as loud as you can. Keep doing this. It will be hard. Keep doing it. A bit longer. It may make you a little dizzy. Do it some more. Talk about the experience—what happened, how did it feel, how did it change? The goal of school at any level is largely to learn how to name things correctly, and this exercise may help break down that expectation of the classroom and so help free the imagination. A Leonard Cohen song has it, "There is a crack in everything. That's how the light gets through."

2. Voice

- After stretching and loosening up, inhale as you imagine your head filling up with air, with helium, becoming a balloon, getting larger and lighter, very large and light, pulling you toward the sky. Then exhale; imagine the balloon deflating, your head becoming smaller, collapsing, smaller and smaller, clenched in tight as a walnut. See if you can inflate and clench your head without affecting the muscles in the rest of your body. Relax. Do it twice more. Shake out your arms and body.

Now inhale to a comfortable depth, and as you exhale, pronounce the *long sound* of each vowel in turn: $\bar{A}$ (as in *play*), $\bar{E}$ (as in *wheel*), $\bar{I}$ (as in *file*), $\bar{O}$ (as in *go*), $\bar{U}$ (as in *cute*). Start on a very high-pitched note, and as you exhale lower the pitch until your voice is as deep as you can make it. Practice relaxing as you go deeper. Keep expelling breath on the long vowel sound for as long as you can.

Do the same exercise, but this time go around the circle, each person in turn announcing on the inhalation a one-syllable word to be said on the exhalation, first with $\bar{A}$, then with $\bar{E}$, and so forth. You might pronounce three words one after each other for each vowel—for example: *Day, Pale, Place,* then *Greet, Steal, Mean . . . While, My, Shine . . . Toe, Bold, Moan . . . Feud, Cure, Mute.*

Do the same with the short vowel sounds: ă (as in *cat*), ĕ (as in *bell*), ĭ (as in *hit*), ŏ (as in *frog*), ŭ (as in *sunk*), first pronouncing the vowels themselves on a descending pitch, then using each in words. Discuss the exercise. What happened? How difficult was it to come up with a word with the right vowel sound? Were some vowels more difficult than others?

Practice in class and/or in your journal coming up with words that fit each vowel sound. Make nonsense sentences with each vowel sound repeated:

> *They lay the mane on the pale gray whale.*
> *He meets and wheels the cream of creepy green deals.*
> > *. . . and so forth to the last short vowel sound . . .*
> *Up! jumps the funky bunch of ugly sunstruck grubs.*

• Have someone bring in a variety of short (nonvocal) musical passages. These should be spliced onto a tape or CD so that they play in succession, with the chance to pause in between. Play one passage, then have everyone write a line of dialogue the music suggests; another passage, pause to write, and so forth. Discuss what happened, what images arose in people's minds, how the music suggested emotions, attitudes and personalities. Play each piece of music again, pausing to read some of the lines of dialogue.

• Bring in a line of dialogue that you overheard this week. Write it both on a sheet of paper and on a 3 × 5 card. Pass the cards four places to the right. Now everyone has two lines of dialogue. Briefly describe the person who says each; mention at least one physical characteristic, one item of clothing, and one action. Write the dialogue between them. "Cast" the parts and read them in class.

3. Character
• Stretch, shake out, sit and relax, centering yourself. Close your eyes. The instructor or someone else designated to do so will gently prompt you to visualize a scene in which you come upon a character. The important thing about the scene is that it should encourage you to focus on specifics. Here is a sample of a visualization: *You are walking along in a place where you are quite comfortable. Notice your surroundings, the land- or town-scape to the left. Now to the right. Note where the light is coming from, and the quality of the light. Feel the weather. Be comfortable in what you are wearing. Now, up ahead you begin to hear a sound. It seems to be made by a person. Where is it coming from? What is it like? As you get nearer it becomes clearer. Begin, yourself, softly to imitate that sound. What is the mood of it? Is it music, or speech, or something else? Is it made with an instrument, a voice, or otherwise with the body, or by tapping one thing on another? Continue to make the noise and increase its volume. You turn a corner and see the person making this noise. Look at the person. How is the body arranged? How does the light fall on the person? How is s/he making the noise? How is s/he dressed? Step closer. Focus on the hair, the forehead, the eyebrows, then the eyes. What is the look in those eyes? Observe the ears, nose, mouth, jaw, neck. Is there any jewelry? Any other ornament? Look at what the person is wearing on the torso. How the arms are arranged? Focus on the hands, the nails, then the disposition of the legs and feet. Are there shoes, socks, stockings? Pull back again so that you can see the whole person. You speak to her/him. What do you say? Does the person reply?*

When you are comfortable that you see the character clearly, open your eyes. Now fold a sheet of paper in quarters. Hold it in front of your face so that one fold runs exactly down the center of your nose and the other across the center of your eye. Grasp the paper (through four layers at the fold) in front of your eye. Tear a small hole there. When you open the paper you will have a mask. Draw on it the face of the person you have visualized. Drawing skill is irrelevant. Just try to focus as you draw, to reproduce as many focused details as you can of the face you saw—hair, eyebrows, eyes, nose, cheeks, mouth, perhaps teeth, jaw, chin, perhaps jewelry, collar—whatever you can remember of what you saw.

Give this character a name. Write the full name on the back of the mask and put the initials on the front.

Play "impressions." Go around the room, choosing categories to fit in this sentence: *If this character were a* _____, *he or she would be a* _____. (For example, *If this character were a color, he or she would be sky blue; if this character were a tool, he or she would be a pair of pliers; if this character were a dog, he or she would be a Scottish terrier, and so forth.*) On the back of your mask, write only the last image of the sentence (*sky blue, pair of pliers, Scottish terrier*). Keep going, making up new categories, until you have a list of fifteen or twenty impressions of your character.

Read out a few of the lists. Discuss what you know about each character from the list of impressions. What age, sex, ethnicity, nationality? What moods, desires, attitudes, interests?

On the back of your mask, fill in this sentence: _____(name)_____ is a _____(adj.)_____ ____-year-old _____(noun)_____ who wants _____.

Save the mask.

4. Setting

• Stretch, relax, sit and center yourself. Take a deep breath and exhale it on a vowel sound, starting in a high register and descending the scale to your deepest bass. Meanwhile let your muscles relax, let your body slump. Continue exhaling till all the breath is pushed out of your body—more, more; a little bit longer—all the while relaxing. Still relaxed, take a deep breath and do it again, letting the tension flow out of your toes, calves, knees, thighs; out of your shoulders, arms, hands; out of your head, neck, chest, stomach. Do it once more. You are a lump of putty, practically melting off the chair. Now take a deep breath and sit up again; center yourself.

Close your eyes. Imagine the inside of your stomach. What is the light like? Where is it coming from? What colors are there? What is the landscape like? Is there vegetation? Water? Architecture? What is the weather, the mood? How far is the horizon? What objects do you see? Is there anyone there?

Draw that scene. As with the mask in the preceding exercise, artistic ability is irrelevant; just try to be faithful to the place you have imagined.

Your drawing is a stage set for a scene with two characters. One wants to stay there. One wants to leave. Write their dialogue. Does either one convince the other? Do they separate?

If your dialogue starts to flag, pick up one of the triggers lines below and keep going:

- I know about this
- You never listen to me
- I'm sorry I didn't tell you before
- But what will happen when
- Look at it more closely
- This is a strange thing

5. Story
• Stretch, relax, sit, center yourself. Close your eyes. Someone slowly suggests a visualization of a journey and an encounter, once more encouraging you to imagine the specifics. Here is a sample: *You are on a journey. What is your mode of travel? How does your body feel? What can you see to the left, the right, in front of you, as far as the horizon? Where is the source of light? How does it fall on the things you can see? What is the weather? Vegetation? Architecture? What are you wearing? What are you carrying? You arrive at a place where you can see, up ahead, a border. There is a guardian at the border. What is the nature of the border? What is the guardian like? Wearing what? Doing what? You know that you must leave something behind. What will you leave behind? Look at this something in detail. Examine it. Look at it on all sides, be aware of it through several senses.*

Take a sheet of paper and draw the thing you must leave behind.

Write a short paragraph or monologue explaining why you must leave it.

Write a short dialogue with the something. It does not want to be left behind. It gives you all the reasons you must take it along. You reply. Is agreement reached?

You approach the border. What is the nature of your exchange with the guardian of the border? The guardian gives you something. What is it? You pass over the border.

Write a poem about: what you have left behind, or crossing the border, or the guardian's gift, or the land beyond the border.

6. Development and Revision
• Bring in the *worst* thing you have written in your journal. Distribute copies of it or read it aloud. Tell everyone what's wrong with it. The job of the class is to tell you what's good about it, where the language works, where an image has potential, where a character is interesting, what use it might be put to, which germ of an idea in it you might explore.

• Make a book. Gather the ten to thirty journal entries you like most, arrange them in some order that makes sense to you, print them in some way that pleases you. Find a title. Bind the book. Invent. Go a little wild in terms of color, texture, font, paper, materials, appendages, and décor. Think what extra-literary skills you might have that you can use to enhance and express. If you become a published writer you will not have this much freedom to design the presentation of your work, so take advantage of it now. Bring it to class.

What you have made is a *collage, montage, bricolage or quodlibet*—all describing ways of putting elements together into a whole that remains a *miscellany*, not based on internal coherence, nor a timeline that begins at the beginning. *Collage* and *montage* refer to art (usually still photos or mixed media in the former and moving pictures in the latter); *bricolage* means making something out of whatever materials happen to be at hand; and *quodlibet* is a Latin term that originally meant some philosophical point picked at random for debate and later came to mean a musical medley; a fair translation of the Latin would be "whatever."

A *"whatever"* is of course a literary form (also called an *omnibus, anthology, collection,* or *garland*), unified most of all by its being physically bound together. Usually, you'll work at developing and crafting your ideas toward greater internal coherence through the literary forms of *essay, story, poem* and *stage play.* But by making a book you have already accomplished a unified work.

7. Essay
• Over the course of your journal writing, you have identified some subjects on which you might write an essay. Your training in the writing of essays has probably led you to think toward unity and coherence as admirable goals, which they are. This

exercise, however, is designed to thwart those aims and "crack open" your idea. Choose one of the subjects that attracts you. Take a sheet of paper and at the *bottom* of it, write down the title of an essay beginning with the word *On: On Rap Music, On Envy, On the False Notion that Dogs are Loyal,* or the like. Pass the sheets around the room, each person writing one sentence on each subject named. The sentence should be written at the top of the sheet and folded over before passing it on, so that the subject remains visible but the sentences are hidden. When your sheet comes back around to you, you will have as many perspectives on the subject as there are people in the room. How many could be useful in *your* essay on the subject? Some will be interestingly close to your perspective; some may be so close as to suggest that the idea is banal and needs rethinking. Some will be irrelevant and not useful. Some may offer interesting digressions and add to the texture of the argument. Read a few of the pages aloud and discuss what happened during the exercise.
• Pick one of the sentences and write a paragraph that might find a place in your essay on the subject.

• Over the course of the next week, write *and send* a postcard a day that deals in some way, and in various techniques, with the idea you have chosen. The postcards can go to the same person or different people. On one, evoke a place, on another a character, on another an image, using more than one sense. Write one postcard all in dialogue. One couched as a question. One as a metaphor. One that states an abstraction. One that tells a story. It does no harm if you mystify your recipient(s)—they'll probably like it—but you should try to impart some picture, info, idea, or impression with each card.

8. Fiction
• This is an actors' exercise, designed to teach—and to test—cooperation, trust, and balance of status, all of which are relevant both to the power struggle that occurs among characters in a story and to the connections and disconnections among them.
    Divide up into pairs. Each pair face each other and arrange your faces, hands, and bodies in a mirror image of each other. Look into each other's eyes. Decide (without words) who is to be leader. The leader will begin to move *so slowly* that the other may mirror every slightest motion with no time lag at all. No talking. Slow down. Slower. An observer should ideally not be able to tell who is leading, who following. *S l o w e r.* Now switch leader and follower and do the same thing over again. Now do it a third time but this time *there is no leader.* Every motion is a mutual decision, every movement a silent agreement. An observer sees only simultaneous movement.
    Discuss what happened during the exercise. What was difficult? How was it decided who was first leader? Was there a natural leader, a natural follower in your pair? How did you know? How hard was it not to have a leader? If you laughed, when and why? How uncomfortable were you? What other emotions occurred? When and why? Was there conflict, connection, disconnection, change?

• A status game: one student is wearing a hat. Another must get the hat without asking for it.
    Another student has the hat. There are three students trying to get it.
    Discuss what happened. What techniques of persuasion were used? What alliances formed? What emotions aroused? What worked?
    How might your characters employ similar transactions?

• Put two characters in a situation in which they make small talk. Write a brief dialogue in which they vie for status, one-upping each other in the smallest possible increments. Example:
    A: Have you been waiting long?
    B: Don't worry about it.
    A: I wasn't worrying, I just asked.

B: Sorry, I didn't mean to offend you.
A: It takes more than that to offend me.
B: You've changed, then.
A: In more ways than you know.
B: I'm glad to hear it.

Now add all the elements of scene: setting, image, action. Show your characters' subtext in any way you choose.

9. Poetry

• Stretch, shake out, relax. Walk in a circle around the room, clapping on every other step: *and-**One**, and-**Two**, and-**Three**, and-**Four**.* Once the rhythm is established, have someone read a strongly iambic poem in time to the walking and clapping: Robert Frost's "Stopping by Wood on a Snowy Evening" is a good choice. "*Whose **woods** these **are** I **think** I **know**. / His **house** is **in** the **vil**-lage **though***"—the poem is quite tough enough to survive this treatment. When you have done this you will bodily have demonstrated the meter of iambic tetrameter.

Now clap on every third beat: *and-a-**One**, and-a-**Two**, and-a-**Three**.* Try taking two small steps, then a big step on the clap. Move freely out of the circle, sidestepping and turning. You're now waltzing. Have someone read or recite a limerick. This one will do: "— There **once** was a **man** from Khar-**toum** / — Who **kept** a tame **sheep** in his **room**. / 'To re-**mind** me,' he **said**, / '— Of **some**-one who's **dead**, / But I **nev**-er can **re**-col-lect **whom**." The dashes represent a pause; the reader should adjust, leaving a beat for that step. When you can follow this rhythm with ease, you are demonstrating anapestic meter.

• Have someone make three copies of a lesser-known sonnet by Shakespeare, cut each copy into its 14 lines, and shuffle. Divide into three groups. Each group reassemble the sonnet according to sense and rhyme (you may consult the rhyme scheme below). Gold stars to the group that comes closest to the original.

• As a class, pick the rhyme words for a Shakespearean sonnet. Here is a sample, together with the letters that designate the rhyme scheme:

road	a
vain	b
decode	a
plane	b
speaker	c
hulk	d
squeaker	c
bulk	d
connection	e
undone	f
perfection	e
stun	f
craving	g
saving	g

Take the words home and each individually fill in the lines. Write in sentences. The syntax should be grammatically correct and the words English words, but don't strive to make sense, nor to adhere to a particular rhythmic pattern. Read a few of the results in class.

10. Drama

• *Making a machine*. This is an exercise that actors and dancers often do to make themselves aware of the physical space they must fill, the composition of levels and shapes within it, the rhythms of movement and sound that make for interesting viewing. First stretch, relax. Divide into groups of five to eight people. A volunteer from the first group enters the space designated as the "stage" and begins making a repetitive movement, accompanied by a regular rhythmic sound. A second person enters close to or almost touching the first and adds a repetitive movement and rhythmic sound. A third person joins them, and so forth. Each person tries to add to the interest of the "machine," perhaps standing on a chair, facing away, lying on the floor and so forth, both fitting into the pattern and making it more complex. Let the machine run for a while. When it is done, discuss what happened. Did one part seem to cause the action of another? Was the space interestingly filled visually? Did the machine have a recognizable quality or personality, and did that change as it grew? Was it funny? Menacing? Purposeful? What, as a playwright, might you take away from such an exercise to use in the writing of a play? Let the next group make a machine; discuss it, and so on through as many groups as there are.

• Everyone in the room write down a situation involving a place and two characters, each of whom wants something but does not want to come right out and say so. (Examples: A shoe store; A wants a pair of shoes that will make her feet look smaller; B, the clerk, wants to go to lunch. At home; X wants to borrow Y's car, Y wants to go out for cigarettes. A customs shed; M wants to smuggle in a Swiss clock, N wants to fill a drug-confiscating quota.) Collect the ideas. One person volunteers as director and two others as actor. The director picks one of the papers, takes aside each actor, tells both the setting but each one only what his/her character wants. The two actors improvise the scene. Discuss what happened. Could you tell what each wanted? How? What verbal clues were there? What visual clues? Was the power struggle equal? Was it resolved?

Appendix B

Formats

"Clean copy" is the first and very visible sign of the professional. Your manuscript should be carefully proofread, neatly printed or copied, and stapled or paper clipped in the upper right-hand corner. Your name need ordinarily appear only on the cover sheet; page numbering can be done in the upper or lower center or right corner of the page. Copyrighting of literary manuscripts is not necessary—essays, stories, poems, and plays are, alas, rarely worth money enough to be attractive to thieves. If your work is published, the magazine or publisher will apply for copyright, and you will have a contract that specifies what rights belong to you.

To cut copying costs, some teachers will ask you to omit a cover page, and/or to single space for class submission. Otherwise, use the formats described below, and in any case keep in mind that these are the formats expected by editors and directors when you submit for publication or production. You should familiarize yourself with them and become comfortable using them.

Always keep a copy of your work.

1. Prose fiction and nonfiction

Title and author's name and address (or class identification) should appear on a cover page.

Manuscripts should be double-spaced, with generous (approximately one inch) margins, on one side of 8½ by 11-inch white paper. The first page of the story or essay should begin about one-third of the way down the page.

2. Poetry

Whereas prose is always double-spaced in manuscript for ease of reading, poetry often is not. Because the look of the poem-as-object is important to its effect, most poets strive to produce a manuscript page that looks as much like the printed poem as possible. Single spacing usually achieves this better.

Poems do not require a title page. Center the title above the poem and put your name and address at the end, toward the right side of the page. If your poem spills over onto a new page and the new page begins with a new stanza, make sure that the stanza break is clear.

3. Drama

The formats for prose and poetry are relatively straightforward and easy to master. The format for plays, unfortunately, is not. It is nevertheless necessary to learn because every peculiarity annoying to the writer is an aid to the actors, director, and designers who must interpret the script in living action. For instance, the names of characters (except when used as a form of address in dialogue), and the pronouns that refer to them, are always in capital letters and are centered before speeches because this visually helps actors spot what they say and do. Short stage directions are put in parentheses and long ones to the right of the page because that signals where the action is indicated. Pages are numbered not merely consecutively but also by act and scene because in rehearsal a director specifies "Take it from the top of scene two" rather than "Take it from page 38," which has less meaning in the structure of a play. And so forth.

The format thus designed for production is not necessarily the same one you will encounter in a printed "trade" or textbook edition (including this one), where there's a higher priority on saving space than on convenience to the company. But as a playwright your goal is production and your allegiance to the theatrical troupe; your manuscript should reflect that.

Playwrights often feel that they *do* need to copyright their work because it may be circulated to many people, and could be produced without their knowledge; it's difficult to prove production after the fact. If you intend to send your work out to production companies and feel more comfortable with a copyright, you should write for "Form PA" to: U.S. Copyright Office, Library of Congress, Washington, D.C. 20559.

Plays should have a cover page with title, some sort of designation such as "A play in two scenes" or "A comedy in one act," and the author's name and address. Plays should be typed in 12-point (or "pica") font, and should be (at least for submission—probably not for class) sent in a sturdy binder.

There follow a few sample pages of a play in the standard "Dramatists' Guild" format.

THE LAST RESORT

a Play in Two Acts

by

Julia Sophocles

class info or
your agent's
name and address or
your address

CAST OF CHARACTERS

Lem Lemming

Early thirties. Skinny and shabby, a former hippie down on his luck. He is normally lackadaisical and apathetic, but when roused can be bad-tempered, even violent.

Eliadne Appleby

Thirty-eight. A do-gooder, caught between her hotshot job and a nostalgia for the simple life. She dresses as if she was set to break the glass ceiling, but her cheery, lilting voice gives her away.

Sam Callahan

The local farmer. A well-preserved sixty, with a spread of sixty acres and a practical take on life.

Lillian Callahan

His wife. Some ten years younger than SAM, but about forty years younger in attitude. She wears peasant blouses and dirndle skirts, dances rather than walks.

SCENE

A farmhouse on SAM CALLAHAN's *spread in the Lower Joaquin Valley.*

TIME

The late 1970s. Early autumn

Act I

Scene 1

> *The living room of a remote farm-house, with autumn leaves showing through the windows. Stage right is a door to the outside, upstage left another to the bedroom. A couch, tattered; a smoking wood stove; sink, table and chairs. General chaos of gear and garbage.*
>
> *LEM is asleep under the bed. ELIADNE appears in the door right, carrying a basket of flowers. SHE is in a chic riding outfit with high-heeled boots.*

ELIADNE

Helloo! Anybody home? (*Pause.*) Lem, are you there?

> *(SHE enters cautiously, sets the basket on the table, rummages in the sink for a vase.)*

ELIADNE (Continued)

This place is disgusting! I swear to god I don't know how any one human being can bear to go on day after day in a . . .

LEM

> (*Waking.*)

Get outta here! Out! Out!

ELIADNE

Ah, there you are! Are you going to be quarrelsome, pet?

LEM

You are asking me if I'm going to be quarrelsome? Am I going to be quarrelsome? What else would I be if I want to get a play going? Do you know what a crummy, goony, loony partner you are to have in a playscript, with your benevolent bunny hugs and your gooey do-goodery and your honey-pie sweetie-pie

LEM (Continued)

sickening way of talking? You bet your boots I'm going to be quarrelsome, because if there's gonna be any chance of a conflict here, it's up to me!

*(HE picks up an axe. SHE holds out the
basket to him.)*

ELIADNE

I brought you some daisies.

(SAM enters through the door right. HE has a shotgun in one hand and a bunch of carrots in the other.)

SAM

Anyone for exposition?

. . . and so forth . . .

Appendix C

A Basic Prosody

In my sensory education I include my physical awareness
of the *word*. Of a certain word, that is; the connection it
has with what it stands for. At around age six, perhaps, I
was standing by myself waiting for supper . . . There
comes a moment, and I saw it then, when the moon goes
from flat to round. For the first time it met my eyes as a
globe. The word "moon" came into my mouth as though
fed to me out of a silver spoon.

Eudora Welty

Prosody is the study of versification, the metrical and auditory structure of poetry. What
follows here is a very basic prosody, outlining the major units of sound and meter, the
basic principles of rhyme, and a few common stanza patterns.

To begin with, these are the building blocks of poems:

• A **phoneme** is the smallest unit of distinguishable sound: *b, m, a*. Phonemes are
either **vowels**, produced by relatively free passage of air through the oral cavity—for
example, *a, o, e*; or **consonants**, produced by a partial obstruction of the air stream: *t,
p, g*. Vowels may be pronounced as **long** sounds (ā, ē, ō, as in *place, wheat, own*) or
short sounds (ă, ŭ, ĕ, as in *cat, up, when*). Consonants may be *labial, dental, guttural,
nasal,* or *plosive* and so forth, depending on which parts of the mouth are used in their
utterance.

• A **syllable** is a unit of sound uttered in a single expulsion of breath, typically containing one or more consonants and a vowel: *mup-, done, ba-*. A syllable may be either
stressed or **unstressed** (**accented** or **unaccented**) according to the relative force with
which it is pronounced. *be-GUN, PO-e-try*. In the **scansion** or measuring of poetry, the
stress is marked (avoiding the cumbersome capitals) as follows: bĕgún, pŏétry. The double accent mark indicates a **secondary stress** (lighter than a stressed, heavier than an
unstressed syllable; some prosodists hear a secondary stress in most three-syllable
words).

• A **poetic foot** is a measure of syllables usually containing one stressed and one or
more unstressed syllables. The poetic feet are marked by slashes:

Í hăve / bĕgún / tŏ wríte / ă vérse.

• A **poetic line** is a unit of verse ended by a typographical break. It may have a given
number of syllables (**syllabic verse**), or a given number of stresses (**accentual verse**),
or a given number of poetic feet (**metered verse**), or its length may be determined by
the poet according to the needs of the particular poem (**free verse**). A **caesura** is a
pause that occurs within the line. In a line that is **end-stopped**, the line break coincides
with a pause; if the sense continues from the end of one line to the next, it is called a
run-on line, or **enjambment**.

• A **stanza** is a grouping of lines within a poem, often predetermined by the chosen
form, with a space break between such groupings.

Try This

With no attempt to make sense, write a four-line verse in which the vowel sounds are all short. (For example: *Flat on his back /the summer shop cat runs/ His love and supper pot./ What fickle chumps.*) Then a four-line verse in which all the vowel sounds are long.

Time

Three terms having to do with the time element of poetry are sometimes used interchangeably, though in fact they differ in meaning.

- **Tempo** refers to the speed or slowness of a line.
- **Meter** comes from the Greek "measure," and refers to the mechanical elements of its rhythm, the number of feet, stresses and unstressed syllables; it is a relatively objective measurement.
- **Rhythm** refers to the total quality of a line's motion, affected by tempo and meter but also by emotion and sound.

Meter is something that can be measured, whereas rhythm is a feeling, a sense. It would be appropriate to say of a line or poem that the tempo is *fast* or *slow*, the meter is *iambic pentameter* or *trochaic dimeter*, and that the rhythm is *lilting, urgent, effortful*, or *sluggish*.

Stress and Scansion; the Poetic Foot

English is a stress language, the pattern of speech determined by the emphasis given to some syllables over others. This fact is so ingrained in us that it's difficult to understand a language otherwise constituted, but Greek, for example, is a language measured in vowel length, and Chinese is patterned in pitch rather than stress.

- **Accentual verse** employs a meter in which only the stresses are counted:

  When the watchman on the wall, the Shieldings' lookout
  whose job it was to guard the sea-cliffs,
  saw shields glittering on the gangplank
  and battle-equipment being unloaded
  he had to find out who and what . . .

  > *Seamus Heaney's translation of Beowulf*

  (Here, each line has four stresses, but they have 12, 9, 9, 11, and 8 syllables, respectively.)

- **Syllabic verse** employs a meter in which only the syllables are counted, as in these lines by W. H. Auden, which keep to nine syllables each although the number of stresses diminishes from five to four to three:

  Blue the sky beyond her humming sail
  As I sit today by our ship's rail
  Watching exuberant porpoises . . .

Try This
Write a "phone poem" as syllabic verse. Use as the title a phone number (of any length you choose) real or invented. The subject of the poem is a phone call to that number; it may be a narrative about the call, or in dialogue, or a monologue of one side of the conversation, or any combination. Each line has the number of syllables of each consecutive digit. So if the phone number is 587-9043: The first line has five syllables, the second eight syllables, the third seven and so forth. A zero is silence.

Most formal English verse counts both stresses and syllables and is **scanned** by measuring the line into stressed (or accented) and unstressed (or unaccented) syllables.

- A **poetic foot** is a unit of measurement with one stress and either one or two unstressed syllables, scanned in these basic patterns:

  - An **iamb** has one unstressed syllable followed by one stressed: around.
    Iambic is the most common meter in English, probably because we tend to begin sentences with the subject, and most nouns are preceded by an article, as in: the girl, the sky, an apple.

    His house / is in / the vil/lage though.

    Note that when the scansion is marked, the feet are separated by slashes even if the foot ends between two syllables of a word.

  - A **trochee** is the opposite of an iamb—a stressed syllable followed by an unstressed: heavy.
    Trochaic rhythms do tend to be heavy, hitting hard and forcefully on the stress.

    Double, / double /toil and / trouble;

  - An **anapest** consists of two unstressed syllables followed by a stress: undefined.
    Notice that *anapest* is not an anapest, though it would be if I say: *you're a nuisance and a pest!* Anapestic rhythms tend to rollicking frolic and light verse; it is the meter of Gilbert and Sullivan.

    From my head / to my toes / I'm all cov/ered in ros/es.

  - A **dactyl** is a poetic foot that begins with a stress followed by two unstresses: carpenter.
    Dactylic meters tend toward the mysterious or incantatory and are rare, though you are likely to have encountered a few in school:

    This is the / forest pri/meval, the / murmuring / pines and the / hemlocks.

  - A **spondee** is a foot with two stresses, which can be substituted for any other foot when special emphasis is wanted (you won't want to, and can't, write a whole poem in it):

    One, two. / Buckle / my shoe.

  - A **pyrrhic** foot is the opposite, a substitute foot with two unstressed syllables:

    Thou art / indeed / just, Lord, / if I / contend
    With thee . . .

Sometimes, as here, a spondee is balanced with a pyrrhic, so the number of stresses remains the same as in a regular line.

Those are the feet, four basic and two substitute, that you need to begin with, although infinite variations are possible, many of which have names (*chiasmus, ionic, amphibrach, anacreusis*) if your interest inclines you to seek them out.

Try This

Practice scanning anything at all, marking the stresses of a sentence or a cereal box, exaggerating as you pronounce the words to hear the stresses. Although scansion is not a science—people pronounce words with different emphasis according to region and habit—the more you practice the more you will hear the pattern of stressed and unstressed syllables, and the more you will be able to direct the stresses of your own poetry.

A line of poetry in a regular **meter** will be scanned according to the number of feet in that line (the following examples are in iambs):

- *Monometer*—one foot: Ĭf Í
- *Dimeter*—two feet: Ĭf Í / dŏn't gó
- *Trimeter*—three feet: Ĭf Í / dŏn't gó / ăwaý
- *Tetrameter*—four feet: Ĭf Í / dŏn't gó / ăwaý / tŏdaý
- *Pentameter*—five feet: Ĭf Í / dŏn't gó / ăwaý / tŏdaý / Ĭ wón't
- *Hexameter*—six feet: Ĭf Í / dŏn't gó / ăwaý / tŏdaý / I'll név/er gó
- *Heptameter*—seven feet: Ĭf Í / dŏn't gó / ăwaý / tŏdaý / I'll név/er gó / ăt áll.

You're unlikely to run into (or write) a metered line longer than this.

Try This

Practice meter—remember not to worry about making sense—by setting yourself more or less arbitrary rules: write three lines of iambic tetrameter, six of trochaic trimeter, and so forth. Mark the scansion of your lines; read them aloud until you're confident you hear the stresses.

Pick a favorite nursery line or lyric (country, Irish, rock, Shakespeare, hip hop, opera . . .), write it down and mark the scansion. Then substitute other words in the same pattern of scansion.

Rhyme

Rhyme is to sound as metaphor is to imagery—that is, two things are at once alike and unlike, and our pleasure is in the tension between that likeness and unlikeness. In the case of rhyme, there are patterns of consonants and vowels that correspond to each other, usually involving the accented syllable and whatever comes after it; and there is a diminishing order of correspondence.

- For instance, in **rich rhyme**, the whole accented syllable sounds alike—any consonants before the vowel, the vowel, and any consonants after. So *tend* would be a rich rhyme with *pretend* and *contend* and *intend*. Because so many sounds in these syllables correspond, they quickly tire the ear, so whole poems in rich rhyme are rare.
- In a **true rhyme**—the sound of nursery rhymes and the first word-play most of us indulge—the vowel sounds of the stressed syllable are alike, and the consonants after the vowel, but not the consonants before it. So *tend* is a true rhyme for *mend* and *lend* and *offend*. Because true rhyme also requires that the unaccented syllables after the stressed syllable correspond, *tender* rhymes with *spender* and *tendency* with *dependency*. When the accented syllable ends a rhymed line, it is called a *masculine rhyme* (out of some outdated notion of strength): *tend, send*. When it is followed by an unaccented syllable, it is called a *feminine* or *weak rhyme*: *tender, blender*; and when followed by two unaccented syllables, a *triple* or *treble rhyme*: *tenderly, slenderly*. (Perhaps these are androgynous?)
- In **slant rhyme** or **off-rhyme**, the final consonant corresponds, but not the vowel that precedes it. So *tend* is a slant rhyme for *bland*, and *tender* a slant rhyme for *grinder*. The use of slant rhyme exponentially increases the number of available rhymes in English and can introduce unexpected effects, subtle aural surprises, and interesting variations in tone.
- **Assonance** is the opposite; the vowel corresponds but not the consonant. *Tend* assonates with *spell* and *weather* and *met*. As with slant rhyme, assonance teases the ear with subtle correspondences.
- In **alliteration**, consonants (usually at the beginning of the word or stressed syllable) correspond: *Tender, tickle, take, entreat*. Alliteration is often used to try to reproduce the sound or emotion of the content:

> The mildest human sound can make them scatter
> With a sound like seed spilled . . .

- Rhymes may be **end rhymes**, coming at the ends of lines, or **internal rhymes**, within the lines. Often the end rhyme of one line will rhyme into the middle of another:

> Body my <u>house</u>
> my <u>horse</u> my hound
> what will I <u>do</u>
> when <u>you</u> are fallen
> *May Swenson, "Question"*

In general, poetry tends toward **euphony**, the change of one quality of sound to another, from consonants to vowels and back again to facilitate pronunciation and so contribute to flow. But sometimes you will want to produce a sound that is not mellifluous or euphonic but effortful. One way of doing this is the **consonant cluster** demonstrated in the Pope line:

> Whĕn Á/jăx stríves / sŏme róck's / vást weíght / tŏ thrów.

Here the consonants butt up against each other at the end of one word and the beginning of the next, so you have to stop between in order to pronounce both: *Ajax \\ strives; rock's \\ vast; weight \\ to*. At the same time, the two spondees give the line especially heavy stress: *sóme róck's vást weíght*. A different sort of **cacophony** is achieved when vowels end one word and begin the next:

And oft / the ear / the o/pen vow/els tire.

Try This

Do, or return to, the exercise on p. 319, the list of words related to your area of expertise. Are there any rich rhymes? True rhymes? Slant rhymes? Arrange a short list to form a line that alliterates: (my list of spices might yield *Cardamom, cayenne, curry, cloves*); and a line that assonates: (*Sage, bay, carraway, arrowroot*); and a line with rhymes true or slant: (*Dill weed, poppy seed, cumin seed, bay leaves, cloves*). Play around with combinations of rhyme, alliteration, and assonance: *Chili, cilantro, oregano, cinnamon, / Carraway, cardamom, gumbo, garlic, / Cinnamon, cumin, sesame, rosemary.* Can you find consonant clusters? *Nutmeg / gumbo; bay leaves / turmeric / cayenne.*

Stanzas

The most common form of English poetry is **blank verse**, unrhymed iambic pentameter—iambic probably because of our habitual arrangement of articles and nouns, pentameter probably because that length represents a comfortable expulsion of breath, unrhymed probably because it is the freest and most flexible of the formal patterns—the nearest to free verse. It is the form of Shakespeare's plays, of Milton's *Paradise Lost*, of Robert Frost's "Mending Wall," Wallace Stevens's "Sunday Morning," and innumerable modern poems. Blank verse runs to any length and is not broken into set blocks of lines. But most patterned verse is written in stanzas.

A **stanza** is a division of lines in a poem, usually linked by a pattern of meter or sound, and usually repeated more than once. It is beyond the scope of this book to enumerate the various, multifarious, loose and strict, simple and elaborate, Eastern and Western stanza forms. But here are a few that are basic to English verse, and a few from other cultures that have attracted a good deal of poetic play in the English of the twentieth century.

• **Couplet.** A two-line stanza, usually consecutively rhymed, although unrhymed couplets are also common in modern verse. A **heroic couplet** is two lines of iambic pentameter, consecutively rhymed:

> The little hours: two lovers herd upstairs
> two children, one of whom is one of theirs.
> *Marilyn Hacker, "Almost Aubade"*

• **Tercet**, or **triplet** is a stanza of three lines (rhymed or unrhymed):

> While mopping she muses over work undone,
> Her daily chores. The blue floor tiles
> Reflect where she cleans and her thoughts run . . .
> *Wendy Bishop, "The Housekeeper"*

- **Quatrain** is a stanza of four lines, of which the **ballad meter** is famous in English, usually four lines of iambic tetrameter, or alternating tetrameter and trimeter, rhymed only on the second and fourth lines (though there are many variations, of both meter and rhyme scheme). The ballad tells a story, often of betrayal and violence:

> Put your hand behind the wainscot,
> You have done your part;
> Find the penknife there and plunge it
> Into your cold heart.
> *W.H. Auden*

- The **song** or **lyric** is often in quatrains of iambic tetrameter with a rhyme scheme of ABAB or ABBA.

- And so forth. A **quintet** has five lines, a **sestet** six, a **septet** seven and an **octave** eight.

- The **sonnet** is a poem of fourteen lines, usually printed without a stanza break although the lines are internally grouped. The sonnet gained its popularity as an import from Italy during the Renaissance, where it was densely rhymed and usually dealt with the subject of love, especially unrequited (something like Country 'n' Western today.) Because of the paucity of English rhymes, the Italian or Petrarchan rhyme scheme (ABBA ABBA CDECDE) was adapted in English to the looser scheme ABAB CDCD EFEF GG. The sonnet is a good example of the way form influences meaning. Petrarchan sonnets have a strong tendency to develop an idea in the first eight lines (or **octet**) and then to elaborate or contradict or alter it at some length in the last six lines (**sestet**). But the English sonnet, including Shakespeare's, developed in such a way that the three quatrains develop an idea, which must then be capped, or contradicted, or changed in a punchy couplet at the end.

Stanzas are arranged in many set, traditional—and many more invented and original—groups, to form the poems. Like the sonnet, most of the forms that we think of as typically English were actually adapted from other languages. Terza rima, rondeau, sestina, ghazal, pantoum, villanelle—any and all of these are worth seeking out (the books recommended on page 332 at the end of Chapter 8 will provide definitions and examples). Meanwhile, of the non-English forms that have become popular, none is more so than the shortest of them, the Japanese **haiku**, an unrhymed verse of seventeen syllables arranged in three lines of five, seven, and five syllables. And none of them provides better practice for encapsulating an emotion or idea in a sharply etched observation, whether reflective:

> Escaped the nets,
> escaped the ropes—
> moon on the water
> *Buson*

—or cynical:

> a bath when you're born
> a bath when you die,
> how stupid.
> *Issa*

—or contemporary:

These stamps are virgins—
not even licked yet. Date night
alone at my desk.
>   *Devan Cook*

Try This

Write a series of quatrains. Choose some meter and rhyme scheme in advance—
iambic tetrameter in a pattern of abba rhymes, for example. This will be an "altar
poem" to someone you want to honor. In the first line, name or describe a place that
would be appropriate to honor this person. In subsequent lines, list or describe the
objects you would bring and assemble in that place. Try slant rhymes to augment
your possibilities. Play around to see if you can use and identify caesura, enjambment, alliteration, assonance.

Write a sonnet as a story: in quatrain one, introduce two characters in a setting; in
quatrain two, they are in conflict; in quatrain three, a third character arrives and
complicates things; in the couplet, all is resolved.

Write a haiku. Write another. One more.

Glossary

Note: Technical terms to do with **prosody** (the study of meter and sound in poetry) will be found in Appendix C.

Antagonist In narrative, the character who provides the major impediment or obstacle to the main character's desire. See **protagonist.**

Aside A theatrical convention whereby a character says something that the audience hears but the other characters do not.

Atmosphere The tone and attitude, as well as the setting, period, weather, and time of day, of a story. The background to the characters' foreground.

Authorial interpretation; authorial intrusion The author speaks directly to the reader, rather than through the point of view of the character. By and large, the device is interpretive any time the author tells us what we should think or feel; it is intrusive if we mind this.

Backstory Past events that are necessary to understand a narrative or its significance.

Brainstorm A problem-solving technique that can also generate ideas for an imagined situation. The writer free-associates a list of ideas, connections, solutions, then uses these as prompts for writing. Often takes the form *"What if . . . ?"*

Character A fictional person. The basis of literary writing.

Cluster A technique for focusing and shaping a freewrite. The writer puts the word that represents the subject in the middle of a blank page, free-associates around it, circles and connects related terms and ideas. This provides a spatial, rather than a linear, sense of structure for the writing that follows.

Complications Aspects of the conflict that build the plot toward its climax. The *"nouement"* or "knotting up" of the action.

Conceit A metaphor in which the connection between the two things compared is not immediately clear. In Samuel Johnson's words, "yoked by violence together," as in John Donne's comparison of a flea to the holy trinity, or Nathanael West's "love is like a vending machine." The author must explain the similarity.

Concrete, significant details Specifics that address the senses in meaningful ways. The basic building blocks of imaginative writing, and what is meant by the advice *show, don't tell.*
- *Concrete* means that there is an image, something that can be seen, heard, smelled, tasted or touched.
- *Detail* means that there is a degree of focus and specificity.
- *Significant* means that the specific image also suggests an abstraction, generalization or judgment.

Connotation The complex of meanings and ideas that come to be associated with a word, as "rose" suggests not only the flower but beauty, fragrance, womanhood, perhaps ephemerality and/or the hidden threat of thorns.

Conflict The struggle between protagonist and antagonist, or between two opposing forces. Considered necessary to narrative, because it generates a desire in the reader to find out what is going to happen.

Creative nonfiction   The essay, enlivened through attention to stylistic and dramatic devices, personal voice, and a search for range and resonance. Also called **literary nonfiction.**

Crisis   The point of highest tension in a story, at which a discovery or a decision is made that decides the outcome of the conflict.

Dead metaphor   A metaphor so common that it has lost the original sense of comparison and acquired a further definition, as "sifting the evidence" no longer calls a sieve to mind.

Denotation   The most direct or specific meaning of a word; how it is defined.

Denouement   The resolution at the end of a story. The return to order after the conflict, its complications and climax have passed.

Density   In literature, the arrangement of words and images to pack maximum meaning into minimum space.

Dialogue   The characters' talk. Dialogue may be:
- **direct,** the spoken words quoted: "No, I can't stand the little monsters and I won't herd a bunch of them to the damn park unless I'm paid."
- **indirect,** the words related in third person: She said she couldn't stand kids and wouldn't take them to the park unless she got paid.
- or **summarized,** reported at a distance: She claimed to hate children, and irritatedly demanded payment for taking them to the park.

Diction   A combination of *vocabulary*, the words chosen, and *syntax*, the order in which they are used. Diction will convey not only the facts but also the tone and attitude of the person whose voice speaks to us from the page.

Diegetic   Musical or other effects that occur naturally as part of the dramatic narrative (a character turns on the radio and a song comes out). **Nondiegetic** effects occur when there is no such natural or realistic link (a suspenseful scene is accompanied by music to enhance the tension).

Distance   The position, close or far, of the author in relation to the characters or narrator, often implying the degree to which we are intended to identify with or trust them. Distance will be affected first of all by diction and tone, and may involve a literal distance in time or space (the narrator, for example, is telling a story about himself as a child) or a psychic distance (the author is describing the exploits of a psychopath).

Dramatic irony   The audience (or reader) knows something that the character doesn't know.

Emotional Recall   A theatrical convention in which one character tells another about an incident from the past, and the story changes the attitude of the second character in some dramatically significant way.

Essay   From the French word meaning "a try," a prose piece with a basis in fact, on a single subject, presenting the view of the author. Kinds of essay include the expository, narrative, descriptive, persuasive, article, feature, profile, literary nonfiction, and creative nonfiction.

Exposition   In narrative and especially theatre, the laying out of the situation at the opening of the action.

Falling action   The portion of a plot that follows the climax and leads to the resolution. A "walking away from the fight." Also called **denouement.**

Figure of speech (or **figurative speech**)   A non-literal use of language, such as metaphor, simile, hyperbole, personification and so forth, to enhance or intensify meaning.

Flashback　In narrative, film, or drama, a leap into the past. The earlier scene is inserted into the normal chronological order.

Formal verse　Verse written in a predetermined pattern of rhythm and rhyme.

Fourth-wall realism　A theatrical convention in which the stage represents a room with the fourth wall removed. Both actors and audience pretend that what is happening onstage is "really" happening at the present time.

Free verse　Verse that lacks a regular meter or rhyme scheme, and uses irregular line lengths according to the demands of the particular poem.

Freewrite.　A piece of writing undertaken without any plan or forethought whatever; writing whatever comes into your head at the moment. Gertrude Stein called this "automatic writing." A **focused freewrite** is a piece written with the same unplanned freedom, but on a chosen topic.

Genre　A form of writing, such as poetry, drama, or fiction. The term is problematic because "genre fiction" and "genre writing" are terms used differently, to indicate writing in narrow plot-driven conventions such as the western, romance, detective story and so forth.

Idiom　An expression that is grammatically peculiar to itself and can't be understood by understanding its separate elements. English abounds in idioms: *put 'er there*, *keeps tabs on*, *of his own accord*, and so forth. The line between idioms, clichés, dead metaphors and figures of speech is often not distinct.

Inciting incident　The event that has created the situation in which the protagonist finds him/herself at the beginning of a drama. For example, Hamlet's father has died and his mother has remarried.

Intensity　In literature, the raising of tension or emotion through character conflict, language, rhythm, situation, irony or other artistic device.

Line　A series of words after which there is a typographical break. In prose, the line ends because the type has arrived at a margin, and may vary from one edition or font to another. In poetry the line implies a slight pause and is used in conjunction with or opposition to the sentence as a means of creating significance. Consequently the line is considered an integral feature of the poem, and will remain the same in each reprinting.

Line editing　Careful, often final, revision of a manuscript at the level of checking punctuation, spelling and grammar as well as the nuance of final word choice.

Literary nonfiction　See **creative nonfiction.**

Metaphor　The comparison of one term with another such that a tension is created between what is alike and what is unlike between the two terms.
- A *metaphor* assumes or states the comparison, without acknowledging that it is a comparison: *my electric muscles shock the crowd; her hair is seaweed and she is the sea*. The metaphor may come in the form of an adjective: *they have a piggy and a fishy air*. Or it may come as a verb: *the bees shouldering the grass*.
- A simile is a type of metaphor that acknowledges the comparison by using the words *like* or *as*: *his teeth rattled like dice in a box; my head is light as a balloon; I will fall like an ocean on that court.*

Monologue　A speech of some length by a single character.

Mood　See **atmosphere.**

Narrative　A story; the telling of a story.

Narrator　The one who tells the story. We often speak of the author as narrator if the piece is told in the third person, although literally a story "has a narrator" only when it is told by a character. This character may be:

- the **central narrator,** the *I* writing *my* story as if it were memoir, or
- the **peripheral narrator,** someone on the edge of the action, who is nevertheless our eyes and ears in the story and therefore the person with whom we identify, and with whom we must be moved or changed.

New journalism   Tom Wolfe used the term in the 1960's for a kind of reporting in which the reporter becomes a character in his report, and which relies on all the techniques of a novelist including—importantly, for Wolfe—the details of dress, gesture, speech and ownership that reveal social status.

Nondiagetic   See **diagetic.**

Omniscience   The narrative convention by which the author knows everything—past, future, any character's thoughts, the significance of events, universal truths. It is the God-like authorial stance.

Onomatopoeia   The use of words that sound like what they mean: *buzz, whine, murmur.*

Oxymoron   A figure of speech that combines or juxtaposes two contradictory words: *burning ice, shouting whisper, plain decoration.* The term comes from the Greek meaning "sharply foolish," which is itself an oxymoron and expresses the potential of the figure to reveal although it appears not to make sense.

Person   In grammar and narrative, any of three groups of pronouns identifying the subject. **First person:** *I look out the window.* **Second person:** *You look out the window.* **Third person:** *He looks out the window.*

Persona   A mask adopted by the author, which may be a public manifestation of the author's self; or a distorted or partial version of that self; or a fictional, historical, or mythological character.

Plot   A series of events arranged so as to reveal their significance. See **story.**

Point of attack   In drama, the first event that sets the plot in motion: for example, the ghost speaks to Hamlet, demanding revenge against Claudius.

Point of View   A complex technique of narrative involving who tells the story, to whom, in what form. Importantly, the **person** in which the story is told, and the vantage point from which the story is told, contribute to the ultimate meaning of events.

Prosody   The study of meter and sound in poetry. See **Appendix C.**

Protagonist   The main character of a narrative; usually, one with whom we identify.

Realism   A narrative or dramatic convention that aims at accuracy and verisimilitude in the presentation of period, place, speech and behavior.

Resolution   The end of conflict, usually involving the restoration of order, at the end of a plot.

Scansion   The measuring of verse into poetic feet, or a pattern of stressed and unstressed syllables. See **Appendix C.**

Scene and summary   Methods of treating time in fiction. A summary covers a relatively long period of time in relatively short compass; a scene deals at length with a relatively short period of time.

Self-reflexivity   Referring back to the self. Generally used to indicate that the work, rather than pretending to represent a true picture of real events, acknowledges in some way that it is a fiction, an artifact, a work of imagination.

Setting   The place and period in which a story or drama takes place.

Simile   A comparison using the terms *like* or *as*. See **metaphor.**

Short-short story   A plotted fiction of no more than three hundred words, usually fewer. Also sometimes called *flash fiction* or *microfiction.*

Soliloquy   A theatrical convention in which a character alone onstage makes a speech that we understand to represent his or her thoughts.

Stage lie   A theatrical convention in which the character says one thing but betrays the opposite through contradiction or visible behavior.

Story   A sequence of fictional or remembered events, usually involving a conflict, crisis and resolution. Humphry House, in his commentaries on Aristotle, defines story as everything the reader needs to know to make coherent sense of the plot, and **plot** as the particular portion of the story the author chooses to present—the "present tense" of the narrative.

Summary   See **scene.**

Symbol   Something, usually an object, that stands for something larger, often an inter-related complex of ideas, values, and beliefs. For example, the flag stands for love of country. In literature, this object is particular to the work. The golden bowl in Henry James's *The Golden Bowl* stands for a situation involving deception, self-deception, betrayal and flawed marital love.

Syntax   The arrangement of words within a sentence.

Theatricalism   The dramatic convention by which the actors acknowledge that the stage is a stage, the play a play, and themselves players of parts.

Undrafting   A technique for showing the strengths of a passage by spoiling it—replacing specifics with generalizations and active with passive verbs.

Unreliable narrator   The narrator of a fiction who, through inappropriate tone, contradiction or other self-betrayal, reveals to the reader that he or she cannot be believed.

Vocabulary   The sum total of words known and used by a writer (or a person or group of people); the choice of words in a particular work.

Voice   The recognizable style of a particular writer or character, composed of syntax, vocabulary, attitude and tone.

Voiceover   In film and theatre, the voice of an unseen character providing narration, usually by mechanical means.

Credits

Photos

Page 002 ©Laurie Lipton

Page 042 ©Saul Steinberg, "Figures Speaking in Abstractions," 1957. Courtesy The New Yorker, June 1, 1957. ©2002 The Saul Steinberg Foundation/Artists Rights Society (ARS), New York.

Page 086 Photo by John Grant

Page 128 ©Jerry Uelsmann

Page 178 ©Adam Shemper

Page 216TL ©Pam Valois

Page 216TR ©Reuters NewMedia Inc./ CORBIS

Page 216BL ©Dirk Westphal

Page 216BR ©Pam Valois

Page 229 Vassar College Libraries, Special Collections, (Ref. #3.1534)

Page 233 Courtesy Janet Burroway

Page 234 Courtesy Janet Burroway

Page 242 ©Clemens Kalischer

Page 272 ©Laurie Lipton

Page 306 ©Jerry Uelsmann

Page 336 ©William Nolan

Readings

"Ghazal", from THE COUNTRY WITHOUT A POST OFFICE by Agha Shahid Ali. Copyright © 1997 by Agha Shahid Ali. Used by permission of W.W. Norton & Co.

"The Female Body", from GOOD BONES AND SIMPLE MURDERS by Margaret Atwood, copyright © 1983, 1992, 1994, by O.W. Toad Ltd. A Nan A. Talese Book. Used by permission of Doubleday, a division of Random House, Inc. and McClelland & Stewart Ltd. *The Canadian Publishers.*

Imamu Amiri Baraka, *Dutchman.* Reprinted by permission of Sterling Lord Literistic, Inc. Copyright by Amiri Baraka.

Donald Barthelme, "The School" from *60 Stories.* Copyright © 1976 by Donald Barthelme, reprinted with the permission of The Wylie Agency, Inc.

"Snow", from A RELATIVE STRANGER by Charles Baxter. Copyright © 1990 by Charles Baxter. Used by permission of W.W. Norton & Company, Inc.

Act Without Words, by Samuel Beckett from *Collected Shorter Plays* by Samuel Beckett. Copyright © 1959 by Samuel Beckett. Used by permission of Grove/Atlantic, Inc.

Laurie Berry, "Mockingbird" from *The Southeast Review* Vol. 10.1 Copyright 1989. Reprinted by permission.

"Dream Song #117" from THE DREAM SONGS by John Berryman. Copyright © 1969 by John Berryman. Copyright renewed 1977 by Kate Donahue Berryman. Reprinted by permission of Farrar, Straus & Giroux, LLC.

"One Art" from THE COMPLETE POEMS: 1927-1979 by Elizabeth Bishop. Copyright © 1979,1983 by Alice Helen Methfessel. Reprinted by permission of Farrar, Straus & Giroux, LLC.

Robert Olen Butler, "Missing" from *A Good Scent From A Strange Mountain,* (New York: Grove Press) Copyright © 2001 Robert Olen Butler. Reprinted by permission of the author.

Raymond Carver, "Locking Yourself Out, Then Trying to Get Back In," from *All of Us.* Reprinted by permission of International Creative Management, Inc. Copyright © 1996 by Tess Gallagher.

John M. McDaniels, "Frontiers" from *Quarterly West,* Issue #42, Spring/Summer 1996. ©1996. Reprinted by permission.

Lydia Davis, "A Mown Lawn" is reprinted by permission of International Creative Management, Inc.

Rick DeMarinis, "Your Fears Are Justified" from *Micro Fiction,* edited by Jerome Sterns. Reprinted by permission of Rick DeMarinis.

"Israel", from DROWN by Junot Díaz, copyright © 1996 by Junot Diaz. Used by permission of Riverhead Books, a division of Penguin, Putnam, Inc.

"At the Dam" from THE WHITE ALBUM by Joan Didion. Copyright © 1979 by Joan Didion. Reprinted by permission of Farrar, Straus & Giroux, LLC.

abstractions, 4, 5
Accidental Tourist (Tyler), 8
action
  character and, 94–95, 98
  setting as, 137–139
active verbs, 6
Act Without Words (Beckett),
  37–40
"Advice from the Extractor"
  (MacBeth), 159–160
Ali, Agha Shahid, "Ghazal,"
  331–332
alliteration, 308, 320
anapest, 319
Angela's Ashes (McCourt),
  55–62
Angell, Roger, 250
antagonist, 182
Anzaldua, Gloria, "*sus plumas
  el viento*," 90
appearance, character revealed
  through, 98
Aristotle
  on desire, 87
  on story segments, 181–183,
    273
  on thought in relation to de-
    sire, 96
Artaud, Antonin, 339
article, as essay, 244
Art of Fiction, The (Gardner), 8,
  53
Art of the Personal Essay, The
  (Lopate), 245
aside, in drama, 346
Aspects of the Novel (Forster),
  274
assonance, 308, 320
Atwood, Margaret, 5, 231
  Cat's Eye, 5–6
  "Female Body, The," 231,
    254–257
  Lady Oracle, 277–278
Auden, W. H., 307, 321
authorial interpretation, of character, 97–99
authorial intrusion, 251

backstory, 278–279
Ball, Pam, 219
Baraka, Imamu Amiri, 136, 314
  Dutchman, 136, 161–177
Barry, Dave, 47
Barthelme, Donald, "School,
  The," 72–74
*Battle of Bull Run Always
  Makes Me Cry, The"*
  (Real), 208–215

Baxter, Charles
  First Light, 220
  "Snow," 147–155
Beckett, Samuel, *Act Without
  Words*, 37–40
Bellow, Saul, *Seize the Day*, 98
"Belongings" (Lester), 268–271
Berry, Laurie
  "Mockingbird," 290–291
Berry, Wendell, 249
  "In Distrust of Movements,"
    249
Berryman, John, "Dream Song
  14," 333–334
Bishop, Elizabeth
  "One Art," 230
  "One Art" (edited example),
    229–230
"Black Hair" (Soto), 75–76
"Black Silhouettes of
  Shrimpers" (Smith), 329
blocking, of stage movement,
  342
Bly, Carol, *Passionate, Accurate
  Story, The*, 54
body language, 91
Brontë, Charlotte, *Shirley*, 52
Brother (Gallagher), 121–126
Browning, Robert, 47
  "My Last Duchess," 188–189
Burke, Carol and Molly Best
  Tinsley, *Creative Process,
  The*, 244, 307
Burroway, Janet, *Time Lapse* re-
  vision, 231–234
Busch, Frederick, "For the Love
  of a Princess of Mars," 248
Butler, Robert Olen, 3, 87
  "Missing," 194–201
Butler, Samuel, *Erewhon*, 130
Butley (Gray), 340–341

caesura, 318
Caine Mutiny, The (Wouk),
  98–99
camera, setting as, 133–135
Canin, Ethan, *For Kings and
  Planets*, 52
"Car Crash While Hitchhiking"
  (Johnson), 26–31, 51
Carlson, Ron, 132, 134
Carver, Raymond, "Locking
  Yourself Out, Then Trying
  to Get Back In," 327–328
"catalogue poem," 231
Catcher in the Rye, The
  (Salinger), 48
Cat's Eye (Atwood), 5–6

central narrator, 50
change agent
  discovery and decision as,
    94–95
  thought as, 96–97
character, 87–126. *See also*
  story
  as action, 94–95
  authorial interpretation of,
    97–99
  as conflict, 98–99
  as desire, 87–89
  in drama, 121–126
  in essays, 99–105
  in fiction, 106–114
  as image, 89–91
  language and, 54
  in poems, 115–121
  point of view of, 47–49, 91
  of protagonist and antagonist,
    182
  as thought, 96–97
  as voice, 91–94
chronology, of story, 274
Churchill, Caryl, 92
Cinderella, story progression in,
  185–188
cinema, screenwriting for,
  347–348
Cisneros, Sandra, 135
clarity, of writing, 224
cliché, 54
  metaphor and, 13
Closely Observed Trains
  (Hrabel), 50
clustering, 218
"Columbia The Gem" (Stern),
  313
comic persona, 47
"Coming from the Country"
  (Sanders), 46–47
comparison, metaphor, simile,
  and, 11–13
complications, in story, 182–183
conceit, in poetry, 311
concrete, defined, 7
concrete, significant details,
  7–10
conflict, 49
  character as, 98–99
  in Cinderella, 185
  connection/disconnection and,
    184
  in story, 181–183, 182
connection/disconnection, in
  story, 183–190
connotation, in poetry, 310–311
consonant clusters, 317

consonants, 317
contrast, 49
creative nonfiction, 244, 245.
    See also essay
Creative Process, The (Burke
    and Tinsley), 244, 307
crisis action, in story, 183, 187
critique of writing, in workshop,
    226–228
Crooked River Burning
    (Winegardner), 93

dactyl, 319
D'Aguilar, Fred, "Son in
    Shadow, A," 252
Daniel, John M., "Frontiers,"
    180, 200
Davis, Lydia, "Mown Lawn, A,"
    79–80
dead metaphors, 312
"Death of a Salesman" (Miller),
    340, 343
decision, change through, 94–95
"Deer Ghost" (Harjo), 156
DeLillo, Don, *Underworld*,
    136–137
DeMarinis, Rick, "Your Fears
    are Justified," 289–290
denotation, 310
denouement. *See* falling action
    (denouement)
density, in poetry, 313
description, setting and, 131
descriptive essay, 244
desire
    character as, 87–89
    thought in relation to, 96
details, 7–10
    for characters, 90
    defined, 7
    metaphor and, 12
    in setting, 132
development and revision,
    217–240
    of draft, 218–222
    examples of, 229–240
    of poetry, 229–230
dialogue, 92–94
    character's voice and, 49
    in creative nonfiction, 248
    in drama, 342–346
"Diamond Mine, The"
    (Gordimer), 283–289
Díaz, Junot, "Ysrael," 106–114
diction, 43
Didion, Joan, 3
    "At the Dam," 139–141
    "Why I Write" (Didion), 43
diegetic sound and music, 343
"Digging for China" (Wilbur),
    202–203
Dillard, Annie, 223, 273
    Giant Water Bug, The, 14–15

Writing Life, The, 223
dimeter line, 320
direct dialogue, 92
discipline, in writing, 217
disconnection. *See*
    connection/disconnection
discovery
    change through, 94–95
    story and, 179–180
distance
    between author/reader and
        characters, 53
    degree of, 53–54
Doctorow, E. L., 253
    Ragtime, 252, 253
Donne, John, 311
Dove, Rita, "Vacation," 158
Drabble, Margaret, 219
draft
    development of, 218–222
    examples of, 229–240
    revision and editing of,
        222–226
    un-drafting and, 238–239
drama, 337–378. *See also* spe-
    cific works
    character in, 121–126
    development of, 218
    fiction compared with,
        337–339
    imagery in, 37–41
    samples of, 349–378
    screenwriting and, 347–348
    setting in, 161–177
    sight in, 339–342
    sound in, 342–347
    story in, 208–215
    voice in, 82–85
dramatic irony, 343–344
dramatization, in creative non-
    fiction, 249
"Dream Song 14" (Berryman),
    333–334
Dresser, Richard, *Road to Ruin,
    The*, 349–356
Drummer, The (Fugard), 40–41
Duet for Bear and Dog (Rosen),
    357–362
Dufresne, John, "Nothing to Eat
    but Food: Menu as
    Memoir," 134–135
Dunn, Stephen, "My Brother's
    Work," 116–117
Dutchman (Baraka), 136,
    161–177

"Earthmoving Malediction"
    (McHugh), 157
editing, 222–226
    for clean copy, 225–226
    examples of, 229–240
    line editing, 239–240
Eggers, Dave, *Heartbreaking*

*Work of Staggering Genius,
    A*, 15–18
Einstein, Albert, 132
emotional recall, in drama, 346
end-rhymes, 321
end-stopped line, 318
Engle, Paul, 217
enjambment, 318
Epstein, Joseph, 243
Epstein, Julius, 179
Erdrich, Louise, "Sister
    Godzilla," 19–26
Erewhon (Butler), 130
essay, 243–271. *See also* mem-
    oir; personal essay; specific
    works
    character in, 99–105
    defined, 243–244
    development of, 218
    fact and truth in, 251–254
    imagery and metaphor in,
        14–18
    kinds of, 244–247
    personal, 250
    samples (readings), 254–271
    setting in, 139–146
    story in, 190–194
    techniques for, 247–251
    transitions in, 251
    voice in, 48, 55–64
Eukiah (Wilson), 367–370
"Everyday Use" (Walker),
    137–138
exposition, 337
    in story, 182, 185
expository essay, 244

"Facing It" (Komunyakaa), 33
fact and truth, in essays,
    251–254
Fairchild, B.H., "Old Men
    Playing Basketball,"
    118–119
falling action (denouement), in
    story, 183, 187
"Falling in Love Again"
    (Galloway), 248
"Father" (Raz), 78–79
feature, as essay, 244
"Female Body, The" (Atwood),
    231, 254–257
fiction, 273–305. *See also* spe-
    cific works
    authorial intrusion in, 251
    author's and character's voices
        in, 48–49
    backstory in, 278–279
    character in, 96, 106–114
    drama compared with,
        337–339
    flashback in, 279–280
    historical or regional fact in,
        252

imagery in, 19–31
samples (readings), 283–305
setting in, 147–155
story in, 194–201
text and subtext in, 281–283
voice in, 64–74
figures of speech, 308
First Light (Baxter), 220
first person, point of view of, 50
flashback, 279–280
For Kings and Planets (Canin),
52
formal verse, 308–310
Forster, E.M., *Aspects of the
Novel*, 274
"For the Love of a Princess of
Mars" (Busch), 248
fourth-wall realism, 339
Frankl, Victor, 98
Frazier, Ian, "Tomorrow's Bird,"
302–305
free verse, 308–310, 321
freewriting, 218, 220
"Frontiers" (Daniel), 180, 184,
200
Fugard, Athol
Drummer, The, 40–41
*"Master Harold" ... and the
Boys*, 90

Gallagher, Mary, *Brother*,
121–126
Galloway, Terry, "Falling in
Love Again," 248
Garcia, Kim, "Priest, The," 239
Gardner, John, 94, 179
Art of Fiction, The (Gardner),
8
on concrete details, 8
on distance, 53
Gas (Rivera), 362–366
generalizations, 5
Gerard, Philip, 245
"Ghazal" (Ali), 331–332
"Giant Water Bug, The"
(Dillard), 14–15
Glass Menagerie (Williams), 54
Glück, Louise, "Vita Nova,"
206–207
Gombrowicz, Witold, *Ivona,
Princess of Burgundia*, 9
Good Morning, America
(Sandburg), 134
Gordimer, Nadine, "Diamond
Mine, The," 283–289
grammar, 225
"Grammar Lesson, The"
(Kowit), 323
Gray, Simon, *Butley*, 340–341
Griffiths, D. W., 348
Gutkind, Lee, 244–245

Ha Jin, "In the Kindergarten,"

64–71
Hall, Donald, 313
Hamby, Barbara, "Language of
Bees, The," 80–81
"Hammock, The" (Lee),
205–206
Hampl, Patricia, "Red Sky in
the Morning," 190–194
Harjo, Joy, "Deer Ghost," 156
Hass, Robert, 318
"Images," 248
"Story About the Body, A,"
200, 202
"Haunted Ruin, The" (Pinsky),
32–33
"Hawk in the Rain, The"
(Hughes), 31–32
"Hawk Roosting" (Hughes),
76–77
*Heartbreaking Work of
Staggering Genius, A*
(Eggers), 15–18
Hemingway, Ernest
"Hills Like White Elephants,"
52–53
Moveable Feast, A, 136
"Here" (Tall), 129–130
"Her Kind" (Sexton), 46
hexameter line, 320
"Hills Like White Elephants"
(Hemingway), 52–53
Hirsch, Edward, "Portrait of a
Writer," 119–120
Hoagland, Edward, 251
Hoagland, Tony, 11
Hoeg, Peter, *Smilla's Sense of
Snow*, 12
Housman, A.E., "II" from *A
Shropshire Lad*, 95, 134
"How to Be a Writer" (Moore),
50–51
"How to Use This Body"
(Kirby), 35
Hrabel, Bohumil, *Closely
Observed Trains*, 50
Hughes, Ted
"Hawk in the Rain, The,"
31–32
"Hawk Roosting," 76–77

iamb, 319
idioms, 311–312
in poetry, 311–312
"II" from *A Shropshire Lad*
(Housman), 95, 134
"I Knew a Woman" (Roethke),
115, 314
image and imagery
character as, 89–91
concrete, significant details
and, 7–10
in drama, 37–41
in essay, 14–18

in fiction, 19–31
imagination and, 3–7
metaphor, simile, and, 11–13
in poetry, 31–37, 310
setting and, 132–133
"Images" (Hass), 248
imagination, image and, 3–7
inciting incident, 337
indirect dialogue, 92, 93
indirect method, of presenting
character, 97–98
"In Distrust of Movements"
(Berry), 249
informal verse, 309
"Inheritance of Tools, The"
(Sanders), 99–105
intensity, in poetry, 313
internal rhyme, 321
interpretation, authorial, 97–99
"In the Kindergarten" (Ha Jin),
64–71
invention, literary, 219
"Invitation to a Transformation"
(Nabokov), 63–64
irony, 49
dramatic, 343–344
"It's Water, It's Not Going to Kill
You" (Sellers), 291–302
Ives, David, *Philadelphia, The*,
371–378
Ivona, Princess of Burgundia
(Gombrowicz), 9

jargon, 54
Jennings, Elizabeth, "One
Flesh," 118
Johnson, Adam Marshall,
"Watertables," 238–239
Johnson, Claudia, 183, 184,
219
Johnson, Denis, 51
"Car Crash While
Hitchhiking," 26–31
Johnson, Samuel, 311
journalism. *See* essay; new jour-
nalism
Joyce, James, *Ulysses*, 252
judgments, 5
Justice, Donald, "Order in the
Streets," 74–75

Kemper, Betsy, "This Is How I
Remember It," 182
Kincaid, Jamaica, "Those Words
That Echo...Echo...Echo
Through Life," 257–261
Kingsolver, Barbara,
Poisonwood Bible,
281–282
Kinnell, Galway, "Why
Regret?", 36–37
Kirby, David, "How to Use This
Body," 35

Kizer, Caroline, 308, 314
"Knife, The" (Selzer), 261–268
Komunyakaa, Yusef
    "Facing It," 33
    "Nude Interrogation,"
        158–159
"Kong Looks Back on His
    Tryout with the Bears"
    (Trowbridge), 77–78
Kowit, Steve, "Grammar
    Lesson, The," 323
Kumin, Maxine, "Woodchucks,"
    204–205

Lady Oracle (Atwood),
    277–278
"Landscape and Narrative"
    (Lopez), 141–146
language
    impoverishment of, 54
    use in writing, 224
"Language of Bees, The"
    (Hamby), 80–81
"Language of the Brag, The"
    (Olds), 332–333
"Lecture on the Elegy, A"
    (Stafford), 318
Lee, Li-Young, "Hammock,
    The," 205–206
length, of writing, 224
Lester, Susan, "Belongings,"
    268–271
Levertov, Denise, 318
"Like This Together" (Rich),
    324–326
limited omniscient narrator, 51
line, in poetry, 318
line editing, 239–240
linking verbs, 6
"list poem," 231
literary invention, 219
literary nonfiction, essays as,
    244
"Locking Yourself Out, Then
    Trying to Get Back In"
    (Carver), 327–328
Logan, William, 88
long shot opening, 133, 134
long vowels, 317
Lopate, Philip, Art of the
    Personal Essay, The, 245
Lopez, Barry, 249
    "Landscape and Narrative,"
        141–146
lyric poet, voice of, 48

MacBeth, George, "Advice from
    the Extractor," 159–160
Mackall, Joe, 251
malapropisms, 54
Martin, Jane, Talking with ...
    Handler, 82–83, French
    Fries, 84–85

"Master Harold" ... and the
    Boys (Fugard), 90
McCourt, Frank, Angela's Ashes,
    55–62
McHugh, Heather, 317
    "Earthmoving Malediction,"
        157
McInnis, Susan, 132
McNeel, John, "On the Fedala
    Road," 134
meaning, in text and subtext, 91
mechanics (language), in edit-
    ing, 225
Meinke, Peter, "Poet, Trying to
    Surprise God, The,"
    323–324
memoir, 245
    development of, 218
    fact and truth in, 251–253
    voice of memoirist, 48
memory. See memoir
metaphor, 11–13, 308, 309
    dead, 312
    in essay, 14–18
    in poetry, 311
meter, 308, 320
Miller, Arthur, "Death of a
    Salesman," 340, 343
Milton, John, Paradise Lost,
    318
"Missing" (Butler), 194–201
mnemonic language, 308
"Mockingbird" (Berry),
    290–291
monometer line, 320
mood, setting as, 136–137
Moore, Lorrie, "How to Be a
    Writer," 50–51
Moveable Feast, A
    (Hemingway), 136
movies. See cinema
"Mown Lawn, A" (Davis),
    79–80
Munro, Alice, 217–218
music, in drama, 343
"My Brother's Work" (Dunn),
    116–117
"My Last Duchess" (Browning),
    188–189
"My Uncle Guillermo Speaks at
    His Own Funeral" (Sapia),
    334–335

Nabokov, Vladimir, "Invitation
    to a Transformation,"
    63–64
narrative essay, 244
narrative sequence, 220
narrator
    central, 50
    peripheral, 50
Neff, Carissa, 12
"New Formalism," 309

New Journalism, Wolfe on, 96,
    245
nondiegetic sound, 343
nonfiction, essays as, 244
"Nothing to Eat but Food: Menu
    as Memoir" (Dufresne),
    135
"Nude Interrogation"
    (Komunyakaa), 158–159

objective narrator, 51
O'Brien, Tim, 247
O'Connor, Flannery, 89
Oedipus Rex, story of, 273–274
off rhymes, 317
"Old man Hansen comes in at
    ten to" (Wah), 117–118
"Old Men Playing Basketball"
    (Fairchild), 118–119
Olds, Sharon
    "Language of the Brag, The,"
        332–333
    "One Girl at the Boys Party,
        The," 315
Oles, Carole Simmons,
    "Stonecarver," 116
Oliver, Mary, 226, 307, 308,
    321
    Poetry Handbook, A, 309
omniscient narrator, 51
"One Flesh" (Jennings), 118
"One Girl at the Boys Party,
    The" (Olds), 315
"On the Fedala Road"
    (McNeal), 134
"Order in the Streets" (Justice),
    74–75
organization, of writing,
    220–221
orientation, setting and, 134
Our Country's Good
    (Wertenberger), 50
outline, 220
    advantages and disadvantages
        of, 221
overstatement, 54

Paley, Grace, on voice, 55
Paradise Lost (Milton), 318
paragraph, reorganizing se-
    quence of, 220–221
Passion, The (Winterson), 138
Passionate, Accurate Story, The
    (Bly), 54
Passion of Artemisia, The
    (Vreeland), 133
passive verbs, 6
pentameter line, 320
peripheral narrator, 50
person, point of view and,
    50–51
persona, 45–47
personal essay, 245, 250. See

also creative nonfiction; essay
development of, 218
fact and truth in, 251–253
voice in, 48
persuasive essay, 244
Philadelphia, The (Ives), 371–378
phonemes, 317
Pinsky, Robert, "Haunted Ruin, The," 32–33
Plath, Sylvia, "Stillborn," 4, 322
plays. *See also* drama
characteristics of, 339
Plimpton, George, 250
plot, 273–276
in Browning's "My Last Duchess," 189
"Poet, Trying to Surprise God, The," (Meinke), 323–324
poetic foot, 319
poetry, 307–335. *See also* specific works
character as thought in, 96
character in, 115–121
connotation and metaphor in, 310–312
density and intensity in, 312–316
development and revision of, 218, 229–230
free verse and formal verse in, 308–310
imagery in, 31–47, 310–312
prose poems as, 200
prosody, rhythm, and rhyme in, 316–322
samples, 322–335
setting in, 156–160
story in, 189–190, 202–207
voice in, 48, 74–81
Poetry Handbook, A (Oliver), 309
point of attack, 337
point of view, 49–55
of character, 91
detail for, 53–54
Poisonwood Bible (Kingsolver), 281–282
Pope, Alexander, 316, 317
Porter, Katherine Anne, *Ship of Fools*, 97
"Portrait of a Writer" (Hirsch), 119–120
power struggle
in Cinderella, 185
story as, 181–183
prequel, backstory as, 278–279
"Priest, The" (Garcia), 239
profile, as essay, 244
proofreading, 226
prose poem, 200

short-short story compared with, 200–201
"Prose Poem" (Tate), 328–329
prosody, 316–317
protagonist, 182
punctuation, 225

Ragtime (Doctorow), 252
Raz, Hilda, "Father," 78–79
Real, Carole, *Battle of Bull Run Always Makes Me Cry, The*, 208–215
"Red Sky in the Morning" (Hampl), 190–194
reflection, in creative nonfiction, 249
"Repetition" (Stone), 330
resolution of conflict, in story, 181–183, 189–190
revision, 222–226. *See also* development and revision
examples of, 229–240
of opening of *Time Lapse* (Burroway), 231–234
from student journal, 237–238
of *Time Lapse* (Burroway), 231–236
rhyme, 308, 320–321
off, 317
end-, 321
internal, 321
slant, 317, 320
true, 320
rhythm, 308
Rich, Adrienne, "Like This Together," 324–326
Rivera, José, "Gas," 362–366
Road to Ruin, The (Dresser), 349–356
Roethke, Theodore, 314
"I Knew A Woman," 115, 314
"Romantic, at Horseshoe Key" (Shomer), 326–327
Rosen, Sybil, *Duet for Bear and Dog*, 357–362
Rosencrantz and Guildenstern Are Dead (Stoppard), 130

Sable, Josiah, 49
Sackville West, Vita, 309
Salinger, J.D., *Catcher in the Rye, The*, 48
"Salvador Late or Early" (Cisneros), 135
Sandburg, Carl, *Good Morning, America*, 134
Sanders, Scott Russell, 46–47
"Coming from the Country," 46–47
"Inheritance of Tools, The," 99–105
Sapia, Yvonne, "My Uncle

Guillermo Speaks at His Own Funeral," 334–335
scansion, 308, 319, 321
scenery, 340
scenes
in creative nonfiction, 247–248
in story, 276–278
Schoen, Steven, 130
screenwriting, drama and, 347–348
second person, point of view of, 50–51
seduction process, Carlson on, 132, 134
Seize the Day (Bellow), 98
self-reflexive script, 348
Sellers, Heather, "It's Water, It's Not Going to Kill You," 291–302
Selzer, Richard, "Knife, The," 261–268
sense impressions, 5, 8. *See also* details
of characters, 90
setting, 129–177
as action, 137–139
as camera, 133–135
in creative nonfiction, 248
in drama, 161–177, 342
in essays, 139–146
in fiction, 147–155
as mood and symbol, 136–137
in poetry, 156–160
story and, 179–180
as world, 130–133
Sexton, Anne
"Her Kind," 46
"Young," 45–46
Shange, Ntozake, *Spell #7*, 90
Ship of Fools (Porter), 97
Shirley (Brontë), 52
Shomer, Enid, "Romantic, at Horseshoe Key," 326–327
short-short story, 180, 182, 200
prose poem compared with, 200–201
"Short Story" (Voigt), 203–204
short story, development of, 218
sight, in drama, 339–342
significant, defined, 7
simile, 11, 308, 311
"Sister Godzilla" (Erdrich), 19–26
slant rhyme, 317, 320
Smiley, Sam, 94
Smilla's Sense of Snow (Hoeg), 12
Smith, Dave, "Black Silhouettes of Shrimpers," 329
"Snow" (Baxter), 147–155
soliloquy, 346

"Son in Shadow, A"
(D'Aguilar), 252
Soto, Gary, "Black Hair," 75–76
sound, in drama, 342–347
space-time-continuum, setting
and, 132–133
Spacey, Kevin, 337
specificity, 7
speech, 92
character revealed through,
98
Spell #7 (Shange), 90
spelling, 225
spondee, 317
Stafford, William, "Lecture on
the Elegy, A," 318
stage. *See* drama; plays
stage directions, 341–342
stage lie, 341
stanza, 308
Stern, Gerald, "Columbia The
Gem," 313
Stern, Jerome, 136, 276, 311
"Stillborn" (Plath), 4, 322
Stone, Ruth, "Repetition," 330
"Stonecarver" (Oles), 116
Stoppard, Tom, *Rosencrantz
and Guildenstern Are Dead,*
130
story, 179–215
beginning of, 275–276
in Browning's "My Last
Duchess," 189–190
chronological order in, 274
as connection and disconnection, 183–190
in drama, 208–215
in essays, 190–194
in fiction, 194–201
plot and, 273–276
in poetry, 202–207
as power struggle, 181–183
progression of Cinderella,
185–188
scene and summary in,
276–278
segments of, 181, 182–183
short-short, 180, 182, 200
"Story About the Body, A"
(Hass), 200, 202
stresses, in poetry, 317, 319
structure of writing, 220
reorganizing writing,
220–221
Strunk, William H., 7
subject, of writing, 224
subtext
in fiction, 281–283
meaning in, 91
summarized dialogue, 92
summary, in story, 276–278
"Surface, The" (Swenson), 34
"sus plumas el viento"

(Anzaldua), 90
Swenson, May, "Surface, The,"
34
syllabic verse, 319
syllables, 317
symbol, setting as, 136–137
syntax, 43

talking. *See* speech
*Talking with...Handler, French
Fries* (Martin), 82–85
Tall, Deborah, "Here," 129–130
Tate, James, "Prose Poem,"
328–329
tetrameter line, 320
text
in fiction, 281–283
meaning in, 91
theatricalism, 339–340
theatricalist technique, 344
third person
distance in, 53
point of view of, 51
"This Is How I Remember It"
(Kemper), 182, 184
"Those Words That
Echo...Echo...Echo
Through Life" (Kincaid),
257–261
thought
character as, 96–97
character revealed through,
98
in relation to desire, 96
Time Lapse (Burroway)
revision of opening, 231–234
"Transit: Ostend-Dover"
from, 235–236
Tinsley, Molly Best, and Carol
Burke, *Creative Process,
The,* 244, 307
to be, forms of, 6
"Tomorrow's Bird" (Frazier),
302–305
"Top Girls" (Churchill), 92
"Transit: Ostend-Dover," from
Time Lapse (Burroway),
235–236
transition
in essays, 251
to flashback, 279–280
Trevor, William, "Visiteur, Le,"
280
trimeter line, 320
trochee, 319
Trowbridge, William, "Kong
Looks Back on His Tryout
with the Bears," 77–78
true rhymes, 320
truth
in essays, 251–254
in fiction, 252
Tyler, Anne, 87

Accidental Tourist, 8

Uelsmann, Jerry, 217
Ulysses (Joyce), 252
Underworld (DeLillo), 136–137
un-drafting, 238–239

"Vacation" (Dove), 158
verbs, 6
verse
free and formal, 308–310
syllabic, 319
villanelle, 229–230
"Visiteur, Le" (Trevor), 280
"Vita Nova" (Glück), 206–207
vocabulary, 43
voice, 43–85
of author, 44–45
of character, 47–49, 91–94
in drama, 82–85
in essays, 48, 55–64
in fiction, 64–74
of first person, 50
of limited omniscient narrator, 51
of narrator, 50
of objective narrator, 51
of omniscient narrator, 51
persona and, 45–47
person and, 50
in poetry, 48, 74–81, 314
of second person, 50–51
voiceover, 346
Voigt, Ellen Bryant, 230, "Short
Story," 203–204
Vonnegut, Kurt, 226
Vreeland, Susan, *Passion of
Artemesia, The,* 133

Wah, Fred, "Old man Hansen
comes in at ten to,"
117–118
Walker, Alice, "Everyday Use,"
137–138
Wallace, Ron, "Worry," 200,
201–202
"Watertables" (Johnson),
238–239
Welty, Eudora, 129
Wertenberger, Timberlake, *Our
Country's Good,* 50
Whitehead, John, 43
"Why I Write" (Didion), 43
"Why Regret?" (Kinnell), 36–37
Wilbur, Richard, "Digging for
China," 202–203
Williams, Tennessee, *Glass
Menagerie,* 54
Wilson, Lanford, *Eukiah,*
367–370
Winegardner, Mark, *Crooked
River Burning,* 93

Winterson, Jeanette, *Passion, The*, 138
Wolfe, Tom, 96, 245
"Woodchucks" (Kumin), 204–205
workshop, on writing, 226–228
"Worry" (Wallace), 200, 201–202
Wouk, Herman, *Caine Mutiny, The*, 98–99
writing. *See also* draft

as art, 3–4
development and revision in, 217–240
freewriting and, 220
organizing, 220–221
revision and editing in, 222–226
structuring, 220
un-drafting and, 238–239
unity and shape in, 222
workshop for critiquing and

improving, 226–228
Writing Life, The (Dillard), 223

yearning. *See* desire
Yeats, William Butler, 317
"Ysrael" (Díaz), 106–114
"Young" (Sexton), 45–46
"Your Fears are Justified" (DeMarinis), 289–290

Additional Titles of Interest

Note to Instructors: Any of these Penguin-Putnam, Inc. titles can be packaged with this book for a special discount up to 60% off the retail price. Contact your local Allyn & Bacon/Longman sales representative for details on how to create a Penguin-Putnam, Inc. Value Package.

Albee, *Three Tall Women*

Allison, *Bastard Out of Carolina*

Alvarez, *How the Garcia Girls Lost their Accents*

Austen, *Persuasion*

Austen, *Pride & Prejudice*

Austen, *Sense & Sensibility*

Bellow, *The Adventures of Augie March*

Boyle, *Tortilla Curtain*

Cather, *My Antonia*

Cather, *O Pioneers!*

Cervantes, *Don Quixote*

Chopin, *The Awakening*

Conrad, *Nostromo*

DeLillo, *White Noise*

Desai, *Journey to Ithaca*

Douglass, *Narrative Life of Frederick Douglass*

Golding, *Lord of the Flies*

Hawthorne, *The Scarlet Letter*

Homer, *Illiad*

Homer, *Odyssey*

Hwang, *M. Butterfly*

Hulme, *Bone People*

Jen, *Typical American*

Karr, *The Liar's Club*

Kerouac, *On The Road*

Kesey, *One Flew Over the Cuckoo's Nest*

King, *Misery*

Larsen, *Passing*

Lavin, *In a Cafe*

Marquez, *Love in the Time of Cholera*

McBride, *The Color of Water*

Miller, *Death of a Salesman*

Morrison, *Beloved*

Morrison, *The Bluest Eye*

Morrison, *Sula*

Naylor, *Women of Brewster Place*

Orwell, *1984*

Postman, *Amusing Ourselves to Death*

Raybon, *My First White Friend*

Rose, *Lives on the Boundary*

Rose, *Possible Lives: The Promise of Public*

Rushdie, *Midnight's Children*

Shakespeare, *Four Great Comedies*

Shakespeare, *Four Great Tragedies*

Shakespeare, *Hamlet*

Shakespeare, *Four Histories*

Shakespeare, *King Lear*

Shakespeare, *Macbeth*

Shakespeare, *Othello*

Shakespeare, *Twelfth Night*

Shelley, *Frankenstein*

Silko, *Ceremony*

Solzenitsyn, *One Day in the Life of Ivan Denisovich*

Sophocles, *The Three Theban Plays*

Spence, *The Death of a Woman Wang*

Steinbeck, *Grapes of Wrath*

Steinbeck, *The Pearl*

Stevenson, *Dr. Jekyll & Mr. Hyde*

Swift, *Gulliver's Travels*

Twain, *Adventures of Huckleberry Finn*

Wilson, *Joe Turner's Come and Gone*

Wilson, *Fences*

Woolf, *Jacob's Room*